KEYFAX
Omnibus Edition

BY JULIAN COLBECK

MIXBOOKS

6400 Hollis Street, Suite 12
Emeryville, CA 94608

Library of Congress Card Number: 96-79301

Book design: Michael Zipkin

Production staff: Mike Lawson, publisher; Lisa Duran, editor; Sally Engelfried, editorial assistance; Teresa Poss, administrative assistant; Georgia George, production director; Tom Marzella, production assistant; Tami Needham, book production

Special thanks to Pete Sears for the Foreword

Cover art: Allen Wallace

MixBooks
6400 Hollis Street, Suite 12
Emeryville, CA 94608
(510) 653-3307

Also from MixBooks:
The AudioPro Home Recording Course
Modular Digital Multitracks: The Power User's Guide
Concert Sound
Sound for Picture
Music Producers
Live Sound Reinforcement

Also from EMBooks:
Making the Ultimate Demo
Tech Terms: A Practical Dictionary for Audio and Music Production
Making Music With Your Computer

Also from CBM Music and Entertainment Group:
Recording Industry Sourcebook
Mix Reference Disc
Mix Master Directory
Digital Piano Buyer's Guide

MixBooks is a division of Cardinal Business Media Inc.

Printed in Ann Arbor, Michigan

ISBN 0-918371-08-2

Contents

Foreword

More than 25 years have passed since Bob Moog figured out a way to shape raw, electronically generated sound by the use of control voltages and develop it into a sophisticated musical instrument called the Minimoog. Since those early pioneering years, the synthesizer has inspired many innovations, from early FM synthesis and MIDI to digital sampling and physical modeling. Even some kind of direct brain-to-midi connection, which until recently was firmly delegated to the science fiction shelves, is now a conceivable technology.

With this book, Julian Colbeck gives us a fascinating overview of 100 classic synthesizers, including detailed specifications on each instrument, information on their development and profiles on the people who conceived, designed and built them. Old schoolers will smile knowingly as they read the book's detailed descriptions of old but familiar instruments like the Minimoog, ARP Odyssey and Prophet-5 but will probably wince a little at the memory of trying to individually tune three unstable internal oscillators, usually right before showtime. Many of these early synthesizers still hold up today with a uniqueness of sound and flexibility that can make them a valuable addition to your arsenal of sounds.

Because of the many different brands of synthesizers now available on the market, a visit to the keyboard department of your local music store can be a mind-boggling and not always productive experience. This is especially true if the salesperson, in their natural enthusiasm for the latest technology, tries to steer you towards the store's newest product, replete with a plethora of whistles and gadgets and sporting a hefty price tag. *Keyfax* will prepare you for the experience with a good working knowledge of the many different features available to you; this, in turn, will help you work with the salesperson to choose an instrument that is best suited to your needs. If you expect to spend a lot of time on the road, for instance, or plan to come within five miles of any airline baggage handlers, you may want to choose an instrument for its sturdiness and light weight rather than its extra features that might be better suited to your home or recording studio environment.

After you've taken the initial plunge and purchased your first synthesizer, take the time to peruse the manual and understand the instrument as fully as possible, so you can better utilize its many dimensions; it will be time well spent. When you recover from the wonderland of colorful sounds that are provided, you'll soon realize that, as with any musical instrument, the synthesizer is only as creative, original and innovative as the person at the controls. The more you understand the synthesizer's many features, the more creative options will be available to you.

In the last 20 years, designers have made considerable progress in developing user-friendly synthesizers (and manuals, thank goodness), but it still takes considerable study and effort to design your own sounds or modify factory-preset patches. These patches are carefully designed by technicians (who are usually musicians themselves) and are often difficult to improve on. But it's still nice, and sometimes necessary, to change the parameters a little to suit your needs. Many amateur and professional musicians have been content with, or more likely only capable of, twiddling a few knobs or perhaps pushing the odd button or two on their synthesizers. However, some hardy souls have managed to plunge courageously into the abyss of sacred words like "envelope generators," "lowpass filters" and "dynamic amplitude." Marching defiantly and unflinchingly into the face of threatening phrases such as "sawtooth waveforms" and "attack transients," they have been rewarded with the discovery of new horizons for their creativity. Many of us end up unable to face all the technical jargon and wind up using three or four stock patches out of the vast array of preset sounds that come with our instrument. I owned my old DX7 for several years before I got around to reading the manual and really coming to grips with the instrument.

The interaction between science and the arts has always held fascinating and creative possibilities. One of the more exciting collaborations, spurring many ingenious innovations, has been the application of the computer in the world of music. This is all thanks to the violent gangs of marauding and unruly computer scientists and musicians who, in the 1960s and '70s, started holding subversive, illicit meetings in back-street cafes and the vegetable departments of certain supermarkets. These eccentric weirdos, who up to now had been content to bury themselves (with the exception, perhaps, of Albert Einstein) in the relative obscurity of their Bela Lugosi, dungeon-like laboratories, were able to gather their creative forces together and add considerable color to the realm of 20th century music. There are many interactive music software programs now available on the market capable of bringing a level of sophistication to our home recording setups that we could once only dream of. Luxuries such as multitrack recording and the convenience of being able to write and print out our own professional quality music lead sheets are now relatively commonplace, along with CD-ROMs and enhanced CDs.

All the fuss started when the first working computer called E.N.I.A.C. (which stands for Electronic Numerical Integrator and Computer) was unveiled to the public on St. Valentine's day, 1946. It took up an area 30 by 50 feet, weighed 30 tons and used 17,418 vacuum tubes (or valves). E.N.I.A.C. was developed for the U.S. Army Ordnance Corps by a team of scientists at the Moore School of Electrical Engineering in Pennsylvania. Its initial purpose was to compute lengthy and complicated firing and bombing tables. However, the computer's enormous potential for peacetime applications was quickly realized, and it soon added a high level of efficiency to many of our daily tasks. Over a few short years, in fact, computers have become so interwoven with our personal lives that, like telephones, it is difficult to imagine life without them.

The recording industry was turned radically upside down with the advent of digital recording and the compact disc or CD. Although digital is able to provide relatively noise-free recordings, many artists and producers still prefer to record in studios that use the old tried-and-true multitrack tape machine. Most major studios have digital and analog recording available and often combine the two mediums in some way. The debate over analog recording with Dolby noise reduction on two-inch tape, with its wide dynamic range and warm sound, versus the supposedly harsher digital recording will probably continue for many years to come. It's difficult to argue against some of the more obvious benefits of the digital approach, such as supplying affordable, professional-quality multitrack recording equipment for portable or home use or providing sophisticated computer editing techniques for the studio. Progress is also being made in capturing the natural warmth and ambience of an instrument being digitally recorded, which can sometimes be difficult to capture when breaking down waveforms to binary numbers. Compact disc technology is also improving and, at the very least, enables music lovers to now enjoy their favorite classical recordings without the intrusion of the unmistakable sound of "frying bacon" caused by scratched vinyl or a dirty stylus. Although here again, many staunch audiophiles will fight to the death over the warmth and supposedly superior sound reproduction of an immaculately kept vinyl LP played on an air-ride turntable with a diamond needle.

In all fields, our technology is advancing at a dizzying, breakneck pace. The computer and digital technology will surely go down in history as two of humankind's most important developments, comparable perhaps to the invention of the wheel. It was the computer that was able to handle the necessary equations that enabled man to travel a quarter of a million miles through space, walk on the moon and return to earth again. It is the computer that allows us to instantly match the blood type of a potential organ donor with that of a transplant recipient. However, its vast potential will have to be handled very carefully.

In the meantime, grab this book, lock yourself in a relatively quiet room with your new (old) synthesizer and its manual, fire up your PC and your latest music software, grab a beer (perhaps you'd better make that a soda), plunge in and enjoy the rewarding world of interactive digital technology. You won't be sorry.

PETE SEARS
Keyboardist for Hot Tuna, Jefferson Starship and Rod Stewart

Preface

*I*n 1981, casting around for something rather more substantial than tearing my fingers to shreds night after night in a Los Angeles Top 40 band and writing here-today-gone-tomorrow keyboard reviews for the inky British magazine *Sounds*, I thought a book on the subject of electronic keyboards might be fun to write and useful to read.

I duly assembled—and rewrote in suitably booky form—a collection of reviews into a nice ring binder alongside some arty black-and-white photos of the main candidates shot by my then-girlfriend, Annie.

Having made numerous appointments beforehand, Annie and I excitedly boarded a plane to New York and set about meeting publishers. The average publisher, we discovered—even those in the music book business—knew and cared about synthesizers about as much as they did about rubber grommet inserting on a car assembly line. One or two feigned some sort of interest for a nanosecond, but essentially they deemed there was no market for such a tome. So, back we went to Los Angeles, and back I went to the drawing board and life as a player and part-time writer.

A year or so later we were back in London, and I had what turned out to be a temporary but permanent freelance position with *Sounds* as its technical editor. Eventually the time was ripe for my buyers guide, and it found its way into the Virgin Books office where John Brown, now the head of his own publishing empire, was sufficiently intrigued to give *Keyfax* its first breath of air.

Even in 1984, a book dedicated to synths and string machines was viewed with suspicion. "Imagine anyone getting all misty-eyed over an old synth?" I think I even heard myself say. But *Keyfax* did find a niche and an audience. And in due time, books two, three, four and five have all appeared. There is even a German translation of the series.

Though I certainly take no credit for the shift in perspective on the instruments themselves, these old keyboards, which were at one time thought to be dead meat, just black boxes stuffed with wire and solder, have indeed now become objects of desire, intrigue and fable. People do talk of a good Rhodes piano or Minimoog or ARP 2600.

Why? Part of the reason lies with the keyboard manufacturers themselves; most of whom have systematically squeezed the character out of synth design over the past decade in the never-ending search for that mythical wider audience eagerly waiting to climb aboard the synth train. The subsequent clones, new design re-vamps, price wars, instruments with more computery and less musical user interfaces and the, at times, worrisome fossilization process of sound known as sampling has left a void among dedicated musicians. Musicians need to be moved, need to be inspired, need to move something, waggle something, hit something...and get an instant result.

Keyfax Omnibus Edition is part honor roll and part history of the smaller successes and even heroic failures of synths and their creators that have imposed themselves on my consciousness over the past 20 years or so.

What I have tried to do in my Hot 100 section is find the story behind each of these key instruments. Each was someone's baby. But whose? What were they trying to accomplish? Did they succeed? If not, why? Who played them? Why? Are they still worth hunting down today? I don't expect that everyone will agree with my choice of the 100 most important electronic keyboards ever made. But, by and large, this collection of curios comprises those that have had the most impact on players and, in turn, the most impact on the music they play that we all listen to.

I have also compiled The Product Directory to provide you with thumbnail reviews, specifications and an invaluable price guide to help you navigate your way through hundreds more products.

There are many people who have helped me along the *Keyfax* trail, but the series could never have been written without John Brown, whose accepting words, "I don't know anything about this subject, but

I'm going to give it a go," will remain with me forever; my father, Norman Colbeck, whose irreverent and sometimes irascible sense of humor I appear to have inherited, but who, sadly, died shortly before the first edition was published in 1985; my mother, Patricia McKenzie, whose unshakable belief in her son's talent could have fueled a library full of books—on any subject; my former girlfriend, Annie, who became and, through some quite extraordinary stroke of luck, still appears to be my wife; and, finally, our children, Abigail and Cameron, whose various needs and wants I attempt to finance by these occasional outpourings.

Guide to This Edition

Keyfax Omnibus Edition takes its lead from previous *Keyfax* editions in its spotlight on keyboard and primarily keyboard-driven instruments designed for use in the high-tech, pro and semipro world. Included are all of the most commonly found general release instruments in the following major categories:

Controller keyboards
Digital pianos
Home keyboards
Monophonic synthesizers
Multi-instrument keyboards
Music processors
Polyphonic synthesizers
Samplers
Stage organs
Workstations (listed under polyphonic synthesizers, since that is what they are)

Some variations on these themes will be found, such as duophonic synthesizers, electronic pianos, etc.

HOW TO FIND AN INSTRUMENT

Instruments appears alpha-numerically under their manufacturer's name. The basic sound technology type of each instrument is also listed.

Instrument Variations

Instruments often hunt in packs, with three or more "variations" of an instrument released simultaneously. Unless they are being particularly perverse, manufacturers generally keep to some recognizable formula. So, if you cannot find the instrument you are looking for under its own name, as in XYZ WW-111, try looking under XYZ WW-112 or even XYZ WW-121.

Missing Entries

This edition has been exhausting, but its entries are not exhaustive. Listed are mainly instruments that received a fair day's hearing. Instruments built in ones or twos by a team of misanthropic boffins in Eastern Europe might well be fascinating, but since you are unlikely to ever find them, *Keyfax Omnibus* has seen fit to remove them from your gaze altogether.

TERMS DEFINED

Orig. Price (19XX)

This is the instrument's original list price—or as near such a thing as it is possible to venture. Many entries were listed with no U.S. or UK price. Feel free to scrawl one in if such becomes available at a later date.

Price in 1996

This gives you an indication of what to expect to pay for the instrument at the time of publication. Where an entry was released in 1978, this is clearly based on a second-hand price. Typically, this refers to a good condition unit in working order. Where an entry is only one or two years old, this price is a reflection of a typical discount or even closeout price. This, happily, is also about what you'd pay for a good condition, "still in box" second-hand unit.

All prices are what you should expect to *pay. Selling* price will vary considerably with the condition of the instrument and the desperation factor of the seller.

Keyboard = keyboard length

61-note = 5 octaves

Sound Type

This gives you an at-a-glance idea of the instrument's underlying technology (e.g., analog, digital, sample, etc.). Where such is provided by the manufacturer, a more specific description of the technology is given in parenthesis.

The Hot 100

360 Systems Digital Keyboard

Digital polyphonic keyboard

THE FAX

Keyboard:	48-note
Programs:	32
External storage:	None
Polyphony:	8-voice
Oscillators per voice:	n/a
Effects:	None
Connections:	Stereo audio, pedals, MIDI
Dimensions:	130mm x 800mm x 550mm
Weight:	19.5kg
360 Systems:	5321 Sterling Center Dr.; Westlake Village, CA 91361; tel: (818) 991-0360; fax: (818) 991-1360

THE FIGURES

Chief designer:	Bob Easton
Production run:	1982-84
Approx. units sold:	300
Options:	MIDI board
Sounds:	360 Systems 64KB EPROM library
Miscellaneous:	360 Systems produced Linn LM1s and LinnDrums under license.
Orig. price (1982):	$3995 (no UK price)
Price in 1996:	$1000+ (no UK price)

California company 360 Systems, aside from being a most difficult name to list alphabetically (Do numbers come before letters? Under T for "three-sixty"?), has enjoyed a checkered career in the musical instrument field, producing instruments sporadically and seemingly without any grand design. Recently, 360 Systems has become a world leader in 2-track hard-disk recording systems for the broadcast industry. Musicians, though, will remember the company better for the MIDI Bass, one of the first in the new wave of dedicated instrument modules in the 1990s. But 360 Systems also produced the world's first sample-replay keyboard, a design much derided at the time. "Who on earth wants to just trigger samples?" we all thought back in 1982. Ten years later, it was difficult to find anyone who wanted to do anything else.

Designer Bob Easton was also a recording engineer who became a close friend of Frank Zappa's (he did some engineering on *Apostrophe*). Zappa and Easton had talked since the 1970s about the possibil-

ity of using recordings as the basis for a musical instrument. Zappa discovered the Synclavier; Easton built the 360 Systems Digital Keyboard.

Even in the 1980s, this instrument was ahead of its time, but it is now merely interesting to note the 360 Systems Digital Keyboard's features and failings. So few of these instruments were produced that the chances of finding one are slim. And even if you did, would it be of any value? Read on and decide for yourself.

A smart, clean-lined instrument along Prophet-meets-Chroma lines, the 360 Systems DK is essentially a preset sample-playback keyboard housing a user-definable (read "purchasable") number of samples stored in ROM, offering but a crumb of tweakability via a filter and the chance to custom-mix a pair of sounds.

Much of what the 360 Systems DK does is thoroughly laudable and carried out with the best of intentions. Unfortunately, its slavish devotion to "accuracy," in both sonic and range terms, rendered the instrument limited in appeal. To wit, bow noise on its 18 Violins voice is so loud that it renders the voice unusable, looping is completely absent (not for nothing was this likened to a digital Mellotron) and the keyboard originally literally lacked sensitivity, though ultimately just figuratively.

In the antiseptic 1990s, such features can be overlooked, or indeed flaunted as providing character, but in the 1980s, all eyes and ears were on sampling as a method of "cleaning up" and sharpening the focus of sound.

You can store 32 sounds at a time, the cost of the instrument varying with the amount of samples you insert. Singly, a sound is playable (loosely) across the short-scale, four-octave keyboard in eight-voice polyphony. You have some tonal control with the filter (cutoff) and vibrato can be added using the mod wheel.

The only major piece of user input concerns the merging of two sounds. Not only can you choose two independent sounds and alter the blend, but you can double the same sound upon itself, altering the pitch or delay of one copy to produce chorus or ADT effects. You can also split two sounds left and right.

Some of the samples offered were very good indeed. The Grand Piano, according to designer Bob Easton, was not the Bosendorfer, as quoted in previous *Keyfax* editions (sorry!) but a Steinway B, multi-sampled at minor thirds throughout the range. Easton says that the instrument was a gem, belonging to a CSN&Y member (Nash or Crosby) and housed in a studio in Los Angeles. The resultant piano "sample" required the insertion of some 64 individual chips at the time and is still a cracker of a sound in pure terms.

A shame about the actual instrument's measly keyboard and action, though. The massed-strings sample was taken from a custom sampling session with the Florida Symphony that cost a staggering $10,000 an hour.

This thread of authenticity runs through the entire instrument. Easton says that every sample was recorded by top L.A. session players, though even now he politely demurs when asked to reveal his sources. Intriguingly, though, Roger Linn was the guitarist for the painstakingly created and totally string-accurate acoustic guitar.

Ultimately, technology, rather than the public, was ready for the 360 Systems Digital Keyboard. With too cumbersome a processing system, too unresponsive a keyboard and too little control, the whole prospect of a sample replay keyboard came across as clever but impractical.

Although, 360 Systems can still do repairs, the company points out that for those outside California, shipping costs may be prohibitive. Schematics have not been published freely, so anything other than minor running repairs will be difficult to get elsewhere. According to ex-360 Systems service personnel, the most likely problems will be the voicing boards, which tend to go out of tolerance, causing mistriggering and errant tuning.

Some of these samples have undoubted vintage appeal today (Easton still has the 24-track masters from his sampling sessions), and if capable of being lashed to a decent keyboard, might provide some high-quality tone colors. A ground-breaking instrument that paved the way for generations of E-mu, Kawai, Roland, Yamaha and Korg models to come.

Akai S612 Digital sampling module

THE FAX

Keyboard:	None
Programs:	n/a
External storage:	MD280 Quick Disk (a separate unit)
Polyphony:	6-voice
Oscillators per voice:	n/a
Effects:	None
Connections:	Mono, 6 separate voice outs, MIDI
Dimensions:	483mm x 90mm x 379mm
Weight:	6kg

THE FIGURES

Chief designer:	Dave Cockerell
Production run:	1986-87

AKAI

Name:	Akai Electric Co. Ltd.
Head Office:	335 Kariado, Nakahara-ky, Kawasaki-shi, Kanagawa, Japan
U.S. Distributor:	c/o IMC: PO Box 2344; Ft. Worth, TX 76102; tel: (817) 336-5114; fax: (817) 870-1271
UK Distributor:	Unit 6, Haslemere Heathrow Est., Silver Jubilee Way; Hounslow, Middx TW4 6NQ; tel: 0181-897-6388; fax: 0181-759-8268
Founded:	1929
No. of employees:	400
Business:	Samplers, keyboards, digital audio products (including digital multitrack recorders), sequencers, hi-fi equipment, fiber-optic connections, water purification systems, language labs

Akai started life in 1929 as a manufacturer of electric motors, a product line that steered it first in the direction of tape recorders, then to hi-fi, then on into pro audio equipment and, finally, musical instruments.

The EMI (Electronic Musical Instrument) division was inaugurated in 1984 with the release of the AX80 synthesizer and the MG1212 12-channel mixer/recorder. Without the benefit of years of experience in the musical instrument business, yet quick to spot the potential of sampling, Akai lost no time in acquiring the rights to produce a rack-mount sampler already half in production, relaunching it as the Akai S612.

The S612 became a much-loved device, and Akai's association with one of its designers, Dave Cockerell, has continued throughout the subsequent S series. In fact, Akai's relationship with non-Japanese R&D teams has been one of its key strengths, and when Roger Linn's seminal digital drum machine company foundered in 1985, Akai recruited Linn to produce a series of professional drum/sequencer products under the Akai/Linn banner.

A similar trans-Pacific collaboration resulted in Akai taking on Nyle Steiner's designs for electronic wind instruments, giving them MIDI connections, restyling them and marketing them as the Akai EWI and EVI. Though the EVI concept was not to last, the saxophone-simulating EWI has enjoyed a healthy career, with updates and additional voice modules.

This is not to say that Akai has no R&D team in Japan. Not only have Japanese input and construction quality been essential ingredients to their success, especially on the sampling instruments, but there has been plenty of material developed in Japan, from effects units to digital multitrack recorders.

In a global sense, Akai has only ever been an important bit player, but in sampling (especially outside America, where a tape-recorder licensing deal struck in the 1950s prevented Akai from forming a dedicated "Akai USA"), Akai is perceived as the market leader. The hi-fi division was Akai's largest revenue earner until the 1990s when this division had increasing difficulties that made restructuring inevitable. Eventually, in a 1995 deal that gave Akai controlling interest in Sansui, the Hong Kong- and Toronto-based Semitech (Global) Ltd. acquired a controlling interest in Akai.

Part of the musical instrument division's substantial success in England has been Akai UK's ability to assess and service the music market at close hand. With only a distributor in the U.S., this has not been possible, though it will be interesting to see if the R&D satellite established in California in 1995 will prove the necessary vantage point from which to capture the valuable U.S. market as well.

Approx. units sold:	12,000
Options:	MD280 Quick Disk
Sounds:	Akai, Soundsations
Miscellaneous:	Editors from Internal Music, Soundfiler (ST), Mississippi Filemaster QD V3.2 (ST)
Orig. price (1986):	$1000 (£799)
Price in 1996:	$300 (£300)

The inclusion of Akai's S612 here may raise the odd eyebrow. But this curious combination of a sampler and a separate storage medium (the Quick Disk-based MD280) is where not only Akai but also many illustrious musicians and producers began.

The S612, a design that grew out of Dave Cockerell's seminal work with Electro-Harmonix, is simplicity itself to operate. You select a sample rate/time by pressing a note on your connected keyboard. You adjust your record level and, using either line or mic inputs, off you go. The 2.8-inch MD280 storage device is pretty much an essential add-on, since without it your sampling is strictly live and real-time. Even so, the MD280 is hardly overburdened with capacity, housing just one sample per side. Quick Disks themselves are quite hard to find in the 1990s, though since Roland and Korg have also used the format, stocks do seem to exist.

The S612's top sample rate is 32kHz for a one-second sample. To squeeze out the full eight seconds, you'd need to drop down to the subterranean level of 4kHz, which will make most samples other than kick drum sound like they've been recorded through several layers of wool. Samples can be truncated and looped using primitive start- and end-point sliders. There's even limited analog-style editing using a (sine wave-only) LFO with depth, speed and delay parameters; high- and lowpass filtering (the highpass filter option, a rarity on any sampler old or new, particularly valuable here since highs are fairly precious) and a decay control. Further editing can be carried out on Akai synths like the VX990 or AX73 by connecting them to the S612 via proprietary 13-pin Voice Out connectors.

There is no multisampling as such, but two samples can be layered. You can also trigger samples—notably and most commonly drum samples—from an audio signal on tape using the optional audio trigger kit. Bandwidth may be restrictive, yet the S612 is so simple and direct that it still has uses and many friends. The gritty, grainy sound can also be viewed as an advantage in some settings. Newcomers on a severely restricted budget, preferably those who also like gritty, grainy, analog-type sounds, could do far worse than to pick up an S612 system. But do make sure you can get hold of some disks before you part with your cash.

Akai S900 Digital sampling module

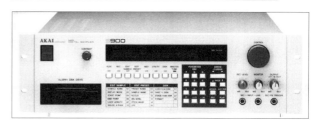

THE FAX

Keyboard:	None
Programs:	32
External storage:	3½" disk drive
Polyphony:	8-voice
Oscillators per voice:	n/a
Effects:	None
Connections:	Mix, L/R, 8 separate audio outs, MIDI, 13-pin voice, RS232C
Dimensions:	482mm x 132mm x 410mm
Weight:	10.8kg

THE FIGURES

Chief designers:	Dave Cockerell, H. Takemura
Production run:	1986-88
Approx. units sold:	15,000
Options:	ASK90 Drum Trigger, IB-101 A/S HD Interface, Marion Systems MS-9C (16-bit upgrade)
Sounds:	Akai library, plus East-West, Greysounds, MIDIMan, Navarrophonic, Northstar, Quantum Audio, Soundsations, 3D Sounds, Four Minute Warning and many more
Miscellaneous:	Internal memory is 750KB and that's it—no upgrades.
Orig. price (1986):	$3295 (£1899)
Price in 1996:	$425 (£400)

The S900 not only served as the blueprint for a couple of generations of Akai samplers, but it has also been a defining influence on sampler design throughout the industry.

Along with Ensoniq's Mirage keyboard (which was, in fact, released slightly earlier), the S900 changed sampling from a rich man's sport to one with, if not mass appeal, certainly mass access. However, radical and successful as the Mirage was, Ensoniq failed to capitalize and build upon its design and appeal. In comparison, Akai saw a good thing, stuck with it and, as a result, went on to establish itself as the de facto standard in the mid- to top-price sampling market, which is a position it holds to this day.

The S900 is a 12-bit sampler with a maximum sample time of 11.75 seconds at full bandwidth. If you're after the full grainy effect or working with non-metallic drum sounds, using the lowest frequency of 7.5kHz can elicit more than a minute's worth of sample time.

In 1986, the S900's good-sized strip of display screen, helpful page buttons underneath, panel-printed parameter list, disk drive, separate voice outputs and mostly logical operating system (which, importantly, is stored internally) made it the immediate choice of professionals.

The eight edit or mode page buttons (Play, Record, Edit sample, Edit program, MIDI, Utility, Disk and Master tune) instantly reveal the scope of the instrument. In a large square to the right of the page buttons are a keypad and cursor keys, plus a useful playback button; and to the right of these is the now-famous large, free-flowing control wheel. Mic and line inputs are also mounted on the front panel (a most sensible arrangement) with record level, monitor and output rotary controls above.

The S900's sampling process goes like this: (1) You record a sample, (2) you insert a sample into a "keygroup" (the name Akai gives to a sort of basket of parameters applied to a particular sample, such as range, MIDI channel, output and volume) and (3) you place keygroups into a program, which is the actual item you store, call up, trigger or play.

Along the way, a good deal of editing and tweaking can take place, of course, starting off with things you can do with raw samples. Actually taking samples is a simple step-by-step process once you have bravely pressed that Record page button with the screen commands as your guide. The questions you will be asked are either logical or straightforward multiple-choice (e.g., desired sample length, level, bandwidth, etc.).

Having taken a sample and, if you like, confirmed that it is there by using the Playback button, the first thing you are required to do is name it. After this, you can snip, tuck and loop it into shape on the edit sample pages. S900 digital edit tools are not sophisticated by later standards, but crossfade looping in all modes was available by Version 2.0, and with a reasonable pair of ears, you can concoct perfectly good results.

In order to apply the many analog-style edit parameters, a sample must be in a keygroup within a program. This is a reasonable request, since it allows you to tweak and fashion the same sample into any number of shapes without altering the raw sample.

The *raison d'être* might be logical, but the actual process of calling up keygroups often foxes people. If this applies to you, here goes: To call up keygroups, go to Page 3 of Edit Program. Put the cursor on Copy, and press Ent until the number of keygroups you need is displayed within the brackets above.

Once in its keygroup, a sample can avail itself of the many edit parameters logged within the Edit Program pages. There is a lowpass filter (no resonance yet—this has to wait until Akai's S3000, some six years hence) with its own ADSR envelope generator, an amplifier with ADSR envelope generator and an

LFO. There's also an interesting doodad entitled "Warp," which is like a preset pitch envelope that makes a sample slide up to pitch. It's simple and fun.

A keygroup can contain two samples, one loud and one soft. Thus, you can velocity-switch between a pair of samples, or you can even layer keygroups. (Either way, such capers, of course, reduce polyphony.)

MIDI channel and output assignments are also made per keygroup. The only potential point of confusion here is that a global MIDI channel can also be set; the keygroup MIDI channels are then offsets of this global channel. This can be confusing at first, but it does allow you to shift a whole group of MIDI channel assignments simply by altering your global channel, which definitely saves time and schlepping around when coordinating a large multitimbral setup. Assigning outputs can be tricky because there are so many options. To start with the physical layout, there's a mix out, plus a left/right pair, plus eight separate voice outputs. The first thing to understand is that the separate outputs are, and can only be, monophonic. If you want more than one note to be sent, you must use the mix or left/right routes.

Another tip to remember is that everything assigned to outputs 1-4 will also appear out of the left output. Similarly, 5-8 and right are linked. If you want to trigger a blend of monophonic and polyphonic parts, use outputs 1-4 for, say, your string pad and use the right output solely for, say, a collection of drum loops. Stereo can be simulated by assigning keygroups to the separate outputs and panning or EQing to order on your mixer.

Management features are generally good. You can load or save programs or samples singly or collectively, and while the operating system can be (indeed, was) revised from time to time on disk, you don't need to reload the OS every time you switch on. The disk drive only accepts DD disks, though.

In its heyday, the S900 found favor with all and sundry, with such sample luminaries as Art of Noise using them extensively on their 1987 tours. (Fairlight? Phooey!) Later, the S900 fell into the role of drum-sample purveyor, partly due to its limited memory and 12-bit status and partly because Akai offered a dedicated drum trigger on the ASK90 that allowed each of the S900's voices to be triggered separately by, among other things, drum pads. For those who found this niche constricting, Marion Systems also offered the MS-9C upgrade, which elevates the S900 to 16-bit.

Although the S900 system is generally understandable to those who bother to get at least their feet wet (and as such became the blueprint for a whole series of Akai samplers), equally as important to its early success was the sample library.

In the UK, Akai pursued a most generous policy of letting owners copy Akai library sounds free if they just called, made an appointment and turned up at Akai's Heathrow offices. In America, such a policy was never feasible ("Where're you calling from? Alaska? Well, next time you're in San Antonio, be sure to look us up!"), and this may well have contributed to the march of Akai sampling being less rampant in the U.S. than it has been in the UK and Europe.

Samples taken and stored in S900 format will generally be playable on models further up the Akai ladder. S900s themselves remain perfectly viable for certain sampling tasks—notably, drums—though most of the instrument's many admirers have by now at least managed to upgrade to an S950.

This was where it began to get serious, though.

Akai S950 Digital sampling module

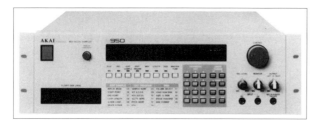

THE FAX

Keyboard:	None
Programs:	99
External storage:	3½" disk drive
Polyphony:	8-voice
Oscillators per voice:	n/a
Effects:	None
Connections:	Mix, L/R, 8 separate audio outs, MIDI, RS-232C, 13-pin voice out
Dimensions:	482mm x 132mm x 425mm
Weight:	10.8kg

THE FIGURES

Chief designers:	Dave Cockerell, H. Takemura
Production run:	1988-1993
Approx. units sold:	15,000
Options:	Digital in, Atari Supra HD Interface, SCSI, 750kHz memory expansion
Sounds:	Akai library, plus East-West, Greytsounds, MIDIMan, Navarrophonic, Northstar, Quantum Audio, Soundsations, 3D Sounds, Four Minute Warning and many more
Miscellaneous:	The author's classic string amalgam, which can be heard on Steve Hackett's live *There Are Many Sides to the Night* album (Caroline), is a scratchy S950 solo violin coupled with a Korg Wavestation Noble Strings preset.
Orig. price (1988):	$2500 (£1349)
Price in 1996:	$1000 (£750)

The S950 emerged in 1988 in a blaze of indifference. In 1988, all eyes were sharply focused on Akai's far more tempting morsel of the S1000. S950? It hardly rated mention as a snack.

But lack of press attention did the S950 no harm whatsoever. You (well, we—I bought one), the public, soon cottoned to the fact that this essentially revamped S900 was perfectly well equipped to meet all manner of sample applications. Sure, it is still 12-bit. Sure, the polyphony has a paltry eight voices. But the sample rate goes up to a sizzling 48kHz, you can squeak out some 2.25MB of internal memory—more than double that of the S900, in other words—and upgrade items from the S900, like cross-fade looping and pre-trigger recording, come as standard. And there's plenty more, too.

Physically, an S950 is almost indistinguishable from an S900. Same strip of green screen, same eight page buttons that take you into the eight main areas of sampling life, same cursor, input and monitor controls. Though the disk drive also looks the same, the S950 will in fact take both HD and DD disks, and the internal memory, 750KB standard, can be upgraded to a respectable 2.25MB. You can also load disks while playing, a feat the S900 is not inclined to perform. The S950 is speedy on the MIDI front, too, with double-speed MIDI communication for sample editing or transfer using an external computer.

Operationally, the S950 works very much along S900 lines. The sample record pages take you through setup procedures one step at a time, the difference here being that you can sample at the lofty 48kHz rate. Though this will give you extra cut and sparkle, it does have the effect of reducing your maximum full-bandwidth sample time on a standard-memory machine.

The S950 expands on the S900's sample edit parameters with crossfade looping and the important pre-trigger recording, which enables you to record razor-sharp front ends.

Having snipped and tucked your sample into shape, you must insert it into a keygroup and then into a program to be played. If you are a little uncertain precisely what a keygroup is, and/or how to call them up on this instrument, please read the S900 entry for additional information. The S950 can hold more samples (99 as opposed to 32), though it's a fair bet you'll run out of memory long before you come close to this many samples.

A feature implemented on the S950 that was not available on the S900 is time stretch. This facility allows you to alter a sample's length (and thus, say, the tempo of a drum loop or how fast someone is talking) without altering its pitch. Well, that's the theory anyway. Experimentation is the order of the day with this facility on any sampler. Once you stray too far away from your original position, samples start to sound metallic and unnatural. The process will invariably muck up your loops as well, so be prepared for this.

For the most part, the S950's facilities are plus, plus, plus. There is one omission from the S900, though: the ASK90 Drum Trigger. In its stead comes the ME35T trigger-to-MIDI interface, which is rather more complex and expensive.

The 13-pin Voice output (also found on the S900) gives you direct access to early Akai synths such as AX73 for additional editing power. I've never come across anyone who has ever done this, though!

The S950 has stood the test of time well. Many people (including your author) have continued to use this sampler well into the 1990s. A scratchy old S950 solo violin sample acts for me as a brilliant "front end" to a lush Korg Wavestation string patch to produce a breathtaking string composite. More resourcefully, perhaps, Norman Cook of Beats International uses a transposed-down S950 Tone Program mixed in with an Oberheim Matrix-1000 for his sub-bass sounds.

As with the S900, the S950 has a simply vast range of Akai and third-party sounds available. Impressively, not only is the S950 fully downwardly compatible with S900 disks, but it's also upwardly compatible with S1000 disks. Though it's 12-bit to the S1000's 16-bit and mono to the S1000's stereo, you'll find that most samples transfer and come out extremely well.

The S950 is not a fancy machine with fancy facilities such as onboard effects, stereo sampling, resonant multimode filters and the like. It is more of a workhorse. The only problem I have personally experienced in several world tours' worth of use is that the EXM006 expansion chips tend to fall out after the instrument has had a hard day of being hurled 20 feet off a 747 at the airport. Luckily, only a couple of screws keep the bottom plate in place, and you can thumb the errant chips back where they belong in a trice. Another tip worth repeating is that if a disk appears damaged and you fear sample data is irretrievably lost, try loading in samples or programs individually rather than using the standard trick of switching on with the disk in place. It'll get you out of jail 50 percent of the time.

Akai S1000 Digital sampling module

THE FAX

Keyboard:	n/a (KB version: 61-note)
Programs:	100
External storage:	3½" disk drive
Polyphony:	16-voice
Oscillators per voice:	n/a
Effects:	None
Connections:	L/R plus 8 separate audio, MIDI, effect send and return, phones
Dimensions:	482mm x 132mm x 425mm
Weight:	9.5kg

Chief designers:	David Cockerell, H. Takemura, Chris Huggett
Production run:	1988-1993
Approx. units sold:	22,000
Options:	SCSI, digital interface, various models (see review); S1000W-A Waveform Manager, S1000P-A Parameter Manager, S1000L-A Library Manager (all for Atari ST)
Sounds:	Akai
Miscellaneous:	Standard memory is 2MB, upgradable to 32MB in 2 or 8MB chunks.
Orig. price (1988):	$4599 (£2599)
Price in 1996:	$1200-1500 (£1000-1500, depending on memory)

What the S900 did for sampling, the S1000 did for stereo sampling. Stereo sampling was seen as a red herring in all but the most crucial circumstances (as with a soloed acoustic piano), but the S1000 was pitched at such a price that the generation that had just cut its teeth on the S900 felt compelled to "move up" to the delights of stereo, 16-bit sound quality and 16-voice polyphony at the earliest opportunity.

Though the S1000 is not radically different from the S900 and S950 in looks, it exudes professional quality. (More so, many feel, than the S1000's replacement models in the 3000 series. But that's another story.) A large number of controls are mounted on the angled front-panel block. The screen, larger than that of previous Akai samplers (40x8 pixels) is bright blue, with two cursor controls that make maneuvering swift and easy.

As with all of the S-series samplers, the S1000's operating system is stored on ROM. Upgrades can be loaded from a disk, but in normal use, all you have to do is switch the unit on and start working.

The process of taking samples begins when you press the Record button, whereupon you are confronted by page after page of logical choices of settings: mono or stereo recording, threshold, bandwidth, etc. Sample frequencies range from 22.5kHz up to industry-standard 44.1kHz, with 24-bit internal processing. Provided you can read, sampling thus far will not be a problem. Akai thoughtfully designed the monitoring to shift automatically from input to output once you have taken a sample, so it immediately becomes playable without having to stab at buttons or move into another mode.

The beauty of the large screen becomes obvious

on your next port of call—the edit sample pages where you can see your sample(s) in graphic form. This is beautiful, but if you work in stereo, it's still no easy matter to trim and loop two samples at a time.

The S1000 has plenty of in-depth automatic looping tools and features. If you have the patience, you can command up to eight loop points, though for most sounds (and most people), selecting a nice long slice of sample and repeatedly pressing Find until you like what you hear will probably suffice. The screen displays both waveform and numerical data and has zoom in and out functions. The S1000 offers a sensible blend of sophistication and immediacy, with enough variables for people with different skill levels and applications to find their own best ways to work.

Samples that are cut to length (and looped, if desired) are then placed within keygroups in order to take up residence in a permanent S1000 program. A keygroup can hold a maximum of four stacked samples, with keyboard zone and velocity information. Analog-style editing parameters at this stage include lowpass filters (no resonance) with a dedicated ADSR envelope generator, an amplifier with an ADSR envelope generator and an LFO. Once again, the generously proportioned screen is excellent for displaying envelope segments and providing a clean, clear environment in which to work.

Equally clean and clear is the process of assembling completed programs for multitimbral playing. In practice, you have two choices: Either you can save a specific MIDI channel in the program, or you can give each program its own channel, used as an offset from the global channel. The system is simple and very flexible. It works particularly well if you want to experiment with sound combinations, since you can simply assign programs to the same MIDI channel and they will sound simultaneously.

The S1000 was one of the first instrumental samplers to push the boundaries of sampling towards studio production applications. Time Stretch was offered as standard on Versions 1.3 and higher and is more detailed than the version offered for the S950. As always, though, if you stray too far from your original speed or pitch, the results sound distinctly unnatural.

Fully loaded with 32MB of internal memory, the S1000 can be fitted with SCSI and even digital I/O, and such an upgraded unit is as powerful as almost any current instrument. Only the polyphony and the inclusion of more detailed editing parameters (notably, resonant filters) give Akai's more recent S3000 series an edge.

The S1000 was released under many guises, from the standard unit reviewed here to the S1000H-D (with a built-in 40MB hard drive), to the S1000P-B (playback only, no actual sampling) to a keyboard version, the S1000K-B, a cumbersome instrument that resembles an industrial steam iron.

Top-flight professionals still tend to be inclined toward Akai's S1100, on which many pro S1000 features like digital I/O and SCSI come as standard along with internal effects, a SMPTE generator and improved A/D converters; but the S1000, loaded and upgraded to meet your own particular requirements, remains viable and a hard act to follow.

ARP 2600 Monophonic analog synthesizer

THE FAX

Keyboard:	49-note (separate)
Programs:	None
External storage:	None
Polyphony:	2-voice (mono on earlier models)
Oscillators per voice:	3
Effects:	Spring reverb
Connections:	Mono audio, phones, CV and gate jacks, trigger input
Dimensions:	740mm x 430mm x 205mm
Weight:	17kg

THE FIGURES

Chief designer:	Alan R. Pearlman
Production run:	1971-1981
Approx. units sold:	3000
Options:	New modules (filter, ring mod, etc.) from third-party companies (see "Miscellaneous")
Sounds:	n/a
Miscellaneous:	Service, repair and modifications from the Audio Clinic/Weyer-Smith Labs: 3461 Canyon Dr.; Billings, MT 59102; tel: (406) 652-1564 or CMS: 1522 Eaton Ave.; Bethlehem, PA 18018; tel: (610) 694-8886.
Orig. price (1971):	$2600 (£1350)
Price in 1996:	$1500-2000 (£1200-1750)

"With the 2600 you never have to listen to the same sound twice if you don't want to," said Joe Zawinul in an ARP promo leaflet. Some would argue that you cannot get the same sound twice even if you wanted to and that this is a good part of the 2600's charm and attraction.

Such debate is symptomatic of the aura of conflicting opinion that has surrounded this classic semi-modular design since day one. The ARP 2600 has grown into an industry of debate, conjecture, folklore and rivalry. Is a "Blue Meanie," one of the garish, garage-assembled earliest models, better than a "Gray Meanie"? Does yours have the old Moog-style filters or the later filters, hastily designed by ARP in response to an impending lawsuit from Moog? Maybe yours even has versions of these filters that were amended and improved after ARP went out of business?

With a 2600, it seems, you're not just buying a piece of musical equipment but also a source of endless speculation—and endless specifications. Indeed, it's tempting to think that ARP 2600 owners must be kindred spirits to the maniacal hi-fi buffs who spend $20,000 on a system and only listen to test tones. But luckily, although this instrument is very much the synth bore's delight, it also happens to sound brilliant. And it is used to great effect even as I write.

The nuts and bolts of the instrument are as follows: Packaged in an oblong case with a lid that detaches to reveal a telephone exchange of sliders, switches and patchbays, this is a three-oscillator analog synthesizer design complete with effects processing and amplification.

Alan Pearlman's first instrument, the 2500, was complex and expensive and never meant to be widely accessible. The 2600 was produced as a more readily available instrument, designed primarily for the education market (hence the handy completeness of its small built-in amplification system and the informative schematics on the front panel). Pearlman built the 2600 so that it could be understood and used. And he did it very well.

There are three voltage-controlled oscillators, a four-pole lowpass resonant VCF, a VCA, two envelope generators, a ring modulator, a sample-and-hold circuit, a white/pink noise generator, a mic preamp input, a spring reverb and unique (and uniquely confusing) voltage processor controls. Most of these modules can be manually cross-patched for an unending display of analog synthesis sounds; each has an input and an output, making the 2600 an excellent instrument on which to learn what each component part of a subtractive-synthesis instrument actually does.

Like all good teachers, the 2600 is also a lot of fun. This is a hands-on machine. It is quite possible to simply stand in front of it and maneuver sliders until you hear something wonderful, but the chance to process external signals throws the sonic possibilities wide open. Rick Smith of The Underworld, a long-time 2600 user, likes injecting the instrument with a blast of shortwave radio (even though the instrument does a fair impression of one on its own). Sample-and-hold effects (the classic bleeps and blurps) can even be clocked externally. Though MIDI was not even a nightmare during the 2600's production, interfacing this instrument with the modern world is not generally a problem; any MIDI-to-CV box should pro-

Name: ARP
In operation: 1969 to 1981
Business: Stage and modular synthesizers

The commercial synthesizer industry was steered into being by two companies: Moog and ARP. For much of the 1970s, the industry saw a Beatles vs. Stones/Pepsi vs. Coke situation, with Moog and ARP appealing to two sides of the same coin.

Founded by electronics engineer Alan R. Pearlman, ARP produced the 2500, a large, modular patch-pin instrument designed and destined for university music labs. A reasonable success, the 2500 inspired Pearlman to produce a more compact, musician-oriented synthesizer, the 2600, which was released the following year.

ARP's "Minimoog" was the Odyssey, released in 1972. The Odyssey never quite soared to the heights of the Minimoog, but it sold well and was the perfect alternative for those who wanted something different. Indeed, much of ARP's motivation seems to have been to do things differently from Moog, however gratuitous that might be.

But whereas Moog instruments maintained a common thread of relatively serious synthesis, ARP diversified into multi-instrument keyboards, strings machines, pianos and, equally disastrously, guitar synthesizers (the Avatar).

It was too much too soon. ARP's reputation was established through powerful and often complex synthesizers. When the public woke up one morning and found ARP instruments in the stores that looked like they fell out of an Italian toy department, it both blew the company's image and unsettled buyers' nerves.

Central to ARP's problems, and quite self-evident from the disparity of its products, was a power struggle within the company. (The details of this conflict are beyond the scope of this book but are outlined at length in Mark Vail's *Vintage Synthesizers*.) Though instruments such as the Odyssey and the Omni were successful, ARP ventured down enough blind alleys to deplete both funds and morale by the end of the 1970s.

ARP was an extremely important company in the development of the synthesizer industry. But its long-term influence has been nowhere near that of Moog, Sequential or Oberheim, those other casualties of the entrepreneurial American electronic-instrument trail.

E-mu's Dave Rossum, relating stories of his early career, once told how he spent more than a year trying to match the specification of an ARP synthesizer. When he actually got his hands on the instrument in question, he found that the specification had been an almost complete fabrication. Such triumphs of style over content are inextricably wedded to a short shelf-life, and while the 2600 and, to some extent, the Odyssey have become prized collector's items, a large slab of ARP inventory was always fairly suspect.

vide MIDI access.

The 2600 changed quite a lot externally during its long production run, from the original "Blue Meanies" (so called due to their distinctive blue panel and metal casing) to more subdued, gray and black models (of which only some 10 were ever made, apparently, during 1972) to the final units, blessed with rather cheap-looking orange markings.

According to ex-ARP personnel, the later models were considerably better-made; their modified internal designs at least allowed them to be repaired, something that the epoxy-entombed circuits of the early models singularly failed to offer. But then there's that trade-off with originality, rarity and sound.

Perhaps the most important ARP-implemented change came in 1975, when a modification from fellow synth designer Tom Oberheim (then only a peripherals designer, actually) was adopted on production models. The mod not only provided a form of duo phony (one oscillator serving the low note, another the high) but also a delayed vibrato feature and a choice of single/multiple triggering.

Another fascinating development in the 2600's history concerns a fault in its filter that engineer Tim Smith discovered that can cause the instrument to sound...well, dull. Smith, one-half of the ARP experts team at Weyer/Smith Labs in Billings, Montana, is quite happy to share the secret of his discovery with anyone who asks, and the result will be a frequency response of better than 22kHz. Weyer/Smith offers a vast range of 2600 improvements and upgrades, including a fixit for the dreaded thump that occurs if you try to set fast attack and release times on the envelope generator. CMS also offers fixits for this and other ARP foibles. (See Miscellaneous for information on both companies.)

In its heyday—or perhaps, seeing as how its popularity has rocketed in the 1990s, I should say its first heyday—the 2600 was a valued axe in the hands of most top players, from Joe Zawinul (top lines from such tracks as "Scarlet Woman" and "Black Market") to Tony Banks. Edgar Winter's monstrous synth sounds on "Frankenstein" are generally credited to the 2600 (as well as ARP's Odyssey), while Stevie Wonder had a modified Braille version built.

The fact that many people are buying 2600s in the '90s says perhaps even more, because the likes of Zawinul and Wonder had everything (correction: *were given* everything). Bands and bods like The Underworld, Orbital and Vince Clarke have truly chosen the instrument and tend to use it because it produces a singular range of sounds (this is the best synth for making stupid, funny noises).

Strictly a real-time animal—don't bother trying to recreate a sound, just create a new one—the 2600 has become one of the classic classics. Highly collectible, the instrument commands substantial prices and, provided you can look beyond professional collector snobbery, purchase is well justified.

ARP ceased trading in 1981.

ARP Odyssey | Analog monophonic synthesizer

THE FAX

Keyboard:	37-note
Programs:	None
External storage:	None
Polyphony:	2-voice
Oscillators per voice:	2
Effects:	None
Connections:	Mono output, pedal
Dimensions:	610mm x 660mm x 152mm
Weight:	8kg

THE FIGURES

Chief designer:	Alan R. Pearlman
Production run:	1972-1980
Approx. units sold:	3000
Options:	CV pedal
Sounds:	You're on your own!
Miscellaneous:	Dave Simmons, the man behind Simmons drums, used to demonstrate and sell ARP Odysseys at London's Boosey & Hawkes in the 1970s. Service and repair from CMS: 1522 Eaton Ave.; Bethlehem, PA 18018; tel: (610) 694-8886
Orig. price (1972):	$1550 (£1250)
Price in 1996:	$500 (£450)

The story of the synthesizer is littered with oddball characters and litanies of disasters, and ARP is a perfect case in point. Headed up by eccentric boffin Alan R. Pearlman, ARP flourished briefly in the mid-1970s before chronic mismanagement saw it dismembered and sold off in job lots to CBS. Personality clashes, strange financial dealings, crazy notions of guitar synthesis...you name it, ARP had it. The curious, go-it-alone monophonic Odyssey was actually one of the company's more normal and more successful outings.

In 1972, there were very few synths that musicians could afford, never mind control or play. ARP produced the Odyssey in response to and as a direct rival to the Minimoog. In fact, the rivalry between Moog and ARP seemed almost stage managed. Everything Moog did, ARP did slightly differently: There was a pitch wheel on the Moog, so there was a pitch knob, and later a pitch pad, on the ARP. Rotary knobs on the Moog—sliders on the ARP. Black color scheme on the Moog—Tic-Tac-like knobs on the ARP.

The Odyssey doesn't have the boffin appeal of most early synths. There are no patchcords, and the front panel, although it comprises a sea of minute switches and sliders (very loosely calibrated, and sporting, as mentioned above, color-coded blobs of plastic about the size of Tic-Tacs, which tend to fall off and get lost), is laid out almost as well.

This is a dual-oscillator monophonic synth, though two notes can be emitted using different pitches for each oscillator. The oscillators offer switchable sawtooth/pulse waveforms; the VCOs are both coarsely and finely tunable . The pulse width can be controlled manually or modulated using an LFO or the ADSR envelope generator. There are both low- and highpass filters, the lowpass offering variable cutoff frequency and resonance sliders. The filter can even be used as a sound source in "self-oscillating" high resonance position. The filter can be shaped by either of two envelope generators (simple attack/release or a more specific attack/decay/delay/release variety) and can be modulated by an LFO, the sample-and-hold circuit, the keyboard CV or a pedal.

The LFO has sliders governing frequency and output lag (delay) and umpteen variations on the theme, "What can you feed into the sample and hold circuit?" Very simply, the answer is VCOs 1 and 2 and/or the VCF but, due to the sliders, the degrees of this modulation are infinitely variable.

In terms of powerful parameters, the Odyssey is well stocked. Noise is available in both pink and white versions, there is a ring modulator, you can set up repeats and auto repeat triggering, and the excellent modulation permutations mean that in the hands of someone who knows what they're doing, this can be a most expressive, lifelike instrument to play. On early models, actual performance controls comprised portamento slider, a four-octave-range transposer and a far-from-accurate pitch bend—a mere rotary control with a supposedly safe central area. Later, these were joined by a rubbery pad called the PPC ("proportional pitch control") that controlled LFO depth. If you are on the lookout for an Odyssey, definitely try to find one of the units with these.

At the other end of the performance scale, the Odyssey is an excellent sound effects synth for wind, steam, seashore or bird noises, space sounds, etc. The Odyssey is big on sample-and-hold. This feature, which is effectively a random note generator, is great fun for sound effects and general space-age noises. Actually, it's somewhat symptomatic of the Odyssey's whole approach to synthesis: great sounds but lousy controllability.

But the instrument's lousy controllability is the main problem, and (in spite of ARP's valiant efforts with little templates that you sling over the panel to mark each knob, switch and slider's setting) replicating a sound even approximately, never mind precise-

ly, is a most unlikely occurrence.

That an Odyssey can be lots of fun, giving you the chance to be really creative, learn about subtractive synthesis, etc., is undoubted. But with no LEDs, and sliders that are calibrated too sensitively, and fairly unstable tuning in anything other than cool studio conditions (tuning is even more difficult because the coarse slider is only approximately marked in Hz, and there's no A=440 guide, button or position), the instrument needs an owner who thrives on the audio version of WYSIWYG (substitute "hear" for "see").

Major plus points are the distinctively rich basic sound—check out Edgar Winter's "Frankenstein" for full-blown Odyssey (the 2600 was also credited), or Ultravox's "Vienna"—the creative sample-and-hold permutations and helpful features such as the pedal you can use to maneuver the filter cutoff for wow effects. A book called *Learning Music With Synthesizers* was written in the 1970s and uses the ARP Odyssey as its source instrument; it's well worth searching out.

Various models were produced, including three distinct panel colors: in chronological order, light grey, dark gray and gaudy orange and black. Later models (those sporting the PPC) are generally perceived as more stable and therefore the ones to buy. The Odyssey is not seen and used to anywhere near the same extent as a MiniMoog is today, but it remains highly collectible.

ARP ceased trading in 1981.

Bit One Analog polyphonic synthesizer

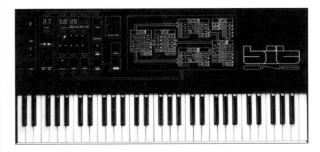

THE FAX

Keyboard:	61-note
Programs:	64
External storage:	Cassette interface
Polyphony:	6-voice
Oscillators per voice:	2
Effects:	None
Connections:	2 audio (upper/lower), phones, trigger, pedals, MIDI
Dimensions:	860mm x 400mm x 80mm
Weight:	12kg

THE FIGURES

Chief designer:	Luciano Jura
Production run:	1984-1986
Approx. units sold:	No figures available

Options:	None
Sounds:	None commercially available
Miscellaneous:	Bit was marketed in the U.S. under the name of Unique. If only...
Orig. price (1984):	$1395 (£799)
Price in 1996:	$400 (£250)

The name "Bit" has a good deal more relevance to keyboards in the 1990s than it did back in the 1980s when the name and a few associated products emerged from Italy. Of course, there was no such company as Bit. Bit was Crumar in disguise, the perceived logic being that the synth fraternity would not be seen dead with an instrument made by an Italian piano and organ company. (Italian companies remain masters of this type of caper to this day.)

Whatever the name, the Bit One caused quite a stir in 1984. It had big, flashy sounds, and it was easy on the eye, brain and wallet. In Britain, the instrument was distributed by a flash-in-the-pan outfit called Chase Musicians, who delighted in preposterously hyped marketing and absurd price slashes ("Originally $3 million, now only 50 bucks!"—that type of thing).

But the marketing front couldn't completely overshadow the fact that although the Bit One had some killer sounds and features, it was also, like so many Italian synths at the time, pretty unreliable. This was early in MIDI's life, and production models only operated in Omni On, though modifications upgrading to full 16-channel MIDI assignments were quick to follow.

In pure programming terms, the Bit One is a powerful exponent of analog subtractive synthesis in stable DCO form. The two DCOs per voice can choose from triangle, sawtooth or pulse waveforms; the 24dB/oct lowpass filter can be shaped by its own ADSR envelope generator (in normal or inverted positions); there are two fully equipped LFOs; and the velocity-sensitive keyboard can control not only volume and brightness, but oscillator pulse width, LFO rate and VCF envelope.

The keyboard can be split at any point (splits are non-programmable), or patches can be layered; both of which render the instrument three-voice polyphonic. Sounds can also be put into heavy, monophonic unison mode.

Produced both in black and white versions, the Bit One looks nothing if not exciting. It was briefly successful until its limited MIDI spec and poor reliability caused resentment to set in. Crumar quickly put together an improved but similar instrument, the Bit 99, along with one of the first successes of the rack-mount market, the Bit 01 Rack Expander.

However, the keyboard market being as perverse as it is, it is the Bit One that has the edge in terms of collectability. Chances are that any model bought today and still working will be a later model with slightly more reliable chips. As with all older synths, a model working today is liable to remain so, and the Bit One produces a nice range of punchy analog tones, many of them with a not wholly offensive metallic ring to them. Distinctive. The keyboard, with its various velocity-controlled modulation destinations, is a particular strength.

The Bit One's designer, Luciano Jura, also worked on the Spirit with Bob Moog, plus assorted Crumar string and organ instruments, before joining Farfisa. There he worked on the F-series synth/home keyboards, then later joined EKO. Such is the complicated life of a designer in the Italian keyboard industry.

Bit, ex-Crumar, is no longer in business.

Casio CZ-101 — Digital polyphonic synthesizer

THE FAX

Keyboard:	49-note (small keys)
Programs:	16 presets, 16 RAM, 16 on cartridge
External storage:	Cartridge
Polyphony:	8-voice
Oscillators per voice:	2
Effects:	None
Connections:	Mono audio out, phones, MIDI
Dimensions:	676mm x 208mm x 70mm
Weight:	3.2kg

THE FIGURES

Chief designers:	Mark Fukuda, A. Iba
Production run:	1985-88
Approx. units sold:	70,000 (CZ-1000: 45,000)
Options:	ROM cartridges
Sounds:	Opcode Librarian and Patch Factory (Mac), Passport Voice Librarian (ST), Kid Nepro, Charles Lauria, Dr. T's, Soundsource, Songwriter, Hybrid Arts
Miscellaneous:	This was the commercial realization of a concept synth called "Cosmo" built for Tomita. The CZ, SZ sequencer and RZ drum machine were all component parts of Cosmo. Books: *Insider's Guide to the Casio CZ-101* by Andrew Schlesinger, *Getting the Most Out of Your Casio CZ-101* by Lorenz Rychner
Orig. price (1985):	$499 (£395)
Price in 1996:	$150 (£100)

What are we going to do about Casio, eh? This mysterious Japanese giant, whose stock in trade is calculators, watches and sundry pieces of musical gadgetry, had one purple patch, so far as serious musicians are concerned, in the late 1980s when the CZ series of digital synthesizers, the FZ series of samplers and finally the VZ synths were built. What these instruments all had in common was that they were innovative, fun and inexpensive. People bought them by the truckload.

Unfortunately, the size of that truck was not the size Casio was used to shipping in. "Only 70,000 units sold," you can hear the Casio bigwigs wailing. "Cancel the project immediately." Now leaf through this book and see how many synths have topped this figure, even before we toss in the 45,000 CZ-1000s they sold.

Rumor has it that management's displeasure was such that some of the design team were banished to far-flung corners of the company to design logos for the staff toilets or something.

The CZ-101 came into the world as a bargain-basement digital synth: unpretentious, uncluttered, accessible to all. However, though the instrument itself might have been street-level, its origins, along with Casio's intentions for it, were of course anything but.

The CZ-101 was hewn out of Casio's much-vaunted but completely unfathomable "Cosmo" concept, a notion floated out of their marketing department that, somehow, all manner of component-part instruments and devices were being progressively extracted from a sort of space-age wonder synth. Aiding this ruse was Tomita's "In Praise of the Earth" extravaganza, a classic piece of mid-'80s money-burning, which saw "The Synthetic One" himself dangling out of helicopters and conducting an electronic orchestra that was floating about on the Hudson River beside Battery Park—or some such nonsense. Poor old Casio, as sponsors of the event, bravely worked in some form of Cosmo tie-in, but in truth they needn't have bothered. The CZ-101 was already a deserved runaway success and needed little help from the likes of Tomita.

Casio's entry in the history of professional-application synths (no speakers or auto-accompaniments) is all too brief: Entered in 1984 with Tomita serenading 80,000 Germans in Linz on the banks of the Danube with the CZ-101. Riotous success ensued upon the instrument's release in 1985 and continued with the CZ-1000 and -5000 and the -3000 in 1986.

Physically, the CZ-101 looks like a most unlikely candidate for success. It is small, tiny almost, with reduced-size keys and little in the way of pro synth aura. But it sounds great—raucous, piercing and with plenty of scope for idle noodlers and serious programmers alike to create new textures. Venturing down to Woolhall Studios near Bath a few years ago

CASIO®

Name:	Casio Electronics
Head Office:	2-6-1 Nishishin Juka, Shinjuka-ku, Tokyo, 160 Japan
U.S. Distributor:	Casio USA: 570 Mt. Pleasant Ave.; Dover, NJ 07801; tel: (201) 361-5400
UK Distributor:	Casio UK: 1000, North Circular Rd., Unit 6; London NW2 7JD UK; 0181-450-9131; fax: 0181-452-6232
Business:	Home keyboards, digital pianos, musical toys, consumer electronics, watches, calculators, cash registers

One word sums up Casio's corporate strategy: volume. This Japanese electronics giant, which made its name and fortune in the calculator and cash register market during the 1970s, first dipped its toes into keyboard waters in 1981, when it launched the VL-1—initially, in fact, a calculator with a keyboard attached. The VL-1 sold in quantities that made sense to Casio bigwigs, and accordingly, an entire range of what became known as "home keyboards" was launched.

From hi-fi stores to department stores to toy stores to garages, for the next few years Casio keyboards sold in large numbers and all was well. Then came Yamaha's DX7.

Until the DX7, the pro synth market was universally recognized as small change. If you could sell 10,000 units, you'd done well. However, 10,000 units to a company like Casio is little more than a loss leader. When DX7 sales went up well into six figures, Casio did not recognize this as the flash in the pan that it was and soon set about producing its own range of not dissimilar digital synthesizers.

The CZ-101 and CZ-1000 swept 1985 off its feet. Inexpensive, innovative and capable of producing a very respectable range of pro-oriented sounds, they didn't rival the VL-1 or the DX7 numbers-wise, but the CZ series sold well. Hot on their heels came a range of dedicated sampling instruments, not bargain-basement cheap this time but innovative and competitive. For samplers, the FZ series sold well, too.

But at this point, all of three years after Casio burst onto the scene in a hail of Tomita-accompanied fireworks (the CZ instruments had all been component parts of the much-hyped "Cosmo" synth, which was featured in a series of overblown multimedia happenings around the globe that were orchestrated by Tomita), the plug was unceremoniously pulled. One minute Casio was talking up a storm about its new VZ series of pro synths and allying itself with ever more creditable professional musicians, and the next minute it was, "We're taking a break from the pro market." (I think that was the phrase they used.) Japanese companies plan long-term, for sure, but Casio's "break" is currently seven year's long, and they show no sign of taking up the fight once more

Back in its familiar arena of home keyboards, and more recently in digital pianos, Casio continues to produce interesting products from time to time. But for serious musicians, Casio remains a frustrating story of what might have been. Doubly so, in fact, considering the about-face the company also did on its excellent range of low-cost pro DAT players.

to interview Tears for Fears producer (and ex-Antperson) Chris Hughes, I couldn't help but remark on the CZ-101 sitting in a place of honor among his grinning racks of state-of-the-art synths and large-screen Macs. "Oh yeah," he said, nonchalantly, "I use it all the time." He and thousands of others to this day.

The CZ-101 is based on Phase Distortion, a proprietary brand of digital synthesis involving messing around with a waveform's phase angle (representing its basic shape) and applying multistage envelope generators to all three of the fundamentals of sound: pitch, tone and duration. PD, as it became known, rivals (and to an extent, shares features with) Yamaha's FM synthesis, first seen by most people on the DX7 a few years previously. It also parallels FM in that there were very few people at the time who had a clue how it all worked. Once again, though, this mattered little in terms of sales and interest. The presets are interesting enough for many applications, but unlike the DX7, it is possible to simply fiddle about with the CZ-101 and get some workable, musical results. Much of this is courtesy of the healthy number of dedicated control buttons and the small but informative display screen.

The three main sections are DCO, for the oscillators; DCW ("W" for Wave), which performs tone-bending, filtering duties; and DCA, for the amplifiers. Each of these sections can be shaped by its own eight-stage envelope generator.

On the DCO panel, there are a number of basic waveforms to choose from: sawtooth (best for brass or string sounds), square (for woodwind or organs), pulse (for thinner, more nasal, reedier tones), double sine (a slightly beefier version of pulse) and sawtooth/pulse (a real rasper), any two of which can be combined. In addition, there are three resonance waves, which are sonic facsimiles of those classic burbling filter patches on the Moog, full of harmonics and whistling.

Having selected a waveform, you can reshape it using the rate- and level-based envelope generator, a task that may seem tedious in print and in prospect, but in practice is beautifully organized and pretty painless to carry out. Indeed, the CZ-101 is a very thoughtful little instrument. You can initialize settings; there's an edit/compare feature; there's key follow, portamento, noise, ring modulation—brilliantly offered, just on or off—and, in quite a killer punch at the time, it can be used multitimbrally, with four monophonic but separately sounding voices.

In 1985, MIDI itself was pretty fresh out of the gate, and multitimbralism was a rare and little-understood notion. The growth of computer-controlled sequencers, notably Steinberg's Pro 16 and Pro 24 in Europe, gave an added boost to CZ-101 sales, because this was (and may still be) one of the most cost-effective multitimbral sound sources available on the market.

If the CZ-101 was snapped up by burgeoning computer hounds, it was by no means sentenced to being stuck in the house all day. With strap holders at either end, the lightweight CZ-101 made a perfect sling-on keyboard for onstage use. Casio demonstra-

tor Hans "Herr" Dryer and his mind-boggling solo-guitar-fading-into-feedback patch were a hit at all the European trade shows at the time. (Hans' patch never made it as a factory preset, but I still remember it. Frankly, it's been seldom, if ever, bettered.)

The CZ-101's quote of eight-voice polyphony is not entirely fair, since almost all patches use the Line 1 + Line 2 routing (an oscillator signal path of DCO-DCW-DCA) for thicker, more complex, more interesting doubled sounds. And if this is not enough, a feature called Tone Mix (you have to be in this mode and on a doubled patch in order to gain the precious four-part multitimbralism over MIDI) renders the instrument full-fat monophonic.

Although in-depth, precision programming on the CZ-101 is generally beyond most people, there's still a forest of literature, videos, organizations, software and sound cartridges around for users to get help at any level they choose.

CZ-101s are notoriously reliable. Yes, reliable. The Casio service department rarely sees any, and when they do, it is often simply a question of pressing the underside reset button, marked "P," while the instrument is switched on in order to reload the factory presets. The CZ-101 can be powered with batteries, but if you let these go flat, the memories will follow.

Less encouragingly, the service departments warn that while it still holds many of the electronic parts, including ICs and such, the physical parts (casing, buttons, screen, etc.) are no longer carried as spares.

Cheap to purchase new, the CZ-101's current second-hand price is still most attractive, because so many units were made. The CZ-1000 is identical internally but has full-size keys and pads rather than panel buttons, while the CZ-3000 is a double-polyphony, 61-note keyboard version and the CZ-5000 adds to this an 8-track sequencer.

Casio FZ-10M Digital sampling module

THE FAX

Keyboard:	None
Programs:	64
External storage:	3½" disk drive
Polyphony:	8-voice
Oscillators per voice:	n/a
Effects:	None

Connections:	Mono audio, mix audio
Dimensions:	482mm x 387mm x 142mm
Weight:	10.7kg

THE FIGURES

Chief designers:	Mr. Sasaki, Mr. Hanzawa, Mr. Fukuda
Production run:	1987-89
Approx. units sold:	3000 (FZ-1: 6000)
Options:	FZ-1 keyboard model, Casio Utilities (Loop Optimizer, Copy Tool, Playbacker Tool, Directory Tool)
Sounds:	2 Casio libraries, Metra Sound, Sample Ware, Kid Nepro, Desert Island, Big Time Productions, East-West, Livewire, Navarraphonic, Jeff Yenter, ProSonus
Miscellaneous:	Casio FZ Users Club in the UK: 53 Linkfield Rd.; Mount Sorrel, Leics, LE12 7DT; book: *FZ-1 + FZ-10: Essential Guide to Practical Applications* by DeFuria & Scacciaferro
Orig. price (1987):	$2499 (£1799)
Price in 1996:	$600 (£600)

- -

As if it weren't enough that Casio, king of kiddie keyboards, started muscling into the synth market with the CZ series in 1985, the company had the audacity to offer up a professional sampling keyboard a couple years later, the FZ-1.

The FZ-1 rattled the competition, all right. Sequential's "revelation" that the instrument was not 16-bit as advertised but was in fact more like 13-bit (because shorting out three bits of the FZ-1's DAC made no difference to a 1kHz tone) was only the most famous piece of flack from a rival company.

All's fair in love and war, you may think, but (a) this piece of information was later to be disproved; the FZ is a 16-bit machine even though it has an 8-bit processor and (b) such slings and arrows made no difference to the FZ-1's wide acceptance in the mid-priced pro and semipro market. The FZ-1 was received well and, for a keyboard sampler, sold well. (It wasn't the critics or the competition that mortally wounded Casio's pro division a year or so down the line. It was simply the market—it was too small for the company's executives.)

Keyboard samplers have always had a limited appeal, though, and the instrument that best survived for almost a decade, in spite of being out of production for half of this time, is the rackmount version of the FZ-1, the FZ-10M.

Aside from obvious physical differences, the major difference with the FZ-10M is the use of professional XLR connectors for sample mic input and the 2MB of standard RAM (the FZ-1 had 1MB but could be upgraded). The bulk of this review is, then, equally applicable to both machines.

Both the look and the feel of the FZ-10M are those of a quality instrument. This large, 4U module appears robust. The control panel is clean and clear, and the display screen (96x64 pixels, dot matrix,

blue) is a good size.

Though billed as a 16-bit sampler, much of the FZ-10M's lasting charm actually comes from a certain graininess in the sound. Indeed, when it comes to gritty, rasping string samples—scrubbing cellos and the like—none better has come along since.

The operating procedures are reasonably familiar: You have to run through an onscreen table of sample setup pages, such as sample rate (36kHz, 18kHz, 9kHz), intended sample time (these max out around 28 seconds at full bandwidth), sample levels and modes. This hierarchical system of screen pages runs right through the instrument for all its many features and is clear enough to let you dispense with the manual for most day-to-day tasks after a few minutes.

Logic does not necessarily equal speed, though. The system may be obvious, but for times when you want to access one particular parameter or see all the sounds on a disk, for example, you still have to scroll through an inordinate number of extra pages beforehand. The days of cut-and-jump had not arrived yet.

Having taken a sample, the first thing most people tend to do, initially at any rate, is lunge for the auto-loop. Not here you won't. At least, not unless you have access to the Loop Optimizer software that Casio later introduced alongside the final instrument in this series, the FZ-20M. Even so, tasks like manual looping and truncating are made quite easy, thanks to the clear screen layout and step-by-step operating system. You are always kept well posted with graphic displays, and the ability to zoom in and out is helpful (and was rare at the time).

Manual looping facilities include crossfade looping and eight-loop-point multi-looping, with each mini-loop programmable to repeat before the next loop kicks in. This is not an everyday feature, but it is indicative of the power under the FZ-10M's hood. Samples can also be cross-mixed, or even cross-fertilized with built-in synthesized sounds.

So much for the digital parameters. Analog-style editing is offered along the lines of CZ synthesizer programming—not surprisingly, seeing as the design team was the same—with eight-stage DCA and DCF envelopes. Not the easiest paths to follow, though the graphic display definitely helps.

What sets the FZ-10M apart from almost all other samplers is the degree to which it caters to and interacts with actual synthesis techniques. The so-called Wave Synthesis section of the instrument lets you create your own digital waveforms, such as Preset Waves. Here, after making your choice of sawtooth, square, pulse, double sine, sawtooth/pulse or random waves (all of which tend to be of the thin and buzzy variety), you can edit using the same analog-style editing parameters (envelopes, etc.) to which the samples have access, including graphic waveform display.

There's also additive harmonic synthesis, in which up to 48 harmonics are specifiable in individual levels ranging from 000 to 256. Again, the graphic display helps present this type of synthesis, always liable to cause head-scratching, in an easy-to-view manner. You can even draw waveshapes by hand.

Once you've created your sounds by one of these methods, some 64 programs can be on tap (memory permitting) at a time. The meager 2MB of internal memory may not allow too much in the way of big setups, but programs are stored across eight banks with all levels, MIDI channels, splits and output assignments intact. There are even eight separate (mono) audio outputs in addition to the mix output.

The FZ-10M continues to be used by many a seasoned pro, from Dee-Lite to Matt Clifford to influential British keyboardist and *Keyboard* columnist Dave Stewart. Maverick electronic composer Steve Reich owns five FZ-1s; his affection for the grit and grime of New York is captured perfectly in the FZ's earthy textures.

FZ sound libraries are not hard to come across, and although Casio has never so much as dipped its toes back into high-tech waters since the SCSI-sporting FZ-20M sampler came out in 1989, the FZ remains a viable instrument. At the time, certain companies advertised boards that raised the FZ's memory to 4MB, but these, according to Casio in the U.S., never actually materialized. Casio engineers say that such a board was not really practical, which is why Casio never offered one itself.

There's no question that the FZ is a classic sampler. How valid any classic sampler is in the cut-and-thrust world of 1990s sampling is another matter. Luckily, the FZ performs very well as an instrument that just happens to be a sampler. Judged solely on its sampling capability, memory limitations plus a mid-'80s operating system tend to make the FZ-10M a little restrictive.

Cheetah MS6 Analog monophonic synthesizer

THE FAX

Keyboard:	No keyboard
Programs:	320 ROM, 96 RAM, 64 multi
External storage:	None

Polyphony:	6-voice
Oscillators per voice:	2
Effects:	None
Connections:	Mono output
Dimensions:	420mm x 240mm x 42mm
Weight:	3.2kg

THE FIGURES

Chief designer:	Ian Jannoway
Production run:	1989-1993
Approx. units sold:	5,000
Options:	None
Sounds:	None
Miscellaneous:	Cheetah closed its musical instrument division in 1993.
Orig. price (1989):	$669 (£399)
Price in 1996:	$400 (£300)

Successful up to a point, British company Cheetah's MS6 module never quite lived up to its promise. The MS6 was released at a time when analog was not particularly hip—as it became a year or so later—and accordingly, the prospect of a low-cost analog synth in module form was not especially tempting.

The modular design notwithstanding, the MS6 is easy to operate (call up a parameter numerically, using the parameter list, then tweak) and chock-full of rich, punchy analog sounds. The programmers drew on the best from yesteryear—Juno, Jupiter, Moog, Prophet-5, Oberheim—for inspiration.

Unlike most of the above units, though, the MS6 does not drift horrendously out of tune, nor does it weigh a ton, nor was it ever expensive, even if current second-hand prices threaten to make it so eventually. In addition, the MS6 has a well-developed MIDI spec, including multitimbralism, and is capable of responding to velocity, aftertouch and MIDI overflow. Sacrifices were made, of course, including the use of a lone mono output and an LED screen and the absence of a volume knob (seriously!).

Sounds are stored in numbered banks. Banks 1-5 are ROM and house sounds grouped loosely according to instrument type (strings, pianos, etc.). None of the pianos rival any modern sampled piano, but for bell-like or cheesy electronic versions, you will be well served. Basses are probably the MS6's finest suit, and you can take encouragement from the fact that Tony Levin was an enthusiastic user until his last MS6 blew up on him. Stars here include all manner of acid basses, fat Moog types, raw funk, woody, metallic, clunky, clicky... You can edit sounds in the ROM banks, too; you'll just have to store edits in Banks 6 and 7.

Bank 8 is reserved for multipatches, each of which can comprise a stack of six tones, layered on top of each other on the same MIDI channel, split across the keyboard or sent multitimbrally on different MIDI channels.

The dual-oscillator MS6 sports a fairly standard parameter list: two full ADSR envelope generators per voice; one four-pole, 24dB/oct lowpass VCF (a Prophet-5-type Curtis) per voice; and one multi-mode LFO per voice. There's some limitation here in the filtering department should you want to apply specific filtering to each of the two DCOs (i.e., you can't), but there are some nice touches, like the option of EG control over oscillator mix and pressure control over pitch. The full parameter list is stenciled onto the top of the casing, so if you don't have a manual, don't even think of racking the instrument.

Even without the aid of a single knob to twiddle, programming is direct and obvious, which is just as well since the designers maintain that putting together a computer editing package would be impossible.

In its brief heyday, the MS6 was used to good effect by Mr. Rick Wakeman as a handy and cost-effective replacement for his Minimoog and remains a firm favorite with the dance fraternity for sundry squelchy bleeps and blurps, mainly in the area of bass. An MS6 II was threatened around the time of Cheetah's demise and may even be revived by Soundscape, the company formed by ex-Cheetah employees in the wake of the speedy one's flagging and eventual collapse with respect to musical instruments.

Designer Ian Jannoway went on to form Novation Music Systems, producers of the BassStation keyboard and BassStation Rack.

Cheetah is no longer in the business of producing electronic musical instruments.

Crumar Spirit — Analog monophonic synthesizer

THE FAX

Keyboard:	37-note
Programs:	None
External storage:	None
Polyphony:	Mono
Oscillators per voice:	2
Effects:	Arpeggiator
Connections:	Mono audio
Dimensions:	700mm x 400mm x 80mm
Weight:	8kg

THE FIGURES

Chief designers:	Bob Moog, Jim Scott, Luciano Jura
Production run:	1983-86
Approx. units sold:	50
Options:	None
Sounds:	None
Miscellaneous:	One of the last, and evidently least successful, monos ever built.
Orig. price (1983):	$895 (£450)
Price in 1996:	$400 (£175)

Italian synthesizers are frequently shrouded in some sort of mystery. Either the name has been plucked out of International Marketing's book of "names likely to appeal to the American market" (i.e., it doesn't actually exist as a company), or it is made under license by or for another company. Sometimes the same instrument can appear a number of times wearing a number of different suits.

Scratching away beneath the surface of the Spirit, we find none other than that well-known Italian, Bob Moog. Though Crumar had been extremely successful in the past, it felt that a man of Moog's clout would launch the Spirit into the sky.

And did it?

No.

Several things went wrong. First and foremost, the release year was 1983, not noted for rabid interest in monophonic synthesizers. Even Britain's OSCar, a far more eye-catching and radical design, had a tough time fending off the polyphonic competition in 1983. This was the year of the DX7.

Also, the Spirit's control panel is highly complex-looking—far too complex for the average musician. This would have been permissible if the instrument had memories or featured some "modern" keyboard control features. But it didn't. The Spirit was faithful to its roots, which were real-time and sound-based as opposed to performance-based.

There are two oscillators, offering sawtooth, triangle and variable-pulse waveforms. There's some limitation in the pitch department, since the pitch of both oscillators is governed by a single control. Though oscillator pulse width is variable, it is not smoothly variable, as is more common; the design here offers four click-stopped widths that you can select, from 50% square to narrow-pulse 6%. Oscillators can be hard-synced.

Filtering is the Spirit's best attribute, with its choice of 12dB/oct or 24dB/oct filter slope not just in lowpass mode but also in highpass and bandpass, with cutoff and resonance controls; the filter section has its own dedicated ADSR envelope generator that can function in normal or inverted position. There's even an overdrive control for those fat, "overdriven," Minimoog-type sounds, and the filter can track the keyboard. This is pretty much anybody's wish list of filter parameters, and it gives you maximum control from broad sweeps to the subtlest changes in tone.

The VCA is attached to a second ADSR envelope generator, which it can bypass for a flat gated output.

While the filter is comprehensive yet comprehensible, the LFO and accompanying modulation routings and options will be fathomed only by the extremely knowledgeable or extremely patient. Part of the reason for this is the panel itself, which is laid out in a confusing fashion. Also to blame is a lot of idiosyncratic, or at least unfamiliar, terminology—X and Y shapers, red noise, mod X, etc. LFO waveshapes include sawtooth, triangle and inverted sawtooth. Under the so-named umbrella of mod X comes a useful sample-and-hold generator, plus an arpeggiator and "red noise," a digitally generated variation of pink noise. There is also a ring modulator.

Laudably, the Crumar Spirit contains almost every classic subtractive synthesis module and feature, which is the reason for its appearance in these pages. Not so laudably, the instrument could not be accused of being encouraging or even friendly to use. Provided you have some knowledge of analog synthesis or are using a Sprit with the express purpose of gaining some, this instrument is well worth tracking down, but it's not for those looking for easy analog.

Much was expected from this design—Bob Moog approached Crumar with the idea, as opposed to the other way around—and very little was delivered in terms of response and sales.

The Spirit has some collectability, but it's not old enough to be ranked alongside Minimoogs or Oberheims. Its current value is based on features more than fashion.

Crumar ceased trading in 1987.

Digital Keyboards Synergy
Digital synthesizer

THE FAX

Keyboard:	74-note
Programs:	24
External storage:	Cartridge, disk with Kaypro II computer
Polyphony:	16-voice
Oscillators per voice:	2
Effects:	None
Connections:	Stereo audio (¼" and XLR), seq out, rec out, pedal
Dimensions:	1200mm x 550mm x 200mm
Weight:	20kg

THE FIGURES

Chief designer:	Stoney Stockell
Production run:	1982-85
Approx. units sold:	800
Options:	RS-232 interface, Kaypro computer software
Sounds:	Voice cartridges #1-6 (Wendy Carlos Set)
Miscellaneous:	Wendy Carlos' albums *Digital Moonscapes* and *Beauty in the Beast* were largely created with the Synergy. A most informative chapter in Mark Vail's book *Vintage Synthesizers* (GPI Books) is devoted to the Synergy and its forerunner, the GDS.
Orig. price (1982):	$5295 (no UK price)
Price in 1996:	$700 (no UK price)

Neither the Synergy nor Digital Keyboards Inc. is exactly a household name. In fairness, both were confined to that rarefied world of wealthy musicians, university electronic music departments and big-budget research laboratories. But for all that, the Synergy is an important milestone keyboard, albeit one that's hardly likely to surface in your neighborhood thrift store.

The Synergy marks the beginning of all-digital synthesis on a (vaguely) commercial scale. It also marks the start of the (vaguely) commercial synthesizer's love affair with external computers, even if the Synergy's choice of the Kaypro II computer looks a bit radical to eyes that, in the 1990s, are used to Macs and PCs.

The Synergy is a large, shiny black monster of an additive synthesis instrument. Baldly, it offers some 24 preset sounds with additional sounds retrievable from special cartridge. But it's not so much what the Synergy has that's impressive as what it does with what it has. For a number of reasons, this is a highly expressive instrument, capable of enormous tonal subtlety over its keyboard range. Wendy Carlos has possibly spent more time with the Synergy and its forebear the GDS than she has with Moog systems, employing these instruments on numerous albums and film scores. Carlos even produced a set of 72 new voices on cartridge.

The controls are set into the shallow, almost vertical panel between the keyboard and the high-gloss top, which is presumably reserved for the odd glass of chilled "DP" or the even odder Kaypro computer. 24 push-buttons activate the tones, which can arrive in several "performance" modes set up by the four-channel programmer. Four sounds can be stored in each location and assigned to arrive in unison, in various split positions or activated sequentially by successive keys. There is also a "floating split" mode, wherein the internal computer reckons it can assign a particular voice to left and right hands no matter where you are playing on the keyboard. Provided you don't deliberately try to fool it (it is based in part on the assumption that most people can stretch to a tenth), it works pretty well.

Other front-panel controls include keyboard sensitivity over amplitude and timbre, a joystick (up/down for modulation, left/right for pitch bend—somewhat awkward in this position) and vibrato controls (speed, depth and delay).

The character of Synergy sounds is definitely big and definitely digital. Definitely ahead of its time, too, with splendid string patches complete with bow noise and the capability to interpolate between one tone and another (effectively morphing) across the keyboard range. Remember, we're talking here not about physical modeling, or E-mu's three-dimensional filtering, but about an additive synthesis machine built at the beginning of the 1980s. Though it was never billed as such, the Synergy's system of additive synthesis is not dissimilar to FM, used and patented by Yamaha, or even PM, as employed by Casio on the CZ-series synths. But whereas both Yamaha and Casio produced financially accessible, fully programmable instruments with these technologies, Digital Keyboards never got beyond the starting block with the Synergy, which was expensive and, until the Synergy II+ came along with a Kaypro in tow, gave you editability, effectively preset.

Even so, the Synergy was way ahead of its time in a number of key areas, such as the inclusion of a four-channel sequencer that could store real-time note, pitch bend, modulation and program information, as well as impose some (admittedly intransigent) quantizing. Wendy Carlos used the Synergy's sequencer extensively on her *Beauty in the Beast* album, a recording that also shows off the Synergy's microtonal capabilities. Synergy was also used extensively by Donald Fagen on his timelessly superb *Nightfly* album. With volatile memory, though, the sequencer is hardly likely to be employed for much beyond compositional aid by Synergy users today.

Digital Keyboards was basically an offshoot of Crumar, the Italian giant that set up Music Technologies and subsequently Digital Keyboards in New York in the late '70s and early '80s. These companies have bitten the corporate dust, though one of the Synergy's designers, Stoney Stockell, now works for Korg in New York and is still on hand to answer the odd question and supply sound files.

The Synergy itself went on to MIDI status (Synergy II+) by 1985, and a modular version, the Slave 32, was also produced.

Though stalwarts like Wendy Carlos merrily soldier on, the legacy of the Synergy and the techniques and technologies it helped to popularize are worth more than an actual instrument these days. It's not sought after as such, but most existing users are still well pleased with this highly individual, highly musical instrument.

EDP Wasp — Analog monophonic synthesizer

THE FAX

Keyboard:	25-note
Programs:	None
External storage:	None
Polyphony:	Mono
Oscillators per voice:	2
Effects:	None
Connections:	Mono audio, phones, 7-pin DIN Wasp-to-Wasp connection
Dimensions:	408mm x 312mm x 60mm
Weight:	1.5kg

THE FIGURES

Chief designers:	Chris Huggett, Adrian Wagner
Production run:	1978-82
Approx. units sold:	3000
Options:	Spider sequencer
Sounds:	n/a
Miscellaneous:	Over 50 Wasps were once successfully linked by their 7-pin digital interfaces.
Orig. price (1978):	$695 (£199)
Price in 1996:	$200 (£150)

The story of the Wasp will be a familiar tale to observers of things British: great idea, not enough money, production problems, collapse. The classic "if only..."

The Wasp was the brainchild of musician Adrian Wagner (a direct descendent of composer Richard) and electronics designer Chris Huggett. It flew into action in the late summer of 1978 and, in England at any rate, immediately devoured hundreds of column inches of press space and hundreds of musician hours as everyone set about fooling around with this crazy-looking (bright yellow and black) and tiny, but great-sounding, little synth. Prior to the Wasp, synthesizers were deemed fairly serious instruments and priced accordingly. The Wasp made synthesis available to all and fun as well.

The cheapness factor came down to a number of items, most prominently that the Wasp has no movable keyboard, just a two-octave strip of silkscreened contact keyboard like something you'd now see in a children's book. It was clearly never intended to be played in a traditional keyboard style. The best way to "play" a Wasp is to sort of press and slide a finger about over the keyboard, almost in the manner of Stylophone playing. Resting on a note allows you to trill, simply by fluttering an adjacent finger. It's fast, that's for sure.

Above the fake keyboard, the control panel has a couple of dozen knobs and switches activating an impressive roster of features from digitally controlled oscillators to low-, high- and bandpass filtering, a pair of envelope generators, sophisticated LFO and more.

The two oscillators span a six-octave range and offer sawtooth, pulse and square waveforms. VCO2 doesn't have a pulse width control; it's replaced by a pitch control allowing you to set up the two oscillators in fourths, fifths or whatever. Not only can you use powerful 24dB/oct lowpass filtering with resonance (printed "Q") and cutoff frequency controls, but you can also use highpass or bandpass. The filter has its own dedicated envelope generator, offering attack, decay and sustain level/repeat parameters. The amplifier is lashed to a second envelope generator with similar separate attack and decay controls; the third knob this time governing delay rather than sustain level. The third EG control on both VCF and VCA envelope generators being shared does make life a little more complex than if the parameters had been straight ADSR. The LFO, or "control oscillator," features square, sine, sawtooth, ramp up/down and sample-and-hold waveshapes and can be routed to the oscillators or filter. Noise can simply be added to the signal flow going into the filter. Classic analog synth sound types like glide (portamento) and repeat triggering are readily available. Real-time pitch bending is quite an art, since it has to be carried out by simply twirling a control knob—hardly conducive to great, grimacing feats of expression.

The Wasp can be mains- or battery-powered, and for the totally impecunious, even heard through its own transistor radio-sized speaker, though this method does indeed tend to imbue the instrument with a worrisome "vesparic" tone. Hook it up to a decent amp and speaker, though, and it's no wonder musicians as varied as Bomb the Bass, Genesis, Thomas Dolby and The Stranglers have all taken this little instrument into their hearts at one time or another.

The Wasp's reliability record is another matter, one that sapped the company's strength to the point of exhaustion by the early 1980s. (Ironically, reliability was one of the company's main selling points early on, one notable "test" involving a Wasp being run over by a Volvo outside Trident Recording Studios in London.) A favorite fault is that the keyboard mistriggers horrendously; the second fault (normally following) is an endless drone.

Two or more Wasps can be linked together via 7-pin DIN interfaces, two of which are mounted flat on the instrument's main panel. By this method, a real keyboarded instrument can also be connected. EDP produced such a thing itself in the Wasp Deluxe, but this almost doubled the price, and since by this time a swarm of low-cost Japanese monophonics were already winging their way in from the East, for EDP, that was largely that.

EDP's full complement of released products also includes the digital, 256-note Spider sequencer, whose reliability record made even the Wasp look dependable, and the dainty Gnat, a single oscillator with a range of powerful sounds that's little short of miraculous for the time, size and price. Various other insect-named contraptions were thought about, or even mocked up in ones or twos, but essentially this is the EDP catalog in full.

If you can find a working Wasp, give it a prod and you'll be totally amazed at its range and power. If you can find a Wasp that's working, it'll probably remain that way for a while and therefore is worth buying. Though it was highly successful at the time, relatively few were made, making this a highly collectible, if not widely sought-after, instrument.

The Wasp broke the expensive, serious mold in which the synthesizer had been encased. For this, and for its (when working) superb range of sounds, the Wasp's place in synth history is deserved and assured.

EDP is no longer in business.

Elka Synthex Analog polyphonic synthesizer

THE FAX

Keyboard:	61-note
Programs:	40 preset, 40 user
External storage:	Cassette
Polyphony:	8-voice
Oscillators per voice:	2
Effects:	Chorus, built-in sequencer
Connections:	Stereo ¼" jacks
Dimensions:	985mm x 110mm x 350mm
Weight:	12kg

THE FIGURES

Chief designer:	Mario Maggi
Production run:	1982-85
Options:	MIDI as retrofit
Sounds:	None commercially available
Miscellaneous:	A model is on exhibit at the UK's Museum of Synthesizer Technology.
Orig. price (1982):	No U.S. price (£2500)
Price in 1996:	No U.S. price (£500)

Geoff Downes called the Synthex: "A cross between a Prophet-5 and a Solina string machine. It has those warm string sounds that only the preset string synths used to have." Downes was not the only one in the high-powered, high-tech fraternity to take advantage of Elka's ahead-of-its-time polyphonic synth during the 1980s. Keith Emerson used a Synthex to recreate the sound of his fabled GX-1 onstage for "Fanfare for a Common Man" when the GX-1 went on one of its customary breaks. Jean-Michel Jarre splashed Synthex all over his *Rendez-Vous* album, in particular the now famous "laser harp" sound. Even Stevie Wonder managed to pry one last Synthex out of Elka for his 1987 album *Characters*.

Yet for all its illustrious users and endorsees, the Synthex did not prove popular with the general public. The Synthex came out at the wrong time, at the wrong price and under the wrong name. Substitute "Sequential" for "Elka" or even "Roland" or "Korg"...

Released just prior to the establishment of MIDI, the Synthex quickly assumed the position of yesterday's news. Perhaps its most newsworthy feat initially was to arrive fresh off the boat from Italy in the UK without sounds. UK programmer Paul Wiffen hurriedly, of his own admission, put some sounds together, and these duly became the factory presets. Very good they are, too.

Sporting DCOs but still very much an analog instrument, the Synthex is surprisingly powerful, employing two oscillators per note; separate envelope generators for its razor-sharp, multi-mode VCF and VCA; and multimode chorus and a simple 4-track sequencer, all controllable from a front panel containing real knobs and switches.

The filters in particular deserve high praise, since you are offered not only standard 24dB/oct lowpass but also 12dB/oct highpass and even 6dB/oct or 12dB/oct bandpass. Such an array might be commonplace on a monophonic synth, but no polyphonic synth of this era, or any other, generally offers such scope. With bandpass filtering, you can produce a complexity of sweeps and swooshes quite beyond that of instruments endowed with mere lowpass filters. With full keyboard tracking, polyphonic glide, a digital ring modulator, cross-modulation between oscillators and ADSR envelope generators, the Synthex is capable of extreme complexity. It is also, thanks to the multimode chorus—almost heresy in its day on a "professional" instrument—capable of extreme weight and thickness. The clean, simple panel layout makes it pretty much a cinch to program, too.

The Synthex's 4-track sequencer is not the thing for storing and reproducing masterpiece compositions on, though it's great and quick as a real- or step-time scratchpad and quite excellent as an accompaniment tool. Even when programming in step time (notes input direct from the keyboard, rests from

small buttons on the left-hand "performance" panel), you can set up a groove or a series of "chords" in mere seconds, over which you can then play. Sounds can be substituted retrospectively, as can a new tempo. Whether Keith Emerson actually employed the Synthex for the *bass part* on "Fanfare for a Common Man" is uncertain, but he certainly could have.

You can both split and layer programs, and once MIDI was grafted onto the instrument as a standard feature, a pair of voices could be sent out on separate MIDI channels. Similarly, the sequencer functions multitimbrally. Ironically, although professionals used it as a substitute for the "professional instruments," whose sound and power—but fortunately not reliability record—the instrument could mimic so adeptly, the press and public viewed it as not quite "pro," due to its Elka name tag.

Unfettered by such nonsense, today's player can now judge the Synthex on its merits, which are many and varied. It's not only good for full, fat analog brass and string sounds but also for swirling filter sweeps; it also does a mean line in digital rasps and rumbles, all without too many tears. Quite an instrument, really.

EMS Synthi 100
Monophonic analog synthesizer

THE FAX

Keyboard:	2 61-note
Programs:	None
External storage:	None
Polyphony:	Mono
Oscillators per voice:	3
Effects:	Spring reverb
Connections:	Stereo audio outputs
Dimensions:	1896mm x 888mm x 792mm
Weight:	Incalculable
EMS (U.S.):	11 N. Main St.; Williamsburg, MA 01096; tel: (413) 268-3588

THE FIGURES

Chief designers:	Dave Cockerell, Pete Zinovieff
Production run:	1971-1983
Approx. units sold:	34
Options:	n/a
Sounds:	n/a

Miscellaneous:	A working Synthi 100 occupies a large amount of space at the Museum of Synthesizer Technology in England. Servicing available in the U.S. from EMSA: 11 N. Main St.; Williamsburg, MA 01096; tel: (413) 268-3588 and in the UK from EMS: Trendeal Vean Barn; Ladock, Truro, Cornwall TR2 4NW UK; tel: 01726-883265; fax: 01726-883283
Orig. price (1971):	$25,000 (£10,000)
Price in 1996:	n/a

Britain's role in the development of the synthesizer has been a vital one, though rarely acknowledged, much less publicized. Britain has also long been king of the perverse. It's appropriate, therefore, that honors for both the smallest and biggest instrument in the Hot 100 go to Britain.

EMS is the very quintessence of the British synthesizer industry: resourceful, dogged, innovative, influential and minute. The Synthi 100 is all of these except the last; the Synthi 100 is *massive*. This is what a synthesizer should look like: vertical panels smothered with large industrial sized knobs and switches, a pair of pin matrices that look as if they could handle the New York telephone system and all manner of preposterous dials and counters. It would fit in just fine if the Synthi 100 had a Van de Graf generator at the end of the line.

You don't have to wear a white coat, sprout wild, wiry hair and speak in a thick German accent, but...

For a number of fairly obvious reasons, the Synthi 100 is not exactly a gigging instrument. It was designed as a sound generator and manipulator for universities and electronic music studios. Among the 34 buyers of the Synthi 100 EMS were Radio Belgrade, the BBC's Radiophonic Workshop (*Dr. Who* theme, etc.) and Karlheinz Stockhausen.

This leviathan of an instrument, for which most customers had to take down walls in order to install, makes suitably monstrous noises, most of them accompanied by atrocious hums and buzzes, all of them unrepeatable by anyone less than the almighty. On a Synthi 100, you get what you get.

A list of features and parameters makes interesting reading, up to a point: 12 voltage-controlled oscillators, 4 lowpass filters, 4 highpass filters, 3 ring modulators, an octave filter bank of no less than 8 resonating filters, limiters, amplifiers, envelope shapers and a 256-event sequencer. But it is not until you are standing before such a sea of knobs, hearing the resultant phantasmagoria of sound, that an instrument like this starts to make any sense at all.

But as for making sense as to "why?" "what?" or "how?" Forget it.

The oscillators, of which three are primarily designed for low frequency modulation purposes (the first functioning, if you can imagine this, at frequen-

cies between 0.025-500Hz), are hopelessly unstable. You're not likely to want (or be able) to bash out Mozart on a Synthi 100, though, so oscillator drift becomes part of the character of the sound.

With synchronization inputs available on all the oscillators, plus the trio of ring modulators, noises of the more additive, clangorous inclination are a Synthi 100 specialty. No less than three noise generators, variable from white to "dark" using filtering, allow you to create textures of enormous depth.

"Who invented the digital sequencer?" is a popular parlor game among synth enthusiasts. While EMS make no special claims towards this, the Synthi 100 predates Oberheim's DS-2 and, if not the first digital sequencer, is certainly the first to appear on anything approaching a commercially produced instrument. The memory, splendidly displayed in a semi-circular bubble meter, like a sort of depth gauge-meets-barometer, holds 256 events. This is not a lot, and the sequencer must be of very dubious worth today, but it can record and play back three simultaneous monophonic lines, allowing you to hear previous passes as you overdub, plus you can edit events and even reverse playback. The sequencer records in real time.

Fundamental to enjoyment of the Synthi 100 is the pair of pin matrices that present literally thousands of patch possibilities. Anything can be connected to anything. Even seasoned users admit they frequently just fire in the tiny pin connectors, stand back and see what happens.

Keyboard playing is basically redundant here. A double-manual keyboard was made and is the only way to program the sequencer, but for most of the Synthi 100's duties—providing textures, atmospheres, effects—notes, as such, do not need to be played.

The theme song of the British television space serial *Dr. Who* is often credited to the Synthi 100. Sadly, this seems unlikely, as the first episode of *Dr. Who* predates the instrument by some considerable time. The BBC's Radiophonic Workshop did purchase one of these instruments, though, and used it for the much of the incidental music during the run of the show.

A working Synthi 100 lies in the Museum of Synthesizer Technology in England, a visit to which is a must for all serious synth historians, as the cost and scarcity of this instrument renders the chance of seeing it elsewhere in a league with winning the lottery. I mean, how many instruments can you think of that have their own oscilloscope? The Synthi 100 is no mere machine. It is a snarling, gurgling, living animal. It could have been designed by Lewis Carroll. A triumph!

EMS VCS3/Putney
Monophonic analog synthesizer

THE FAX

Keyboard:	37-note (with optional DK1, DK2 keyboards)
Programs:	None
External storage:	None
Polyphony:	2-voice (with DK2 keyboard)
Oscillators per voice:	2
Effects:	Reverb
Connections:	Stereo outputs, VCA signal outputs, phones, scope, 2 input channels
Dimensions:	430mm x 440mm x 420mm
Weight:	9kg
EMS (U.S.):	11 N. Main St.; Williamsburg, MA 01096; tel: (413) 268-3588

THE FIGURES

Chief designer:	David Cockerell
Production run:	1968-1994
Approx. units sold:	800 (Synthi A: 1000)
Options:	Octave filter bank, random voltage generator, pitch-to-voltage generator, phase frequency shifter
Sounds:	n/a
Miscellaneous:	U.S. distributor is EMS: 2409 Hassler Rd.; Snellville, GA 30278; tel: (404) 972-9176; servicing in U.S. from EMSA: 11 N. Main St.; Williamsburg, MA 01096; tel: (413) 268-3588; servicing in UK from EMS: Trendeal Vean Barn; Ladock, Truro, Cornwall TR2 4NW UK.; tel: 01726-883265; fax: 01726-883283
Orig. price (1968):	$825 (£330)
Price in 1994:	$2400 (£1500)
Price in 1996:	$1000-1500 (£500-1000)

Welcome to the longest-running saga in synthesis. The VCS3, or Putney as it is more commonly known in the U.S., is the ultimate electronic gadget. It looks like a nice piece of laboratory equipment, with its large control knobs and pin matrix patch bay encased in a real wood frame, and it delights in making spacey, whoop-whoop-blip-swoosh noises that are totally unusable in any musical setting—aside from rhythm or sound effects, at which it is totally brilliant. It's redolent of Tangerine Dream, Klaus Schulze, Gong, David Vorhaus—the Germans would love it, you'd think, and you'd be right.

In fact, over its long and frequently illustrious

life, the VCS3 has found favor with most of early synthesis' movers and shakers: Eno, during early Roxy Music days; Pete Townshend, who had the VCS3 trigger the organ sound on The Who's seminal "sequencer synthesizer" track "Won't Get Fooled Again"; Todd Rundgren; and Jean-Michel Jarre, who still has a phalanx of them in his armory. Shooting forward a few decades, Julian Cope continues to be a loyal customer, and the Aphex Twin and Pete Namlook are recent users.

Designed in the UK by Dave Cockerell, who went on to giddier heights with Akai's S series of samplers, the VCS3 was instantly popular among the European avant-garde because (a) it was affordable; (b) it could supply an endless and unrepeatable selection of high-quality electronic bleeps and blurps; and (c) it was small, if not exactly portable (due to its unique L-shaped design, which makes it awkward to pick up or to box).

In the '60s and '70s, if it could even be argued that synths had a role at the time, it was as providers of unusual and normally other-worldly noises.

The VCS3's basic range of tools exudes high quality in their scope and performance, with its three independent oscillators—independent not only in range (frequency) and level but also in their waveforms and applications (the VCS3 can be used as a sub audio LFO)—white and "variable-colored" noise generator, self-oscillating lowpass filter, ring modulator, envelope shaper and even a dual spring-line reverb unit. The exception, it must be said, is oscillator stability. If all you want to produce are interesting noises, then drifting oscillators can be part of the sound, but for an accurate pitch performance, this problem makes the VCS3 a high-risk animal.

Though the oscillator and filter panels should seem familiar to anyone with a degree of subtractive synthesis experience, the envelope shaper panel, featuring a pair of attack controls, decay/"off" and "trapezoid" and "signal" level controls will probably fox most—including me. With its variety of triggering modes and a decay time parameter that can be set from the patchboard, this simply has to be viewed as an area for experimentation by modern, ADSR-inclined users.

Indeed, much of the pleasure in playing a VCS3 lies in the panel's patchboard pin matrix, which allows you to connect up each of the instrument's "modules." It's a bit like playing solitaire, with equally unpredictable results for most people. But it is the VCS3's ability to be cross-patched in an almost limitless number of permutations and routings that accounts for its enduring mystery and appeal.

Other surprises include the internal reverberation unit, which ranges from 25-millisecond delays up to 2-second reverbs (again, voltage-controllable via the patchboard), and the stereo outputs, which effectively let you set up and deliver two separate but simultaneous sounds. Also, in the days before MIDI, the only way to expand your sonic horizons beyond the wire-covered lump of metal you actually purchased was to drive or be driven by other audio sources. Thus, external signal inputs on the VCS3 let you process signals from a mic or a guitar, and the control outputs let you trigger external sounds using the envelope shaper or the third oscillator LFO. The VCS3 was also one of the first instruments to offer joystick control, governing independent parameters on its X and Y axes.

But joystick or not, unless your performances do not entirely depend upon defined Western musical pitches, the VCS3 cannot be recommended for live use. Tuning is inherently hairy, and the prospect of a hardworking musician under stage lights sweating profusely into the patchboard as he leans over the controls is frightening. Frankly, the VCS3 is most at home at home; there's even a small internal speaker system.

The VCS3 can be played from a separate 37-note keyboard (either the DK1 or the DK2, the latter providing two-voice polyphony). It was also made available in "briefcase" form, as the Synthi A. The KS Sequencer keyboard can be fitted into the lid of a Synthi A (thus turning it into what EMS sold as the Synthi-AKS). This 2½-octave touch keyboard (no movable keys) also throws a 256-note sequencer into the proceedings. The many illustrious Synthi-AKS users include Alan Parsons and Pink Floyd.

As of this writing, EMS is assembling what it says will be one final batch of Synthi As—final because there will be no more ABS casings left. The VCS3 is officially deleted, but only because EMS cannot find a local woodworker capable of producing the French-polished afromosia hardwood case for a sensible (or possibly any?) price.

EMS has gone through a few changes since beginning life as the manufacturing arm of an electronic music studio (hence the initials) owned by electronic composer Peter Zinovieff in the leafy London suburb of Putney. The VCS3 (Voltage Controlled Studio Version 3) has become an icon in synthesizer history. Though an instrument can still be commissioned today, it is no longer the bargain it was in the 1960s. Even so, it's still capable of sonic surprises and, for sound effects, still hard to beat.

E-mu EII Digital sampling keyboard

THE FAX

Keyboard:	61-note
Programs:	99 presets per bank
External storage:	5¼" disk drive (optional 20MB hard drive)

Polyphony:	8-voice
Oscillators per voice:	n/a
Effects:	None
Connections:	Mono mix, 8 separate audio outs, RS422, SMPTE Out, metronome
Dimensions:	1000mm x 460mm x 225mm
Weight:	25kg

THE FIGURES

Chief designer:	Dave Rossum
Production run:	1984-87
Approx. units sold:	3000
Options:	Double memory, second disk drive, CD-ROM system
Sounds:	E-mu library, plus Optical Media CD-ROM, Northstar
Miscellaneous:	At one time, it was reported that 50% of studios in the U.S. owned an EII.
Orig. price (1984):	$7995 (£5175)
Price in 1996:	$900 (£800)

In 1984, sampling was a far cry from the scratch 'n' sniff, instant formula it became in the 1990s. It was a sedate rich man's sport, studio-bound and serious. Previously, sampling instruments had been the Fairlight and the original Emulator; Kurzweil's 250 came out this year as well.

The EII was still way out of reach for the average muso, but for a gung-ho working pro, it was just about affordable. It represented a ticket to freedom from the stylized leading synths of the day, such as Yamaha's DX7, Roland's JX-3P and Oberheim's OB-8. As such, it was not just a ticket to freedom, but a ticket to huge amounts of work. The first EII owners wrote their own paychecks; such was the clamor for this wonder instrument in the studio.

Viewed dispassionately 10 years later, it is hard to believe that the EII was ever regarded as a wonder instrument. For a start, it is only 8-bit; in other words, the accuracy with which it inspects incoming sounds in order to turn them into digital samples is half the norm of the 1990s. Listen to an EII alongside any 16-bit machine, and in pure sound quality terms, the EII sounds muffled, dull and indistinct, though "grainy" is the rather more positive spin aficionados tend to put on it. The EII works in mono and at 512KB, the standard memory is positively pea-brained.

What was so good about the EII? Incredibly enough, it was the sound quality. Quality plus range,

E-MU

Name:	E-mu Systems Inc.
Head Office:	1600 Green Hills Rd.; Scotts Valley, CA 95066; tel: (408) 438-1921; fax (408) 438-8612
UK Distributor:	E-mu Systems Ltd.: Suite 6, Adam Ferguson House, Eskmills Park; Musselburgh, East Lothian, EH21 7PQ, Scotland; tel: 0131-653-6556; fax: 0131-665-0473
Founded:	1972
No. of employees:	120
Business:	Synthesizers, samplers, digital audio products, custom VLSI

For almost the first 10 years of its life, E-mu was a well-kept secret, known only by a favored few wealthy musicians like Frank Zappa, Pat Gleason and Peter Baumann (who could afford the company's hand-built, large-scale modular analog synths) and by the California synthesizer industry, for which E-mu worked variously as consultants and OEM designers.

At the helm was UC Santa Cruz biology major Dave Rossum, who had been drawn into the field of electronic musical instruments purely by chance when asked, as a "scientist," one day, to help unpack and set up the UCSC Music Department's new Moog 112 single-oscillator synth. Out of his field but not out of his depth, Rossum not only showed the department all about its new purchase by the end of the day, but, intrigued by the whole notion of music synthesis, soon set about building an exponential generator of his own.

It was at this time that Rossum and his university cohorts came up with the name E-mu (electronic music), not because they had any corporate aspirations but because they needed a name in order to persuade manufacturers to sell them components not normally available to the public.

Dave's dorm room at Santa Cruz was transformed into a printed-circuit repackaging lab, and by the end of the year, his ad hoc team had actually built a synthesizer. They called it the Black Maria, and it was designed along similar lines to the ARP 2500. However, once completed, the Black Maria ended up being smashed into a million pieces on the ground after being thrown out of UCSC's library window.

The next project was more ambitious: an ARP 2600 clone Rossum dubbed the Model 25. About as good and stable a synth as anyone was building at the time, the Model 25 had definite sales potential, and Rossum teamed up with an old high school buddy, Scott Wedge, in order to market and sell the instrument.

E-mu went official in November of 1972. The story goes that Rossum and Wedge flipped a coin to decide who'd be president. Wedge lost and became president, a post that he retained for the next 15 years.

Early E-mu products consisted of advanced analog synthesizers and circuits. The company divided its time between product manufacture and OEM design work and consulting. Though E-mu's clients ranged from Oberheim (on the 4-voice) to chip manufacturers SSM, Rossum's most notable outside triumph was work carried out with Dave Smith on the Prophet-5.

As they explained, "Nobody had any money in those days, so our deal was to get paid back in royalties." For a while, everything was hunky dory. The Prophet-5 was a runaway success and the royalties flowed. Then came a major software revision, and suddenly Sequential decided that it was a completely different instrument. Enough was enough—the royalties stopped.

The resultant cloud of litigation, financial shortfalls and strained relationships had a golden lining: At the precise moment that Sequential royalties stopped, Rossum saw the Fairlight at the 1980 AES show. Rossum figured that (a) there was a market for an instrument dedicated to sampling, and (b) if he used memory-sharing chip technology, he could build one for a fraction of the cost of a Fairlight. And so the Emulator was born, and along with it, the age of the sampler.

The Emulator begat the Drumulator, which in turn begat the EII, E-mu's first commercially successful product. Thereafter came the SP-12 and SP-1200, followed by the less expensive Emax series of samplers.

Like so many garage-founded American synthesizer companies, which swung from peak to trough depending on the state of their newest release, E-mu zig-zagged through the 1980s, nearly coming to grief after the slow start of the original Emulator and again after an abortive association with the Swedish company ddrum.

Somehow, the company's resolve and plain ingenuity always managed to pull it clear—first, a lucrative sound licensing deal with Matsushita, then the world-beating success of the Proteus range of sample replay modules. Stability finally came in 1993, when E-mu was acquired by Creative Labs Ltd. of Singapore, the company behind the Sound Blaster cards. The deal, which gave Creative an almost unassailable edge in audio technology, has enabled E-mu to diversify and make long-term plans, luxuries seldom afforded outside the Japanese musical instrument business.

E-mu's twin towers of strength are the undoubted brilliance of its founder and "technologist" Dave Rossum, whose series of chip designs has fueled E-mu's (and others') products since day one, and its exceptional skills in the recording and post-production of audio sample data.

at any rate. E-mu very sensibly made a large and splendid sound library available as soon as possible. Samples like the Marcato strings, bird-tweeting atmospherics, gamelan bells and ripping brass instantly became highly prized and highly sought-after by every self-respecting recording band and studio. Indeed, by the end of the decade, *Mix* magazine published a survey that revealed that 50 percent of U.S. studios actually owned an EII.

If EII sounds instantly captured everyone's imagination, so did its basic layout and operating style. Although only E-mu itself may have perservered with the EII's precise terminology, its fundamental approach to sampling, from recording to processing, has been largely followed by most subsequent sampling instruments.

E-mu's terminology is unique to E-mu, though; it includes Voices (raw samples) and Presets (collections of processed samples). The initial sampling procedure is simple enough; it's merely a question of following instructions on the (admittedly minute) display screen. Since the sample frequency is fixed, you don't have to worry about sample length-to-quality issues; on a standard instrument, you have 17.6 seconds to play with. Under the title of Voice Definition—its table of contents is printed on the control panel, as are those of most other "modules" (i.e., sections of the instrument's software)—you can truncate, loop and generally nip and tuck your basic sample into shape. Samples can be crossfaded, reversed, spliced together…this was no small feat in digital processing terms. In "analog" editing terms, the EII is equally well equipped. There is one four-pole lowpass filter, one VCA, two ADSR envelope generators and one LFO per voice. The filter features frequency and resonance parameters and can be controlled by the LFO or the EGs, by keyboard tracking or indeed in real time by the mod wheel. The eight LFOs offer true polyphonic vibrato and feature some unusual parameters, like random variation, whereby different LFO rates can be applied to successive played notes.

Combining and coordinating Voices into a Preset can encompass velocity switching or crossfades, zoning, transpositions and even arpeggiations (the EII's arpeggiator was the springboard for much crazy composition at the time). The arpeggiator is relatively straightforward to operate; the EII's sequencer, on the other hand, is somewhat less friendly. However, you have eight polyphonic tracks to record on, with each track able to trigger its own Preset. You can punch in and out, tracks can be bounced together, and the EII even comes with a SMPTE reader/writer built in for when (or if, given the sequencer's complexity) it comes to synchronizing sequences to other material recorded on tape.

The basic EII came with 512KB of internal memory. The EII+ doubled the memory. E-mu pioneered work on hard drives for musical instruments; the EIIHD was the first production instrument to offer this mass-storage device in 20MB Winchester form. E-mu was also the first instrument company to organize a CD-ROM storage facility, hooking up with fellow Californians Optical Media to offer the equivalent of some 500 floppy disks worth of sounds on a single CD. E-mu's forward-looking attitude didn't stop here,

either, with computer-based sample editing soon available from Digidesign (Sound Designer) and Turtle Beach (Sample Vision), both for the Mac.

With its radical design casing, the EII was destined to be featured on film as well as at the music production end of moviemaking. The most high-profile of its numerous appearances was as the sound effects generator in *Ferris Bueller's Day Off*. The EII also made a notable appearance in a Paul McCartney video, dressed up with an extra slice of white tape as the then-completely-mythic EIII. (The generally fun-loving E-mu was not at all pleased at this jape, as it happened.)

Here in the 1990s, the EII is of course a little stranded, even if prices have drifted up a bit from the $500 of two or three years ago, and spares and servicing—indeed, even the upgrades—are still available. The EII's most enduring characteristic is its now-fashionable "grainy" sound, which injects instant substance and texture, especially to richly timbral samples like strings or vocals. Scrubbing cellos from the Marcato series is still probably about as powerful and authentic as it gets.

As a general-purpose sampler, the EII has chronic limitations today, but for particular types of sound and as a miracle of ahead-of-its-time engineering, it is still in a class of its own.

E-mu EIII Digital sampling keyboard

THE FAX

Keyboard:	61-note
Programs:	n/a
External storage:	3½" floppy disk drive
Polyphony:	16-voice
Oscillators per voice:	n/a
Effects:	Arpeggiator, chorus
Connections:	Stereo audio, 16 separate audio outs, RS422, SCSI, SMPTE I/O, stereo sample inputs, footswitches
Dimensions:	972mm x 444mm x 170mm
Weight:	22kg

THE FIGURES

Chief designer:	Dave Rossum
Production run:	1988-1993
Approx. units sold:	1200 (EIIIXP: 2000+)
Options:	WORM optical/CD-ROM storage systems, 8MB RAM, System Expander, 50-pin SCSI
Sounds:	E-mu library (on disk and RM45 cartridge)

Miscellaneous:	Sound/sequence editors: Digidesign Q-Sheet A/V, Sound Designer, Softsynth; Blank Software's Alchemy
Orig. price (1988):	$9995 (£8784)
Price in 1996:	$3000-3500 (£1800-2500)

Possibly as a legacy of its days in modular analog synthesizer design, E-mu has always favored options, upgrades, add-ons and alternatives. When you buy an E-mu instrument, far from purchasing a closed book, you buy a library card.

For both E-mu and its customers, this approach has proven to be a mixed blessing.

E-mu's EII sampler created the mold for professional quality sampling back in 1984. Although E-mu kept pace with what became the competition (the Akai S900 and Ensoniq Mirage DSK) for Emax, the company still had a loyalty toward and a belief in the high-end market. And whereas Akai and Ensoniq upped the ante in 1988 to include stereo sampling, expandability, good libraries and mid-level editing on the S1000 and EPS, E-mu went all out on the EIII in order to produce the very best that available sampling technology could offer.

The problems were that this was expensive, perhaps more than most people needed at the time and, to cap it all off, the EIII had major reliability problems, which, though later solved, saw to it that the EIII fought a rearguard action for much of its life.

The EIII story begins in 1986, when E-mu founder and designer Dave Rossum was wandering about on an Italian beach one morning after a particularly industrious evening of sampling (sampling Italian wine, that is). During his fresh air stroll, Rossum essentially came up with the plans for E-mu's F chip, on which the EIII would be designed. E-mu needed to do something special after the success of the EII, and the F chip, used one per channel, made the electronics practical for 16 channels (voices) with, as Rossum put it, "free" digital filtering (which was necessary to improve some problems that the system inherently created for sound fidelity).

The EIII was developed alongside Emax, and there is a noticeable overlap in terminology and style, including its system of "modules" (groups of controls dedicated to particular purposes), a list of which is helpfully printed onto the control panel. Not so welcome, however, is the EIII's tiny display. Front panel controls include management buttons, cursor keys and a keypad, plus volume, data entry and sample input level sliders. The 3½" floppy disk drive is supported—uniquely, at the time—by a 40MB hard drive. The five-octave keyboard is semi-weighted. At the back are a full 16 audio outputs—all mono—plus stereo mix outputs and stereo sample inputs. The EIII's mass of mono outputs was viewed with suspicion at the time (people generally preferred separate polyphonic outputs), but E-mu steered drummer/percussionists (for whom this is obviously not a problem) towards the EIII. The EIII's lack of digital I/O, however, proved to be more of a problem.

The EIII can sample in mono or stereo. Aside from a few operational refinements, E-mu wisely retained the same basic system as on its earlier models. Sample rate is flexible on the EIII, from 33.1 to 44.1kHz, which, even with the standard RAM of 4MB gives 48 to 63 seconds of (mono) sample time. The RAM can also be increased to 8MB.

In the digital processing module are the truncating and looping controls and playback options, plus a very useful sample rate conversion facility operating from 7 to 50kHz (again, useful in particular for percussion samples), gain normalizing and Undo.

Samples can be crossfaded and cross-switched, and zones can be repositioned; there's also an arpeggiator and plenty of room for expression with assignable wheels and footswitches.

Analog processing is what E-mu calls zone-applicable (a "zone," in E-mu-speak, is a keyboard range, irrespective of where multisamples lie). Included are resonant filtering, three five-stage envelope generators (ADSR plus H for Hold), an LFO, full keyboard tracking facilities, velocity-controlled panning and chorus.

The EIII also has a sequencer, though there is a tradeoff between sample time and sequencer memory. The sequencer has a nice, easy, ongoing feel, with track looping, overdubbing, track offset and a real-time track mix display for adjusting track volumes. Add in full SMPTE cue list features for precision matching of sound-to-picture, and E-mu's description of the EIII as a "Digital Sound Production System" was not conferred in vain.

MIDI Song Pointers, Song Select and MTC were implemented on subsequent software releases, as were features such as loop compression, dynamic two-pole digital filtering, digital compression and 20-band EQ.

The EIII was, and to some extent still is, a mighty machine. So why didn't it sell in vast quantities?

Problem number one was chronic unreliability on initial units. And it was the worst type of problem: intermittent. Eventually a frantic E-mu traced its problems to a third-party company that had revamped its stock of parts and sent E-mu vast numbers of unreliable "old ones." After a massive chip removal and re-insertion operation, EIIIs in fact became relatively reliable animals, but the damage to their reputation had already been done. That was the last time E-mu trusted such discrete technology.

Problem number two was price and performance. The EIII was considerably more expensive than the Akai S1000, which also offered 16-bit stereo sampling, albeit in a less complete package. Unfortunately for E-mu, the market wasn't ready for bells and whistles in 1988.

Proteus, whose sample playback sounds E-mu readily touted as coming "from the EIII library," ironically saved the day somewhat for the EIII. Even before the EIII appeared, E-mu had a huge library of 16-bit digital samples stored on Sony's F1 digital format that had been created for the EII. The EII could not reproduce this fidelity, of course, but the EIII could. The subsequent success of the Proteus range effectively drove the EIII for the next four or five years and kept EIII customers supplied with new material.

The EIII's problems, coupled with Proteus' success, understandably shifted the company's focus of attention. This explains why it took almost four years before an upgraded modular EIII, named the EIIIXP, finally appeared, using the same operating system but with Rossum's G- and H-chip technology. The EIIIXP is a very different proposition from the EIII, with digital I/O, 8MB of RAM (expandable to 32MB) and the option of a 105 megabyte hard drive.

The EIII may not have served E-mu well in a direct sense, but it formed a vital link in a chain of products bridging the EII to the present day.

E-mu EIV Digital sampling module

THE FAX

Keyboard:	None
Programs:	1000 presets per bank
External storage:	3½" floppy disk drive
Polyphony:	128-voice
Oscillators per voice:	n/a
Effects:	Chorus, compression, parametric EQ, Doppler, exciter, arpeggiator
Connections:	Stereo sample inputs, stereo ¼" and XLR outputs, 6 separate sub-mix outputs, digital I/O, 2 50-pin SCSI connectors, ASCII keyboard interface, MIDI
Dimensions:	312mm x 120mm x 456mm
Weight:	11kg

THE FIGURES

Chief designers:	Bob Bliss; technologist: Dave Rossum
Production run:	1995-present
Approx. units sold:	No figures available

Options:	3 expansion ports (additional MIDI port, plus future applications), HD version, SIMM RAM expansion up to 32MB, 16MB Flash RAM
Sounds:	E-mu library (disk/CD-ROM), CD-ROMs from Q Up Arts, InVision, Northstar
Miscellaneous:	The first 128-voice instrument in the world of synths and samplers
Orig. price (1995):	$5995 (£4695)
Price in 1996:	n/a

The EIV is one of the most current instruments featured in this Hot 100 and as such may cause a few eyebrows to be raised. But E-mu's Professional Digital Sampling System represents the pinnacle of dedicated sampling instruments as of this writing, and while it is far too early to confer classic status, the EIV's rewriting of the scoresheet in terms of polyphony, organization and exemplary sound quality merit this brief inclusion. This is not just another sampler!

The EIV's roomy 240x64 pixel screen displays graphics (computer-type icons and waveforms) as well as numbers, and the panel is angled up and easy to work with. An "easy operation" theme runs through the instrument. If you install the 16MB of Flash RAM, you can even switch on the instrument and call up sounds instantly—no loading of anything from anywhere. The EIV can also read Akai S1000/1100 format over SCSI.

Operationally, the EIV is informatively laid out, from its desktop-type browser, where you can scroll through items stored on external drives, to a most useful Find operation that allows you to search for a particular folder, bank, preset or even sample (in very much the same way as you can ask to Find a document on a Macintosh). In fact, even while a sound is still on an external drive, you can listen to it using the dedicated audition button (which plays one note that you can choose in the tune pages). Assembling sounds for multitimbral use is also smooth sailing, with presets called up hardwired to MIDI channels and viewed *en masse* on a special multi page.

If you already know E-mu sample-to-preset hierarchy, the process of sampling and assembling a "finished" preset on the EIV will be swift. Key help facilities include auto placement, crossfade looping and auto normalization, all of which save time and fiddling.

Ease of use should not be confused with limited options, though. The EIV has an almost over-the-top number of digital fixits, from compression to crossfading and auto-correlate, which somehow persuades even unloopable samples like Mellotron strings or heavily vibratoed guitars to toe the line. The serious sound designer will also appreciate the resonant, multimode filters, envelope generators, LFOs, arpeggiator, portamento, digital chorus, all manner of modulation routings and more.

For post-production, the EIV's 24 minutes of sample time, with both analog and digital source input rates up to 48kHz, and 18-bit DAC, should be enough for any pro audio environment. As a gift to remixers and programmers, you can "scrub" a sample using a (connected) keyboard pitch wheel, while the EIV's stunning pitch transposition, advanced cut-and-paste tools, reverse sample playback, powerful envelopes and filters and time compression manage to solve most of the practical problems in this field. Time compression, in particular, can work its magic from 50 to 200 percent; this not only renders sample beats fully usable through an enormously wide range of tempos, but it does so quickly, processing data in a matter of seconds.

E-mu Emulator Digital sampling keyboard

THE FAX

Keyboard:	49-note
Programs:	2 per disk
External storage:	5¼" floppy disk
Polyphony:	8-voice
Oscillators per voice:	n/a
Effects:	None
Connections:	Mono audio outputs
Dimensions:	900mm x 450mm x 225mm
Weight:	36kg

THE FIGURES

Chief designer:	Dave Rossum
Production run:	1981-83
Approx. units sold:	500
Options:	Genmod analog processing
Sounds:	E-mu library
Miscellaneous:	Stevie Wonder bought serial number 001.
Orig. price (1981):	$7995 (£8050)
Price in 1996:	$750 (£1000)

The Emulator is the godfather of samplers. This was not the first instrument to offer sampling; in fact, the word "sampler" was never used in its literature, even though that was the code word for the instrument during its design stage. But a sampler is what it is. Prior to its release in 1981, no one felt that being able to record snippets of real sound into computer memory and play them back polyphonically was a very practical basis on which to build a commercial musical instrument.

E-mu had been around for a number of years prior to the Emulator and had carved out a very successful niche for itself, both as a builder of analog modular synthesizer systems and as an OEM design house. The late 1970s were boom years: E-mu modular systems were selling for up to $40,000 apiece, and royalties for design work on the Sequential Circuits Prophet-5 exceeded all expectations.

But in 1980, it all suddenly went wrong. Sequential decided that the Prophet-5 (rev. 2) was different enough from the original design to stop paying E-mu royalties. And the latest E-mu design, a giant computer-controlled analog called the Audity, that was inspired by Tangerine Dream's Peter Baumann was shaping up for a $70,000 price tag.

At the 1980 AES show, E-mu noticed the Fairlight, almost as fabulously expensive as its own products but, so far as E-mu founder and designer Dave Rossum was concerned, primarily of interest because of its digital "sampling" capability. (The following Monday morning, the Sequential Circuits "no more royalties" bombshell dropped in through the mail.)

The Fairlight effectively contained eight monophonic samplers, providing eight voices. Rossum figured that by concentrating on the sampling and employing a system of memory-sharing on the currently available DMA chips, he could create an eight-voice polyphonic instrument for around one-third the price of a Fairlight. And so the Emulator was born.

Featuring a pit into which you can lob 5¼" floppies, this large gray blob of an instrument (for whose external design E-mu paid a top industrial design company handsomely) has very few controls on its dashboard-type control panel. Two samples can be stored per disk, one playable over the upper octaves, the other over the lower. Four switches next to the disk drive juggle which sound appears where. For one sound to appear over the whole keyboard range, you must record the sound twice.

There's no display screen at all, so all input levels, loops and truncate points have to be set "blind" using the panel switches. The truncate controls are shared by a filter activator (lowpass), which is one of the few analog-style editing facilities, though a mod (Genmod) from JLCooper later offered an ADSR envelope generator and a full-fledged filter. Cooper's mod, incidentally, acted as the blueprint for the analog-style editing parameters that were required by, and would be featured on, the EII and all samplers thereafter.

Vibrato can be added to either keyboard half, with speed and depth controllable; a mod wheel for depth sits alongside a one-tone range pitch wheel. Each keyboard half can be detuned.

E-mu was forging new territory here, and mistakes and oversights were inevitable. One of the most drastic was that on the original instrument, a sample always played to its end. You couldn't stop playback simply by taking your fingers off the keys. Clearly, this would render the instrument almost unplayable in a conventional keyboard style. Having initially said this was impossible to cure, the resourceful Rossum eventually found a "release mode" fixit, which was included some 10 months after the initial launch. At this time, polyphonic sequencing was introduced as well.

Stevie Wonder caused quite a stir trying out the Emulator at the Winter NAMM show, and placed an order. Wonder's unit (serial number 001) was delivered in May of that year.

With its 8-bit companding processing, four-second maximum sample time and 21kHz sample rate, the Emulator's specifications would hardly grace a children's toy in the mid-1990s. Yet, with a resourcefulness equaled only by the instrument's creator, top musicians such as Stevie Wonder, Michael Boddicker, Vangelis and many more used the Emulator on what are now considered landmark recordings. Boddicker used it extensively on Michael Jackson's *Thriller*, and the instrument was featured on Vangelis' soundtrack for *Blade Runner*. (One sound, a reggae loop heard in the bar scene of *Blade Runner*, was sampled off an AM radio station in E-mu's then-hometown of Santa Cruz. E-mu used this sample essentially just to demonstrate the power and effect of looping, and its eventual appearance in so illustrious a setting caused much amusement up at the factory.) More recently, bands such as Depeche Mode have employed the instrument.

E-mu's sound library went on not only to fuel world-class instruments like the Proteus but also became a marketable entity in its own right. E-mu learned the value of a sound library during the Emulator's first few months of life when, after a brief flurry of activity comprising no more than a couple of dozen sales, the Emulator "hit a brick wall," as Dave Rossum puts it. There just didn't seem to be any interest left. The release mode fixit helped, and the price dropped a little, but what really clinched the unit's eventual success, according to Rossum, was upping the number of sound disks it shipped with from 5 to 25. Up until this turnaround, the Emulator's sales had been so disastrous that E-mu had come within inches of selling out—and for a song, too.

In the early 1980s, although E-mu met with occasional reticence from musicians whom they recorded for sampling purposes (many local musicians, locations and studios were used, including the concert hall at UC Santa Cruz), phrases like "sample clearance" had not yet been invented. E-mu got a taste of what was to come at the first Emulator user group party in 1982, to which Todd Rundgren was invited. Eager to please, E-mu played Todd a small sample they'd taken from his latest album. "He seemed to be rather impressed," said the engineer, "but he had to leave. Then about an hour later, we got a call from his attorney..."

The Emulator is massively limited compared to 1990s technology, but technical excellence is not necessarily the whole story. The Emulator is riddled with character and, with so few made, is now highly collectible.

E-mu Morpheus Digital synthesizer module

THE FAX

Keyboard:	None
Programs:	128 ROM, 128 RAM
External storage:	PCMCIA card (128 program)
Polyphony:	32-voice
Oscillators per voice:	2
Effects:	None
Connections:	6 audio outs, 4 sub-mix inputs, phones, MIDI
Dimensions:	456mm x 200mm x 42mm
Weight:	2.4kg

THE FIGURES

Chief designers:	Dana Massie, Neil Warren, Scott Ruder; technologist: Dave Rossum
Production run:	1993-present
Approx. units sold:	No figures available
Options:	16MB ROM
Orig. price (1993):	No U.S. price (£1195)
Price in 1996:	$750 (£700)

When most people go away on vacation, they go to forget work. Not so, it seems, with E-mu's co-founder and senior designer Dave Rossum. If you read the EIII review, you may recall we found Dave strolling along a beach in Italy and coming up with the plans for the F chip. Cut to a skiing trip in 1989, and we find Dave pondering the problem of inherent noise on recursive digital filters (worrying about the phone bill or how to fix that leaky bath is for wusses).

"Thinking about the nature of multiplication, I came up with the realization [that is now in a patent somewhere] that if you just look at it this way [a closely guarded 'simple math trick'], it's real obvious what you have to do about it. I didn't even have a calculator with me, so I sat down and did all the math on paper." Rossum's idea went on to become the H chip, which was first used on the Emax 2 for digital lowpass filtering and subsequently on the EIIIXP.

Rossum built a lot of flexibility into this filter chip, and E-mu data processing specialist Dana

Massie eventually came up with the idea of Morpheus as a sophisticated, almost patchcord-type synthesizer platform through which the H chip's power could begin to be unleashed.

Physically, Morpheus looks a lot like one of E-mu's Proteus units, Vintage Keys in particular, with its eight panel buttons and large data control knob. Since it's a 1U module, the screen is unavoidably small, which has to be one of the main reasons that this innovative and challenging instrument has not sold as well as it might have. (Complex, patchcord-type synthesis is difficult enough to sell, but complex synthesis through a pinprick display is like fighting with one hand tied behind your back.)

Terms like "Morphing" and "Z Plane Synthesis" sound interesting but forbidding, and the truth is that to take Morpheus to anywhere approaching its limits requires understanding and patience.

True, Morpheus is still a sample+ synthesis instrument presented along Proteus lines—and so makes light work of flipping through presets, grouping presets together multitimbrally or even doing stage one-type tweaking, like substituting ROM waves or filter types—but this somewhat misses the point of the instrument. Moreover, judged as just another s+s module, Morpheus' price tag begins to look steep; this conundrum must also share the blame for modest sales.

What really kicks Morpheus into life is an 8MB slab of waveform ROM (expandable to 16MB) culled from the ever-growing E-mu library of EIII samples, on which the Proteus was fed and nurtured.

But whereas the typical s+s instrument uses its waveform ROM to take the headache out of sound programming, Morpheus argues that this takes out the pleasure as well. Accordingly, although there are plenty of harmonically interesting starter waves like acoustic piano and brass and such, these are very much starting-off points. The power of this instrument lies not so much in its waveform ROM but in the way you can present and process it. (Action required of the player? A brave move, given the spoonfed users of the 1990s!)

As with the Proteus, a Morpheus preset consists of one or two basic waves that are processed "digitally," in terms of sample length, playback direction, loop, etc. and "analog," in terms of filters, amplifiers, LFOs, etc. However, though there are structural similarities with Proteus, Morpheus expands on the design at every turn. The framework is also augmented in two key areas: multitimbral memories (here there are 16, while on Proteus there is but one current setup) and effects processing (Morpheus offers two channels of multi-effects, while on the Proteus, sounds are delivered squeaky clean and naked as the day they were born).

Single-preset programming seems straightforward enough: You choose either one or two waves from the waveform ROM and then set about processing them individually using the various digital and analog-style edit parameters. But when you apply this individual processing to capabilities as deep as Morpheus' range of almost 200 filter types, then the range of possibilities begins to look limitless.

Filters, even on powerful synthesizer engines like the Oberheim Matrix-12 or Prophet-VS, are generally limited to two or three types (lowpass, bandpass and/or highpass), plus cutoff frequency and resonance parameters. Morpheus takes a more three-dimensional approach, using the effects of keyboard scaling and keyboard velocity over time and wrapping them in with the filtering process. By these means, you can seamlessly change from one type of sound into another. This is not a simple process to explain or understand. In theory, it allows you to program sounds that evolve and change with similar results to vectoring or "wavesequencing," which, for those who are prepared to spend time with the system, can be highly creative and expressive.

How these 14-pole interpolating filters change can be dependent upon a number of sources, including a multistage envelope generator, an LFO, the mod wheel and more, all of which form part of the instrument's MIDIPatch system of modulation routings.

There are simpler routes to audio satisfaction, of course—namely, finding a sound and swapping filter types without regard to any other parameter. Such a random approach is not what the designers had in mind, perhaps, but can be invigorating all the same. These filter types range from instrument simulations to effects to filter shapes.

Proteus allows you to link presets to create bigger and more complex sounds. Morpheus expands on this concept with 128 Hyperpresets that can each comprise up to 16 presets with individual key range, velocity, pitch and volume data.

These are not to be confused with multitimbral memories, of which 16 can be set up and stored; this is the stage at which Morpheus' mult-ieffects are applied. This is a very sensible choice, because it removes the age-old annoyance of having to remove effects applied to a single sound when it is used in a multitimbral setting. Here, single sounds are not dependent upon effects, and in multi mode you can simply apply a top coat of reverb or delay, much as you might do over a mix. There are two channels of multi-effects, A and B, which together offer reverbs, early reflections, flanging, chorus, delay, fuzz and even a ring modulator. The reverb editing is very broad, but you can tweak the modulated time-based effects quite sufficiently for most applications, in terms of speed and depth.

The main appeal of Morpheus has to be its detailed level of sound sculpting via the Z Plane filtering, which offers sound analysis not far from physical modeling. Morpheus filters are undeniably powerful, if not wholly stable (one of the inherent pitfalls of time-variant filtering). Bouts of self-oscillation are frequently wanted on an old analog synth, but for the filters to "blow up" here, as is possible, is not a pretty sound. In fact Morpheus contains a little circuit that monitors every sound and, if it predicts a blowup, shuts it off quickly.

But the main problem with this instrument is related more to application; even E-mu accepts that it was hard to steer its sound design team in directions that do the system justice.

Morpheus may never sell in huge quantities, but as a source of challenging and unusual sounds and capabilities, it is, in its class, unparalleled.

E-mu Proteus Digital synthesizer module

THE FAX

Keyboard:	None
Programs:	128 ROM, 64 RAM
External storage:	SysEx
Polyphony:	32-voice
Oscillators per voice:	2
Effects:	Chorus
Connections:	6 audio outs, 4 submix inputs, MIDI
Dimensions:	456mm x 200mm x 42mm
Weight:	2kg

THE FIGURES

Chief designers:	Byron Shepherd, Josh Jeffe; technologist: Dave Rossum
Production run:	1989-1994
Approx. units sold:	50,000 (plus 20,000 Orchestral/World models)
Options:	8MB ROM (XR)
Sounds:	E-mu Orchestral Expander, Protologic 2MB Expansion Board, Livewire patches on disk (ST/PC/Mac), Many MIDI disk (ST/PC/Mac/Roland MRC)
Miscellaneous:	Proteus started off life as a "filler" product.
Orig. price (1989):	$995 (£629)
Price in 1996:	$325 (£300) (Proteus 2: $425 [£350]; Proteus 3: $475 [£375])

The key factor in the life of most instruments is timing. Great ideas presented before their time don't sell; mediocre ideas or even blatant copies with better tim-

ing can sell very well. Great ideas with great timing take the place apart, and the Proteus series was just that.

After the EIII, E-mu founder and designer Dave Rossum became less involved in the day-to-day management of the company and concentrated his efforts on technology. In 1987, Rossum shut himself up in his office and emerged a year later with the G chip. In the spring of 1988, this new chip came back from testing and sounded great. Now, what to do with it?

At this time, the EIII was not doing well for E-mu, and it took a long time to gestate a new high-end sampler. The company needed a filler product, something simple that could be designed fast to incorporate the new chip. E-mu needed what this product was first known as at the factory: the plug.

Said plug soon took shape as a band-in-a-box type of product and its code name became the slightly more dignified "Bubba." All hands went to work on the project, with Rossum's brother drafted to design new packaging (on which E-mu took out a patent).

At this period in its history, E-mu formed an alliance with giant Matsushita, the company behind the Technics and Panasonic brands. Midway through the design, E-mu became doubtful about its own ability to market a product like Bubba, and offered it on a plate to Matsushita. Matsushita turned it down flat as a dumb idea. "No one wants to buy this," was their reply.

Come the Winter NAMM show in 1989, the ugly duckling had turned into a swan. Proteus was the hit of the show, with orders exceeding E-mu's expectations by a factor of ten. "How much memory have you got in there?" asked Bob Moog after his personal demo from Dave Rossum. "Four megabytes," replied Rossum. "You're kidding," said Moog as he walked away, shaking his head. By then, everyone knew they had a winner.

The basic premise of Proteus is indeed deliciously simple: Take a range of top-quality 16-bit samples (which E-mu already had, thanks to its high-end sample library); provide just enough editing capability so that people won't get bored but also won't get lost; make it immediately and permanently multitimbral and don't bother with effect. By 1988, people were buying software sequencers by the truckload, and being able to extract all the meat-and-potatoes sounds you needed from one slimline module was the answer to a thousand prayers. Many thousands of prayers, in fact.

At Proteus' heart is a large ROM bank of what E-mu calls "instruments," which form the building blocks for constructing sounds. A standard unit offers 69 full looped and/or multisampled sounds, 21 harmonic waveforms, 20 single-cycle waveforms and 12 multicycle waveforms (sample snippets). You can combine a "primary" and a "secondary" instrument, then tweak this and that—envelopes, volume and such—and store the result in a "preset," the term for a finished sound.

In a stroke of unparalleled genius, the tiny Proteus display's main page reveals the barest of essential information: a preset's name, its MIDI channel, its volume and its pan position. By cursoring around the screen, you can stop off and alter any of this data. Proteus can operate in a permanently multitimbral mode, so assigning new patches to MIDI channels involves placing the cursor over the MIDI channel, using the data entry knob to select a new channel, moving the cursor to the preset and flipping through the presets until you hear what you want. Similarly, you can have the cursor resting over the MIDI channel and spin through all 16 channels to see which sounds are currently assigned. It's completely idiot-proof.

With its expansive pianos, gripping and raspy string sections, pleasant acoustic guitars, multi-mapped drums, choirs, brass and definitive collection of basses, most people have been content to use Proteus for its range of well-constructed, if never exactly sparklingly crisp (Proteus can tend to sound a little dull), presets. (Weyer/Smith Labs offers an op amp upgrade which enhances Proteus' high-end performance considerably.)

The curious will discover that this is not entirely a playback machine, though. Editing goes as far back as primary or secondary instrument selection (though opting for a dual sound halves polyphony). Per instrument, however, you can reshape a sound with a five-stage envelope generator or apply some wobble with a multiwaveform LFO. There's chorus, and you can change the start point of a sound (lop off the front end), reverse it or even route mod sources like the pitch and mod wheels of your controller keyboard to any stage of the envelope, LFO, volume, etc., in what E-mu calls a "MIDI Patch."

Notable for its absence is any form of filtering. The only form of tonal control comes from the keyboard follow parameter or keyboard velocity.

Invariably, most of the best sounds use two instruments. But these are not necessarily plain sound sandwiches. Even those with a modest amount of creativity can cut and paste one sound into another using delay, envelope shaping, reverse play, etc. For even more impressive results, up to four presets can be linked to sound together.

A master mode on Proteus takes you into global territory, where you find overall tuning and transposition, pitch bend range settings, velocity curves (a choice of four) and output selection (there are six to choose from, including the ever-handy option of using two of the auxiliary sends as returns when you run out of channels) and the simple but quite adequate MIDI functions.

The one-at-a-time multitimbral status of Proteus, plus its refreshing lack of internal signal processing—which neatly circumvents the age-old problem on all effects-laden synths of having to dump a single sound's effects when in multitimbral mode—means that this is a lightning-quick instrument to use. Proteus almost invariably gets you out of trouble.

There is no card facility. Though even a standard Proteus has plenty of room internally for new presets, external storage is via SysEx only. Upgrades to the waveform ROM, called Sound Sets, come in 4MB chunks and have been offered not only by E-mu but by third-party companies as well.

Though Proteus got off to a flying start at the Winter NAMM show, E-mu experienced near-catastrophic problems with delivery. Between a supplier who trashed one entire stock of chips and lost a second batch and the great California earthquake of October 17, 1989, whose epicenter was but a rockslide away from E-mu headquarters, it wasn't until a full year after its release that Proteus supply began to meet Proteus demand.

Although this clearly let in the competition, notably Roland's U-110 module, E-mu soon made up ground with the release of a large number of Proteus versions and variables, all of which looked and performed like the original but had different sound sets. These include the Proteus XR, which has a large RAM area for user-programmed presets; the Proteus 2/Orchestral, featuring orchestral sounds; and the Proteus 3/World, featuring all manner of ethnic instrument samples (many of them recorded on E-mu's doorstep in the world/ethnic percussion haven of Santa Cruz). There was even a keyboarded version, the Proteus MPS, which was one of the rare failures of this series.

As a development system, Proteus has outlasted its four or five years of production. Instruments designed along very similar lines include, to date, the ProCussion drum and percussion module, Vintage Keys, Classic Keys, Morpheus, Proteus FX and UltraProteus.

Not bad for a filler!

Ensoniq ESQ-1 Polyphonic synthesizer

THE FAX

Keyboard:	61-note
Programs:	40 RAM
External storage:	Cartridge, cassette interface
Polyphony:	8-voice
Oscillators per voice:	3
Effects:	None
Connections:	Stereo audio, MIDI (no Thru)
Dimensions:	980mm x 90mm x 340mm
Weight:	12.7kg

Name: Ensoniq Corporation

Head Office: 155 Great Valley Parkway; Malvern, PA 19355; tel: (800) 553-5151; fax (610) 647-8908

UK Distributor: c/o Sound Technology Plc: Letchworth Point; Letchworth, Herts SG6 1ND; 01462-480000

Founded: 1982

No. of employees: 167

Business: Samplers, synthesizers, effects processors, custom VLSI

Many American electronic musical instrument companies started out as hobbies in the basement of someone's house on a capital investment of $50. Ensoniq, however (founded in 1982 by three ex-Commodore executives: Bruce Crockett, Al Charpentier and designer Bob Yannes), from the very beginning, had much more grandiose intentions.

The key to Ensoniq's success lies in custom chip design. The Q Chip, a reported one-million-dollar investment in itself, gave birth to the world-beating, cost-slashing Mirage sampler and the innovative ESQ-1 synthesizer; and in recent times, a large slice of the company's income has come not from the sale of complete musical instruments but from sales of "wavetable synthesis" chips for the burgeoning computer/sound card market.

The instant successes of the Mirage and ESQ-1 were not exactly flashes in the pan, but Ensoniq was soon to learn that (a) the music industry is a good deal smaller than they'd thought and (b) sales of 30,000 and 50,000 units, respectively, were extremely rare.

Notwithstanding a few occasional forays into related areas of the instrument business, both abortive (in the case of the Ensoniq Piano) and worthwhile (the DP/4 effects processor), Ensoniq has largely focused its attention on synthesizers and samplers.

In synthesizers, the ESQ-1 and subsequent SQ-80 were replaced by a line of instruments that began with the VFX in 1989 and has twisted and turned through the VFX-SD, the VFX-SDII, the SD-1 and, in the 1990s, the SQ series. The more recent TS series has shifted to a different perspective, interestingly, blurring the distinction between synthesizers and Ensoniq's second major product line, samplers.

In pure sampler terms, Ensoniq had a rethink after the Mirage and its many guises that led to a new generation of Ensoniq instruments that began with the EPS in 1988. The EPS series, with its unusual (for a sampler) emphasis on performance, endeared itself to a generation of working musicians throughout America. Ensoniq's efforts to produce a major sound library and continual offers of upgrades, add-ons and general support material offset the EPS series' less-than-perfect reliability record to some extent.

Perhaps due to its computer-industry origins, Ensoniq has been loathe to trot along tried-and-tested music biz paths, preferring to plot its own course in terms of exhibiting at industry trade shows (which it doesn't); offering hands-on, personal dealer training (which it does); and showing active interest in independent newsletters (the excellent *Transoniq Hacker*) and Internet newsgroups and forums. Perhaps less wisely, Ensoniq's go-it-alone philosophy has also made it slow to embrace GM and reluctant to do away with proprietary disk and sequence formats that could hinder interplay with non-Ensoniq instruments and systems.

Although Ensoniq has a reasonable global presence (indeed, all of its keyboard mechanisms are made in Italy), America remains the company's highest profile market.

THE FIGURES

Chief designer:	Bob Yannes
Production run:	1986-88
Approx. units sold:	50,000
Options:	Ensoniq RAM cartridges, Ensoniq Voice Cartridges, Sequencer Expansion Cartridge (+7,600 notes), sustain and CV pedals
Sounds:	Ensoniq VPC cartridge, Cesium, Maartists, Many MIDI
Miscellaneous:	Book: *ESQ-1 Advanced Programming Guide* by Bob Wehrman; video: *ESQ-1 Made Easy* with Walter Holland; the independent club/newsletter *Transoniq Hacker* can be contacted at 1402 SW Upland Dr.; Portland, OR 97221
Orig. price (1986):	$1395 (£1080)
Price in 1996:	$350 (£400)

The year was 1986, and the young Ensoniq corporation was still reeling from its success with the Mirage sampler. But many new products were trailed when they burst onto the scene, and the ESQ-1, the synthesizer that was initially planned as the company's debut product, was obviously going to be foremost among them.

Similar to what Korg was doing on the other side of the world with the DW-8000, Ensoniq experimented with the use of digital sampled waveforms as starting-off points for otherwise quite standard subtractive analog synthesis. Indeed, everything looked and felt new on first sighting of this instrument back in 1986, from its early s+s design to its large fluorescent blue display screen (inspired in part by Oberheim synths) to its built-in 8-track sequencer. The name "workstation" hadn't been coined in 1986, but that's what this was.

Upon powering up, the large screen reverts to your last used set of programs or parameters. In patch programming terms, the display reveals the names of ten sounds at a time that, in Ensoniq-speak, correspond to a complete "bank." Just 40 sounds can be stored internally, but the factory presets are fresh and vital, and with room to store a further 80 on cartridge, there were few complaints.

Programming may not be idiot-proof, but it is not too daunting, especially since the screen can display a reasonable amount of information at any one time. At the heart of the instrument, sounds can be generated by up to three oscillators, with each oscillator able to choose a particular type of waveform: analog, digital or multisampled, the latter fully looped and ready for action.

The choice of waveform ROM is arranged in five overall categories under the headings Classic Synth (analog); Sampled (various instruments, plus voices and kick drum); Additive Synthesis; Formant Waveforms (multisamples with set peaks) and Sound Limited Waveforms (bandwidth-limited versions of the previous lot). There are 32 ROM waves in all. Forbidding though the list looks in print, selection can be simply a matter of auditioning: "Yes, I like that sound. No, I don't like this one."

This jump start on sound creation was new and different in 1986, and the ESQ-1 attracted a good deal of press attention. Although the waveforms are inherently interesting next to comparatively plain-faced sawtooth and sine waves, you are still offered interactive features, such as oscillator sync and ring modulation and oscillator amplitude modulation.

Complementing these perfectly are resonant analog filters (four-pole, lowpass) with a dedicated six-stage envelope generator. The idea is that sounds can be as fresh and clean as samples without losing the timbral richness of analog. Access to analog sounds and sensibilities in a digital setting makes the ESQ-1 a good choice if you want analog elements in your work without making a full commitment to analog, with its severely dated technology, lack of stability, MIDI shortcomings, etc.

For the most part, the ESQ-1 is intuitively easy to program, the only likely stumbling block being the multistage envelope generators, of which there are no less than four available per voice.

The ESQ-1's 8-track sequencer took the whole concept of built-in sequencers to new heights, way beyond the songwritery scratchpad device. Here it is possible to actually demo parts of a song. Without getting carried away, the sequencer tracks feature quantizing facilities and a basic storage capacity of 2400 notes, which can be expanded to 10,000 with an upgrade. Tracks can be mixed down and sent out on their own MIDI channel. Up to 30 (pretty short) sequences can be stored and even chained together to form up to 10 songs. I say "without getting carried away" because the total instrument polyphony is just eight-voice; the unit has some inherent and fairly major limitations as viewed from the 1990s.

The keyboard has light action (Ensoniq hadn't quite moved into its lumpy weighted action phase yet) and responds to velocity, though not aftertouch. Sounds can be layered or split.

The modular version, the ESQ-M, loses the sequencer but offers the MIDI Thru missing on the keyboard.

Obviously the ESQ-1 has been superseded in pure performance terms by generations of Ensoniq synths. But the ESQ-1 sold in considerable quantities at the time, and it remains important not only as a source of particularly rich hybrid tones but also as a landmark product that introduced or crystallized many synth concepts that Ensoniq and others have subsequently enlarged upon.

Ensoniq Mirage Digital sampling keyboard

THE FAX

Keyboard:	61-note
Programs:	4 sounds per bank (2 banks)
External storage:	3½" disk drive
Polyphony:	8-voice
Oscillators per voice:	n/a
Effects:	None
Connections:	Mono audio (stereo on later models), MIDI
Dimensions:	1090mm x 90mm x 305mm (DSK model slightly smaller)
Weight:	13.2kg (DSK model slightly lighter)

THE FIGURES

Chief designer:	Bob Yannes
Production run:	1985-88
Approx. units sold:	30,000
Options:	Advanced Sampler's Guide, MASOS Advanced Sampling software; Input Sampling Filter (50kHz sample rate) available on original Mirage model only
Sounds:	Ensoniq Sound Library disks, Actronic, Livewire, Northstar, Desert Island, 3D Sounds, Synthware
Miscellaneous:	Software editing via Mirage Visual Editing System (Apple IIe), Blank Software Sound Lab (Mac), Steinberg Mirage Soundworks Editor (ST), Sonus Sonic Editor (Commodore), Turtle Beach Vision (PC); Syntaur (Ensoniq Sound Library): 11116 Aqua Vista #2; N. Hollywood, CA 91602; tel: (818) 769-4395
Orig. price (1985):	$1695 (£1695)
Price in 1996:	$350 (£300)

A Mirage is not a Mirage is not a Mirage. This ground-breaking sampler, which launched both Ensoniq and the whole concept of affordable sampling, appeared in many guises during the second half of the 1980s, in both keyboard and module form.

The Mirage marked Ensoniq's debut, but it was not the first product that the three ex-Commodore men who founded the company—designer Bob Yannes, software engineer Al Charpentier and executive Bruce Crockett—had in mind. Originally set to launch the company was the ESQ-1. On closer inspection, however, the trio decided the synth market was too crowded, opting instead for the (at the time) completely empty path of entry-level samplers. Fortunately, both instruments were based on the same custom chip technology, so the change of heart was by no means a major turnaround.

Although "Mirage" became a hook on which the company would hang several low-cost sampling instruments, in the beginning there was a plain Ensoniq Mirage keyboard. Plain indeed it was, comprising a vast expanse of empty front panel on which there was but a keypad, a two-digit LED, eight dedicated sample and sequencer buttons and a volume slider.

The Mirage appeared with a rather wonky keyboard that Ensoniq was forced to buy from the ailing Pratt-Read (in an all-too-familiar story, it seems Japanese manufacturers placed so many trading restrictions on the purchase of their keyboards that import was wholly impractical) and a totally forbidding user interface. But the Mirage was ludicrously cheap, and it gave thousands of players who had hitherto only been able to observe sampling from the sidelines their first taste of the sport.

Judged by modern-day sampling specifications, the Mirage's 8-bit, 30kHz sampling capabilities, providing just two seconds of sample time, seem positively absurd. But perception of audio quality changes with time, and diving down to the realm of an 8kHz sample rate in order to squeeze in a decent amount of sample time was not the joke it seems today.

Digital edit parameters are fairly rudimentary, but you can nip and tuck and loop samples with a bit of patience, and in terms of analog-style editing, the instrument is well provided for, with its 24dB/oct lowpass resonant filtering with dedicated ADSR envelope generator, plus a separate amplifier ADSR envelope generator and LFO. It also includes the ability to detune and layer voices and even record parts into a small playsequencer, whose meager capacity of 333 events could be enlarged to 1333 via an expansion cartridge.

The two main complaints about the Mirage, after the euphoria that greeted its very existence had died down a little, were the feel of the instrument's keyboard (Ensoniq later bought much better keyboards from Italy) and the primitiveness of the operating system (unless you like programming in hex), especially with respect to MIDI.

The success of Ensoniq's custom VLSI Q chip—responsible, said Ensoniq at the time, for the redundancy of some 20,000 transistors—plus the fact that the operating system was disk-loaded, meant that upgrades and improvements to the original design were bound to happen.

Within a year or so, Ensoniq repackaged the Mirage as the Mirage DSK-8, featuring not only a weightier-action keyboard but also the delights of Local On/Off, the ability to send and receive MIDI program changes and, impressively, polyphonic aftertouch.

In 1987, the DSK-1 arrived, sporting physical alterations like a recessed disk holder and stereo audio outputs. The DSK-1's final specification may still only reach the giddy heights of a 33kHz sample rate, but you can record and map up to 16 samples across the keyboard range, use the instrument multitimbrally, and store sounds and sequences from Ensoniq's ESQ-1 synth on disk using the Mirage's disk drive. In addition to the new keyboards, Ensoniq also produced the DSM-8, a module version.

Ensoniq upgrades notwithstanding, the user interface of a keypad and a two-digit screen, on which all the parameters must not only be accessed but also altered, provided the impetus for many third parties to release editing packages for then-current computers such as the Apple IIe and the first Apple Macintoshes. In the 1990s, this sounds perfectly natural, but in the mid-1980s, the terms "computer" and "musical instrument" were uttered in the same breath only by the brave.

Though Ensoniq itself produced some software for the Apple IIe, even better is Blank Software's *Sound Lab* for Mac, which not only circumvented the Mirage's keypad and screen entirely but provided waveform redrawing, full onscreen editing of filters and envelopes and sample naming. This was, and possibly still would be if you were hellbent on owning a Mirage today, a most useful utility to track down.

Which leads one to that very question: What is the Mirage's value today? Truthfully, the Mirage had its heyday and is best left at that. Unlike other early samplers like Akai's 612, which at least has an element of hands-on, real-time operation about it, the Mirage needs serious fiddling with unless you're perfectly happy slotting disks in and out all day long. However, the inevitably grungy sound—not due to the 8-bit technology, insist the designers, so much as to the problems of aliasing—is something of a cachet on the mid-'90s dance scene.

In the 1990s, Syntaur has taken over distribution of the Ensoniq Sound Library.

Fairlight CMI Sampling/recording system

THE FAX
Keyboard:	73-note (Series III)
Programs:	n/a
External storage:	8" floppy disk

Polyphony:	16-voice (Series III)
Oscillators per voice:	n/a
Effects:	Reverb, delay, flanging
Connections:	Variable
Dimensions:	Variable
Weight:	Variable
Fairlight USA:	626 N. Beachwood Dr.; Los Angeles, CA 90004; tel: (310) 287-1400
Fairlight ESP Pty. Ltd.:	30 Bay St.; Broadway, NSW Australia 2007; tel: 61 (2) 212-6111; fax: 61 (2) 281-5503

THE FIGURES

Chief designers:	Kim Ryrie, Peter Vogel, Tony Furze
Production run:	1985 (original CMI introduced in 1979)
Approx. units sold:	200 (Between CMI, Series II and Series IIx: 300+)
Options:	Inputs, digital video, storage (HD, magneto-optical), record channels and much more
Sounds:	Fairlight Library
Miscellaneous:	The machine on which sampling was first spotted as a viable technology base
Orig. price (1979+):	$40,000—175,000 (depending upon system)
Price in 1996:	Depends on system (no UK price)

The Australian Fairlight had its day in the mid-1980s when, with Trevor Horn production in tow, bands like Frankie Goes to Hollywood and the Pet Shop Boys ruled the airwaves. At that point, the Fairlight represented the cutting edge of technology. In Britain during this period, if not so much in America, every two-bit group that scored a couple of Top 10 hits dashed out and spent their life's advances on one of these outlandishly priced music computers in the hope that it would bolster their position.

The Fairlight quickly assumed the position of dream machine for a generation of "tech novices" and professional programmers, but it was also the favored weapon of more established artists like Peter Gabriel (whose Fairlight Shakuhachi sample on "Sledge-hammer" became the first sample cliche), Kate Bush, Thomas Dolby (during the *Aliens Ate My Buick* period) and many more. For a while, it was easy to dismiss the Fairlight as a rich boy's toy, and when both instrument and company fell from grace at the end of the decade, boy, did they fall. Fairlights, in all their high-priced glory, could be found operating as doorstops and dinner tables in studios all over the world, with second-hand prices all but nonexistent. Yet this is the instrument that introduced musicians to the notion of keyboard sampling. E-mu picked up on this at the 1980 AES show, and it was what inspired them to build the first Emulator. More than that, the Fairlight, with its fluid, upgradable, system-based format, not only served as an inspiration for a generation of street-level workstations but also surely sowed the seed for the subsequent generation of dedicated hard disk recording systems that share instrument and recording device status.

The Fairlight also said that it was okay to hang a five-figure price tag, provided that you could convince musicians that this was where their next hit would be generated. And for four or five years, an awful lot of people paid up and did just that.

A thorough description of the Fairlight's development would occupy a small book in itself. Despite its high-gloss image and brief flirtation with high-profile users, Fairlight itself has always been quite a small, personal operation. Accordingly, there have always been lengthy periods of time between upgrade announcements and their delivery, with specifications, options and future developments scattered about like confetti.

The distinctive feature of a Fairlight system, even the initial CMI released back in 1979, is its multi-component design—a musical keyboard, an alphanumeric keyboard, a processor unit and a monitor with a light pen—most all of it dressed in creamy white livery. The effect is at once high-tech and somewhat other-worldly.

Though sampling is what the Fairlight would become known for, this was by no means its original primary purpose. The CMI began life as an all-digital synthesizer, distinctive in that you could redraw waveshapes and envelopes on its dedicated screen. This early instrument was, in effect, eight monophonic synths strapped together with, by today's standards, a minute sampling capability.

By 1982, Fairlight had created the Series II, which upgraded not only the capacity but also the quality of sampling. This, Fairlight had realized by then, held the key to its popularity and was the version used on the infamous Frankie Goes to Hollywood sessions, courtesy of programmer Andy Richards, engineer Julian Mendelsohn and producer Trevor Horn.

Fairlight hovered on the brink of MIDI for a while—I remember talk of "we don't need MIDI," as if it were some sort of hobbyist plaything, from the Fairlight's snobby UK distributors at the time—before it was implemented, along with faster processors, on the Series IIx.

The Series III appeared in 1985, and it is this version that continues in some form to this day, though the name has changed to MFX-2. The Series III consists of a light-action 73-note keyboard; an alphanumeric keyboard; a high-resolution graphics tablet with stylus; a high-resolution monitor; and the processing unit, containing the microprocessors, disk drives, power supply, MIDI ports, outputs, etc.

The Fairlight is very much a custom-built concept, which allows you to purchase the memory, polyphony and storage facilities that suit your particular application. Whatever your system, its day-to-day operation is quite straightforward, using a number of pages to access and work on the various facilities. Among these pages are sampling, editing, filtering, mapping and MIDI, including some spectacular tools like resynthesis and waveform drawing with Fast Fourier Transform, as well as Waveform Edit, much of which later became available on Digidesign's sample-edit software packages.

Upon release, much was made of the sequencing capabilities of the Fairlight's Page R, which takes its lead from the friendly, ongoing style of sequencing of the Linn drum machines. Although not overtly designed to do so, Page R has a distinctive groove, and those familiar with the Fairlight are generally able to tell which Kate Bush, Thomas Dolby or Peter Gabriel track was put together thusly. Somewhat less intuitive are the Fairlight's MCL step-time sequencer and giant CAPS polyphonic sequencer.

In its prime, the Fairlight's complete working environment represented the pinnacle of technology, its potential maximized by artists like Thomas Dolby, who pushed it to its limits on such tracks as "Pulp Culture," "Ability to Swing" and "Budapest by Blimp," where almost everything is a Fairlight sample being driven by Fairlight sequencing. But in due course, the expansion of dedicated sequencing programs (especially those from Akai and E-mu) quickly overtook the Fairlight's Page R in tracks, features, capacity, fidelity and polyphony.

The bottom dropped out of the high-priced musical instrument market by the end of the 1980s, and indeed Fairlight itself teetered on the brink of extinction. In a perfectly logical transformation, however, the Fairlight morphed into a digital audio workstation. Hard disk recording began simply as one track with cut-and-paste editing on mid-version Series IIIs, but impressively, even owners of early 16-voice Series III instruments can still upgrade to the 24-track random-access hard-disk recording system that is the MFX2.

Fairlights have only ever been available to the wealthy few, so perhaps this development system's most lasting legacy is the collection of sound samples with which it established itself. Fairlight sample CDs are far more readily available than the systems themselves; Digital Domain's Series IIx sound library

(audio CD and CD-ROM) contains some 700 multi-sampled sounds where the full glory of these classic 8-bit samples can be heard.

Fairlight purists, if such can now be delineated, tend to feel that Series II and IIx instruments have a clearly defined character that later models progressively ironed out.

Farfisa Compact Organ Organ

THE FAX

Keyboard:	49-note
Programs:	9
External storage:	None
Polyphony:	Full
Oscillators per voice:	n/a
Effects:	Vibrato, reverb
Connections:	Mono audio, pedalboard, volume, phones
Dimensions:	912mm x 432mm x 216mm
Weight:	25kg
(Farfisa) Comus S.P.A.:	Viale Don Bosco 35; 1-62018 Potenza Picena, MC, Italy; tel: 0733-8851; fax: 0733-885302
Comus UK:	12 Churchill Way; Lomeshaye Industrial Estate, Nelson, Lancs BB9 6RS; tel: 01282-606600; fax: 01282-606660

THE FIGURES

Production run:	1964-1970
Options:	13-note pedalboard
Sounds:	n/a
Miscellaneous:	The sound used on Percy Sledge's "When a Man Loves a Woman" was a Farfisa Compact Organ; the earliest Compacts in America were badged CMI (Chicago Musical Instrument Co.).
Orig. price (1964):	$800 (£200)
Price in 1996:	$500 (£300)

Much of the Italian organ business is a mystery—even to the Italians. This was the case even in its heyday in the 1960s. Instruments came and went, were up- or downgraded and were replaced or superseded on a scale that makes the 1990s look staid and solid.

Of the many famous names of this era, Farfisa stands out. And of the colossal Farfisa series comprising all manner of organs, such as the Ballata, the Transicord and Transivox, the Gulliver, the VIP and the Synaccordian (used by Vangelis), the Compact is the name most people remember.

Although there is a plain Farfisa Compact, essentially a portable version of the Ballata, the Compact appeared in many guises, from the large double-manual Compact Duo to the Compact Deluxe to the slimline Minicompact (also called the Compact

Minor). The standard-model Compact was also made in a variety of colors, certainly the most striking being blood red. Named after its ability to be neatly folded away—legs, lid and all—for transportation purposes, the Compact sets up in seconds via a beautiful piece of engineering. It also sits quite sturdily on its tubular steel legs, a board boldly proclaiming the words "Compact" and "Farfisa" unfolding and facing out into the audience.

Though the sides and underneath of the instrument are Tolex-covered wood, the top is curvy molded plastic and about as deliciously '60s-looking as it gets. Rocker switches jut out from the slope just above the keys that control both tones and tone enhancers.

This is an electronic transistorized organ, and its sound is totally different from the human throaty roar of a tone-wheel Hammond. The Farfisa sound is shrill and distinctively cutting. It's the sound of "When a Man Loves a Woman" (where it was played by Spooner Oldham), early Elvis Costello (Steve Nieve), Blondie and more. A Farfisa can rarely be accused of prettiness, but it adds instant character.

On the Compact, there are nine tabs that correspond to instruments and footages: Bass and Strings at the 16' pitch range; Flute, Oboe, Trumpet and Strings at 8'; and Flute, Piccolo and Strings at 4'. None sounds remotely like its name, with Strings and Oboe sounding intriguingly similar in a quacky, ducklike sort of way. Equally mystifying, the piccolo is quite rich and fruity. But this is hardly the point. Tones can be mixed and matched by flipping the rocker switches on and off, and by far, the most classic Farfisa sound can be had by switching all of them on at the same time.

An important element of the Farfisa sound is vibrato, available in light or heavy, slow or fast settings. The heavy setting is somewhat over the top. The spirited "fast" and "light" positions do the trick nicely.

Spring reverb is offered in either medium or long types. Spring reverb has become a sound in itself and is again very much part of the overall '60s vibe of this instrument. A bass section, marked by almost an octave's worth of reverse-color keys, can use its own tones, or you can plug in the optional 13-note pedalboard. A volume swell pedal was included in the original package and tucks away neatly into the lid.

You can "boost" the tone at various pitch ranges via a special knee lever beneath the keys, which you activate by bending your knee outwards. This patented "multitone booster" feature gives the instrument much of its classic edge and bite. Though the Compact is designed for the stage, a jack mounted on the small panel to the left of the keyboard is reserved for, as Farfisa called them at the time, "earphones."

The Farfisa Compact and the Vox Continental

carved up the pop instrument market between them in the 1960s. (At this time Hammond organs were the domain of jazz players; it wasn't until the end of the decade that pop, then in its progressive phase, allied itself to the Hammond's greater power and range.) The Farfisa sound made a brief comeback in the New Wave era of Blondie and Elvis Costello but only as a means of conjuring up images of the past.

Prices are rarely high, and though, judged by today's audio standards, the average Compact is hideously noisy and limited, these are delightful instruments to own as pieces of '60s memorabilia.

The Farfisa name took a battering in the 1980s with its production of none-too-illustrious organ-cum-synths. In the 1990s, as part of the giant Bontempi-owned Comus organization, the brand is being revived, thanks to massive injections of capital and new technology from Comus' internationally renowned IRIS research center just outside Rome.

Fender Rhodes Stage 73
Electro-mechanical piano

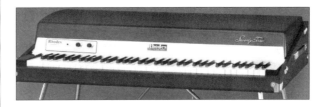

THE FAX

Keyboard:	73-note
Programs:	n/a
External storage:	n/a
Polyphony:	Full
Oscillators per voice:	n/a
Effects:	Varies with model: some have active EQ, some tremolo
Connections:	Audio out
Dimensions:	1150mm x 250mm x 600mm
Weight:	60kg
Harold Rhodes:	5067 Topanga Canyon Blvd.; Woodland Hills, CA 91364; tel: (818) 340-8483

THE FIGURES

Chief designer:	Harold Rhodes
Production run:	1968-1984
Options:	Many third-party modifications
Sounds:	n/a
Miscellaneous:	Service and repairs from Steve Woodyard: (714) 821-7859
Orig. price (1968):	$995 (£800)
Price in 1996:	$300 (£300)

It's common among American synth manufacturers for companies to bear the name of their founders: Oberheim (Tom), Moog (Bob), Kurzweil (Raymond), Buchla (Don), even ARP (which stands for Alan R. Pearlman). But in terms of influence, only the name of

Moog rivals that of Rhodes (Harold), which is renowned not just for a line of instruments but also for a sound, perhaps even a mood. Now that's what you call fame.

Harold Rhodes produced something at least akin to what became this seminal electric piano during World War II, when he was a trainee flying instructor stationed in Greensboro, North Carolina. It all began in 1942, with a pile of aluminum tubing that Rhodes salvaged from a B17 bomber on the airbase and then fashioned into a sort of xylophone. After the war, Rhodes remodeled his xylophone into more of a piano, using spun metal rods called "tines"—an idea he'd hit upon after taking a chiming clock apart.

Rhodes' first marketed design was the 32-note Piano Bass, launched in the mid-1960s under the guidance of Leo Fender and used subsequently and enthusiastically by Ray Manzarek of The Doors. In 1965, this design was modified and enlarged into a full piano (complete with an amplification system, the Suitcase 88), upon which the instrument sat. Of the various models to emerge over the years (see following entries), the Stage 73 was definitely the best known and is the best preserved. Even so, this model underwent constant refinement and modifications during its 15-year run, culminating in the rare Mk 5 MIDI version, produced only in small quantities in 1984.

Thereafter, the Rhodes marque was sold to Roland, which manufactured a range of completely different instruments under the name. Although Harold Rhodes appeared as a consultant in Roland advertising, the "Roland Rhodes" instruments bore little or no resemblance to any previous Rhodes design, and the association was always an incongruous one. As it turns out, Rhodes is now questioning the legality of Fender's sale of the marque to Roland, and it's not due to some whim: At the age of 84, Mr. Rhodes is currently poised to resume manufacture of his fabled instruments, though on a limited scale.

The Stage 73 is the quintessential Rhodes piano: it's a unique-looking instrument with its curvy black lid (flattened out somewhat on models produced from 1974 onwards), weighty wooden chassis and screw-in legs that can be packed away into a small compartment in the top lid for transportation. Such a design, once packed away, renders the instrument a compact, if still murderously heavy, oblong box.

As on all the Rhodes pianos, sound is generated by the key action activating rubber hammers that hit not strings but thin metal rods called tines. Vibrations are then picked up and transferred using a system of individual magnets positioned close to the tip of each tine. The tines are cut to rough length and then fine-tuned using little springs jammed on the ends, which

you have to scrape up or back in order to make the tine effectively longer or shorter. The classic Rhodes sound is highly expressive but hardly what you'd call precise; when you hit a note really hard, you can produce anything from a harmonic to a clear, loud tone to a dull sort of thwack. This is both the pleasure and the pain of the instrument. You could call the classic Rhodes sound part bell, part xylophone and part piano.

Aside from a curious sustain-pedal affair comprising a collapsing metal rod that you have to insert simultaneously into the base pedal unit and a hole in the underbelly of the instrument (the bugger always slips out anyway), there is not much to worry about technologically with the instrument except broken tines. Tines do break, quite frequently, though the process of fitting and tuning new ones is laborious rather than difficult.

Aside from some of the later models, which had active tone controls, a lone passive tone control means you are largely stuck with the sound as is. Third-party and user modifications abounded, though. Perhaps the best known being Chuck Monte's Dyna-My-Piano from California, a complete workover of the action and the sound, adding active tone controls, power and relative stability along the way. A new Fender Rhodes had an action that was wrist-breakingly stiff (never mind "weighted"), and it generally took months for both it and you to settle down.

Many a Rhodes would quickly go from stiffly new to knackered (the most common term among users) in a matter of only a year or so. Accordingly, no two instruments feel or sound the same. There are good ones and murderous ones.

Quite the worst I ever played belonged to Michael McDonald. Back in the '70s, when the band I played in toured America with the Doobie Brothers, we used to jam onstage for the last couple of numbers. McDonald's Rhodes only had about 80 percent of its notes working and a lumpy action of cobblestone proportions. Who knows how, but he could still make it sing!

The MIDI Mk 5 model (produced in both 73- and 88-key versions, though in small quantities) was a vast improvement on early models in many respects: bright new Torrington tines, harder neoprene rubber hammers and an ABS vacuum casing, making it immeasurably lighter.

In the early days, the Fender Rhodes was a bit of a jazzer's instrument, used by players like Herbie Hancock and Chick Corea (in Harold Rhodes' opinion, the finest exponent of the instrument he ever heard), not the least because actually being able to hear the soft, muted tones of a Rhodes in anything approaching a rock context was nigh-on impossible.

After a period of deep unfashionableness in the late 1980s, the retro revolution of the 1990s revived an enormous interest in the instrument, helped by Donald Fagen's 1993 *Kamakiriad* album and his almost exclusive use of the instrument.

Of course, the Rhodes sound has become a cliche, still sported today by every single digital piano on the market. This didn't have quite the same devastating effect that it had on the Clavinet, possibly because, although both instruments are far more expressive and colorful than any sample can do justice, the Rhodes has always remained valid as a stand-alone, main-axe instrument.

Checking out a Rhodes for potential purchase is more an aural examination that anything else. There was a period during the late 1970s when CBS (now owners of Fender) substituted lead alloy for the special steel originally used for the posts—the tone generators into which the tines are inserted. Harold Rhodes eventually spotted the substitution, whereupon manufacture reverted to the original design. But many late-1970s instruments have what Rhodes, anyway, regards as an inferior tone as a result.

Keyboard action is a matter of personal taste, but an action that is too flappy and loose is probably on its way out. Don't worry too much about a degree of unevenness; this can be smoothed out. Unevenness in individual note volume, too, is a relatively easy thing to cure. It's simply a matter of adjusting the angle and/or distance between the end of the tine and the pickup.

Rhodes pianos were produced in large quantities and are therefore still in plentiful supply. Prices shouldn't tax even modest budgets, and most repairs can generally be carried out yourself with a modicum of intelligence and patience. If you want to hear, see and feel how instruments used to be before the march of digitization made everything "virtual" as opposed to "real," a Rhodes piano will present the lesson perfectly.

Main (Fender) Rhodes Models:
Fender-Rhodes Piano Bass (1964): 32-note piano-action keyboard, stand optional
Rhodes Stage 54: 54-note keyboard, not particularly successful
Rhodes Stage 73: See previous entry
Rhodes Stage 73: Mk III EK-10 (1981)
Rhodes Stage 73: Mk V (1984)
Rhodes Suitcase 73: Included built-in amplification
Rhodes Stage 88: 88-note version of the Stage 73
Rhodes Suitcase 88: Big version of the Stage 88, with built-in amplification

Gleeman Pentaphonic — Polyphonic synthesizer

THE FAX

Keyboard:	37-note
Programs:	100
External storage:	Cassette interface
Polyphony:	5-voice
Oscillators per voice:	3
Effects:	Chorus
Connections:	Mono audio, phones
Dimensions:	592mm x 318mm x 138mm
Weight:	8kg
A&B Design:	140 San Lazaro Ave.; Sunnyvale, CA 94046

THE FIGURES

Chief designer:	Al Gleeman
Production run:	1981-82
Approx. units sold:	70
Options:	"Clear" model, hewn out of plexiglass; joystick controller
Sounds:	None commercially available
Orig. price (1981):	$2795 (£1530)
Price in 1996:	$2500 (no UK price)

The Gleeman Pentaphonic probably owes much of its latter-day fame and fable to its name. It's redolent with images of early synthesizers, of knobs and switches and flashing lights, of wild-haired boffins in white coats exclaiming, "Yez, I zink I have it!"

But in fact, the Brothers Gleeman released their Pentaphonic synthesizer in the early 1980s. The Pentaphonic is a quite modest-looking instrument, not wholly unlike, say, a Moog Multimoog, except for its rather spindly pitch bend lever. That is, black Pentaphonics look modest; Gleeman also produced a wonderful see-through plastic model, of which no more than 10 were ever made.

The four Gleeman brothers (Al, Tom, Bob and Dan) hailed from Minnesota. When they traveled cross-country to California in the late 1970s, their shared fascination with the music industry combined with their wide range of technical, engineering and marketing skills led them to the crazy notion of building a synthesizer.

Keyboards—the physical mechanism, that is—proved a perennial thorn in Gleeman's side. The company's first design had only a touch keyboard, like a Wasp. Then, throughout the development of the Pentaphonic, Gleeman had problems purchasing the keyboards they wanted. The Japanese, they maintain, refused point-blank to sell to them. Eventually they found and used the instrument's short-scale, 37-note keyboards. The short scale was a deliberate choice; the thrust of the design being a self-contained instrument capable of being carried about and played anywhere—an "electronic version of an accordion," as brother Bob explained.

After some five years in development, the Pentaphonic hit the market as a five-voice instrument offering a meaty three VCOs per voice, each with their own gain controls and eight waveform selectors. A (lowpass) filtering panel features cutoff frequency, resonance and envelope amount controls along with a dedicated ADSR envelope generator. The small modulation panel has rate and depth controls, plus a three-position toggle switch for its destination: pitch, filter or gain. The amplifier has its own ADSR envelope generator.

A fast/slow chorus adds still more depth to this three-oscillator synth, and a simple 300-note-capacity sequencer, over which you can play live, rounds off what is an admirably streamlined and fathomable instrument.

There are no trimmer pots, so adjusting Pentaphonic tuning, theoretically at any rate, is not an issue. Quality of parts and stability were important factors in the design. The wooden parts of the casing even used the same wood as the Ovation guitar. The Pentaphonic was not built to a price or a marketing scheme. It was simply built. When the Gleemans set about designing it, they deliberately avoided all contact with other instruments. All research came instead from books.

The nature of the Pentaphonic's design meant that Gleeman could and did make many custom modifications. With so few instruments made, there is a fair chance that each model in existence may be unique. One general-purpose optional extra was storage for 100 program memories. Fifty memories are presets and 50 are user-programmable; the presets can be overwritten using a secret red lever tucked away at the back. MIDI was also made available as a retrofit.

Operationally, everything on the Gleeman Pentaphonic is very straightforward. The sounds are generally strong and interesting, the Pentaphonic's rendition of a cathedral organ particularly impressive, though you may need something a little beefier than the instrument's 5-watt internal speaker system to hear that.

In its day, the Pentaphonic was used by the good and the great. The ubiquitous Stevie Wonder bought one, of course, and country stars Alabama used one extensively on *The Closer You Get*. Gleeman even has the platinum record to prove it.

The Pentaphonic's build quality is what inspired its most glorious permutation, the "clear" model. According to Gleeman, the boards looked so high-tech, with all the silver- and gold-coated contacts and components, that it seemed criminal to hide it all from view. After much research into finding a clear plastic suitable for vacuform molding, around ten clear models were built. Hand-built, that is. Even the knobs are hand-machined and tapped.

Although the Gleeman Instrument Co. ceased producing Pentaphonics after a year or two, the Gleemans continued to support their customers until 1994, when all remaining parts and rights were sold to the Mellotron Archives.

Al went on to become a top dental laser electronics specialist, and Bob now runs A&B Design. The company produces a gadget called the VMB/60 Voice Message Bank, a record-and-playback tool built in response to America's wearisome obsession with voice mail systems. "It looks kind of like a little Pentaphonic," says Bob. I guess you just can't keep a good team down.

Gleeman Instrument Co. is no longer in business.

Hammond B-3 Organ

THE FAX

Keyboard:	2 61-note
Programs:	12
External storage:	None
Polyphony:	Full
Oscillators per voice:	n/a
Effects:	Vibrato, chorus
Connections:	Leslie multi-pin
Weight:	193kg
Hammond Suzuki USA Inc.:	1121 N. Main St.; Lombard, IL 60148; tel: (708) 620-6633; fax: 708-620-6905
Hammond UK Ltd:	Potash House; Drayton Parslow, Bucks, MK17 0JE; tel: 01296-720787; fax: 01296-728156

THE FIGURES

Chief designer:	Laurens Hammond
Production run:	1954-1974
Approx. units sold:	275,000 (between B-3 and C-3)
Options:	None
Sounds:	n/a
Miscellaneous:	Service and repair specialists at Goff Professional: 32 Boswell Rd.; West Hartford, CT 06107; tel: (203) 667-2358; CAE: 285 N.

Amphlette; San Mateo, CA 94401; tel: (415) 348-2737; Keyboard Products: 2708 W. Seventh Street; Los Angeles, CA 90057; tel: (213) 387-2205; in the UK, Hammond Organ Service (Clive Botterill): 2, Pine Grove, Bricklet Wood; St. Albans, Herts AL2 3SS; tel: 01923-675782

Orig. price (1954): $2365 (no UK price)
Price in 1996: $2000-3000 (£1500)

Only those who have never stood in front of a B-3 in full flight, Leslie cabinet screaming, could fail to understand why this instrument was what it was and is what it is. In a world where even scraps of character are hungrily devoured by manufacturers, programmers and musicians, the Hammond organ—the B-3 its zenith—is Ali, O.J., Kennedy and Jagger all rolled into one. A big, bad, beautiful instrument, it has both inspired musical movements and forged careers and continues, even in this digital age, to fascinate, yet somehow still elude, the world's foremost sound designers.

This particular piece of musical magic sprang to life in the 1950s when erstwhile clockmaker Laurens Hammond introduced the B-3, and its more solidly cabineted brother the C-3, into the company's lineup of tone-wheel organs.

The tone-wheel design—literally using a spinning steel wheel whose relationship with a magnetic coil produces different voltages and pitches—was been inspired many years earlier by Hammond's fascination with the synchronous motor, which was used in the earliest known "synthesizer," the giant Telharmonium (1907). The B-3, too, has a synchronous motor, as all Hammond players well know, since the organs have a pair of toggle-type "on" switches: one for the starter motor (which whirs away and drags the synchronous motor up to speed) and one for the main motor itself. (Seasoned players will also be familiar with the flipside of this particular coin—switching the motor off—wherein the sound slowly drops away in pitch like a wounded animal.)

Why the B-3, rather than Hammond's earlier models, should have inspired such adulation is a subject beyond the scope of this book and its writer. True, the B-3 was the instrument to add Percussion, a feature that adds transient harmonics, and thus "interest," to the front end of each note. Then again, the launching of Jimmy Smith's career a year or so after the B-3's release must have helped. Or perhaps it was just the explosion of youth culture in the late 1950s, establishing and eventually immortalizing a variety of noises that happened to be around, from the electric guitar to the jukebox.

Sifting fact from fiction with an instrument like this is hard, but there is genuine mystery in the B-3 sound. B-3's didn't spin off a robot-driven production

line in Japan like milk cartons. They were hand-built, and you can find good ones and bad ones. Although there are presets—called presets, too, and recallable using the bottom octave's worth of reverse-color keys, which only function as switches—the way you play any Hammond is to footle around with the drawbars, each one of nine within a set corresponding to a particular pitch or harmonic and capable of being "pulled out," thus progressively increasing in volume. Estimates vary, depending upon whether you consider overall volume changes, vibrato, chorus and the like, but the general consensus of opinion puts the number of variables in the eight-figure bracket. If you've heard one B-3, you have definitely not heard 'em all. And one B-3 player does not sound anything like another. The chances of two players using the exact same settings by accident is slim. Many books have been written about Hammond drawbar settings, and older players can be as snippy about how they get "their sound" as a modern-day record company's legal department is about sample clearance.

The electronic organ industry looked to the pipe organ—both its inspiration and its competition at the time—for terminology to describe organ pitches, settings and effects. Thus, the B-3 has "drawbars" grouped in nines and each is colored white, brown or black, depending on its pitch. Each drawbar has a name printed on it, corresponding to a different pitch. When you pull out a drawbar, you progressively increase the volume of that particular pitch. It is a direct form of additive synthesis.

In a set of nine drawbars, four are white and correspond to the fundamental pitch or higher octaves (8', 4', 2' and 1'). Two are brown and correspond to a lower octave (16') and a fifth above the fundamental (5-1/3'). And three are black and correspond to the third (2-2/3'), fifth (1-2/3') and sixth (1-1/3') harmonics. Each of the B-3's two manuals has two sets of these drawbars; the idea is that you can switch between two configurations quickly using two of the black preset keys.

The beauty of drawbars is that the system is quick. No, not just quick—immediate. A sound can be set up with one grab at the drawbars. And while you continue to play with the right hand, the left hand can snake up and boost or cut some harmonics to completely alter the sound. All classic B-3 players, from Jimmy Smith to Booker T. Jones to Rod Argent to Keith Emerson (though Emerson preferred to stab and manhandle the smaller L series onstage), have their own "secret" configurations and settings. The range of noticeable sonic variations (never mind the theoretical ones) is fantastic. A B-3 can deliver from the end of the world to the end of the pier. From a crystalline, high, harmonics-only sound to one that's clarinety and pure. From low and slow to razor-edged and attacky.

Threading the drawbars in and out is not the end of the story. There are a number of tone enhancers, from vibrato to chorus to the percussion effect (which immediately says "jazz"). The percussion effect, available only to the upper manual, adds transient harmonics to the sound, either the second or the third harmonic. You can vary the speed of decay, and you have some broad control over volume, but this effect only works on the first note played. In other words, it is single-triggering. If you play in a legato style, no notes after the first played will harness the percussion. Percussion once got me out of a terrible situation when, as an eager young backing player, I discovered that the act whom I played for had agreed to back the support act—a fearsomely paced Irish comic with a routine in which musical cues were intertwined like rampant periwinkles. Taking one look at the mass of black on the charts I was handed—minutes before we took the stage at London's Drury Lane theater, incidentally—I figured I could cop either the rhythm or the chords but not both. I plumped for the rhythm, set my Hammond on its most percussive sound and played the entire show by stabbing the keys so gently that all you could hear was this percussive effect. It was a nightmare, but it worked like a dream, and afterwards the comic, delighted with my prowess, strode up to me and shook me warmly by the hand. Guilt and elation is a strange but heady mix.

On/Off rocker switches control vibrato for either manual, and a rotary switch offers you three strengths of vibrato alone, plus three strengths of vibrato-plus-chorus. Hammond was, by all accounts, quite pleased with its vibrato effect, which replaced a gentler tremolo effect found on earlier Hammond organs. But vibrato pales to complete insignificance in comparison to the most prominent Hammond organ effect, made not by Hammond but by one Don Leslie.

Hammond and Leslie are like cheese and pickles, pancakes and syrup, Abbott and Costello: One was quite clearly destined to perform with the other, although, like many a double act, there was little love lost between the actual companies. A Leslie cabinet consists of two amplified, revolving speakers in a big wooden box. The bass speaker drum spins around in one direction, and a pair of horns spin around in the other. There are two speeds, slow and fast, and there is a speed-up and slow-down factor in either direction. (Most B3's were retrofitted with a switch that toggled between slow and fast Leslie.)

The resultant, swirling Doppler effect brings a B-3 to life in a way that defies description; a B-3 without a Leslie is flat and one-paced. Leslies, like B-3s, are large and cumbersome, and they're a pain. But they're kind of indispensable if you want the "genuine" B-3 sound. Leslie simulators exist, and some of them are good, but please don't confuse them with the real thing.

One final attribute of note is what has come to be known as "key click," a percussive, popping, spitting noise that is very much a part of the B-3 sound. It wasn't supposed to be there, of course—it was a design fault—but there it is, and there it will always remain. This noise—which is, essentially, the electrical switches making contact—gives the B-3 a distinct edge (literally and figuratively) over the competition.

From spit to split: The B-3 is a monster in terms of its bulk. Eventually it became popular to saw them in two horizontally, making them easier to cart about. A "split" B-3 is one that can come apart in such a fashion.

Perched on its spindly, neo-Georgian legs, the B-3 looks like no other organ. Practically, it has long passed its sell-by date, but for studio use, or on tour with an army of road crew, there is no substitute. Organ samples can sound wonderful...until you hear a B-3 and Leslie in full swing.

Hohner Clavinet D6 — Stage electric clavichord

THE FAX

Keyboard:	60-note
Programs:	Multiple
External storage:	None
Polyphony:	Full
Oscillators per voice:	n/a
Effects:	Damper lever
Connections:	Mono audio (100mV)
Dimensions:	1190mm x 150mm x 380mm
Weight:	31kg
Hohner Inc. (USA):	PO Box 15035; Richmond, VA 23227-5035; tel: (804) 550-2700, fax: 804-550-2670
Hohner Vertrieb GmbH:	Andreas-Koch-Strasse 9; D-78647 Trossingen, Germany; tel: 07425-200; fax: 07425-20510
M. Hohner Ltd. (UK):	Bedwas House Ind Est.; Bedwas, Newport, Gwent NP1 8XQ; tel: 01222-887333; fax: 01222-851056

THE FIGURES

Chief designer:	Ernst Zacharias
Production run:	1971-1985
Approx. units sold:	No figures available
Options:	AC adaptor
Sounds:	n/a
Miscellaneous:	The first Clavinet, the Clavinet 1, was built in 1966. UK servicing and repair at John Andrews at Hohner: 157-159 Ewell Road; Surbiton, Surrey KT6 6AR; tel: 0181-399-1166; fax: 081-390-

8796. In the U.S., the modern-day Hohner won't be remotely interested in hearing from you.

Orig. price (1971):	$700 (£350)
Price in 1983:	$1150 (no UK price)
Price in 1996:	$200 (£450)

The Clavinet has had a topsy-turvy ride through keyboard history. It began life as yet another curious invention (first the Cembalet, then the first Pianet) from Hohner staff designer Ernst Zacharias, a man with a life-long quest to modernize and electrify a whole battery of baroque keyboard instruments. The Clavinet's eventual appeal, to R&B musicians playing loud, raw funk, must have been a great shock to the genteel ice maidens of the German home market for whom the instrument had originally been planned. But when the lights went down on the disco and the strains of "Superstition" screamed nothing but "dated," you couldn't give a Clavinet away. I know, I tried.

Yet the Clavinet survived and has been revived. In Europe in the mid-1990s, buoyant on the crest of the retro wave, the instrument actually commands higher second-hand prices than its last new sticker cost.

The first Clavinet 1 arrived in the early 1960s with built-in amplification, followed by the Clavinet L, a brilliant, triangular, three-legged period piece complete with '60s reverse color keys. But it was the D6, with its distinctive light wood casing, flip-top lid and screw-in legs, that was the big one. (The E7 retained the same innards, but sported a new Tolex livery and more modern-looking tubular steel legs.)

Why the popularity? The Clavinet is murderously heavy. It requires a silly little battery for power. It effectively only has one tone. It needs tuning. It's ancient. And as for MIDI, forget it. Yet even today, no digital piano, synth or home keyboard would dare leave the factory without a "clavi," " clav," "funky cl" or some other form of litigation-avoiding variation onboard. To appreciate the complexity and power of this unique instrument, you have to play one. A real one. Only then will the full weight of this percussive, catchy, edgy, eminently playable tone become apparent.

And when you do, you'll quickly notice that the 60-note, firm-but-fast keyboard is not just velocity-sensitive, but also, mechanically, aftertouch sensitive. Simply leaning hard into a note presses the hammer hard up against a string and (pitch) bends it; a serious player can even produce vibrators by further waggling. Also, polyphony is full. But the main advantage of owning an actual Clavinet, as opposed to a set of clavi samples or a digital piano with a clavi tone, is that there is a whole range of tones at your fingertips.

To quote from Hohner literature of the time, "When a key is depressed, a plunger underneath touches the string and presses it onto an anvil. The string impinges on the anvil with greater or less strength according to the heaviness of the key pressure, thus affecting the dynamics of the sounding string. Immediately the key is released, contact between plunger and anvil is broken, leaving the wool-wound part of the string (left of the anvil) free, so that the string's vibration is immediately muted."

Magnetic pickups lie at the other end of the string, and six rocker switches on the top panel control the instrument's pickup arrangement and polarity. These are marked Brilliant, Treble, Medium, Soft, A/B and C/D, and they are able to concoct a vast array of tones. A slider-operated string damper can either let notes ring or progressively muffle them.

Aside from knowing which pickup configuration produces what tones, there's not much in the way of technical skill needed in order to play a Clavinet. A lot of muscle is needed in order to pick one up, and no small amount of skill also, in order to keep the substantially weighted lid from becoming unhinged and cleaving into your foot.

Sound is produced by hammers hitting strings, so two more skills come into play: tuning and replacing broken strings. Tuning needs checking on a regular basis and although string replacement is achievable by the user, it is somewhat of a drag. Strings don't break often, luckily.

One of the Clavinet's less endearing attributes is that it requires a small amount of power to function; most commonly this is left to a small 9V battery (there is an AC adaptor socket, but good-quality batteries actually provide a quieter play, with less mains buzz). As long as you remember to switch the instrument off when you're not using it, batteries can last six months or so.

Of course, Stevie Wonder blew the world of the Clavinet wide open with his splendid, funky playing on the main riff of "Superstition." Immediately, Clavis became synonymous with groove and funk. This was enhanced by the addition (just in-line) of some sort of effects pedal—normally a chorus or phaser.

Remarkably, D6 design did not change throughout its long production run. Equally remarkably, the instrument was made to such a high specification that repairs are minimal; even today, almost all parts are still available. The rubber hammer tips are no longer produced by Hohner, though; resourcefully, the company recommends O-rings from a Chevy engine, cut to size, as a perfectly adequate substitute. Jeff Jetton informs browsers on the Internet that changing broken strings can be facilitated by weaving a plastic drinking straw through the yarn, then passing the string through that.

When examining a prospective purchase, obviously, check that the strings are not rusty (as on some long-unplayed models) and that the bed in which the keyboard sits is not distorted. Both problems are curable, but adjust the price accordingly.

Clavinet users are countless. One of the more interesting uses was conceived by Frank Dunnery of It Bites, whose first two albums feature a "Rose Marie" guitar-like contraption that was—and still is, no doubt—essentially a fretted Clavinet bed.

The Clavinet also appears as half of the Hohner Duo (the other half is the Pianet), unbelievably heavy instruments highly prized by their owners.

There is no off-the-shelf Clavinet MIDI kit, though the instrument, like any mechanical keyboard, is perfectly MIDI-able.

Here in the mid-1990s, Clavinets are in great demand and can command good prices. A good buy, but watch your back!

Hohner Pianet Electronic piano

THE FAX

Keyboard:	60-note
Programs:	1
External storage:	None
Polyphony:	Full
Oscillators per voice:	n/a
Effects:	None
Connections:	Mono audio
Dimensions:	900mm x 350mm x 80mm
Weight:	17kg
U.S. distributor:	Hohner Inc. (USA): PO Box 15035; Richmond, VA 23227-5035; tel: (804) 550-2700, fax: 804-550-2670
Hohner Vertrieb GmbH:	Andreas-Koch-Strasse 9; D-78647 Trossingen, Germany; tel: 07425-200; fax: 07425-20510
M. Hohner Ltd. (UK):	Bedwas House Ind Est.; Bedwas, Newport, Gwent NP1 8XQ; 01222-887333; fax 01222-851056

THE FIGURES

Chief designer:	Ernst Zacharias
Production run:	1976-83
Approx. units sold:	No figures available
Options:	Legs ($90)
Sounds:	n/a
Miscellaneous:	The first Pianet model was produced in 1962. UK servicing and repair from John Andrews at Hohner: 157-159 Ewell Road; Surbiton, Surrey KT6 6AR; tel: 0181-399-1166; fax: 081-390-8796.
Orig. price (1976):	$525 (£295)
Price in 1983:	$649 (no UK price)
Price in 1996:	$250 (£150)

Unless you are keenly interested in period sounds, you won't have much reason to search out a Hohner Pianet. The Pianet is an archetypal one-trick pony—that one trick being a thinnish piano sound that's only a loose approximation of an acoustic piano. But for a considerable slice of the '70s, a Hohner Pianet was the nearest you were going to get to an acoustic piano (Fender Rhodes and Wurlitzer pianos may be more professional, but their tone is more classically "electric") at a sensible price.

Though the Pianet T was the most popular model in rock 'n' roll circles and was definitely the most likely to have survived into the next couple of decades, Hohner made an assortment of other models, dating back to the early 1960s. The Pianet N looks like a cross between a school desk and a night storage heater, and re-examining photographs of the Pianet L, I still stand by my description of it in *Keyfax 3* as a plank of wood balanced on pipe cleaners.

What all the various Pianets have in common is their rather peculiar method of making sound, namely vibrating reeds being plucked by plastic suction pads. The vibrations are then converted into electrical energy via a pickup. There is no mains electricity required or even batteries. You just plug it into an amp via a single 1/4-inch output (amps with input impedance between 10KB ohms and 100KB ohms are recommended), and that's that. Amazingly enough, the sound is not un-pianolike. There are no tone controls. In fact, there are no controls whatsoever on board—not even a volume knob. I think we can safely say the Pianet is idiot-proof in its operation.

Idiot-proof but not bulletproof in terms of performance. Minor repairs can probably be carried out yourself. Hohner gave some user maintenance/servicing hints in their promotional literature. If some notes go quiet, make sure the reed plucker is positioned correctly. Make sure there is no grease or dirt on the reed or plucker. Make sure the gap between the reed and pickup is correct. If you get buzzes, the pickup is probably too close to the reed or there is gunk stuck in between them. Adjust this or remove that. Suction pads can get dirty; remove and wash with soap and water.

The minimalist Pianet is an interesting animal of more historical than musical relevance in the 1990s. Cost and production volume mean they are not exactly sought after. Hohner also produced the Duo, which is a mix of Pianet and Clavinet; the two sounds can be layered or split across the 60-note keyboard. The Duo is a hipper instrument, but it weighs a ton. Almost literally.

Kawai K1 Digital polyphonic synthesizer

THE FAX

Keyboard:	61-note
Programs:	64 single, 32 multi
External storage:	Card
Polyphony:	16-voice
Oscillators per voice:	2
Effects:	None
Connections:	Stereo audio, MIDI, phones, hold
Dimensions:	936mm x 260mm x 80mm
Weight:	6.8kg

THE FIGURES

Chief designer:	Unknown
Production run:	1988-90
Approx. units sold:	50,000
Options:	K1m, K1r modules
Sounds:	Kawai RAM cards, also Eye+I, Voice Crystal, Kid Nepro, K-Wonder
Miscellaneous:	Books include *The K1 Cookbook* from Pro-Arts Productions, *The K1 Sound Making Book* by Maestas & Walker and *Kawai K1 Operations & Tweaking Sounds* by Dan Walker; editor/librarians available from Steinberg (K1 Synthworks, for ST), EMC (ST), Big Noise (PC), James Chandler (Mac), Sound Quest (ST, PC, Mac)
Orig. price (1988):	$795 (£599)
Price in 1996:	$250 (£200)

Kawai's K1 was the Korg Poly-800 of its generation. This small, inoffensive, inexpensive unit is not your classic heart-stirring synth. It is simple, has good sounds, didn't cost a lot and was obviously just what the doctor ordered at the time, because it sold extremely well. Unlike Korg, though, Kawai did not go on to greater heights and newer technologies. This lumbering giant of a company continues to stumble about between outright winners like the K1 and a succession of limp rehashes and copycats. The key is that Kawai is not dedicated to synthesizers like Korg or Roland or even Yamaha. Sometimes it stumbles across a good synthesizer design; sometimes it doesn't. And when it doesn't, it just carries on making squillions of acoustic pianos.

On a brighter note, the K1 emerged into the arena in 1988, a year later than Roland's D-50, which it vaguely resembles physically and in operation. Stopping short of calling it "LA synthesis," of course, Kawai nonetheless based the K1's sound creation on the analog-style processing of a number of PCM transient and looped multisampled waves, except that here you can layer up to four separate sounds. So it can be viewed, as indeed it was, as a sort of multitimbral D-50 at around half the price. Roland must have been thrilled.

This is a very easy instrument to work with. There are some 256 digital waveforms (52 one-shot PCM samples, plus 204 cycled waves) stored in ROM.

KAWAI

Name:	Kawai Musical Instrument Manufacturing Company
Head Office:	200 Terajima-cho, Hammamatsu, Japan; fax: 053-457-1218
U.S. Distributor:	Kawai America Corp.: 2055 East University Dr.; Compton, CA 90224; tel: (310) 631-1771
UK Distributor:	Kawai Europe: Centre, Europark Fichtenhain, Ais; D-47807 Krefeld, Germany; tel: (49) 2151-37300
Founded:	1927
No. of employees:	5400
Business:	Acoustic pianos, electronic organs, synthesizers, wind instruments, digital pianos, computer music equipment, athletic equipment, toys and furniture

Kawai is Yamaha without the global perspective. Kawai is a billion-dollar company, a large employer in the city of Hammamatsu (which it shares, as it happens, with Yamaha). But while Yamaha's presence is felt, if not pushed, wherever it goes, Kawai quietly gets on with the business of making and selling musical instruments and other (occasionally) related products and leaves it at that. In the electronic music instrument field, Kawai is a walking PR nightmare.

Founded by master engineer and piano builder Koichi Kawai in 1927, Kawai's main focus and source of income has always been acoustic pianos. The company's first foray into electronics came with organs, a sister line to its range of acoustic pianos.

When synthesizers first appeared to have sales potential in the 1970s, Kawai produced a small range of instruments under the brand name Teisco (a company with whom it had joined forces in 1966). Synths and samplers may not have occupied too much of the thoughts of the chairmen, but Kawai harbored plenty of canny engineers—a fact first evidenced by the company's early support of MIDI and its innovative range of electroacoustic MIDI pianos in the mid-1980s and later substantiated by such exciting and challenging products as the K5 additive synth and the entry-level K1 sample replay keyboard.

However, synth spotters have been frustrated by Kawai's sporadic technological record, which has always been dogged by inconsistencies and abrupt curtailments and makes it very difficult for the company to generate any long-term loyalty from either the high-tech dealer or the end user.

The simple explanation of this phenomenon is that electronic musical instruments have not been of paramount importance to Kawai, a company that produced its two-millionth acoustic piano in 1990. However, Kawai's acquisition of Lowry Organs in 1988 and the steady increase in importance of music within the computer and multimedia market (for which Kawai seems to have a reasonable appetite) may yet see Kawai consolidate its efforts in the electronic field.

A true dynasty (the current president is Shigeru Kawai, the founder's grandson), Kawai's traditional belief in the harmony between mind and body manifests itself in its 3,000 gymnastic schools scattered throughout Japan in which exercise, play and music are combined in a unique fashion.

One of the K1's few irritating features is that the precise makeup of this waveform ROM is only revealed (named, anyway) in the manual. Onscreen, waveforms only appear as numbers.

In single mode, you can combine two separate ROM wave "Sources" and still have 16-voice polyphony. Four waves can also be harnessed, with still-respectable eight-voice polyphony. Each of the sound Sources can be edited and processed separately, including unusual items like being able to delay the ADSR-styled envelope generators in order to produce multicycling sounds with almost a Wavestation feel. Also separately controllable are tuning, fine-tuning and LFO modulation. Waves can even interact for ring modulation effects.

Notably absent from the list, though, is a filter. What this means is that it's hard to alter the basic character of any chosen waveform aside from using ring modulation. You can re-envelope the waveform and delay it, but you cannot alter its fundamental tone. With 256 waves to choose from, though, this is not as restrictive as it might seem, especially when you realize that each wave might only represent one-quarter of your final sound.

A K1 multi patch is a combination of single patches, either playable from the keyboard in a layer or split or controlled externally on separate MIDI channels. As on Kawai's K5, setting up multitimbral patches here is easy. A selection of windows highlights different groups of parameters, with each sound in a multi patch capable of fixed or flexible polyphony, playable over its own keyboard zone and sensitive to its own velocity rate, and each has its own MIDI channel, transposition, fine-tune, volume and pan selections. You can even link up to eight multi patches together in a chain, which is useful for live performances. Another helpful facility is being able to set up pitch and mod wheel assignments specifically for one patch in a multi.

In terms of final patches, the K1 is strongest on acoustic instrument facsimiles, the strings being especially luscious. Synth sounds are not very convincing, partly due to the lack of a controllable filter. The K1 bravely ignored both drum sounds and internal effects, which evidently did not hurt sales, though both were to appear on the subsequent K1 II.

The keyboard is not immensely satisfying to play but is still velocity and aftertouch sensitive. There are separate pitch and mod wheels set deep into the top left hand of the control panel, plus a joystick.

Flushed with the success of the initial model, Kawai went on to produce the K1m, a tabletop module of the K1 and the rackmount K1r.

The significance of the K1 is its range and cost-effectiveness. This is not a great synth in the class of a Minimoog, ARP 2600 or M1. It has no collectability whatsoever in current terms. It is a purveyor of well-proportioned, interesting sounds, singly or multitimbrally. It does what it does simply, leaving any song-and-dance aspect entirely up to you. It's a shame Kawai didn't do things like this more often.

Kawai K5 — Additive polyphonic synthesizer

THE FAX

Keyboard:	61-note
Programs:	48 single, 48 multi
External storage:	Card
Polyphony:	16-voice
Oscillators per voice:	2
Effects:	None
Connections:	Stereo, plus 4 separate audio, MIDI, phones, hold
Dimensions:	1040mm x 339mm x 99mm
Weight:	12.8kg

THE FIGURES

Chief designer:	Unknown
Production run:	1987-89
Approx. units sold:	1500
Options:	K5r (rackmount version)
Sounds:	Kawai DC-32 RAM cards (pre-programmed), Bo Tomlin Harmonic Spectrum
Miscellaneous:	Pro-Sample ST is an Akai sample-to-harmonics conversion program for the ST; editor/librarians: Dr T.'s K5 Editor/Librarian (Mac), Kawai K5 Librarian (PC), Opcode K5 Librarian (Mac), Syntonyx Overtone, Graphic Librarian/EditorSample Analyzer (PC)
Orig. price (1987):	$1995 (£1495)
Price in 1996:	$400 (£300)

Though second-hand prices are hardly spectacular, the K5 is a rare and very interesting instrument. It is not, to use that nice old English expression, everyone's cup of tea.

The K5 is rare because it is fueled by additive synthesis. Rare because it presents its multitimbralism (a rarity itself in 1987) crystal clearly. Rare in that it fails to flatter in its factory programs, taking the more adventurous route of providing the raw material and saying "Get on with it."

The K5 is a bulky instrument with a very large display screen—far larger than anything else in its day—around which are grouped a number of control buttons taking you in and out of the various operating modes.

On power-up you see the names of a dozen single sounds from one of the instrument's four sound banks. Choose a bank, press one of the 12 keypad buttons and up comes a name in writing large enough to read at 50 paces alongside patch-relevant data like pitch and mod wheel values, routings and pedal assignments. The things you actually need to know, in other words. Someone did their homework here.

Additive synthesis is a bit like knitting or pointillist painting: You need to be very patient, or knowledgeable, or experienced, to slog through the tedious process of assembling a sound in the reasonable hope that at the end of it all something worthwhile awaits. The process here involves adding together some 126 sine wave harmonics generated by Kawai's Digital Harmonic Generator, each with individual volumes between 0 and 99.

The quickest way to learn the basics is to access a single sound and then press Edit, followed by DHG 1 on the keypad. What then appears onscreen is an easy-on-the-eye bar graph, plus a whole slew of gobbledygook that is explained—somewhat—in the manual. Each one of the lines on the bar graph corresponds to one harmonic. Using the cursor keys and the free-flowing incremental wheel, a harmonic can be selected and increased or decreased in level. The harmonic will accordingly grow or shrink onscreen and you'll hear the resultant sound change in real time.

Luckily you are not left completely on your own; some shortcuts are offered. In "twin" mode, you have two sets of 63 harmonics, one of which can be offset against the other. This is important, because the harmonics Kawai offer are all in the natural harmonic series, which is not ideal for producing the weird and wonderful. If this is what you need, such offsetting (detuning) starts to produce dissonant, atonal frequencies.

Even so, tweaking and twiddling 63 harmonics is no instant solution. You can create patterns (using odd harmonics only, even ones only or octaves only) using such parameters as All Harmonics. You can also set an automatic high- or low-end roll-off curve by selecting a particular roll-off angle. (Parameters like this sound dangerous in print, but they're timesavers in practice.)

More traditional, analog-style programming skills are not completely redundant, since after these additive harmonic adjustments, the K5 starts to behave more like an analog, subtractive instrument. A DDF (digital dynamic filter) features familiar-looking cutoff, slope, envelope amount, keyboard scaling, velocity and aftertouch parameters. The DDAS (amplifier) can be controlled by keyboard dynamics, release velocity, the LFO or keyboard scaling or by its own six-stage envelope generator. A second envelope generator is reserved for the filter, and a third functions as that most underused but powerful tool, a pitch envelope generator.

The above might be familiar, but on the whole, the K5 is neither a quick nor an easy synth to pro-

gram. Kawai didn't make things any easier at the time with its generally lackluster collection of factory programs. By 1990, Kawai programmers around the world had been busy creating new volumes of sounds that showed off the true potential of this instrument. But by then they were only servicing existing owners; there were no new customers. The K5 was dead meat.

Although K5 sales cannot have overburdened Kawai coffers, the instrument enhanced Kawai's reputation considerably. K5 users are rightly proud of and loyal to their instrument. Jan Hammer used a K5 extensively during his *Miami Vice* soundtrack period, and the instrument's big, bright, bristlingly metallic patches are hard to come by anywhere else.

Operating the instrument in multitimbral mode is pure joy. Hitting Edit in multi mode reveals a list of single sounds, each with its keyboard zone, polyphony count (which can be fixed or variable), internal or external triggering mode and MIDI channel. Up to 15 single sounds can be combined in a multi memory, with the above and individual detune and velocity information intact. Simple to set up. Quick to alter.

In a completely out-of-the-blue move, the K5 also allows you to load in samples to form the basis of new sounds. The system is not instant and does require the use of external computer software (see above). But such a facility was, like many of the K5's features, way ahead of its time.

The K5 remains a bit of a well-kept secret. As I said at the beginning, it will not appeal to everyone—neither its sounds, nor its programming depth—but the K5 is a most rewarding instrument for those who dive in. The K5r is a 4U rackmount version, fully compatible with the K5 keyboard.

Kawai SX240 Analog polyphonic synthesizer

THE FAX

Keyboard:	61-note
Programs:	48
External storage:	Cassette interface
Polyphony:	8-voice
Oscillators per voice:	2
Effects:	Ensemble
Connections:	Stereo audio, phones, clock in/out, seq stop/start, prog up, sustain, MIDI
Dimensions:	886mm x 380mm x 130mm
Weight:	12.9kg

THE FIGURES

Chief designer:	Unknown
Production run:	1984-85
Approx. units sold:	1000
Options:	None
Sounds:	None commercially available
Orig. price (1984):	$1695 (£1245)
Price in 1996:	$400 (£350)

The Kawai SX240 is not a classic instrument. But it is an unusual and worthwhile synth for several reasons. First, it is one of the very few "original" analog synths to sport MIDI as standard. Kawai was very active in the creation of the MIDI standard, and the SX240 was in the first run of instruments to offer the new interface. Secondly, it has some great sounds—almost in the Prophet-5's class; less controllable perhaps, but more reliable and more accessible. Third, it commands quite modest prices, and thus makes a good buy on the second-hand market.

The SX240 isn't vastly different from the SX210 which preceded it. It's a bright and cheerful-looking soul with an early Ensoniq-type display that just manages to spell out program names. It also has a good selection of dedicated panel switches and diagrams to help you through the voice and sequencer programming routines. The only negative is the curious positioning of the "bender" on the control panel. "My God, where's the pitch wheel?" You can almost hear the team leader wail in horror as he is about to sign off on the design. "You idiots! Well, you'll have to stick it on the control panel now, as you've not allowed any room beneath the keyboard." This lone, Roland-type lever activates all forms of pitch or amplitude modulation as directed within the programming setup of a patch.

Meanwhile, above the actual keyboard are 0-9 keys, plus an alphabet and associated squiggles so you can name your patches. This is okay, but it does somewhat give the instrument the look of a home keyboard, which it is not.

Armed with two digitally controlled oscillators per voice, you can choose variable pulse or sawtooth waveforms. A sub-oscillator can be added. Lowpass filtering is the main dish of the day, with its resonance, cutoff frequency and modulation (from keyboard, LFO, envelope or bender) parameters, but there is also a simple variable-cutoff highpass filter. This is rather in the manner of the simple highpass filter control on a Roland Juno-60. (You might begin to wonder if Kawai ever did anything "new.") Useful, nonetheless.

Both filter and amplifier have dedicated ADSR envelope generators. There is a three-waveshape LFO with (rare) reverse, speed and delay time parameters. Further spicer-uppers come in the shape of ensemble (gentle chorus), portamento, glissando and hold. There's also a noise generator.

This is by no means a stingy tally, and you can put together some meaty patches in the string synth, bass and brass departments. Patches are stored in the 48-bank memory, and you can either layer or split any two—another attribute that lifts the SX240 out of the ordinary. Furthermore, there's a small sequencer with eight memory banks capable of storing 1500 notes. The adroit can set up repeats, with timing offsets, breaks and rests, all ultimately controlled from a footpedal if need be.

The SX240 smacks a little of design by committee (how else could they have forgotten that pitch bender? "I thought *you* were going to do it...!") and accordingly lacks a bit of oomph or spark. Still, at today's bargain prices, this is one of only a few dedicated analog, dedicated MIDI synths and would make a good buy for a beginning player on a tight budget who wants to tap into the 1990s craze for analog without sacrificing MIDI control.

Korg 01/W
Digital polyphonic workstation/synthesizer

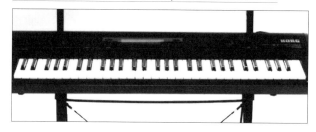

THE FAX

Keyboard:	61-note
Programs:	200 single, 200 multi
External storage:	Card, disk drive
Polyphony:	32-voice
Oscillators per voice:	2
Effects:	2 multieffects processors
Connections:	Stereo, plus 2 separate audio outputs, footswitches, MIDI
Dimensions:	1059mm x 344mm x 115mm
Weight:	13.4kg

THE FIGURES

Chief designer:	Mr. Ikeuchi
Production run:	1991-95
Approx. units sold:	100,000+
Options:	XSC PCM/Program cards, XPC Program cards, SRC-512 RAM card, ST-LV stand, FC-01/W Flight Case, HC-01/W Hard Case
Sounds:	Pro Rec, Eye+I, Sound Source, Soundtraxxe, Technosis, Metra Sound, AMG Producer Series
Miscellaneous:	Korg's *Best of the 01/W* CD features custom sequences from Tom Coster, Rick Wakeman, Dave Stewart, Keith Emerson and Chuck Leavell.
Orig. price (1991):	$2799 (£1799)
Price in 1996:	$1400 (£1000)

How do you follow a bestseller? Authors and film-makers happily work on a formula if they can hit upon it. With musical instruments, it's not quite so easy...or perhaps it is. True, the M1, the world's best-selling synth, was followed by the less than rampageously successful T series, but very soon after came the 01/W ("terrible name," everyone said and says). And the 01/W is not an international departure from the M1, but more a local hop, at best.

Rounded and smooth like the M1, the 01/W is a workstation based on Korg's own AI2 sample+ synthesis design. There's more polyphony, a disk drive and some improvements and additions to the parameter list and basic waveform memory. Korg's trusty joystick controller turns into the more conventional pitch lever, and the slit screen becomes a decent-sized 64x240-pixel display.

AI2 involves the processing of one or two sampled waveforms chosen from a vast pool of samples and DWGS waveforms (called "multisounds") through analog-type filters and envelope generators and finally two spankingly bright and breezy multi-effects processors. It's a classic sample+ synthesis design. A patch employing a single "oscillator" per voice will be 32-voice polyphonic. Many of the best sounds employ two, of course, thereby cutting this tally in half.

Having selected your oscillator waveforms from the 6MB treasure trove of multisounds, the oscillator can be fine-tuned, balanced, sent through the pitch envelope (this parameter is used infrequently, but can add considerable interest to a sound and is well worth investigating) and then processed further using low-pass filtering with its own dedicated envelope generator, keyboard tracking and keyboard dynamics settings, plus an overall envelope generator, LFO and multieffects.

Notwithstanding the odd cutback from the M1, such as the EG, which is now single-pitch for both oscillators, improvements and additions to the M1 system are everywhere.

Although 01/W filters do not possess a resonance parameter, it offers an amplitude modulation feature called waveshaping; some of its waves (used to interact with your PCM samples) are called "resonant" and do go a long way toward providing a similar audio result. There's an additional LFO for pitch modulation, and each oscillator can be routed through its own effect and output.

Although the 01/W is by no means difficult to program, if you want instant results, use the Quick Edit parameters that appear on the main screen, which can be speedily tweaked with eight soft buttons and include octave, waveshaping intensity, filter EG, VDA level, attack, release and effects level. Having

stabbed at one of these buttons, you can either make adjustments using the data entry slider or control parameters continuously in real time from a footpedal. Either way, this is one of the 01/W's most attractive features.

The 01/W's standard waveform memory holds 255 multisounds and 199 drum sounds. At the time, the quality, range and sheer quantity of this arsenal, stored in 6MB RAM, took everyone by surprise. How did Korg do it? The answer was not via some hitherto unused form of data compression so much as the cunning use of bandwidths and sample rates. Even within one multisound, there are splits between 16-bit and 8-bit processing and bandwidths between 32 and 24kHz. By this means, Korg was able to use every last drop of space for this library of waveform data. (Everyday musicians might be quite familiar with this level of resourcefulness, but manufacturers, in the thick of a forest of available technologies, specifications and engineering anal retention, generally are not.)

If the M1 had its trademark "Lore" multisound, the 01/W had "Tron," actually created in SoftSynth and invariably heard, in addition to everywhere else, in bubble gum commercials. Multisounds might be the seeds, but the fruits of your labors lie in the basket of "Programs" and "Combinations"—single and multi patches, respectively. As ever during this period of Korg instruments, the factory patches are iridescent. The splendid Total Kit drum amalgam is replete with big, gutsy, angry drum samples; the samples in Dance Kit are a kaleidoscope of gongs, orchestra hits, scratches, stabs, acid flicks and whipcrackaway snares. Tuned patches range from misty, Elgar-ish pads to vibrant guitars to complete Scottish landscapes with bagpipes, drones and crisp, fluttering snares.

Up to eight Programs can be combined in layered or split form in a Combination. There are limits in terms of effects processing, because the Program effects are removed in Combination mode and replaced by a new pair of Combination effects settings. Setting up a new Combination involves simply scrolling through a list of pages, setting MIDI channels, key ranges, velocities, volumes, effects routings and outputs. The system is both flexible (you can stack up to eight sounds on the same MIDI channel) and methodical; most people come to grief only over effects routings, which are a bit befuddling.

The 01/W offers a choice of 47 single or combined effects, each of them programmable with its own set of relevant editing parameters. The effects processing is of a very high quality. Too high, some might argue, in that sounds removed from their own effects can be somewhat cut off at the knees. Why

KORG

Name:	Korg
Founded:	1963
Head office:	1-15-12 Shimotakaido, Suginami-ku, Tokyo 168 Japan; 81-3-5376-5207; fax: 81-3-3324-5697
U.S. Distributor:	Korg U.S.: 316 South Service Rd.; Melville, NY 11747-3201; tel: (516) 339-9100; fax: (516) 333-9108
UK Distributor:	Korg UK Ltd.: 9, Newmarket Court, Kingston; Milton Keynes, MK10 0AU UK; tel: 01908-857100; fax: 01908-857199
Products:	Synthesizers, electronic pianos, general key boards, rhythm machines, signal processors, tuners, multimedia, music production facilities

The name "Korg" doesn't sound very Japanese, and indeed Korg is not a traditional close-knit, closed-shop Japanese company in the mold of a Yamaha or a Kawai. Korg has a unique history of welcoming foreign expertise through endorsees, programmers, OEM companies and even non-Japanese personnel working in Japan.

Korg was founded by Tokyo nightclub owner Tsutomu Katoh and Japan's top accordion player, Tadashi Osanai (a regular attraction at Katoh's club). The initial motivation was to produce a better backing-rhythm device than Osanai's erratic Wurlitzer Sideman. With this goal in mind and bolstered by Osanai's musical and technical expertise (he was a graduate of Tokyo University), Katoh's money and four employees, the team set up shop alongside the Keio railway line in central Tokyo in 1963. The original company traded under the name of Keio Gijutsu Kenkyujo Ltd. and later Keio Electronic Laboratories, not officially changing to Korg—derived from the first letter of each founder's name plus "RG" from the oRGan market they planned on assaulting and also the name under which almost all their products were marketed—until the mid-1980s.

The inaugural product was a "disc rotary electric auto rhythm machine," christened the Doncamatric because it went "donca, donca, donca..." (Seriously!) This was one of the first such machines built in Japan, and the Doncamatic and its subsequent versions and reworkings sold very well domestically. During the 1960s, Korg's success with this first rhythm machine spawned a large number of beatboxes, culminating in the MiniPopos series.

Korg soon moved on to organs and eventually synthesizers, along the way creating more than its fair share of innovative products and features. We have the key transposer, for instance, courtesy of a lady singer at Katoh's club who always had difficulty hitting high notes. Unfortunately, her accompanist was not sufficiently accomplished to play in a different key. Having recently discovered what a capo does for a guitar, Katoh asked why there wasn't something similar for keyboards, "to put us all out of our misery." Korg was also the first company to feature effects parameters on a synth and the first to use what we now know as "sample+ synthesis" design, using PCM samples for starter waves in an otherwise subtractive synthesis environment.

Korg's diversification into the synthesizer market in the 1970s was initially fueled by recruiting engineers from Berklee and fanned by long and close associations with all of the top players of the day: Keith Emerson, Rick Wakeman, Joe Zawinul and Tom Coster. These were not window-dressing recruits, either; they were working professionals whose feedback, ideas and concepts were listened to, supported and frequently implemented.

Korg has rarely gone for rehashes and lengthy series like Yamaha or even Roland, preferring one-off single designs and specially targeted products. "We want to build musical instruments," says Tom Katoh. "But instruments should have personality. Take a hundred musicians, and I think at least ten should definitely not like an instrument. If, out of that number, even just two or three top-flight musicians really like a product, then I'm satisfied."

Korg's synthesizer line in the 1970s comprised large, complex, expensive modular systems, like the PS series, and instruments strictly for the home or hobbyists, like the Mini Korgs. It took until the 1980s for the company to score its first major international successes with the Polysix and the Poly-800.

With the coming of the digital age in the mid-1980s, digital pianos became a natural extension of the synth market; Korg began production of its Concert series in 1987. Though Korg acquired many notable admirers in this field (Dave Grusin, Henry Mancini), the company has done well without doing spectacularly.

However, huge success came in 1988 with the M1 workstation, an instrument that has sold about 250,000 units and, as such, has the honor of being the world's best-selling synthesizer ever. A large part of the M1's appeal was, and remains, its range of sounds. Korg makes no secret of the fact that both the M1 waveform ROM and the factory programs relied heavily on Korg's crack team of international programmers in Europe and America.

Shortly before the M1 was released, Yamaha acquired a large portion of Korg stock. The presidents of the companies had long been friends, and the association, drawn up by Katoh, allowed each company to retain independence and competition as far as design and marketing strategies were concerned.

In 1988, Yamaha purchased the remains of top California synth company Sequential, but the association started off flat and went nowhere. Less than a year later, Yamaha decided to pull the plug on the remaining Sequential design team. It is said that when Katoh learned of this, he asked one favor of Yamaha: simply tell him the day on which the Sequential team was to be let go. The day after the Yamaha bombshell was delivered, the men from Korg dropped by. "Anyone want a job?" they inquired. And what a move! The Wavestation, the first instrument to result from the newly formed Korg R&D team in San Jose in 1990, went on to become the most influential new sound in synthesis for the first half of the decade. The team, now residing in Milpitas, California, continues to work on new technology, including the physical-modeling Prophecy.

Though Korg has become rather more corporate and less whimsical in recent years, the company's penchant for the unusual is still alive. The Wavedrum, resembling nothing so much as a wooden toilet seat but in fact an electronic, physical modeling-based conga, was released in 1994. Korg also continues to fight an almost solitary battle for the potential professional home keyboard market with its i series of instruments and struggles bravely in the overcrowded digital audio workstation market with the SoundLink.

But Korg's skill, first and foremost, lies in keyboard products. Over the years, the company has diversified into professional digital effects, tuners and karaoke sing-along systems, but it has not to date ventured directly into acoustic instruments or any further into pro audio territory than its narrow but excellent range of multi-effects processors.

Korg has enjoyed a long association with Marshall, distributing Marshall products from its American base in New York. Korg Inc. Guitar products, from Korg pedals, processors and tuners to actual distributed lines such as the Parker Fly, have clearly been a long-term interest.

A tiny company by Japanese standards, Korg's influence on the history of electronic keyboards has been substantial. It is also a company that likes to keep you guessing and, in the hands of its founder's son, long may it remain so!

remove effects, then? Well, you may have to in the studio (cue engineer request numbers three and four: "If we record it dry, we can tailor the effects later on/use the Lexicon." And blah, blah, blah). More commonly, you will just lose Program-specific effects when using the instrument multitimbrally with Combinations. You'll also lose Program-specific effects when you use the sequencer, which also taps into Combinations.

The 01/W's sequencer can coordinate a full 16 tracks, and standard memory is 48,000 notes. The instrument's decent-sized screen helps you pick your way through the edit pages so an 01/W makes a lot more sense as a workstation than an M1 ever did. Like the M1, though, the sequencer does a nice line in drum machine-type, pattern-style sequencing, plus you can set up loops, overdub, tempo edit, etc. For a workstation, the sequencer is quite powerful. But compared to even the most basic software sequencer, it is, of course, hopeless. The only sensible applications are for those who simply cannot afford/abide a computer and software sequencer, for scratchpad composition or for live gigs where you simply load in sequences recorded and tweaked elsewhere.

Back in 1991, the General MIDI and Standard MIDI File formats had yet to be formalized, so access to such has had to arrive by upgrade. Instruments with Version 6.2 software or higher are able to load SMF. If your instrument has no Page 4 on its disk-loading pages, then your instrument is an earlier version. Fortunately, the XPD-50 disk costs only about $15 from Korg dealers and gives you this access as well as reconfigures some of the program data to GM.

Program, Combination and sequence data can be stored on card or, more cost-effectively, on disk. New PCM data is loaded in from card.

The 01/W has been presented under many different guises from an early version with no disk drive to the regular 01/W FD, the 01r/w module, the 01/W Pro and the Pro X. These last two instruments, 76-key and 88-key models respectively, added a new slice of acoustic piano sample plus some extra drums in their waveform ROM.

People said, as they mused over the squillions of sales of Korg M1, "Yes, but in truth, the M1 doesn't do anything very new." The O1/W does even less, but what is does do is couple a huge range of highly playable, highly musical sounds with reasonably fathomable editing. And this, as always, is a highly potent combination.

O1/W users range from the great and godlike to legions of Joes and Joannas. Korg's endorsee list can be heard twittering away on the Korg-produced CD called *Best of the O1/W*—none of the items recorded use the 01/W's own sequencer, I hasten to add! A classic instrument, though, still very much in favor some five or six years after release.

Korg CX-3 Portable organ

THE FAX

Keyboard:	61-note
Programs:	3 presets
External storage:	None
Polyphony:	8-voice
Oscillators per voice:	n/a
Effects:	Overdrive, rotary effect
Connections:	2 mono (high/low) outputs, FX send/return
Dimensions:	1149mm x 137mm x 315mm
Weight:	10.5kg

THE FIGURES

Chief designer:	Mr. Mori
Production run:	1980-84
Approx. units sold:	5000
Options:	ST-3 stand, volume pedal, rotary effect footswitch, legs
Sounds:	None
Miscellaneous:	The BX-3 is a dual-manual equivalent with added chorus and vibrato effects. Service and repairs from Resurrection Electronics: 3504 King St.; Austin TX 78705; tel: (512) 451-5900
Orig. price (1980):	$995 (£825)
Price in 1996:	$700 (£600)

Think of classic rock organs, and names like Hammond, Farfisa and Vox immediately come to mind. The Korg CX-3? Maybe not, if you're not an organ specialist charged with the job of finding the best portable, reliable facsimile around. But those who are know that the CX-3 and its double manual partner the BX-3 have effectively ruled this particular roost unchallenged all the way up to the early 1990s, when Hammond (itself, by then, under Japanese control) marshaled up a rearguard action with its own "BX-3."

Synthesizers have always fancied themselves purveyors of organ sounds, which is perfectly understandable, not only because the synth industry grew out of the organ market but also because so many classic synth starter waveforms are inherently organ-like in sound. But synthesizers eventually devoured large portions of the organ market, and much, in sonic terms, was lost in the process.

Whether it was by luck or judgment, or simply

thanks to Korg's prime endorsee in the late 1970s being the knife-wielding Keith Emerson, Korg hit the mark in 1980. Ah, so this is how organs are supposed to sound. To borrow from the quip about whether sex should be dangerous and dirty (answer: only if you're doing it properly), authentic organ sounds need menace, unpredictability, dirt and roughness; characteristics that self-respecting synths rightly run screaming from.

Cased in wood and sprouting a fistful of drawbars, the CX-3 looks authentic enough, too. There are three preset tones just to get the nervous novice started. All can, of course, be replicated and improved upon, by instead playing around with the nine drawbars initiating frequencies of 16', 5-1/3', 8', 4', 2-2/3', 1-3/5', 1-1/3' and 1'. The simple theory behind drawbars is that each corresponds to a set frequency or pitch, and as you pull out a drawbar, that particular frequency is activated and increased in volume. Pulling out various drawbars mixes up frequencies and their relative volumes. If you want a more synthesizer-oriented explanation, think "additive synthesis." Okay? To aid this highly addictive and fun form of real-time "programming," each drawbar is click-stopped and numbered. Tips on drawbar settings are offered in the instrument's owners manual from Eddie Jobson and Richard Tee.

The tonal range is already heady, but there's more. Two buttons control the instrument's built-in rotary effect. (For an explanation of the actual effect of which this is an electronic copy, read the Hammond entry and comb it for the word "Leslie.") The CX-3 makes a fair stab at this swirling sound-enhancer, including the all-important speed-up and slow-down factors.

Two more push-buttons control another telltale organ characteristic, namely percussion, which adds a brief harmonic at either 4' or 2-2/3' to the front end of a note. The volume and the decay speed of said harmonic is variable. The point of percussion is to add sparkle and interest to the attack. It works well here.

While percussion is a legitimate device long used by organs, the feature here called "key click" was Korg's (or rather, he claims, Keith Emerson's) idea for replicating the much-loved fault on early Hammond organs whereby dirt trapped in the key contacts produces a sort of spitting or...well, a key click. In a similar vein, an overdrive control progressively distorts the signal.

No particular thanks to actual tone controls of treble and bass, the CX-3 can still deliver a range of organ tones from prissy Christening music to a major-league-stadium howl. Operating a CX-3 is not difficult in technical terms, but knowledge of drawbar settings and of organ technique is a distinct advantage.

MIDI was not even a gleam in the industry's eye back in 1980, but CX-3s can be retrofitted by independent specialists if you are so inclined.

The double manual BX-3 pumps out the same quality of sounds but adds chorus and vibrato effects—nice, but probably not essential for most people.

Neither instrument tends to be relinquished by its owner frequently or freely. These remain sought-after classics of their type.

Korg DW-8000
Polyphonic digital/analog synthesizer

THE FAX

Keyboard:	61-note
Programs:	64 RAM
External storage:	Cassette interface
Polyphony:	8-voice
Oscillators per voice:	2
Effects:	Arpeggiator, digital delay
Connections:	Stereo outputs, phones, portamento, program advance, MIDI
Dimensions:	998mm x 338mm x 101mm
Weight:	10.9kg

THE FIGURES

Chief designer:	Mr. Ibe
Production run:	1985-87
Approx. units sold:	20,000
Options:	MEX-8000 memory expansion, hard case, light bag, pedals, ST-2B stand
Sounds:	Angel City (10 volumes), Solid Sounds, Deep Magic, Kid Nepro, Livewire
Miscellaneous:	Book: *Getting the Most Out of Your Korg DW-8000* by Lorenz Rychner; Mac editor available from Beakertech
Orig. price (1985):	$1295 (£1100)
Price in 1996:	$400 (£300)

The DW-8000 was produced at a strange time in Korg's history: during a run of unspectacular sellers that occurred just after a long series of successes with the Polysix, Poly-61 and Poly-800 and just before the company's crowning glory, the M1. In fact, it was during this period that Korg stock in Japan was acquired by Yamaha. The DW-8000 was not world-class, but new ground was broken here, and the EX-8000 rack version remains a highly prized module to this day.

The DW-8000, like its fatally flawed forerunner, the DW-6000 (no keyboard velocity, over-emphasis on preset sounds), is an early sample+ synthesis instrument that takes snippets of a "complete" sound as the starting-off point for otherwise fairly traditional subtractive synthesis programming. In light of instruments produced at the time of this writing, offering banks of ROM sample data tallying hundreds if not thousands of sounds, the DW-8000's offer of some sixteen waveforms sounds cute, if not absurd. But this is how s+s design began. Prior to the DW series, synthesizers dealt in oscillators offering but a handful of "raw" waveforms, typically sawtooth, square and pulse. To be confronted by a choice of sixteen back in 1985 was revolutionary—so much so that I suspect part of the reason behind printing little graphics of the waveforms on the control panel was so that professionally inclined users could still relate to these predigested sound snippets and take the instrument seriously.

DWGS (Digital Waveform Generator System) is the name Korg gave to this new technology. Essentially, Korg analyzed and recreated, using additive harmonic synthesis, the waveforms of certain key sound types. On the DW-8000, these sound types include sawtooth and square waveshapes, acoustic piano, hard and soft electric piano, Clavinet, organ, brass, sax, violin, acoustic guitar, distorted electric guitar, electric bass, digital bass, bells and sine-wave organ whistle.

Choosing one such type for each of two oscillators, you could then move on through a lowpass, resonant filter with dedicated six-stage envelope generator and keyboard tracking, an amplifier with similar six-stage EG, and a multimode modulation generator (LFO). Plenty of juicy extras lie along the way, too, from the mini-pitch EG "auto bend" to portamento, an arpeggiator, two types of unison mode, the velocity/aftertouch keyboard and what was then billed as the world's first programmable digital delay.

Again, from a 1990s perspective, when built-in digital effects processing has hijacked what was left of people's already slim inclination to assemble sounds from scratch, a smattering of DDL parameters governing time, feedback, mod frequency and effect level looks like peanuts indeed. But, in 1985, this, too, was revolutionary.

With such innovative and wide-ranging parameters at hand, 64 program memories could soon be filled, and in 1986, Korg introduced the MEX-8000 Memory Expander, which bumped up the capacity to 256 programs.

The DW-8000 is still a splendid source of digitally analog (or analog-influenced digital) Sounds: bells that ring out with digital clarity yet analog roundness, basses that fuzz and fart most endearingly, some blistering organs, some screaming lead sounds.

Keith Emerson was a genuine aficionado of the

"8000" (module), and, I noted with interest, among the many Emersonian items logged in the massive VEMIA sale of musical instruments held in the UK in July of 1995, there were several Korg instruments but no EX-8000s.

Korg M1
Digital polyphonic workstation/synthesizer

THE FAX

Keyboard:	61-note
Programs:	100 single, 100 multi
External storage:	Card
Polyphony:	16-voice
Oscillators per voice:	2
Effects:	2 multieffects processors
Connections:	Stereo, plus 2 separate audio outs, footswitches, MIDI
Dimensions:	1058mm x 355mm x 110mm
Weight:	13.5kg

THE FIGURES

Chief designer:	Mr. Ikeuchi
Production run:	1988-1994
Approx. units sold:	250,000
Options:	MSC/MPC PCM/program/sequence cards (numerous); memory expansion: Frontal Lobe's Channel SysEx sample load kit, InVision M1 Plus One Expansion board; sounds: Valhalla, Kid Nepro, Livewire, Dr. Sound, Metra Sound, AMG Producer Series and many, many others
Miscellaneous:	Many books and videos have been produced, including *The M1 Sequencing & Recording Handbook* by Dan Walker, *The M1 Patchbook* by Pro Arts Productions, *The Korg M1 Drum Pattern Handbook* by Walker & Verga and *Getting the Most Out of the Korg M1* (video) by...ahem...Julian Colbeck!
Orig. price (1988):	$2166 (£1099)
Price in 1996:	$800 (£700)

If this Hot 100 had to become a Top 10, or perhaps even a Top 3, the Korg M1's place would still be assured. Viewed historically, the M1 was not so much a ground-breaking design in itself. But what it did, what it had, what it offered, was in such style that for a staggering period of four or five years, every other synthesizer on the market had to be assessed in terms of, "Yes, but is it any better than an M1?"

For Korg, the M1 couldn't have come at a more opportune time. The DS-8 hybrid FM synth, which some thought was the shape of things to come after Yamaha's acquisition of a considerable amount of Korg stock, failed to capture the public's imagination, let alone sales. The colorful 707 synth, similarly, promised a lot but delivered little. Korg even tried sampling, but the DSM-1 was a pig to operate and a lemon to sell.

At the 1988 Winter NAMM show, the expectancy surrounding the "731," as the new Korg was then called, could hardly be described as feverish. The 731's clarity, flexibility and power were interesting. But no one, not even Korg, I think, would have predicted that what we were looking at would in time become the world's best-selling synth ever.

Subdued and unassuming in looks (for the rounded casing we have Korg founder Tom Katoh to thank), the M1 has a tiny display screen with eight soft keys below, the scantest of panel hardware and a fairly unexciting pitch bend/mod stick planted in a little raised dome. The layout is simple, and most operations are easy to understand and execute. Operating the M1 on a day-to-day basis is something even the freshest of faces should be able to handle in a matter of minutes.

At the heart of this sample+ synthesis instrument (AI synthesis, as Korg calls it) is 4MB worth of PCM sampled and synthesized waveforms. From this basis, sounds can be shaped using fairly conventional analog-style editing parameters into the M1's standard currency of a Program. Up to eight Programs can be stored in a Combination, which are used for either stacked or zoned sounds or as a way of storing complete multitimbral combinations with each Program on its own MIDI channel. Throw in a decent pair of DSP chips, for good onboard effects, and a sequencer, and there you have it.

Even back in 1988, this was hardly revolutionary. So why has the M1 sold so well? The simple answer is sounds. The M1's ROM waveforms and stunning array of factory programs (not to mention an endless array from third parties) sounded far better than anyone else's at the time and have weathered well. Some have even gone on to become classics in their own right.

In 1988, the M1's factory programs, replete with acoustic guitars that really sounded like acoustic guitars, haunting oboes, fierce and chunky pianos (the piano on LondonBeat's "I've Been Thinking About You" and a zillion other dance soundalikes), melting strings and sonorous basses, took the world by storm. Re-examined today, there's a certain lack of sophistication even compared to machines like Korg's 01/W series or the Roland JVs, never mind the next generation of physical modeling instruments. But M1 sounds are pleasantly direct and full of character. An M1 will always get you out of trouble.

A single Program sound can use either one or two oscillators, with waveforms plucked from the 4MB pool of Multisounds—the PCM samples and synthesized waveforms. Multisounds range from full multisampled pianos to bells and pan flutes, plus snippets of sound like the famous Koto Trem, Lore (a sample of a jack-in-the-box being wound up, donated by Steve Winwood's keyboard technician) and Pole. There are even synth waveforms hoovered out of that earlier Korg notable, the DW-8000.

If you choose the single-oscillator route, a Program will be 16-voice polyphonic. A double-oscillator program will be eight-voice. After multisound selection, you can alter basic pitch and the relative volume of the two oscillators (where applicable). You can go to work on a four-stage pitch envelope generator; a lowpass filter with cutoff point, EG, velocity sensitivity and keyboard tracking (but no resonance); a similarly endowed set of amplifier controls; modulation controls affecting pitch or tone; aftertouch and pitch/mod wheel assignments; and finally, a pair of digital multieffects processors.

Such a list is, surprisingly, quite sufficient for an endless array of inspirational sounds. Much of the credit for this must be given to the Korg voicing team in Japan and the U.S. who assembled the list of PCM/DWGS multisounds. The range and quality of these fundamental building blocks give the M1 its character and Korg its success. The surprising aspect of this is that the filters have no resonance parameter, there's only lowpass filtering, there's no interaction between oscillators (i.e., no cross-modulation or sync) and there are only limited LFO options. In fact, Korg labored long and hard over the filter—on the original design, the filter had no EG intensity. Fortunately, along with the fixit came the intensity parameter and the interesting positive or negative intensity option.

There's still plenty to do and plenty of tricks that enhance this modest display. You could try using the pitch envelope to give a single oscillator sound an added bit of front end "interest," in the form of a fast slide-up at the beginning of each note. In addition to creating catchy sounds like this, you can do so without having to resort to a double-oscillator sound, which maintains the 16-voice polyphony. Another good trick is to envelope out the body of a full-sample multisound to use as a brand new "front end" in a double-oscillator Program. The tip of the Koto multisound is a good case in point.

Organ patches that use the rotary speaker effect can be dramatically improved by connecting a footpedal to Effect Control 1 (on the Global page), so that you can control the slow/fast "Leslie" effect in real time. Similarly, you can adjust many of the M1's basic controls—filter cutoff, release, effects level, etc.—in real time by selecting one of these parameters on screen (eight of these prime parameters are displayed on the main Program screen and can be accessed simply by pushing the little round function button underneath) and waggling either the edit slider or a connected footpedal.

Effects are found at the end of the regular edit pages in Program mode. They include reverbs, delays, overdrives, chorus, rotary speaker and EQ and are clean, powerful and fully editable.

The only real nightmarish aspect of the M1 is the routing of these effects, because the effects and the overall output routing are inextricably bound together. Choices abound, whether it be series or parallel for the effects or a separate output for each program. There are even a couple of erroneous Program edit pages that don't do anything, just to make things really confusing.

The M1 was one of the first synths to offer a really serious collection of premapped drum kits, thus hammering the nails into the dedicated drum machine's coffin a little further. Not only are the samples first class, but you can remap them to suit your own style or application. Only the development of General MIDI, whose mapping most people now adhere to, has stopped the flow of hit records with drum sounds generated by the M1. Remapping the internal kits to a quasi-GM assignment is by no means impossible, though.

M1 Combinations are made up of M1 Programs. You can almost think of them as memories housing eight independent M1s. A classic M1 Combination would be a set of timpani layered with double basses in the lower registers of the keyboard, moving up to some lush strings in the middle, with a velocity-switched oboe and flutes at the top. Thus an entire orchestra would appear at your fingertips. Combis are also used for multitimbral playing, using either the internal or an external sequencer, whereby each Program contained therein is set to respond to its own MIDI channel. It's easy to step through the edit pages in Combi mode and adjust on the keyboard where a selected Program will trigger, alter its basic pitch, change its pitch bend range, change its MIDI channel, filter out unwanted MIDI data, etc. Unlike many more modern instruments, on the M1, you can assign more than one Program to a MIDI channel. In print, this may not sound like a big deal, but believe me, it is.

As on most multitimbral synths, there's no simple solution to juggling effects that are already part of a Program that you may later want to assemble into a Combination. A Program's effects are automatically bypassed when in Combination mode. Instead, a brand new pair of effects takes over that must service all Programs therein. If you don't want to set up new effects, you can copy the effects assignment across from a Program. Korg's way of dealing with the problem is as good as anyone else's. The sneaky, skilled

programmer can, because some of the effects algorithms are dual effects (e.g., delay plus reverb), set up a situation where each of four separate sounds within a Combination has a single different effect on it. A Program can also bypass effects altogether.

It's a shame that only a few diehards use the sequencer on the M1, because although on the face of it, the sequencer is a standard 8-track device on which you can assign programs to tracks with full quantizing and editing, it has one or two interesting options. These include being able to program and store patterns—bite-sized chunks of a sequence—in a separate slice of sequence memory that you can insert into your sequence wherever and whenever. This phrase-based system saves valuable memory and is highly creative. It's a bit like having a sampler full of loops that you can mix and match and slot in wherever you like.

The M1's success speaks for itself. Even now, when it has been superseded by half a dozen instruments in Korg's own roster, let alone everyone else's, people still buy, use and hire M1s on a regular basis. One reason is the level of support available in terms of books, videos and sound cards, plus Korg options, such as new PCM samples on card. Korg's MSC-1S-16S cards comprise different instrument types—synths, sound effects, drums, etc.—and offer both raw PCM data and Program/Combi data based on those particular sound. The other reason, as mentioned already, is sounds. So it's good to learn that the A-team of Korg programmers around the world who were responsible for this sterling selection (Jack Hotop, Athan Bilias, Ben Dowling and others) were suitably rewarded. Presumably, not feeling they were chancing too much, Korg management promised this international team that if the M1 sold more than 50,000 units in one year, they could hold their next product-planning meeting in Hawaii.

Well, aloha!

The M1r is an otherwise identical rack-mount version, subsequently upgraded to the M1rEX (commonly referred to as "Mirex") with a ROM waveform capacity of 275 multisounds, as compared to the M1 keyboard's 144. The M1 can be upgraded to Mirex status—equivalent to Korg's T-series instruments.

Non-Korg upgrades are also available, ranging from Frontal Lobe's PCM Channel SysEx sample loading kit to InVision's M1 Plus One expansion board. The latter, which you may find pre-installed in the M1 "Plus," offers 4MB of new data comprising sparkling new samples like organs, guitars and flutes.

New PCM sounds jazz up the M1, of course. But it's amazing how much power remains in even a standard unit.

Korg Mono/Poly

Analog mono/polyphonic synthesizer

THE FAX

Keyboard:	44-note
Programs:	None
External storage:	None
Polyphony:	4-voice
Oscillators per voice:	1
Effects:	Arpeggiator, chord memory
Connections:	Mono output, phones, CV in/out, trig in/out, VCO in, VCF in, portamento in, arpeggio trigger in
Dimensions:	744mm x 450mm x 144mm
Weight:	12kg

THE FIGURES

Chief designer:	Mr. Mori
Production run:	1982-84
Approx. units sold:	10,000
Options:	Foot controllers, ST-1B stand, soft or hard case
Sounds:	None commercially available
Miscellaneous:	Avid users in the 1990s include Tim Simenon (Bomb the Bass).
Orig. price (1982):	$995 (£749)
Price in 1996:	$375 (£300)

Time and the fates have looked kindly upon the Mono/Poly. In 1982, this crazy mongrel of an instrument, part monophonic and part polyphonic, was viewed as intriguing. But the reality was that the Mono/Poly was far too unpredictable to be of any use polyphonically, and frankly, the market then for a new synth that played only one note at a time was not so much slim as emaciated. The Mono/Poly was also launched alongside the Polysix, which sold in droves.

With understandably canine tendencies, the Mono/Poly still wasn't a complete dog sales-wise, and, indeed, those who did buy in the 1980s should now be feeling very smug, because the Mono/Poly has become widely sought after and none too available.

Why, you ask?

Well, in 1982, the world's focus was on polyphony. The Mono/Poly can function polyphonically, but only riskily so. In 1982, this was hardly ice cream on a hot summer's day. But in the 1990s, the chance to use an analog synth with no less than four independent oscillators, cross-modulation, sync and an arpeggiator...well, yesireebob!

So the very reasons that made the Mono/Poly so lukewarm in 1982 now reappear as positive advantages, if you're scouting about for perpetrators of fat-assed synth bass or arpeggiated rhythmic weirdness. And those reasons are that controls for monophonic and polyphonic are shared—an accident waiting to happen, as we shall see.

Bass and plinky-plonky gated or arpeggiated parts are very much the Mono/Poly's current stock in trade. Four oscillators are available, each not only able to use a different waveform (triangle, sawtooth, variable pulse) but also independently tunable and mixable. The oscillators may not boast separate envelope generators, but at least there are independent EGs (on which the standard parameters of ADSR are offered) for the resonant lowpass filter (VCF) and amplifier (VCA). There are also two LFOs, which, if not entirely flexible, at least let you set up separate modulation effects for, say, mod wheel and oscillator pulse width. (Good time to mention that pulse width mod affects all selected oscillators; in other words, it is not independently controllable per oscillator.) Oscillators can be cross-modulated or hard-synched into one another. Noise is also on hand.

Features thus far, aside from the proliferation of oscillators, are pretty much standard issue for a mono synth. But the Mono/Poly's busy and beknobbed control panel goes on to offer one or two nice additions for the live performer, namely a couple of "one-touch" buttons to activate the cross-mod and sync features for those moments when you need extra growl or an enhanced weirdness factor. For that classic sliding-between-notes effect, portamento is offered. Then, of course, there's the arpeggiator—a simple but good specimen offering up, down and up/down modes along with latch (hold) controls.

The one-touch and arpeggiator controls aside, the whole panel layout is sufficiently roomy and clear to encourage live tweaking, though not complete manipulation in terms of rebalancing the oscillators, filter resonance, modulation or envelope-shaping. (All of which is just as well, you might say, since there are no program memories.)

Operating in monophonic mode, with the ability to harness up to four fairly independent oscillators per note, it lets you do things like spread the tuning of the oscillators for thick and swirly sounds or even stack sounds in jumps of an octave or fifths. Either way, you are not short of firepower.

But this leads us to the issue of using the Mono/Poly polyphonically. Problems arise when you decide to jump into polyphonic mode, because it's unlikely the current settings for your last monophonic operation will transfer...well, *musically* (remember, everything has to be set up in real time). For instance, if you had previously spread the tuning of the oscillators for a thick chorus-type sound, the tuning in polyphonic terms will be different for each successive note. This is similar in effect to dealing with the completely separate SEMs on an Oberheim 4-voice.

If you do have the patience to operate the Mono/Poly in poly mode—and make sure the instrument is set up sympathetically on each oscillator panel—a couple of tidbits such as the chord memory (which allows you to hold down a collection of up to four notes and then retrigger this "chord" using one note at a time) and the oscillator cycling facility on the arpeggiator will be there to greet you.

In sum, the Mono/Poly is capable of whipping up quite a storm monophonically, courtesy of its oscillator power. Polyphonically, as Vince Clarke observed in a review of the Mono/Poly back in 1982, it's "like four cheap synthesizers all playing together." Hardly a searing recommendation.

In 1982, I observed that the instrument probably acquired its name as much from its operation being akin to the game—requiring no skill and being a matter of complete chance—as from its dual-mode note-playing capability. But perhaps the Mono/Poly was built ten years ahead of its time. Second-hand prices are buoyant, with demand, for the most part, outpacing supply.

Although the Mono/Poly missed MIDI by a whisker, it is worth noting that Korg abandoned its Hz-to-voltage system on the CV connections; here you will find the more commonly used octave-to-voltage type. However, a MIDI retrofit would still make more sense, in most applications.

Korg MS-20 Analog monophonic synthesizer

THE FAX

Keyboard:	37-note
Programs:	None (the SQ-10 sequencer can perform as a 12-channel memory)
External storage:	None
Polyphony:	Monophonic
Oscillators per voice:	2
Effects:	None
Connections:	Mono out, headphones, various control inputs
Dimensions:	595mm x 249mm x 309mm
Weight:	7.7kg

THE FIGURES

Chief designer:	Fumio Mieda, Mr. Mori
Production run:	1978-82
Approx. units sold:	20,000+
Options:	MS-01 foot controller, MS-02 interface, MS-03 signal processor, SQ-10 sequencer
Sounds:	n/a
Miscellaneous:	20 "giant" versions of the MS-20 were built for education.
Orig. price (1978):	$850 (£425)
Price in 1996:	$400 (£200)

The MS-20 had the misfortune to be launched in 1978, when all eyes and ears were straining towards America and a strange new company called Sequential Circuits. Yes, 1978 was also the year of the Prophet-5, and that, quite rightly, overshadowed everything else. Worse for Korg, the Prophet-5 was the first of the last few nails in the coffin of monophonic synths like the MS-20.

The MS-20 was designed in Japan by Messrs. Mieda (who designed Korg's first keyboard product, an organ, back in 1967 and went on to become head of Korg engineering) and Mori (who moved on to a special engineering group working on new synthesis techniques, after leading the design teams on the CX-3, Mono/Poly and Poly-800). The idea behind the MS-20 was to produce a scaled-down version of Korg's bulky PS series of polyphonic patch bay synths produced in the same year. At this time, there were plenty of good small mono synths on the market, but few boasting patch bays like you'd find on the big boys from Moog or ARP, or indeed Korg. (The beauty of a patch bay is that you can physically connect "modules" of the instrument, such as the filter, the oscillator or the LFO, in the precise way you want rather than having to stick to a predefined layout and routing.)

The MS-20 stands out physically, with its steeply sloping control panel (though it doesn't collapse like that of the Minimoog) and tiny, "professional-looking" schematics and labels dotted about on its battleship-gray metal casing. High-quality components were used; the control knobs offer the sort of precision that only money can buy. Compact compared to the PS series, the MS-20 is still an awkward shape, with the lone control wheel tucked down below the bottom C on the final inch's worth of ledge. The design has definite pose value, but once cased, an MS-20 does make a hefty package to cart around.

This is a dual-oscillator synth. Each Voltage Controlled Oscillator, or VCO, has its own marked-out area of panel, allowing you to set up different waveforms and different pitches for each. VCO1 offers triangle, sawtooth and variable-pulse waveforms, as well as white noise (for steam sounds, explosions, breath or wind sounds, etc.). Pitch can be varied over four octaves. VCO2 offers sawtooth, set square and narrow pulse waveforms, and a ring modulator. The ring modulator setting harnesses both oscillators to produce those hard-edged bell and gong-like sounds used in the 1990s by artists like The Shamen. VCO2 is also scaled one octave higher. To the right, there is a small mixing panel with separate control knobs for VCO1 and VCO2 levels. Pitch can be modulated by the LFO or one of the two envelope generators.

Already this has the makings of a powerful system: independent waveforms, ring modulation, noise, independent balance. But the MS-20 also offers separate low- and highpass filtering, each with its own "peak" (resonance) controls. Filtering can be modulated by the modulation generator (LFO) for filter vibrato or wah effects and shaped over time using one of the envelope generators.

The modulation generator itself offers a number of knob-controlled waveshapes, plus full control over mod speed. There are two envelope generators: EG1, which is internally routed to the oscillators, featuring delay, attack and release time; and EG2, which is generally used for shaping both VCA and VCF and offers attack, decay, sustain, release and hold.

Along with Portamento (a lone knob governing time—i.e., speed) and master tune, these are the MS-20's basic sound-generating tools. Features under knob control are simple and direct. If you want to carry out more advanced maneuvers, then you can reel out sundry lengths of spaghetti and start customizing the patching. You can, for instance, reverse the polarity of the EGs; patch in a footpedal to control the filter cutoff in real time; make use of a sample and hold circuit (for crazy, random squeaks and squawks); or harness the (darker) pink noise, either as a source or a modulation signal.

You can also get really adventurous and use the MS-20's own pitch-to-voltage converter and External Signal Processor inputs to trigger the instrument from a guitar or even a microphone, for a form of guitar synthesis or vocoding. You can also fire off an MS-20 sound triggered from, say, a snare drum on tape. The flexibility this offers, both internally and externally, is almost unlimited—provided you have the time, the inclination and a modicum of knowledge to exploit it. If you are lucky enough to find one, the MS-20 manual is extremely concise and helpful on the subject of patching. (What went wrong? Why aren't manuals written like this today?)

What does an MS-20 sound like? The 12db/oct filtering (using custom-designed Korg filters) may not furnish the raw power of a Curtis chip, but the high/low (and even bandpass, from the patch bay) filtering options, plus ring modulation, definitely give the instrument bags of character, in a hard-edged, electronic way that is totally in keeping with its vague-

ly military appearance. In pure sound terms, Korg Japan advises that the signal-to-noise ratio does leave a little to be desired, so you might want to gate out residual white noise inherent in the circuitry. This problem may be particularly apparent on the MS-20's single-oscillator baby brother, the MS-10, whose white-noise generator delivers a sound more like breakup than noise anyway.

A point of interest is that Korg UK's Phil MacDonald sampled his own MS-20 for many of the "spitty" drum noises on Korg's i-series workstations. Phil's is one of the extremely rare "Big MS-20," giant-scale versions of the instrument made by hand for a select number of star endorsees and music colleges. Only around 20 of these instruments were ever produced.

Star endorsees and users at the time included Keith Emerson (a longtime Korg friend), YMO and Kitaro. In recent years, the MS-20 has been rediscovered by all self-respecting synth aficionados, from Vince Clarke to The Shamen to the Aphex Twin's Richard James, who in fact has three of them that he uses undoctored.

Though relatively reliable, the MS-20 can use standard transistors and op amps, rendering spares not a problem, theoretically. When examining a second-hand unit, it might be advisable to check the state of the jack field (sockets can rust, among other things), though even these can be replaced without too much heartache. A number of accessories were produced, including cut-to-length patchcords; the MS-01 foot controller, with which you can operate parameters like filter cutoff in real time; and the SQ-10 analog sequencer, which allows you to program a sequence of up to 24 notes with individual pitch, timing and tone color. (Since this unit can also be used to store MS-20 sounds, it makes a useful addition to your system.)

Interfacing the MS-20 with the outside world was always a bit of a problem, largely because Korg adopted the Hz-to-voltage system rather than the more common one volt-per-octave standard used by other synths at the time. Korg's stout defense was that Hz-to-voltage gives you greater oscillator (pitch) stability. Track down an MS-20 interface, which converts to one volt-per-octave, or more likely a third-party equivalent, if you feel the burning need to interface with other synths and sequencers.

A purist's instrument, not terribly rare or sought after, but a great acquisition all the same.

Korg Poly-61 Analog polyphonic synthesizer

THE FAX

Keyboard:	61-note
Programs:	64 RAM

External storage:	Cassette interface
Polyphony:	6-voice
Oscillators per voice:	2
Effects:	Arpeggiator
Connections:	Mono audio, program up, sustain, audio trigger in, phones
Dimensions:	985mm x 110mm x 350mm
Weight:	11kg

THE FIGURES

Chief designer:	Mr. Iijima
Production run:	1983-84
Approx. units sold:	15,000
Options:	MIDI as retrofit, hard case, ST-2B stand
Sounds:	None commercially available
Miscellaneous:	The Poly-61M, with MIDI standard, appeared in 1984.
Orig. price (1983):	$995 (£895)
Price in 1996:	$250 (£200)

Few people rave about the Poly-61. It's just not that type of keyboard. Korg went for functionality over flash, price over programming permutations, and who can say they were wrong? The Poly-61 sold well and stayed the course. At today's giveaway prices, it still makes a decent noise, providing a nice splash of analog in a semi-digitally controlled environment, and it's reliable.

But even back in 1983, the Poly-61 was a work-horse: dependable, with strong, easy-to-achieve sounds. It was Korg's first instrument to abandon knobs and switches, yet all the main parameter headings and value ranges are etched onto the casing in Korg's '80s-style, pseudo-computer writing. Getting lost on a Korg Poly-61 is, well, unlikely, even for a novice.

The digitally controlled oscillators are streamlined. DCO-1 offers sawtooth, pulse and square waveforms; DCO-2 the same minus the pulse option. The oscillators can be tuned separately, but not set at different volumes. DCO-2 can only be switched off. An equally simple filter section sees lowpass, resonant filtering that has to be shaped by the same ADSR envelope generator available to the amplifier. The filter can track the keyboard, but the shared envelope generator is a definite limiting factor. The LFO can affect the oscillators or the filter, but sine wave is the only option. So smooth vibrato is okay, but hard-edged trills are out.

This modest set of controls makes the Poly-61 a breeze to use, however. Most anyone will be encouraged to start programming from day one; this makes

an excellent synth on which to learn about analog synthesis.

And indeed, people *are* encouraged, because the Poly-61 sounds clean and purposeful. It specializes in harder, Clavi-type analog sounds, but the extra thickness afforded by the dual-oscillator design makes thick, full string patches work well, in a synthy, as opposed to lifelike, style. Unfortunately, Korg ditched chorus (found on the earlier Korg Polysix), which can add greater swirl.

A further loss from the Polysix is the unison keyboard mode. On the Poly-61, you must employ the chord memory to stack up the oscillators, and though this is an undeniably handy feature for instantly creating fat bass sounds, the results are not programmable. Overall volume is non-programmable as well.

This list of losses and omissions must be weighed not only against a range of punchy, usable presets but also against a fine arpeggiator, which can be clocked externally from similar-vintage Korg drum machines and against the luxury of being able to step through the presets from a footswitch, a feature that is an unrivaled plus for live playing.

Along with what was then called "digital access control" design (i.e., no knobs and switches—the dawning of the era of programming as typing), Korg inaugurated the joystick controller for pitch bend and modulation effects. It was and remains a bit dinky, though Korg stalwarts are, by now, well used to this device.

MIDI was right around the corner as the Poly-61 appeared, and Korg was quick to offer a MIDI retrofit. A year later, the Poly-61M came with a retrofit as standard. These were early MIDI days, so anomalies, weirdnesses and limitations on the MIDI side abounded. MIDI also sounded the death knell for the dreaded (and temperamental) cassette interface method of external storage. Ironically, though, the Poly-61's cassette interface is both quick and stable.

The Poly-61 was aimed at the hobbyist, semipro market, so not many hardened professionals admit to owning or using one of these synths. However, many's the time a Poly-61 lay in prime position in a pro's home studio, due to its immediacy and not inconsiderable range and power.

This is not a collector's synth yet, and perhaps never will be, but it's a good buy for analog-hounds on a tight budget. MIDI retrofits are widely available and are recommended.

Korg Poly-800 — Analog polyphonic synthesizer

THE FAX

Keyboard:	49-note
Programs:	64 RAM
External storage:	Cassette interface

Polyphony:	8-voice
Oscillators per voice:	1 or 2
Effects:	Chorus, DDL (on Mk II)
Connections:	Stereo outputs, phones, program advance, MIDI In/Out
Dimensions:	780mm x 286mm x 87mm
Weight:	4.3kg

THE FIGURES

Chief designer:	Mr. Mori
Production run:	1984-86
Approx. units sold:	100,000
Options:	MEX-8000 Memory Expander, strap
Sounds:	Patch/Works Music Software
Miscellaneous:	A reversed color keyboard model was also made.
Orig. price (1984):	$795 (£575)
Price in 1996:	$225 (£200)

It's tempting but dangerous to talk of "Japanese synth companies" as if all are alike. In fact, some, such as Casio or Yamaha, rarely move their corporate eyes off the bottom line; while others, like Korg, are ever-willing—hellbent, almost—on trying something new, even if it doesn't sell in large quantities. Korg founder Tom Katoh once told me that [electronic] instruments should have "personality," and trying to please everyone in a design was crazy.

Such a philosophy has fired many an oddball synth out of the Korg factory—some heroic failures and plenty of runaway successes—and right up at the top in both the oddness and success categories is the Poly-800.

With its green buttons and panel decorations, computer-font parameter numbers, short-scale keyboard and strap handles (so you can sling the little beast around your neck and play it like a guitar), you're not going to mistake a Poly-800 for any other synthesizer. And the bright and breezy image is totally appropriate for this fun-loving but seriously powerful instrument. This is not a synth to pore over, to program laboriously and endlessly. Set it up, fiddle about a bit, sure, but do get on and play it.

The control panel consists of a small display screen, a joystick, a large volume control, three key assign buttons, a smattering of sequencer controls, a small keypad and finally a long string of parameters names, numbers and values. Dedicated knobs and switches might have gone West, but evidently it was still advisable to mark out their ghosts.

Taking some of my own advice: Never mind

what it's got for the time being, what's a Poly-800 like to play? You don't have to play it slung over your shoulder, but if you do, the playing angle is comfortable and the instrument itself is light. The position of the joystick is also comfortable but hardly encourages great expressive feats (nothing to grip or hold onto, just a flimsy stick to waggle). Moving onto a new patch takes two button-pushes (not good), but you can connect a footswitch and literally step through the programs (good). You can also power the instrument via batteries (good). But the juice doesn't last that long, and when it's time to change the batteries, you have no more than five minutes' grace period between removing dead batteries and inserting fresh ones or else your program and sequencer memory will disappear (disaster).

There are two types of patches: a "whole" patch, which uses up all available oscillators, giving you eight-voice polyphony, and a "double" patch, with which you can effectively layer two totally separate sounds in four-voice polyphony. Obviously, the more interesting patches are the dual ones.

The Poly-800 is a refreshingly different-sounding synth due to its hybrid subtractive analog/additive digital blend. Cutting lead sounds are a breeze, it does a nice line in wheezy flutes, you can produce searing if somewhat digital organ tones and there are plenty of hard-edged metallic sounds (at which all Korg instruments of this vintage seem to excel) to be had.

The Poly-800's method of sound creation may not be the norm, but it is not difficult to figure out. Effectively, you build your own waveforms by combining pitches (16', 8', 4' and 2') at different volumes, rather like using drawbars on a organ. You can choose between sawtooth and square waveshapes. The signal then passes through a lowpass resonant filter, with the option of adding noise as you go. The filter is the Poly-800's Achilles' heel, because it has to function for all the oscillators in a bank. This may or may not be of earth-shattering significance, depending upon what and how you play. However, it does render the instrument more like a string machine than a synth at times. (If you're playing legato, for example, the filter will not retrigger for each successive note.)

Offering single/multiple triggering modes goes some way toward disguising this fact, and the VCF can track the keyboard and be shaped by its own six-stage envelope generator. Two further EGs are reserved for DCO-1 and DCO-2. The envelope generators, in addition to standard ADSR parameters, feature B for break point, which effectively gives you a two-part decay, and a second S for slope, governing the time it takes from break point to sustain. The LFO is sine wave only, with speed and delay parameters and routing options to the oscillators or the filter. Chorus can be added progressively to a sound.

Perhaps the last thing you'd expect on a synth like this is a sequencer. But here it is: a 256-event, step-time sequencer that can house notes and chords. The sequencer is great for riffs or motifs, even triggered live, but there is a slight hazard in that the sequencer-enable switch at the back is prone to being moved, in which case the device promptly empties itself when you accidentally select "sequencer" on the control panel. Not so good were this to happen onstage. I speak from experience here.

At its absurdly inexpensive price, the Poly-800 was a resounding success, so much so that not only did Korg produce a non-keyboard version (EX-800) but also a Poly-800 Mk II, which added DDL parameters to its list of (now also programmable) effects. A limited edition with a reverse-colored keyboard was made, too. Sadly, by the time of its arrival, the Poly-800 had really had its day, and I clearly recall these smart black-instead-of-white-key instruments loitering in the bargain basements. Enough Poly-800s were produced for supply to outstrip demand for a while longer. MIDI is included, albeit in a basic (no Thru) style, and do take note of the short-scale, 49-key keyboard. Still an invigorating instrument, however, of genuine quality and great value.

Korg Polysix — Analog polyphonic synthesizer

THE FAX

Keyboard:	61-note
Programs:	32
External storage:	Cassette interface
Polyphony:	6-voice
Oscillators per voice:	1
Effects:	Arpeggiator, chorus
Connections:	Mono out, filter control in, arpeggio trigger in, chord memory footswitch, phones
Dimensions:	980mm x 373mm x 132mm
Weight:	11.5kg

THE FIGURES

Chief designer:	Mr. Nozokido
Production run:	1982-83
Approx. units sold:	30,000
Options:	MS-01/04 foot pedals
Sounds:	Deep Magic "Korg Polysix 3" 640-program cassette

Miscellaneous:	T. Katoh, Korg founder: "More than any other single event, the success of the Polysix moved us into the forefront of the electronic music market."
Orig. price (1982):	$1095 (£899)
Price in 1996:	$350 (£250)

A synthesizer doesn't physically improve with age, like a guitar or a bottle of wine. But tastes change and so do applications and perceptions. Perception of quality can thus shift over a period of time, which is exactly what has happened with the Korg Polysix.

In 1982, the Polysix was seen as Korg's answer to Roland's Juno-60, both scrambling to shore just ahead of the tidal wave of MIDI machines yet priced at a level that gave the average musician their first serious shot at buying a polyphonic synthesizer. But more telling in the long run, Korg engineers had, in fact, set about designing the Polysix in response to the Prophet-5 way back in 1979. Indeed, the Polysix uses SSM chips, as did the original Prophet-5s.

The Juno-60 and Korg Polysix both sold well, opening up the synthesizer market to ages and financial brackets of musicians undreamt of when the Prophet-5 ruled the sine waves. However, the Polysix never seemed to attract rave reviews from the public and pundits. It was just a good synth at a great price.

More than a decade later, the Polysix is remembered and regarded as an altogether more serious proposition. Many a star of the 1990s cut their musical teeth on a Korg Polysix ("The first punk synth," LondonBeat's Willi M called it; "loud and raucous"), and the instrument's second-hand price, undisputed raw analog power and directness endeared it to the retro generation nearly as much as classic American instruments from Moog and ARP.

Korg's final knobs-and-switches instrument, the Polysix has just a single oscillator per voice, offering sawtooth, pulse and variable pulse-width waveforms. Like the Juno-60, the Polysix has just a sub-oscillator, operating either one or two octaves below, for reinforcement. But make no mistake, the Polysix is a rowdy performer. Filtering is 24dB/oct lowpass with full cutoff, resonance and keyboard tracking parameters, though it shares an ADSR envelope generator with the amplifier. This is an admitted limiting factor, as is the sine wave-only LFO. The LFO can be used to modulate pitch, tone or volume; the word "or" here meaning just that.

There are some limitations in pure synthesis terms, but the Polysix also has an effects section, comprising phaser, chorus and ensemble, with speed and intensity variable. It also has the all-important feature of unison, whereby all oscillators join forces for a mass assault on the eardrums. For big, fat bass sounds or really thick, penetrating lead sounds, this is the answer.

A multimode arpeggiator lets you set up rippling mini sequences up and down the keyboard, and users are encouraged to clock arpeggio effects externally via the arpeggiator input jack and, to be safe, a Korg drum machine or sequencer. Unless your name is Vince "MIDI is crap" Clarke, you will most likely want this to take place via MIDI these days, so a MIDI retrofit (which was available from Korg in the early 1980s but must now be obtained from an independent retrofit company) seems sensible.

Part of the reason for the Polysix's extended popularity is that the instrument waved a final farewell to a number of features: not only control-panel knobs and switches but pitch and mod wheels (thereafter, Korg entertained only the joystick) and VCOs (replaced by DCOs until the passing of the analog era).

Warmly old-fashioned, then, the Polysix is nonetheless capable of storing edited sounds in a small 32-location program memory, backed up by cassette interface, and generally has the reputation of being reliable. In terms of control, you can maneuver the filter cutoff or initiate modulation from a connected footpedal, store and "play" (with one finger) chords using the chord memory feature and even advance program memories from a program-up footswitch.

Squared up against its longtime rival the Juno-60, Korg's Polysix holds its own. Perhaps sounds err towards the hard and thin, but this can be offset by the chorus, flanger and ensemble effects. The Polysix does not command high prices, but it is always (and rightly so) sought after. Many were made, so you can usually find one.

Korg PS-3200 | Polyphonic analog synthesizer

THE FAX

Keyboard:	None (48-note PS-3010 sold separately)
External storage:	None
Polyphony:	48-voice
Oscillators per voice:	2
Effects:	EQ
Connections:	Mono audio, modulation, phones, digital input, analog input

Dimensions:	920mm x 445mm x 345mm
Weight:	30kg

THE FIGURES

Chief designer:	Fumio Mieda
Production run:	1977-79
Approx. units sold:	500
Options:	PS-3010 keyboard, PS-3060 remote programmer, PS-3040 dual foot controller, patch cords
Sounds:	None
Miscellaneous:	One of only a few synths to offer control over keyboard temperament
Orig. price (1977):	$7000 (£3300)
Price in 1996:	$3000 (£2000-2500)

Korg made three large PS-series synths in the late 1970s: the PS-3100, the PS-3200 and the PS-3300. All are square, bulky instruments encased in wood. The PS-3100, at least, has the courtesy to arrive attached to its own keyboard, unlike the 3200 and 3300 which require plumbing into a detached, separate keyboard, like Korg's PS-3010. And when I say "plumbing," the metaphor is not used gratuitously; the connectors and cables resemble nothing so much as an industrial water supply. (For some inexplicable reason, Korg mounted the synthesizer's socket on its right-hand side, but the PS-3010's keyboard's connectors are on its left. So beware the healthy length of piping snaking its way along the bottom of the unit.)

The three PS instruments have much in common, design- and soundwise. If you have free rein, the three oscillators-per-voice PS-3300 is the king of the heap for sonic versatility and power—a sentiment endorsed by none other than Bob Moog. But the PS-3200 is the model most likely to have survived into the 1990s. Armed with program memories and microtonal tuning, not to mention its kaleidoscopic range of sounds, it is, therefore, the PS-3200 on which the scrutinizing gaze of *Keyfax* will focus.

Only in the 1980s was the synthesizer invariably a keyboard instrument. For various reasons, the 1990s have opened up control to guitar, wind, drum, glove—you name it—"alternative" controllers. Also, back in the 1960s and 1970s, a serious synthesizer was not so much an instrument for playing music as a device for *creating* music. The PS-3200 appeared on the cusp of this transition.

Serious it looks, indeed. Those reared on a diet of Juno-60s or M1s will be totally put off by the PS-3200's telephone-exchange looks. But in fact, although many of the parameter headings sound foreign to modern ears and eyes, this is not a particularly impenetrable instrument at all.

Fully polyphonic—yes, fully—the PS-3200's signal generators or oscillators can be pitched between

16' and 2' octaves, and you can choose from triangle, sawtooth, square and variable-pulse waveforms. Filtering is resonant lowpass, with keyboard follow. There are standard ADSR envelope generator controls, a sample-and-hold circuit, two modulation generators (LFOs) and remarkably sophisticated EQ facilities, plus the delights of pink or white noise, an adding amplifier, voltage processors and, of course, an extensive patch bay that allows you to literally create "patches."

If all else fails, there are also 16 program memories on the PS-3200, each recallable at the touch of one of the 16 white programmer buttons. Overriding a patch requires that you simply pull out a desired control knob to make, as the brochure says, "temporary adjustments."

What does a PS-3200 sound like? In a word: big. Tones range from panoramic orchestral washes to bells to die for to all manner of multilayered bleeps and blurps. It also does a nice line in organs and ethereal strings. The PS-3200 sounds surprisingly modern, especially if you fancy your chances at some microtonal tunings courtesy of the two sets (one for each oscillator bank) of 12 temperament adjust buttons. It seems wholly appropriate that the American design team behind the Wavestation turned to Korg.

Though the PS-3200 is, and always was, a studio hound, the PS-3010 does sport a number of performance controls and switches, among them (intriguingly, for Korg historians who might wonder where they originally got the idea) a joystick.

In the mid-1980s, the PS-3200 could hardly be given away. You'd occasionally come across a model slumped in the corner or back room of a studio: unloved, unused and, you'd have thought, all washed up. The 1990s have hardly seen the instrument come screaming into fashion, but these are now highly prized synthesizers, rare and expensive. They sound brilliant, too.

Korg SG-1D Digital piano

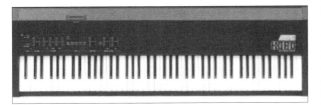

THE FAX

Keyboard:	88-note
Programs:	4, plus cards
External storage:	Card
Polyphony:	12-voice
Oscillators per voice:	n/a

Effects:	Chorus, brilliance, graphic EQ
Connections:	Stereo audio, phones, sustain, MIDI
Dimensions:	1370mm x 400mm x 123mm
Weight:	33.7kg

THE FIGURES

Chief designer:	Mr. Takeda
Production run:	1986-1994
Approx. units sold:	5000
Options:	ST-SGD model (includes a stand with built-in speakers), HC-SG Hard Case
Sounds:	Korg SGC ROM cards
Miscellaneous:	Originally released as 76-note SG-1; 88-note SG-1D released soon after
Orig. price (1986):	$2850 (£2150)
Price in 1996:	$1000 (£1200)

From the look of the specifications, or indeed a look at the instrument, it's not immediately apparent why the SG-1D has proved so popular. Tones are thin on the ground, it looks fairly dull and even Korg can hardly be accused of prolonging its life with an endless supply of new sounds on card. Yet the SG-1D has been enjoyed and employed by many hardened professionals, from rockers like the Stones' Chuck Leavell to precision artists like Alan Parsons keyboardist Gary Sanctuary to jazz maniac Django Bates. In other words, players across the whole spectrum of styles and sensibilities have warmed to the SG-1D's sound and feel. This hardy, professional-quality stage piano offers a small range of piano tones, good MIDI implementation and a medium-weight keyboard action.

The original SG-1 was released in 1986 as a 76-key model, though it offered the same basic range of tones and features as the 88-note SG-1D, which appeared not long after. Just to add to the confusion, by 1990, the "New SG-1D" appeared, "New" referring to the amount of sample memory allotted to and taken up by the new multisampled Steinway grand. Regular SG-1Ds were upgradable to New (subsequently called SGX-1D) status up until 1993.

Physically, the SG-1D is long and large, with only about one-third of the flat panel occupied by controls. These are comprised of four tone select buttons and sliders for volume, three-band EQ, brilliance and chorus speed and depth. Pitch and mod wheels are placed, a little unusually, above the keyboard on the control panel itself. But what's even more unusual is that they're on this piano at all.

The presets are rather blandly named Piano I and II and Electric Piano I and II. Truth be told, there's not a whole world of difference between Pianos I and II, but the sound is firm, substantial, meaty: a sound you can really come to grips with, even if the 12-voice polyphony is a bit limiting (and certainly minimal by current standards). The acoustic piano multisamples are taken from a Steinway grand piano—12-bit, perhaps, but Steinway. The first electric piano tone is the classic Rhodes/DX hybrid, eminently playable. The second tone is more unusual, very edgy and probably has more limited appeal. ROM cards (SGCU 11-16) can be slotted in, enabling the instrument to tap into harpsichord, clavi, vibes and other presets, which is nice (and rare) to find on a stage piano.

The basic sounds are fundamentally classy. You also have excellent real-time control over effects and tone. The chorus may not be terribly smooth and sophisticated, but you have speed and depth controls, and the electric piano sounds both lap it up, as you might expect.

MIDI-wise, the SG is reasonably sophisticated in that you can split internal and external sounds, switch local off, send out Program Changes and transpose data. Okay, let's not carried away—there are no MIDI memories, no banks of assignable controllers, etc., but this piano often makes a perfectly respectable keyboard controller. The keyboard action is weighted but not heavily so. Aftertouch is transmitted, and there are eight levels of velocity to play with, alterable on the rear panel.

People tend to hang onto these instruments, making second-hand models hard to come by.

Korg Trident MkII Polyphonic synthesizer

THE FAX

Keyboard:	61-note
Programs:	32
External storage:	Cassette interface
Polyphony:	8-voice
Oscillators per voice:	2
Effects:	EQ, vibrato, flanger
Connections:	Mix and separate voice audio outputs, VCF footswitch, brass tone pedal
Dimensions:	1012mm x 542mm x 173mm
Weight:	23.5kg

THE FIGURES

Chief designer:	Fumio Mieda
Production run:	1982 85
Approx. units sold:	5000
Options:	Footswitches
Sounds:	None commercially available
Orig. price (1982):	$4595 (£2999)
Price in 1996:	$500 (£500)

Sound has been the Trident's saving grace. By all rights, this cumbersome hybrid synth-cum-string/brass

machine ought to have been consigned to the history books (and not this one, either) years ago. But the Trident makes a big noise, and if you have the space to house such an animal, it will surely repay your not inconsiderable investment.

Korg dumped the plain Trident onto an unsuspecting public back in 1981. It attracted interest, but there were a number of complaints and problems: The programming system was completely unmusical, volume couldn't be programmed at all and there were only 16 memories.

Nowadays a company would summarily fire the designer and move on. But Korg knuckled down, improved the instrument and launched the Trident Mk II a year later. The Mark II remained in production for three years and enjoyed good sales, considering the price of the instrument.

A 1982 ad copy headline describing "Full Synthe Sections" tells you quite a lot about where the Trident was aimed. This was an instrument for the keyboard player who wanted synth(e) sounds without any of the hassle, thank you very much—the type of player for whom "synthe" sounds only just shaded out brass sounds or string sounds in order of importance.

The synthesizer section of the control panel (there are also dedicated brass and strings sections) takes up about half its width and comprises a pair of sawtooth, square or variable pulse wave oscillators; resonant lowpass filters with variable keyboard tracking and dedicated ADSR envelope generator; and a VCA with ADSR envelope generator. There's no programmable LFO as such, vibrato effects automatically coming under joystick control.

Clearly this is not a Matrix-12 or the like, but you can whip up some respectable, substantial synth sounds extremely quickly.

And that's not the end of it. The brass section has its own filter controls and ADSR envelope generator; its sounds can be pitched at either 8' or 16' pitches. Next door, the strings panel features tone activators at 16', 8', 4' and 2' pitch ranges, with slimline envelope controls for attack and release, tone controls, keyboard tracking and vibrato.

Uniquely, the Trident offers a "bowing" effect, which would have been a great idea if it sounded any good. In truth, it just seems to boost resonance.

Moving along, there's a complete flanging panel, offering control over intensity, speed, feedback and manual. Any section can employ the flanger, though not, curiously, more than one section simultaneously.

The Trident's versatility extends to its ability to be set up in a number of keyboard splits and layer permutations, separately controllable in volume and indeed physical output. Seasoned users (OMD, for one) can elicit great things from a Trident. It has presence, both physical and audio. Mark II's are quite plentiful, in absolute terms, but people tend to hang onto them. They're worth snapping up if you've got the room and the back muscles.

Korg Wavestation

Digital polyphonic synthesizer

THE FAX

Keyboard:	61-note
Programs:	150 single, 16 multi
External storage:	Card
Polyphony:	32-voice
Oscillators per voice:	4 max
Effects:	2 multieffects processors
Connections:	4 separate audio outs, MIDI, phones, control pedals
Dimensions:	1000mm x 350mm x 110mm
Weight:	12.5kg

THE FIGURES

Chief designers:	Ray Keller, John Bowen, Scott Peterson
Production run:	1990-94
Approx. units sold:	14,000 (keyboard versions only)
Options:	EXK-WS ROM Expansion Kit (from plain Wavestation to "EX" version)
Sounds:	WSC-1S Piano, WSC-2S Drums and Percussion, WSC-3S Synth and Time Slice, WPC-11-20 Patch and Performance cards, PSC1S-3S for Wavestation SR (all from Korg); Kid Nepro, Valhalla, Voice Crystal, Eye + 1, AMG Producer Series
Miscellaneous:	Editor/librarians: Opcode Galaxy Plus—Wavestation (Mac), Geerdes Wavestation SWS (ST), Steinberg Wavestation Synthworks (ST); book: *Korg Wavestation* by Dan Walker
Orig. price (1990):	$2485 (£1499)
Price in 1996:	$800 (£650, EX model)

Some synths are designed, made, sold and then discontinued. I like that kind of instrument. The nightmare scenario for a synth sleuth is the Wavestation. In its long and colorful career, the Wavestation—if we can even talk in the singular—has evolved from a seed sown in one company in California (Sequential) through a brief period of incubation under the wing of a Japanese company (Yamaha) to its eventual rebirth to another Japanese company, this time official midwife and parent Korg.

Not content with such a complex heritage, the Wavestation has also gone on to appear in a number of guises and versions, both keyboard and modular. A brief chronological breakdown runs like this: The original, plain Wavestation keyboard was released in 1990. In 1991, Korg released the Wavestation EX, featuring additional piano and drum samples. Plain Wavestations could upgrade to EX status (see "Options" above) but were quickly phased out as production moved on to EX instruments only. Also in 1991, the Wavestation A/D module was released, which was similar to the EX version but with the addition of analog inputs. The Wavestation SR, a slimline module brim full of every Wavestation patch ever dreamt of, was created in 1992. More in-depth analysis of each variable can be found at the end of this "all-in-one" review, but this is the short version of the big picture.

The Wavestation concept was unashamedly built on designs and ideas found on Sequential's last major releases, the Prophet-VS and the Prophet-3000 sampler (whose screen and soft keys were promptly purloined). At the heart of these machines is the idea that the waveforms—not just the processing of the waveforms but the actual waveforms themselves—should be allowed to move, cut and paste into each other, evolve, mutate. On the VS, this idea was represented by what Sequential called Vector Synthesis, which meant mixing the balance of up to four waveshapes using a joystick. On the Wavestation, not only can you mix up the waveshapes, but you can string endless numbers of them together sequentially (ha!) to form what John Bowen, the mastermind behind the idea, called "wavesequences." Initially, Bowen saw wavesequencing only in gentle, evolving settings. But Korg programmers in New York were quick to spot wavesequencing's potential for hard-driving, rhythmic patches. And so the full breadth of the Wavestation came into being.

A smart, smooth, rounded machine not unlike the Korg M1 in looks, the Wavestation first offers up sounds as Performances, items that respond on a single MIDI channel. On the earliest models, there are three banks of 50 Performances each: two in RAM and one in ROM. Performances are made up of Patches, which are themselves created by combining up to four oscillators, each complete with its own analog-style filtering, envelope-shaping and modulation parameters. Incredibly, you can use up to eight Patches in a single Performance. This might lead you to wonder how the Wavestation can cope with multitimbralism, because it's only 32-voice polyphonic. Indeed. This is not the instrument's strongest attribute.

At the patch stage comes the Wavestation's vectoring capability: An oscillator mix can be drawn using the joystick and the envelopes used to fade them in and out, with sections looped along the way. You don't need to limit yourself to blending oscillators at the same pitch, either. You can have great fun mixing harmonics or dissonants for madcap, arpeggio-type effects. Anyway, Vectoring can be as serious or as serendipitous as you like, with analytical approaches or blind, random waggling equally likely to throw up an interesting result.

Wavesequencing takes this concept and stretches it out over the time dimension, allowing you to create classic Wavestation patches, from those that glisten and shimmer their way through endless tonalities and textures (New Age heaven, in other words) to in-your-face drum and percussion grooves that actually "play" as you hold down a key. What you are doing is compiling a list of waves, plus a list of commands as to when each wave will start, how loud it will be, what its tuning will be, etc. Depending upon the type of wave chosen—a long, drawn-out one or a transient—and whether you crossfade between waves or not, you can achieve dramatically different results. Wavesequences can be clocked over MIDI. You can even wavesequence up a form of speech, using the many "vowel" sounds in waveform ROM. (Supposedly, senior Korg personnel were highly skeptical of this claim by programmers until one wag programmed up a message telling them to f*** off.)

Although the Wavestation programming system is generally understood by most with a loose knowledge of subtractive synthesis and some spirit of adventure, the occasional booby trap does lie in wait. The first involves the way in which the instrument organizes sounds. Each Performance bank can also hold 35 Patches and 332 Wavesequences. You can use a Patch stored in, say, Performance Bank 1—let's call the Patch "Guitary"—within any Performance stored in any of the Banks, internal or even on card. Let's say that your favorite Performance, in fact, is largely based upon the Guitary Patch.

In time, you are merrily trawling through the Patches looking for a suitable sound to insert into a new Performance, when you come across Guitary. "Nice," you think. "That's almost what I need. But I just need to tweak the attack on that second oscillator." And so you do. You use this edited version in your new Performance and you're very happy. Then you flip past your favorite Performance only to find—quelle horreur!—that it's changed. Yes, it is now based upon your edited Guitary. The original is gone.

The moral of this tale is to store everything, everywhere, every time. It's hard on the SysEx dumps, or the cards, which are expensive, but easy on the frustration level in the long run.

Wavestation programming is nothing if not great fun. On a very simple level, you can call up a Performance and simply substitute new Patches. Solo, a feature that isolates a Patch in this setting, is very useful.

It may take a little head scratching to figure out that when a Patch is in place within a Performance, it is actually called a "Part," and as such comes complete with its own volume, delay start time, unison or polyphonic play mode and MIDI controller responses. This does allow for some flexibility for the same Patch (as referred to in the tale above).

To get to the soul of the instrument, you need to program at the Patch level, where, having selected the starter waves from a pool of hundreds stored in ROM (365 on the original Wavestation, 484 on the EX), you can impose velocity-dependent pitch envelope modulation, do some lowpass filtering (there is an unusual parameter called "exciter," but no resonance as such, plus rate- and level-type envelope generators) and assign two LFOs.

The full list of capabilities is long and extremely comprehensive, but Korg does try to make things easy with such features as "All" (selects oscillators within a Patch so you can instantly address the entire sound while fiddling about with, say, the filter cutoff) and the macros, which are like little templates you can impose on a sound for envelope or filter settings.

As if this weren't enough, the Wavestation has a glittering array of built-in effects, provided by two 55-algorithm multieffects processors. Effects are applied at the Performance stage, and yes, you can interact with many an effects setting from the mod wheel, aftertouch or a foot controller.

And still there were complaints about the original Wavestation. Where's the piano sound? Where are the drum patches? It must have been mighty depressing for the design team to hear such bleatings. But strong men they were, and spanking new piano samples and drum programs duly appeared on the EX model. In the process, a few new effects algorithms were also added: a compressor/gate and some vocoders.

As for who uses this instrument, it's safe to say that anyone who can, does. Peter Gabriel had a unit permanently set up at Real World during the recording of *Us*, and most of the pads on Michael Jackson's *Dangerous* were Michael Boddicker Wavestation patches. From Genesis to Lee Ritenour to George Duke to Jan Hammer to lesser-known mortals like Paul Schutze, on *New Maps of Hell* and *Apart*, Wavestation has been smeared across a generation of recordings.

To close, a few brief words about the A/D and the SR. The two-unit A/D module is notable for its analog inputs, which allow you to process the signal from, say, a mic or direct from a guitar. And this is not just to make use of the splendid vocoding effects, either. An incoming signal is treated exactly as if it were one of the ROM starter waves. Very exciting for those who like life out on the audio edge!

If the two keyboard versions and the A/D represent just about the pinnacle of 1990s sound design possibilities, the Wavestation SR takes the raw material and bundles it up for predigested, preset performances.

Though the SR is fully programmable, to program this tiny module is like—and I make no apologies for repeating the analogy—painting a room by sticking the brush through the keyhole. Doing much more than playing the SR, even altering MIDI channels, is a headache-inducing pastime. But the SR is full to the brim with first-class Patches and Performances culled from the best that Korg's wizardish team of programmers, led by Jack Hotop, could muster. If you just want Wavestation sounds pure and simple (not at all!), then the SR is the weapon to choose.

The whole Wavestation series is classic in its own way. Sales may look insignificant compared to the M1 for Korg, but in terms of influence and professional use, it's Wavestation all the way.

Kurzweil 250 Digital keyboard sampler

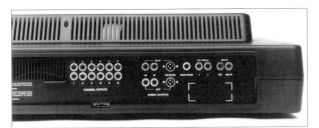

THE FAX

Keyboard:	88-note
Programs:	n/a
External storage:	Via Macattach software (see "Options")
Polyphony:	12-voice
Oscillators per voice:	n/a
Effects:	Chorus
Connections:	Stereo audio XLR/jacks, phones, MIDI, mic/line sample inputs, footswitches, computer port, sync, click
Dimensions:	1296mm x 294mm x 216mm
Weight:	43kg

THE FIGURES

Chief designers:	Ray Kurzweil, Bob Chidlaw, Larry Bodony, Chet Graham, Don Byrd, Neil Marshall
Production run:	1984-89
Approx. units sold:	3000
Options:	Sound Modeling Program, Sequencer RAM, keyboard stand, plexiglass music rack, fan, Macattach and later QLS (Quick Load System) offline sample storage software (250 Pedal Pod was standard)
Sounds:	Kurzweil Sound Blocks
Miscellaneous:	A keyboardless 250 module was produced as well, the K250RMX rack unit. Service and support in the U.S. from Sweetwater Sound: tel: (219) 432-8176

Orig. price (1984):	$16,675 (£10,062)
Price in 1996:	$2500-3500 (£2000-2500)

Sometimes it seems as if Stevie Wonder has single-handedly steered, and even funded, the synthesizer industry. Time and again, his name crops up as having requested this or inspired that. From the number of instruments this influential figure has been given, much less bought, there must be a storage facility somewhere in the United States fairly groaning with the carcasses of instruments he's owned or used at one time or another. And machines with the serial number 00001 could probably constitute a separate collection in themselves.

The Kurzweil 250 is another Stevie Wonder request job. But here the connection is rather more valid, stemming from Wonder's use of a revolutionary reading machine for the blind that scanned the written word and transferred the data into sound via a synthesized voice. The inventor was one Raymond Kurzweil. The gauntlet subsequently thrown down was to produce a music synthesizer with the richness of an acoustic instrument yet employing the latest, modern computer control. In 1984, Kurzweil and his team duly delivered this imposingly large sampling/sample replay keyboard, albeit at a price that only the likes of Stevie Wonder could ever hope to afford.

The Kurzweil 250 is a beautiful instrument to look at; its gently sloping panel is a nice mix of dedicated function and soft control buttons aided by a 10-digit keypad and small (tiny, in fact, by modern standards) display screen.

Pleasing to the eye, the 250's two main areas of focus are, in fact, the ear and the fingers. As a purveyor of samples, there is very little of that scrunched-up, over-compressed feel you certainly expect from an instrument of this vintage. With few exceptions, Kurzweil 250 sounds still ring out, have room to breathe and sound true, and with the keyboard's 256 levels of velocity sensing—far more than MIDI, in other words—the instrument is a pleasure to sit at and play. This is very impressive for the 10-bit machine that is the 250. According to the design team, the quality was achieved by "playing games" with the samples, making sure that the full complement of ten bits was always being employed. In other words, the signal is always swinging between full-scale positive and negative. Even on a piano sound that decays into silence, the processing stays at the same level using compression and expansion techniques. A VCA in front of the A/D chip responds to silence and compensates accordingly.

Out of the box, the 250 arrived with 36 ROM-based sounds in what Kurzweil called the "base block." Additional "sound blocks" can be inserted,

KURZWEIL™

Music Systems

Name:	Kurzweil (Young Chang)
Head Office:	Akki Korea, Seoul/Inchon, Rep. of Korea; tel: 82 2-777-0381
U.S. Distributor:	Young Chang America: 13336 Alondra Blvd.; Cerritos, CA 90701; tel: (310) 926-3200
UK Distributor:	Kurzweil c/o Washburn UK: 15, Amor Way; Letchworth, Herts SG6 1UG UK; tel: 01462-482446
Founded:	1982 (acquired by Young Chang in 1990)
Business:	Samplers, synthesizers, digital pianos, master keyboards

American musical instrument companies tend to be either followers of the open, ultra welcoming school of behavior a la E-mu or Peavey or completely aloof and mysterious like New England Digital...or Kurzweil.

Kurzweil Music Systems was founded in Waltham, Massachusetts, by its namesake, Raymond Kurzweil, in 1982, with the express purpose of building what became the Kurzweil 250, a top-quality keyboard instrument based upon sampling technology.

The company was built upon inordinate amounts of venture capital that had been extracted out of eager investors by Raymond Kurzweil's beguiling mix of soft sell and stratospheric technical claims. When first planned, the K250 was designed to sell at $4,000, but in order to meet the avalanche of advance hype, the instrument finally came in at around $16,000.

A tricky game, that, but one that nonetheless produced a beautiful instrument—indeed, one upon which the entire catalog of Kurzweil products was based for the next eight years.

The K250 was a deserved success, but where to go from there? Essentially, the K250 was first sliced up into its various "Sound Block" components, which were released as a number of dedicated instrument-type modules—a trend that is only now coming into fashion in the mid-1990s. Along the way, Bob Moog was recruited as "chief scientist," whatever that was supposed to mean, and the company subsequently dipped into waters such as master keyboards and even home keyboards.

But there was no real plan. It seems that Raymond Kurzweil was a bit of a loose cannon, and by 1990, with massive debts and no major successes since the K250, rescue was desperately sought. Finally, Young Chang put together a rescue package that gave the company the trading name, stock and staff of Kurzweil but not the millions of dollars' worth of debts. Young Chang licensed Kurzweil Music Systems and its technology on an ongoing royalty basis, leaving KMS to deal with the debts.

Young Chang's production know-how and cash allowed Kurzweil to flourish into a major force in the keyboard industry, marketing the stunningly successful K2000 (in development during the switch to Young Chang), nurturing the K2500 and new master keyboards and expanding Kurzweil's range into high-quality home keyboards and pianos. A temporary glitch occurred a few years after the license agreement, when the new owners decided the current technology was sufficiently new for royalties to no longer be applicable (read "payable"). As with the Sequential/E-mu commotion over Prophet-5 royalties a decade earlier, in came the lawyers, followed by, sensibly, an out-of-court settlement. The details of the settlement are not available, but apparently royalties are no longer an issue of contention.

Free from all the demons of its past, Kurweil's future looks particularly sunny. The mix of American technology and Korean capitol is a heady one to which Kurzweil's rivals in the music industry are increasingly having to pay attention.

providing a large number of instruments that can be configured into an even larger number of presets or variables. Included in the base block is the now-legendary concert grand piano (supposedly Stevie Wonder was not able to tell it from a real acoustic grand, even when he played the instrument—well, I doubt that...) and some superb strings (violin, viola, cello), plus basses and percussion sounds. All are immediately on tap and can simply be punched up and played, yet they can also be redefined in terms of splits and layers.

Bob Chidlaw, in charge of the sound recording, confesses that the supposedly singular grand piano was in fact something of a hybrid. Initially, a seven-foot Steinway grand was recorded, and then the recordings were copied from analog tape to analog tape. Not surprisingly, these recordings were ultimately felt to be too hissy, so the team went back and recorded more pianos, primarily a nine-foot Steinway, on Sony F1. All fine and dandy, except that the digital recording didn't have the warmth and tonal quality of the first recording. In desperation, Childaw went back and designed a program—which he dearly wishes he'd patented, of course, but didn't—to remove hiss from tape so the final sound could be assembled.

Even so, the grand piano sample is an amalgam of several nine-foot Steinways in the bass (except for one note, which is from a seven-foot!), a seven-foot Steinway in the midrange and another nine-foot instrument in the high registers. The sample became known as the Frankensteinway at the factory. Another key sample was the so-named Marcarto strings; no one seems to remember exactly who these scrubbing fiddle players were, but members of the Boston Pops orchestra were often used on Kurzweil's monthly forays into the New England studios.

Though the 250 is regarded as a sampler, actual user sampling was not offered on the earliest models, and even by the end of its career, when it could sample up to ten seconds at 50kHz, this required the use of an external Macintosh. There was never even a disk drive on the 250.

But once you implement the Sound Modeling program, the 250 becomes capable of truncating samples, looping, tuning, velocity crossfading and multisampling—all modest by modern standards, perhaps, but quite sufficient for adding custom sounds to Kurzweil's impressive sound library. Once resident as a mapped sample, a sound can be processed using stereo chorusing (a true sample-on-sample effect and a firm favorite among users, though an inevitable polyphony-eater), a multistage envelope generator (quoted as having 256 segments, though surely no one ever went this far), pitch modulation and numerous keyboard triggering modes and layering options (up to six). Among the instrument's many helpful "real world" features and functions are a variety of transposition types, from broad to chromatic to timbre shift, which is excellent for tweaking a little extra brightness out of a sound.

As with all samplers, though, the 250's strength soon meant the depth of its sound library. Kurzweil produced a body of work that long supersedes the actual instrument. Much like E-mu's EIII-to-Proteus connection, Kurzweil 250 samples went on to fill a succession of dedicated instrument sound modules (HX, PX, etc.) and even swelled the wavetables of the K2000 synth and its library.

One of the 250's most common resting places has been in the film and TV world, where composers have developed a strong affinity for the instrument's range of lush textures and smooth, 88-note, piano-style keyboard. Michael Kamen (*Robin Hood*, *Die Hard*, *Brazil*, *Someone to Watch Over Me*) has been a committed 250 user, and even Paul Shaffer continues to keep a 250 on tap for the *Late Night With David Letterman* show.

As with high-end E-mu sampler customers, many less illustrious investors in the 250 have gone on record as saying they earned their money back, in a matter of days, in some instances.

The 250 comes complete with an onboard sequencer, though it was limited to 12 tracks even by the end, but Version 5 software provided separate audio outputs, full multitimbral voice-to-channel assignments, additional channel-stealing facilities (which help fool you into thinking there's more than 12-voice polyphony at hand) and implementation of MIDI PC transmission. It has a capacity of 12,000 notes, plus quantize, punch in and out, looping, track copy and event editing; you can sync to tape via MIDI or via a variable-rate tape sync. Neither SMPTE nor MTC were ever introduced, though.

The 250 was Kurzweil's debut product, launched in a swell of venture capitol and enough hype to drown in, with phrases like "contoured sound modeling" and "artificial intelligence" sprinkled about like confetti. All complete nonsense, of course, but it imbued both instrument and company with an all-important mystique that even now, a dozen years later, is still somewhat in evidence.

Judged as a self-contained sampler, the 250 never reached the level of top-of-the-range Akais or E-mus, but it is more than a sampler. Part of Stevie Wonder's brief was to produce a musical instrument, and the 250 still feels and sounds like one, outdated and obsolete though much of the technology has now become.

Kurzweil K2000 — Digital polyphonic synthesizer

THE FAX

Keyboard:	61-note
Programs:	200 ROM, 200 RAM
External storage:	3½" disk drive
Polyphony:	24-voice
Oscillators per voice:	4
Effects:	Multieffects processor
Connections:	Stereo audio, plus 4 separate audio, SCSI, analog in, optical in, digital I/O (AES-EBU and S/PDIF formats)
Dimensions:	984mm x 336mm x 96mm
Weight:	11.9kg

THE FIGURES

Chief designers:	Bob Chidlaw, John Teele, Ralph Muh, Geoff Winton, Mitch Dale, Tim Thompson, Jo Lerarei, Jennifer Hruska
Production run:	1991-present
Approx. units sold:	No figures available
Options:	SMP Stereo Sampling Option, P-RAM, Soundblock 1 & 2 (with daughterboard), Fan Kit, V3 software.
Sounds:	Kurzweil Sound Library (Percussion, Mixed Bag, Film Score, Orchestral Sample, Public Domain, Theater Organ, Best Analog Patches, General MIDI); also from Eye + I, Stratus Sounds, Sound Source, Pro Rec, Voice Crystal, Kid Nepro
Miscellaneous:	Kurzweil Users Group (KOG): 5451 Watercress Pl.; Columbia, MD 21045-2455; tel: (410) 964-3548
Price in 1996:	$1500-2500 (£1500-2000): prices depend on options

Hype is the lifeblood of the synthesizer industry. Whether it's about specifications, applications, users or life expectancy, exaggeration is the industry's stock in trade. When Kurzweil trailed the K2000 in 1991, the hype was rampant. At the time, Kurzweil was emerging from a period of confusion and had just been acquired by Korean company Young Chang. Pundits were impressed with the specs being thrown around, but most were rather less inclined to swallow the brags about continual upgradability and how obsolescence was built out.

But fair's fair. As I write, the K2000 shows no signs of flagging. It remains rampantly popular in America and widely used elsewhere. Superseded by the K2500, maybe, but definitely not replaced. In an age when the synthesizer market is widely perceived as having collapsed, the Kurzweil K2000 is one of the rare beacons of success.

In general, it is wise to be skeptical about instruments that claim to be all things to all people. The phrase "jack of all trades" (and master of none, if this epithet has escaped your attention) sums it up. But although the K2000 has a first-rate synthesis engine; can load in and process samples; and even has a multitrack, Standard MIDI File format playback sequencer, it manages to cover all three with considerable élan.

The aptly named VAST (Variable Architecture Synthesis Technology) allows you to configure the editing parameters in a variety of different ways to suit a particular sound or application. There are 31 different "algorithms" containing what Kurzweil calls "blocks," through which the signal flows from basic sample to final output. Blocks comprise parameter groups such as filters (of which there are an amazing variety, from one-, two- or four-pole lowpass with resonance to highpass, notch, bandpass and more), amplifiers, parametric EQ and the like, each capable of being modulated separately by a mod source such as keyboard velocity, mod wheel or keyboard tracking. In simpler terms, the K2000 lets you use its large tool chest of edit parameters as you want and in the order you want.

Though it can sound analog, the K2000 is, in fact, an all-digital machine (as the sparkle of its filters might suggest). Bob Chidlaw, in charge of the DSP, freely admits that most of the design was done visually, without actually listening to what was going on. "How on earth did you do this?" he was asked later. "Used good stuff," came the admirably succinct reply.

The good stuff Chidlaw refers to is not only components, of course, but also the quality of the waveform ROM that lies at the heart of the instrument. The K2000 is not just a "buy your waveform ROM here" machine, mind you, that simply gives or sells you slabs of samples from the factory. In addition to the internal 8MB of waveform ROM (plus optional 16MB ROM soundblocks), you can load in and process samples much as you would on a dedicated sampler. Even more generously, samples can be either recordings you take or sounds purloined from the libraries of other manufacturers.

Although the K2000 is but 24-voice polyphonic, you can layer up to four sound sources within a program and still retain full polyphony. There are, accordingly, 96 "oscillators" onboard.

The K2000 is an unusually deep and sophisticated instrument, but wisely, it doesn't compel you to take a university course before you can have great fun with the instrument. The user interface, with its large screen, soft keys and mode select buttons, lets you accomplish almost any day-to-day job, like selecting

new sounds, changing MIDI channels, even doing basic editing, without having to resort to the manual. (Kurzweil also provides a free video manual, in fact.)

There is a single, stereo multieffects processor, based on a Digitech chip, which has some 47 preset effects while offering the chance to modify and store a further 80, using 26 effects algorithms. The effects themselves cover chorus, reverbs, delays, EQ and flanging, and up to four effects can be applied simultaneously. However, with but one effects chip, there is no completely satisfactory solution to the age-old problem of single sound effects disappearing in a multitimbral setting. The K2000's answer is to select (or edit) sounds that employ algorithms that offer the panner or mixed amps parameters, which will then allow you to remove or apply your own level of effects for each program.

Until recently, this problem has not been as great as it would be on a self-proclaimed "workstation," where you are more likely to want to remain in this one environment. However, the K2000's sequencer, previously only capable of playing back full 16-track Standard MIDI Files with scratchpad recording facilities (essentially, one-track record with continual overdubbing), has now, on Version 3 software, bloomed into a powerful workstation utility. With V3 in tow, the sequencer becomes a 32-track real-, pattern- and step-time recording device, with variable quantize and full note/data edit facilities, event edit lists, nondestructive editing and even performance gadgets like the ability to trigger sequences from the keyboard.

In keeping with the Kurzweil's go anywhere/do anything philosophy, you can buy a K2000 in a number of different versions depending upon how you like to work. A plain K2000 keyboard (there is also a rack version) can have its sample memory upgraded to a full 64MB via cost-effective SIMMs, which let you load in and process a huge amount of sample data to use as, or as the basis for, your sounds. If you want to record samples yourself, you can then buy the SMP sampling option, which hooks up stereo sampling inputs, both analog and digital. K2000S models come preloaded with the user-sampling facility.

On to the thorny question of compatibility. Although Kurzweil's sound library is extensive, it would be nice, would it not, to be able to load in that killer string sample you acquired when you worked on an Akai S900 three hundred years ago?

Well, you can. The K2000 lets you load in—via floppies—sample disks from other manufacturers with a reasonably seamless transition. Formats supported include Akai (from S3000 to S900) and Ensoniq (from EPS to ASR). The K2000 can read raw sample data, sample start and end points/loops, tuning and keyboard mapping. What it cannot read are filtering and envelope assignments. Typically, then, what you will need to do after loading in that killer S900 string sample is reprogram the envelope (or if you're feeling lazy, copy one from another string-like program you already have in your machine). Over SCSI, the K2000 can also read Roland sample data. E-mu? Nada. All things considered, though, this is highly impressive stuff.

The only area of slight disappointment is the keyboard, which, though velocity- and release velocity-sensitive, has a very light action. This is strange, in a way, because Kurzweil has gone to inordinate trouble to offer every conceivable performance device—as in velocity control over *anything* to an assignable controller, no less than 17 velocity scalings and modulation routings to die for.

What does a K2000 sound like? In a random selection of words: big, American, fusion-friendly, analog, digital. The K2000 is big on textures. Kurzweil has been a favorite with the film fraternity since the 250 sampler, and the K2000 has an equally multifaceted "filmic" quality to it.

One of the very rare modern classics.

Logan String Melody   String machine

THE FAX

Keyboard:	49-note
Programs:	5
External storage:	None
Polyphony:	Full
Oscillators per voice:	n/a
Effects:	Chorus
Connections:	Mono audio
Dimensions:	900mm x 350mm x 80mm
Weight:	10kg

THE FIGURES

Chief designer:	Unknown
Production run:	1973-76 (as String Melody II until 1979)
Approx. units sold:	5000
Options:	Pedals
Sounds:	n/a
Miscellaneous:	A classic workhorse keyboard from the pre-polyphonic synth era
Orig. price (1973):	$800 (£500)
Price in 1996:	$200 (£80)

A Logan "string machine" (as they were referred to) ruled the roost of string-part simulation in the mid-1970s. In Britain, if you could afford Ken Freeman personally on a session with his own string contraption, you most certainly did just that. But those who could not and did not have sufficient record company advances to buy a Mellotron used a Logan String Melody.

Chances are String Melodys survived in reasonable numbers because they were sturdily built, the

casing covered in Tolex and topped with a thick wood veneer. The controls comprise string sliders—which sit on a flat area of control panel beneath the keyboard and mix the levels of various stringed instruments, from bass to cello to viola to violin to a percussion (attack) control—push-buttons for additional or modifying tones (mounted on the edge between the keyboard and the flat top) and very basic envelope sliders for each keyboard "half."

The bass and cello sliders activate sound over the bottom half of the keyboard only, which is a sensible limitation. You can elicit a respectable plucked string bass by slamming percussion full on. Individually, the four string sounds are quite passable. Collectively, although two of them occupy their own slice of keyboard, the sound tends to mush up in an irksome, metallic fashion.

Tones can be augmented (or substituted) with an organ tone or an accordion tone and processed using the heavily vibratoed "solo" or one of two choruses. In either keyboard half, sounds can be tailored by their own attack and sustain sliders, with sustain functioning more like decay.

Although this is a well-planned layout, there were limiting factors obvious even at the time. Mainly, these concern the add-on processing controls that strut their stuff over everything played in both right- and left-hand sections, which is not necessarily going to be the effect you're after.

Many years down the line, this may seem a little churlish. The Logan String Melody is only going to cost a few...well, *anythings*, and you'll buy it for the authentic '70s "string synth" sound that it was largely responsible for creating.

A successful instrument in its day (a long one, of course), with a distinctive, influential sound, String Melodys are not especially collectible as of this writing.

Logan is no longer in business.

Mellotron Mark II & 400
Orchestral keyboard

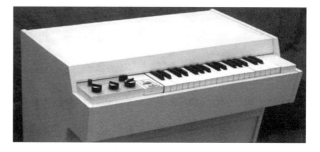

THE FAX

Keyboard:	2 x 35-note (Mark II)
Programs:	3 x 6 sounds (Mark II); 3 sounds (Model 400) at any one time

External storage:	Tapes
Polyphony:	Full
Oscillators per voice:	n/a
Effects:	Spring reverb
Connections:	External speaker (Mark II), high-impedance audio out (Model 400)
Dimensions:	1224mm x 625mm x 940mm (Mark II); 530mm x 820mm x 820mm (Model 400)
Weight:	138kg (Mark II); 55kg (Model 400)
Mellotron Archives (U.S.):	11044 Burbank Blvd., Suite 200; N. Hollywood, CA 01601; tel: (818) 754-1191
Mellotron Archives UK:	tel: (01) 889-22211

THE FIGURES

Chief designer:	Les Bradley, Harry Chamberlin
Production run:	Mark II: 1964-68; Model 400: 1970-1977
Approx. units sold:	Mark II: 300; Model 400: 2000
Options:	Model 400 only: tape frame case ($350), Protect-o-Muff (padded case), pedal, ¼" tape conversion kit, SMS 4 MR Motor Control System ($350)
Sounds:	S1-8 Violins, W1-W5 Woodwind Instruments, B1-8 Brass, V1-5 Voices, O1-3 Organs, AP1-11 Acoustic Percussion instruments, EP1-10 Electronic Percussion Instruments, SFX
Miscellaneous:	A Mellotron tribute album, *The Rime of the Ancient Sampler,* features tracks by Patrick Moraz, Mike Pinder, David Cross and...Julian Colbeck, among others. *Mellotron* by Mike Pinder is an Akai-format CD-ROM of Mellotron samples.
Orig. price (1964):	Mark II: $1500 (£1000); Model 400: $4000 (£850)
Price in 1996:	Mark II: $4000-5000 (£4000+); Model 400: $2500 (£2500): prices are for fully reconditioned models

To give one of these leviathan British precursors of the sampler classic status over the other has defeated me. Given the oddball nature of this instrument, its creator and most of its users, it seems somehow appropriate that an oddball double review has provided the solution.

Oh, the Mellotron. Wherever it goes, it always spells trouble.

I'll admit to finding this entry daunting. This is not an instrument I have owned. Nor have I ever officially reviewed a Mellotron. I have played one as a professional keyboardist from time to time. I have even contributed to the 1993 "Mellotron album," *The Rime of the Ancient Sampler.* Hell, I have even worked with prime Mellotron aficionado Steve Hackett these past five years. But I am not familiar with the Mellotron. Not so as to hope to compete with this instrument's many fanatical followers around the world, who can freely converse in Mellotron chain mechanisms or tape widths—and who can not only quote chapter and verse on Mellotron statistics and memorabilia, but who are *only* interested in Mellotrons. Not vintage keyboards in general, just Mellotrons. Beginning and end of story.

A singular instrument with a singular following,

history has accorded the Mellotron classic British status, a sort of musical equivalent of the London taxi—and not far off in weight, either. But in fairness, the kernel, if not a large part of the shell, of the idea hailed from America, from Harry Chamberlin's eponymous invention built in tiny quantities in California during the early 1960s.

The concept (freely, it seems, adopted and then adapted by a trio of brothers named Bradley in the British midlands) involves producing sound by triggering tape loops. With each key depression, a tape corresponding to that note is stirred into action and "played." The tapes are actual recordings of real people playing real instruments. The strings, for instance, were a collection of genteel ladies from the home counties. (Lord knows how they felt about their sweet bowing being plastered over Led Zeppelin's satanic ramblings in the early 1970s. Perhaps they'd have asked for royalties?)

This ingenious analog system predates but covers precisely the same territory as digital sampling. If the Emulator is the father of sampling, the Mellotron is its great-uncle.

When the Bradleys produced their first Mellotron (the Mark I) in 1962, keyboard players were either organists or piano players. The word "synthesizer" existed only in the rarefied world of academe. Things were no different in 1964, when the Mark II came out, and the opportunity to play theoretically unlimited sounds (you could buy new sounds, or even put your own recordings onto the special Mellotron tapes) polyphonically on a keyboard was little short of science fiction. Like the Fairlight two decades later, the Mellotron had "must have" appeal to the top bands of the day, from The Beatles ("Strawberry Fields Forever") to the Moody Blues to the Beach Boys to the Rolling Stones; the Mellotron was the instrument to be seen with.

The Mark II is on a par with Jethro Tull's (the man, not the group) Seed Drill or some devilish contraption out of a Monty Python cartoon. Things whir and whiz, tapes slither about on their loom-like frame and out comes a concoction of noises that is at the same time absurd and miraculous. To play the aforementioned strings here in the 1990s and realize that what you are hearing now was recorded and played a third of a century ago is strangely moving. The sound quality, though frequently mismatched from note to note because each note is a different recording and a different piece of tape, is often breathtaking. Mellotron "samples" are around eight seconds in duration, over which time it's fair to expect some wavering of tone, tune and volume, but the quality, in terms of being lifelike and having a richness of timbre, can still be an object lesson to most 16-bit digital samplers.

The Mark II looks like a very smart piece of church furniture: polished wood cabinet; dual keyboards placed side by side; a smattering of large, businesslike controls... The whole thing is almost unmovably heavy. Like an eerie glimpse at what both samplers and home keyboards would go on to offer some 20 or 30 years later, the left-hand keyboard was used to trigger a number of recorded rhythms and accompaniment patterns. The right-hand keyboard was used for normal playing. The design, with its built-in amplification and speakers and built-in spring reverb, screams "home entertainment system," even though it was the pop market that embraced the concept. (The pop market was not specifically targeted until the subsequent Mellotron 400.)

The Mark II offers some control in terms of volume and pitch (tape speed), and at any one time three sounds can be called up from a single strand of tape. Six actual banks of sounds can be push-button-selected from the control panel, though you must be careful not to do this in midsound or the tapes will shred.

Because the Mark II was the first vaguely feasible Mellotron to hit the market, this was the model snapped up by eager studios, keyboard players, TV stations and the odd showbiz personality (Peter Sellers, for one). One of its most famous performances was the opening section to Genesis' "Watcher of the Skies," where an amalgam of strings and brass in the right hand and the unlikely but highly effective bass accordion in the left provided the segment with its dense, dark and almost frightening quality. Other classic Mellotron sounds include the flutes (they can be heard on the opening of The Beatles' "Strawberry Fields Forever") and the various male and female choirs.

Mark IIs have become highly collectible, not just because they are rare, but because the chances are good that a surviving instrument will have an association with a famous player or recording. The above price guide rates a model with no illustrious provenance; it should be noted that Bill Wyman's Mark II, used on the Stones' "2000 Light Years From Home," was on auction in the UK in 1995 with a £7000-8000 ($12,000) price estimate.

The Mark II was notoriously tricky to keep in working order in the 1960s and frankly is little better today. Rather more streamlined and, as such, rather more viable, the Model 400 appeared in 1970 as a comparatively portable, single-manual instrument on which just three sounds could be accessed at any one time, on a single bank of tapes. In order to play more sounds—and many were produced—you'd have to whip off the back and insert a new rack of tapes. Further streamlining included the removal of internal amplification and spring reverb, but you can still alter volume, tone and tape speed.

The Mellotron's relevance in today's music-making is unquestionably related to the sound rather than the instrument itself. Whether you can capture the sound without having the instrument breathing its 2-bit (a joke!) sound quality out at you is another matter. In order to sound anywhere near convincing, a sample must be of the full duration (about eight seconds). Shorter loops make nonsense of the Mellotron's distinctive undulations and tonal waverings.

The Mellotron's relevance to the serious collector is another matter. Mellotron Archives, which even has a subsidiary in the UK run by the redoubtable Martin Smith (of *The Rime of the Ancient Sampler* fame), not only restores and rebuilds Mellotrons but also carries a full set of tapes for both Mellotron and Chamberlin instruments.

While a full-scale Mellotron revival seems a little fanciful, interest in these classic instruments shows no signs of abating. Be prepared for continual servicing and tinkering, but these, the musical equivalent of steam traction engines, will surely endure as collectible and talked-about items for as long as people remain interested in pop culture.

Moog Memorymoog
Analog polyphonic synthesizer

THE FAX

Keyboard:	61-note
Programs:	100
External storage:	Cassette interface
Polyphony:	6-voice
Oscillators per voice:	3
Effects:	Arpeggiator
Connections:	2 mono audio, CV, gate, S-trig outputs, CV input, clock in, program up/down, release, hold pedal inputs, cassette
Dimensions:	1016mm x 467mm x 165mm
Weight:	17.2kg
Big Briar Inc.:	Rt. 3, Box 115A1; Leicester, NC 28748; tel: (704) 683-9085

THE FIGURES

Chief designers:	Rich Walborn, Ray Caster
Production run:	1982-85
Approx. units sold:	3500
Options:	Lintronics MIDI upgrade from Big Briar (see

	"THE FAX"), footpedals
Sounds:	Moog alternate preset cassette, Dr. Sound, Walt Whitney
Miscellaneous:	Expensive? The Memorymoog contains $900 worth of components alone!
Orig. price (1982):	$4795 (£3676)
Price in 1996:	$1500 (£1500+)

Everyone loves a Minimoog, but the Memorymoog has people divided. Quite strongly. There are users and aficionados who revere this instrument, who find it capable of extraordinary power yet subtlety and who, in the mid-1990s, continue to work with and use it on a regular basis. Then there are those who view Moog's parting shot as having passed its sell-by date before its release: using old technology, scrappily put together and riddled with imperfections. I'm afraid I'm inclined toward the latter, but my innate sense of fair play is seeing to it that this instrument takes its place in the Hot 100 as a classic of its type.

This is the true polyphonic heir to the Minimoog (forget the Polymoog—please). The Memorymoog's voice architecture is remarkably similar to the Mini's: three oscillators per voice, with hard-sync option between osc 1 and 2 and the third usable in low-frequency mode; time-honored 24dB/oct lowpass filtering with dedicated ADSR envelope generator; well-equipped LFO; noise; and plenty of mode and triggering options, including end-of-the-world, 18-oscillator unison.

So what's wrong with that?

If it all worked just fine and stayed in tune and MIDI hadn't reared its sweet head midway through the design process, nothing. But reliability was the Memorymoog's downfall, and it must have helped and hastened the downfall of the Moog company itself. Yet the Memorymoog was not left stranded after Moog's demise, and here in the 1990s, the instrument is probably enjoying a period of greater stability (in all senses) than at any other time, well catered to by companies and fixits.

The busy anodized-aluminum control panel is carefully sectioned off into areas called Oscillators, Filters, Modulation, etc., making the instrument smooth sailing as far as knowing where to lunge for what. Programming controls occupy three-quarters of the front panel, the remainder is taken up by controllers and their assignments—footpedals, portamento, arpeggiator, displays and a keypad.

The arpeggiator has been a particular hit with the dance fraternity: You can set up and latch a pattern, transpose it freely by pressing new keys and then make real-time changes to the sound using panel controls—increase modulation, alter filter cutoff, etc. British synth composer Mark Shrieve is a specialist at such capers on a Memorymoog.

Though the Memorymoog is rightly noted for strong, deep, large-scale sounds, it is also capable of great subtlety and expression. The ability to use the third oscillator as an audio source or a low-frequency modulation source (as on the Minimoog) can take much of the credit for this, especially when employed for cross-modulation to introduce interesting overtones and harmonics. The 24dB/oct lowpass filtering, too, is razor sharp and has a variety of keyboard tracking strengths.

The flexible third-oscillator modulation option is enhanced by its wide range of modulation destinations (pitch of either dedicated audio oscillator, pulse width, filter cutoff), and the filter's envelope generator can, in turn, control the amount of osc 3's modulation.

All of these combine to make a very expressive instrument, which is all the more impressive because many aspects of the instrument are under- or unspecified. The Memorymoog was released shortly before MIDI and just before the collapse of Moog Music; you should be aware that the keyboard does not respond to velocity and that MIDI was only implemented on the Memorymoog Plus or as a retrofit on early units. Either way, there is no multitimbral capability. Why no velocity keyboard? It seems that Moog stalwart Dave Luce experimented with keyboard velocity, using a ring oscillator system built under the keyboard that extracted a control voltage. It was fast, but it necessitated redesigning the contour generators, and for that, sadly, there was simply no time.

However, this much-loved beast has on its side the Lintronics Advanced Memorymoog Modification, a comprehensive upgrade and MIDI implementation that not only plants MIDI but grants control change status to most of the front-panel knobs and switches. This means, for instance, that you can tweak in real time and have those real-time sound changes recorded and subsequently played back from a MIDI sequencer. For diehard Memorymoog fans, this admittedly pricey upgrade will be like the second coming. Further delights of the upgrade include program data transference via SysEx, some user interface and tone-production enhancements and, it is said, "dramatic improvement" in tuning stability. Amen to that one, at any rate.

One of the Memorymoog's more curious implementations is the security code, designed as a failsafe to protect programs from being accidentally erased as users whir around the control panel stabbing this and pulling that (quite a typical scenario, in my experience).

Never cheap, and with a LAMM upgrade, horrendously expensive, the Memorymoog is (for the time being at any rate) the final instrument bearing the Moog name. Ironically, Bob Moog, who had noth-

Name: Moog Music

Founded: 1995 (Moog Music from 1965-1973, thereafter part of Norlin)

Business: Synthesizers, synthesizer components

As of writing, there exists confusion over the current rights to the Moog trademark and designs. Bob Moog himself runs a company called Big Briar that manufactures Theremins plus carries out modifications to certain Moog instruments. Though Bob has no current involvement in any company styling itself as "Moog," a number of companies incorporating this name have arisen in the 1990s, all of which generally claim to own such rights as are available to produce or reproduce Moog instruments.

Frankly, this is a minefield that *Keyfax* cares not to tread across. Hopefully, a clear and undisputed "new Moog company" will appear in due course, but for the moment, the case remains one of *caveat emptor*.

Bob Moog, a Ph.D. graduate of Cornell University, more or less fell into the business of building synthesizers, having grown up building Theramin kits as a semi-paying hobby. Moog's interest and obvious ability to produce musically appealing sounds electronically was part of a general awareness of the potential of electronic music (a "network of the imagination," as Moog calls it) that developed in the early 1960s.

For a while, Moog's cottage industry building modular synthesizers, notably the giant 3C modules, was a steady, comfortable business. The company sold all the units it could produce, selling mainly custom designs, or at least custom systems, to universities, electronic music studios and composers. One such composer was Wendy (then Walter) Carlos. In 1968, Carlos released the seminal *Switched on Bach* recordings, which single-handedly thrust the word "synthesizer" into the mainstream of musical language.

Switched on Bach did wonders for synthesizers and initially for Moog, whose modules Carlos was using. But it proved a mixed blessing. Within a year it seemed the whole record industry was synthesizer-crazy, indeed Moog-crazy; Moog records and groups were everywhere.

Then the awful truth became apparent: It wasn't the Moog, or even synthesizers, that sounded so great; it was Carlos. *Switched on Bach* could have been recorded using toilet paper and a comb, such was Carlos' painstaking musicality. The records that flooded the market in 1969 revealed the synthesizer for what it really was: horribly limited, complex, capable of almost no expression and very difficult to control.

As quickly as the Moog sound came, it went, and along with it went the chances of Bob Moog's company growing and becoming a viable operation. Staring at a disastrous shortfall of cash, Moog was rescued by an opportunistic businessman named Bill Waytena, who moved the company to, in Bob Moog's words, a "shithole" factory in Buffalo, New York, and slowly fattened up the order book in order to sell it for a profit, which he

did in 1973, to the giant distribution company Norlin.

During this period, Dr. Moog and fellow designers Jim Scott and Bill Hemsath put together the Minimoog, an instrument that regular musicians—once the dust from *Switched on Bach* had settled— welcomed as the next logical, necessary step in synth design. The Minimoog was highly successful and indeed established the synthesizer as a bona fide musical instrument that could be sold in music stores and played in bands.

As part of the Norlin buyout, Bob Moog had to remain *in situ* for four years, which he did, though fairly reluctantly. (Moog is a designer and theoretician, and the constraints of marketing and corporate strategies did not fit him well.)

The success of the Minimoog established Moog at the forefront of the new synthesizer industry. Even so, it was many years before a line of new instruments appeared, by which time Bob Moog himself was long gone. Monophonic instruments like the Micromoog, Multimoog, Source and Prodigy, all sold in respectable quantities, and the company was one of the first to crack the tough nut of polyphony, albeit with the nightmarish (a deeply personal opinion, this) Polymoog.

When Moog started there was no competition. By the 1980s, not only was there domestic competition in the shape of California entrepreneurs like Sequential, Oberheim and E-mu, but the Japanese had come of age, with Roland, Yamaha and Korg all beginning to produce more controllable, more flexible and less expensive instruments with every release.

In a world eagerly looking forward to inexpensive, stable polyphony, microprocessor control and even digital synthesis techniques, the brightly colored Source and its digital access control offered a fascinating glimpse into the future, but for the most part Moog somehow became stuck in monophonic analog-land. The Memorymoog, the company's final act, proved a notoriously difficult birth and was riddled with technical problems. Shortly after the Memorymoog's release, the curtain came down on Moog as an ongoing brand, and that was that.

Until 1995, that is, when the worldly goods of the company were purchased at auction and it was re-established as Moog Music Technology. As of this writing, it is too early to say what MMT is hoping to achieve— whether it will simply service and supply customers who own older Moog instruments or whether it will find the necessary capital to go into production with new products.

Bob Moog is not associated with Moog Music Technology; his current company is Big Briar Inc. Their business includes building Theremins and, ironically, installing upgrade kits for the Memorymoog—an instrument in whose design Bob played no part.

The name Moog will remain synonymous with synthesizers because it was the first. Both with and without Bob Moog on the team, the company produced many superb instruments. If it had been taken over by a Japanese or Korean company in the 1980s, I suspect the brand would have gone from strength to strength. As it is, Moog Music is a song with a beginning and an end, though now with an intriguing coda as well.

ing to do with the original design aside from providing the inspiration for the Minimoog, is the man to turn to for the LAMM upgrade, which is undertaken by Moog's Big Briar Inc. in North Carolina. A word of warning to prospective buyers: Test the whole unit very thoroughly, since as we speak, the availability of Curtis chips, which the Memorymoog employs, may soon be drawing to a close.

Moog Minimoog

Analog monophonic synthesizer

THE FAX

Keyboard:	44-note
Programs:	None
External storage:	None
Polyphony:	Monophonic

Oscillators per voice:	3
Effects:	None
Connections:	Mono out, headphones, CV, S-trigger, audio in
Dimensions:	750mm x 400mm x 375mm
Weight:	6kg
Big Briar Inc.:	Rt. 3, Box 115A1; Leicester, NC 28748; tel: (704) 683-9085

THE FIGURES

Chief designers:	Bob Moog, Jim Scott, Bill Hemsath
Production run:	1970-1982
Approx. units sold:	13,000
Options:	Lintronics Minimoog MIDI Interface from Big Briar (see "THE FAX")
Sounds:	None commercially available
Orig. price (1970):	$1495 (£1150)
Price in 1996:	$750-1500 (£500-700)

Ask the man on the street to name a synthesizer and most will still say—many, many years after the last of Dr. Robert's babies trundled off the production line in upstate New York—"Moog."

Perhaps it's the name, which sounds suitably mysterious and exotic and which people like pronouncing (or perennially mispronouncing; it should rhyme with "vogue"). Perhaps it was Bob Moog himself: a likable, avuncular character full of wit, charm and musical insight and an excellent spokesman for the burgeoning synthesizer industry. Perhaps it was the sterling sales efforts of Moog's super-salesman David Van Koevering, whom Bob Moog himself credits with getting this newfangled contraption into music stores in the first place. Perhaps Moog synthesizers just sounded better that anyone else's.

Or perhaps it was just that Moog got there first. The Minimoog was by no means the first synthesizer, of course, but it was the first synthesizer manufactured for and priced specifically for musicians, as opposed to electronic music studios or universities. For the keyboard player, synthesis arrived with the Minimoog.

The Minimoog is indisputably a wonderful instrument to play. It is simple to understand, yet enormously powerful. Its range of sounds and applications are still almost unmatchable within their own specific areas. Want the fattest, fruitiest bass sound? Go for a Minimoog. Want a classic filter sweep effect? Find a Minimoog. Looking for one of those searing, prog-rock,

portamento-laden "lead synth" sounds? It's a Minimoog you're after. The highs are higher and the lows lower.

In terms of parameters, analog (or analog-type) synthesis may not look vastly different today, but the Minimoog's physical appearance, with its pop-up panel, wooden casing and 44-note keyboard, has remained unique.

The knobs and switches follow a logical signal flow from left to right, from the three multi-waveform oscillators through to the mixer, the filter, the envelope generator and the amplifier.

On the oscillator "bank," two of the oscillators, pitched between 32' and 2', conform to most people's idea of a regular oscillator: choice of waveform from square, rectangle, sine or sawtooth; choice of basic pitch. Oscillator 3 on the other hand can be used either as an audio source or as a low-frequency modulation source (LFO), which, in fact, is its most common application. This said, by opting to use the third oscillator in its regular audio range, the Minimoog is capable of some surprisingly modern, almost digital sounds. Noise is an additional source, which can be switched in or out.

The worst thing about all synths of this vintage is their general lack of stability. Oscillators tend to drift out of tune with astonishing ease. In this respect, the Minimoog was no worse than most of the monophonics that followed it. But even so, Moog redesigned the oscillator board midway through the instrument's production run, greatly improving its tuning stability. Models with serial numbers greater than 10175 contain this board as standard. Bob Moog himself pooh-poohs the folklore that has grown up around this improvement—that it somehow reduced the Minimoog's warmth and power. Not to say you'd be wrong to feel such a thing; designers can be ruthlessly single-minded when it comes to an opportunity to build a technically "better" instrument, even if the cure would kill the character. (If Hammond could have cured the B-3's key-click, it would have.) A handy tuning aid is the A=440 button, emitting this tone on the control panel itself.

The design philosophy behind the Minimoog was to offer gigging musicians the opportunity to manipulate sound as one could on Moog's large, cumbersome and highly complex modular synths. These had recently exploded into the public consciousness through such ground-breaking projects as Walter Carlos' *Switched on Bach*, released to mass acclaim in 1968. Although some components were redesigned for this new application, some, most importantly the filters, remained almost unchanged from the Minimoog's predecessors.

The Minimoog's powerful 24dB/oct lowpass filter, offering cutoff frequency and resonance controls, plus a simple attack, decay and sustain envelope generator, is what gives the instrument its razor edge. Even today, the Minimoog's clarity and high-end fidelity will make many a sample-based preset machine hang its head in shame. Under the subhead of Loudness Contour, the amplifier's ADS envelope generator shapes the overall sound. And a damn fine job it does, too. Again, very few modern instruments are capable of generating attack times quite this fast, which is part of the reason why the instrument is so effective for hard-edged, "attacky" bass sounds.

It has often been said that the Minimoog is a perfect training synthesizer, and certainly the roomy front panel's generously sized knobs and switches are easy to see and obvious to operate. You may not completely understand what you're doing, but you are unlikely to get lost on a Minimoog.

Unlike modern synths, which have tended to become slaves to preset mimicry, the Minimoog was designed as an instrument to be played, tweaked and controlled in real time, producing new, unique sounds. Aside from questions about tuning stability, using a Minimoog in live performance does not present any special problems. The panel layout gives access to even the chubbiest of fingers, two wheels offer modulation and pitch bend and portamento can be switched in or out. The idea of vertically operating pitch and mod wheels was new, and it quickly caught on. (Many years later, when the Sequential team was designing the Prophet-5, a quick call went out to the Moog designers, as much as anything else to confirm their suspicion that this was a patented design. But it wasn't. "Well, do you mind if we use it, too?" asked the Californians. "No, go ahead," came the reply, much to their astonishment. Reassuring, somehow, to find that civilized instruments can be made by civilized people.)

Meanwhile, a generation of fairly uncivilized players, from Rick Wakeman and Keith Emerson to Dave Stewart, Chick Corea and Jan Hammer carved out their careers on this instrument. But in the 1970s, the Minimoog was more often heard swooping and screaming its way through lead lines and blistering solos, replete with elephantine portamento and an only tenuous resemblance to pitch. Its most common application in recent years is bass. Its repertoire ranges from short, deep, rubbery "thunks" to sizzle-edged acid tones and pretty much everything in between.

A Minimoog is monophonic (though you can detune the oscillators) and came out long before MIDI was even dreamt of. It can be MIDIfied, of course, and indeed many have been. Or you can effectively buy it in a modern MIDI/rackmount setting from Studio Electronics, called the MIDImini. This is undoubtedly a more stable proposition than the MIDI-ed original model, and in essence, the sound-generating and

sound-sculpting components are faithfully reproduced. There are, however, some reworkings, such as the loss of a couple of footswitch inputs and some of the audio flexibility on oscillator 3.

If you want to work on an original model, the Lintronics Minimoog MIDI interface comprises a complete, microprocessor-controlled interface system for controlling the instrument via MIDI. The kit comprises a single circuit board installed inside the instrument, giving you MIDI control of pitch, volume, filter cutoff, modulation amount, glide and decay. The company behind this is none other than Bob Moog's Big Briar. If you want BB to do the work, it'll cost you $495, or you can buy the kit for $295 and have a go yourself.

As you can see from the used prices above, there is enormous disparity in Minimoog prices. Because these are highly collectible instruments, a model in pristine condition could be valued at twice the price of an old road dog. In pristine condition does not mean unmodified, though, since a MIDI-ed model will generally command a higher price than an unadulterated unit.

The last Minimoog was manufactured in 1981. The final 25 were produced in walnut cases, with their serial numbers etched into brass plaques; the last of these, number 13259, was presented to Dr. Bob Moog himself.

Moog Multimoog
Analog monophonic synthesizer

THE FAX

Keyboard:	44-note
Programs:	None
External storage:	None
Polyphony:	Mono
Oscillators per voice:	2
Effects:	None
Connections:	High/low audio, S-trig out, keyboard out, ext. keyboard scale adjust, ribbon out, keyboard force out, glide on/off, mod on/off, filter CV in, osc A & B in, S-trig in, audio in (to filter), touch mod effects in
Dimensions:	744mm x 312mm x 120mm
Weight:	12kg

THE FIGURES

Chief designer:	Jim Scott
Production run:	1978-1981

Approx. units sold:	1000
Options:	Pedals
Sounds:	n/a
Miscellaneous:	One of a rare band of mono synths to offer aftertouch sensitivity
Orig. price (1978):	$1595 (£815)
Price in 1996:	$400 (£200)

The fact that Steve Winwood used a Multimoog as the lead-line synth on "While You See a Chance" is passport in itself to the Hot 100. Winwood's haunting, flowing, gently pitch-bending melody is simple and tasteful (and, accordingly, as rare as rocking horse dung, in the *Sturm und Drang* world of the synth solo).

A fine example of sensitive playing and a sensitive synth, the Multimoog is one of the great live mono synths, stable enough to be practical and with controls spaced widely enough apart to invite real-time twiddling. The Multimoog has a mod wheel, a pitch ribbon, an aftertouch-sensitive keyboard and a pepper-pot of a rear panel, on which you find, among other things, glide and modulation footswitches and jacks for CV control over volume and filter cutoff. The VCF pedal was, in fact, used to great effect by Winwood on the aforementioned track.

The panel is encouragingly sparse for the nervous novice synthesist. The Multimoog is actually an upgrade of the Micromoog but with two oscillators. The oscillators choose their waveforms from a smooth-running control knob that moves from a sawtooth wave through a square wave into a narrow pulse. This is unusual, and although it makes replicating precise sounds more difficult, well, who wants to recreate on an instrument like this? Just create! Oscillator A also has an interval knob that allows it to be pitched independently (up to a fifth) from osc B. Meanwhile, osc B can throw a sub-oscillator square wave into the proceedings at one or two octaves below set pitch, which is brilliant for real subterranean bass. There is some streamlining though: Overall oscillator pitch, which can be set from 32' to 2' or "wide" (pitching the oscillator way out of earshot at either end of the audio spectrum), is a shared control between the two oscillators, and their relative balance is set by just one control knob. Noise is an additional sound source that can be mixed in with the tuned oscillators.

Filtering is classic Moog 24dB/oct lowpass with cutoff frequency and resonance (here, as ever, called "emphasis") controls plus envelope generator amount control that can function positively or negatively. The filter envelope is simple: a single attack-release knob plus sustain offered as either short or long and controlled by a white two-way switch below. Simple means fast to set up and modify, but also limited in terms of precise filter movement.

The amplifier envelope generator is similarly curtailed (though there are separate attack and release knobs), and the absence of decay parameter here might be more noticeable than on the filter, while release is offered from a switch. In compensation, there are some interesting triggering and modulation options, including the monotimbral "drone" (no one at Moog ever had a clue what this parameter was for either, so don't worry if you are left puzzled at this point), filter modulation by oscillator B and the ability to "play" the filter without an oscillator note in tow, which is excellent for whistly, spacey effects. Modulation sources include a multiwaveform LFO with sample-and-hold, square and sine waveshapes that can affect pitch or tone in amounts that can vary in speed and depth. The aftertouch keyboard, which, at the time, was called "force sensitive," governs much the same range of parameters as can be attached to the mod wheel (VCOs, VCF cutoff, sync). Though a little heavy-fingered, this is a great feature to have on a set of sounds like this, where human expression is very much the order of the day.

And then there's the pitch ribbon. Pitch ribbons are making a comeback in the 1990s, and this zero-inertia controller just begs to be stabbed at either for straight pitch-bending, as Mr. Winwood displayed, or for the doubly dexterous, finger vibrato or even trills. The pitch ribbon can be routed to either or both oscillators.

Ribbon controllers are fairly expensive to manufacture, requiring extra circuitry and adding another obvious potential failure point. However, Moog Music say that they have a good stock of ribbon assemblies, as well as keyboards, in stock, so a unit whose ribbon is frayed or torn is far from a write-off.

While the construction of the Multimoog is not so lovingly lavish as that of the wooden-cased Minimoog, it remains practical and tough. High, metal-edged sides protect the panel hardware, and the whole construction is solid and built to last. I recall Moog salespeople at the time of its release boasting they could (and indeed did) jump up and down on units to prove their sturdiness.

Instruments can look a bit battle-hardened, but on the whole they have stood the test of time very well, physically and operationally. This is a simple monophonic, not quite providing the timbral richness of a Minimoog, to be fair, but supremely playable and a lot of fun.

Moog Prodigy Analog monophonic synthesizer

THE FAX

| Keyboard: | 32-note |
| Programs: | None |

External storage:	None
Polyphony:	Mono
Oscillators per voice:	2
Effects:	None
Connections:	Mono audio
Dimensions:	552mm x 336mm x 120mm
Weight:	7.5kg

THE FIGURES

Chief designers:	Rich Walborn, Tony Marchese
Production run:	1980-84
Approx. units sold:	11,000
Options:	Later models may feature additional S-trigger and CV inputs and outputs
Sounds:	None
Miscellaneous:	Offers on my original blue "I Dig a Prodigy" sweatshirt, anyone?
Orig. price (1980):	$645 (£295)
Price in 1996:	$175 (£225)

Like a giant can of insecticide, the Moog Prodigy descended on the UK in 1980 and almost overnight consigned the British-made Wasp synth, which had been the big buzz all year, to the history books. The Wasp never took off (sorry!) to quite the same extent in America, so the Prodigy had an even clearer run there. Strangely, the Prodigy itself was a good deal more popular in Europe than it was back home as well.

I'd always regarded the Prodigy as a sharply designed beginning synth—a triumph of marketing. Moog practically created the market for synths in the early 1970s, and a decade later, that market was well-established and, more importantly, gaining large numbers of first-timers. "Now, if we can get 'em while they're young..." you can almost hear middle management plotting.

As it happens, nothing could be further from the truth. The Prodigy is what Moog personnel came to know as the "bootleg Moog." Designers Walborn and Marchese concocted the Prodigy on the quiet. They wanted to see if they could build a "$500 Moog," and they did just that. They simply dumped it on the marketing division weeks before the Winter NAMM show and said, "Here it is, give it a name." To the Moog marketing team's eternal credit, they scraped themselves off the floor and did just that.

This clean-lined synth offers two oscillators and limited but high-quality filter and modulation controls. In 1980, it was an ideal first buy. Fifteen years later, it's hard not to make the same recommendation. The Prodigy was Moog's biggest seller next to the Minimoog.

Both oscillators have a switchable choice of sawtooth, triangle or pulse (narrow on osc 1, square on osc 2) waveforms, and they can be pitched within a two-octave range. Osc 1 calibrates this as 32' to 8' and osc 2 from 16' to 4'. An interval knob can split the voices up to a fifth apart, and a sync switch smartly lashes them back together again for those searing, forced tones that remain de rigeur in the Jan Hammer school of lead synth playing. A small mixing panel offers independent control over the level of each oscillator, plus a master volume.

At the time, Moog made much of its "heated chip" technology—not a culinary term, but a method by which Moog hoped to cure the perennial problem of oscillators drifting out of tune. But the Prodigy made only a negligible improvement in this regard, and prospective purchasers are wise to leave an instrument on for a while to see how well it performs.

The 24dB/oct lowpass filter features standard cutoff frequency and resonance (Moog persisted in calling this "emphasis") controls and a slightly limiting ADS envelope generator. The filter can track the keyboard (fully, half on or off) and is good for self-oscillating, whistly, ghostly noises. Modulation is limited, with a square- and sine wave-only LFO capable of modulating either or both of the VCO and VCF.

There's a lot more Walborn and Marchese could have put on, of course, but that's not the point here. They were designing to a very tight, albeit self-imposed, financial brief, and the spinoff benefit is that no one gets frightened or bamboozled with sample-and-hold or a squillion modulation sources and destinations on a Prodigy.

The basic sound of a Moog synthesizer is still here–not classically so and not particularly flexibly so, but with portamento and a pair of stiffish mod and pitch wheels (which I trust will have eased up a bit on most models by now), you can crank out some nice squelchy bass lines and more. The oscillator hard-sync sounds work particularly well.

Encased in wood, the unit's basic construction was of good quality, which means they stand a chance of survival. Some of the panel hardware was of less sturdy stuff, so some knobs and switches might need to be replaced. No matter—the current street prices suggest that the Prodigy is still something of a bargain for those looking for a piece of history at a price they can live with.

All of this notwithstanding, the Prodigy's lack of

ins and outs can get frustrating, and Moog Music does have an upgrade mod kit that adds a degree of interfaceability.

Moog Source — Analog monophonic synthesizer

THE FAX

Keyboard:	37-note
Programs:	16
External storage:	Cassette interface
Polyphony:	Mono
Oscillators per voice:	2
Effects:	None
Connections:	Mono audio, S-trig in and out, CV in and out, cassette
Dimensions:	670mm x 317mm x 76mm
Weight:	21kg

THE FIGURES

Chief designers:	Dave Luce, Ray Caster
Production run:	1981-85
Approx. units sold:	7000
Options:	None
Sounds:	Jan Hammer alternative set, Deep Magic (cassette & data sheet)
Miscellaneous:	We also have Dave Luce to thank for the Polymoog.
Orig. price (1981):	$1395 (£899)
Price in 1996:	$600 (£400)

This was Moog's first programmable synthesizer. In its own way, the Source was as revolutionary in 1981 as the Minimoog was a decade earlier. Gone were the knobs and switches; gone was the subdued, school-lab design; gone was the compulsion to create your own sounds. The Source was new, and because it was new, it was expensive. Sales figures, given all factors, were impressive.

Always noted as a "good synth," by the beginning of the '90s, Sources were well past their sell-by date and you could pick one up in the low hundreds (dollars) or very low hundreds (pounds). The voyage of rediscovery didn't start until after retro fever firmly took hold, but now the price is steadily going back up again. You've got to pick your spot if you want to play synth dealer—timing, appropriately enough, is everything.

The Source is one of the very few mono synths to employ digital access control in place of knobs and switches and one of not many more to offer program

memories. The first is a bit of a pain, frankly; the second, welcome, provided you are not one of those purists who regard early use of microprocessors as the thin end of an invidious wedge.

First-time spotters should note the free-flowing incremental wheel that Roland later clasped to its bosom and called its own, soon to be followed by the rest of the music industry. The system, by now common as muck but then revolutionary, requires you to stab a parameter "pad" and then spin the wheel to the desired parameter value, as displayed on a small screen. The technology required for the device and system was expensive, because at the time there were no off-the-shelf components within a reasonable budget.

The first thing to strike you about a Source are its radical looks. This rethink from the typically understated classic Moog lines came from the marketing brains at Moog's then-parent company, Norlin Industries (as opposed to Moog itself, which hired a crack industrial design team for the job).

Under this alarmingly garish hood (how the traditionalist Bob Moog, by now long since parted from the company, must have gagged), lie a pair of fully independent VCOs, separately tunable and offering a choice of triangle, sawtooth and variable-pulse waves, which can be forced back together using hard sync. Pink noise is an additional sound source, with its own level control.

As you might expect, the filtering is 24dB/oct lowpass with cutoff frequency and resonance (finally called by this name; Moog had previously stuck to "emphasis") controls, plus the full ADSR envelope generator. This made the creation of filter shapes rather more of a precision exercise than it was on earlier Moog synths. The filter can track the keyboard (fully, half or off). The LFO has sine or square waveshapes, plus a sample-and-hold feature. The amplifier too has the full ADSR collection of envelope parameters.

Viewed today, the parameter list is full without being overly generous, and the user interface...well, fairly commonplace. In 1981, the Source was about as familiar and friendly as a cigarette machine in kindergarten. People pulled this and twirled that and nothing much seemed to happen.

So they resorted to the 16 memories (which is where the rot set in—okay, okay) and amused themselves with the assorted lead synth, string, organ and flute presets. The Source still cops a fair Taurus pedal, and for the terminally lazy, a second cassette of sounds was made available from Jan Hammer's programming. The presets are recallable from buttons that run along the front lip of the panel above the keyboard, sharing duties (in "Level Two" mode) with controls for a small, real-time-only sequencer and an arpeggiator. The sequencer has the neat ability to be transposed in real time simply by hitting a new key on the keyboard. The arpeggiator is fairly limited and can only be clocked internally from the LFO clock.

It's difficult to say whether the recent move in prices is justified in absolute terms. This is a unique instrument in looks, and perhaps this has contributed. Source sounds are fairly powerful and, provided you are happy with the programming system, you should be able to elicit some hard, driving low-end sounds.

The Source has proved a reliable performer, all in all, thanks, no doubt, to Moog's recently implemented process of burn-in aging before final calibration. While internal spares should not be a problem, there are only a few membrane panels left, which is something to bear in mind if confronted by a unit with a trashed panel.

New England Digital Synclavier

Music computer system

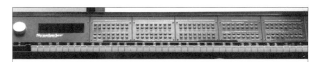

THE FAX

Keyboard:	76-note
Programs:	Variable
External storage:	HD 5¼" floppy disk drive
Polyphony:	32-voice, expandable to 96
Oscillators per voice:	n/a
Effects:	DSP
Connections:	XLR or ¼" audio outputs, individual outputs, SMPTE, clock in/out, MIDI
Dimensions:	528mm x 528mm x 1512mm (Synclavier 9600)
Weight:	296kg (Synclavier 9600 with road case)
The Synclavier Co.:	Rivermill Complex; Lebanon, NH 03766; tel: (603) 448-8887; fax: (603) 448-6350
Synclavier European	
Services:	18 Prince Charles Way; Wallington, Surrey SM6 7BP UK; tel/fax: 0181-669-4265

THE FIGURES

Chief designers:	Sydney A. Alonso, Cameron W. Jones, Jon Appleton
Production run:	1977-present
Approx. units sold:	1600
Options:	Voices, memory (up to 768MB internal), optical disk storage, MIDI Patch Bay, VITC reader, music-engraving software and much more
Sounds:	Synclavier library; also East-West, ProSonus, Universal
Miscellaneous:	Frank Zappa's "Barking Pumpkin Digital Gratification Consort" was none other than the maestro's beloved Synclavier. Synclavier Sampler Library sounds are available on audio CD and CD-ROM for Akai, Kurzweil, SampleCell, Roland and E-mu sample formats from Ilio Entertainment. Disks include Strings, Brass and Winds, Essential Percussion, Keys and Guitars and World Orchestral.
Orig. price (1977):	From $50,000 (£40,000)

Price in 1996: Depends on system configuration. Core system from around $27,000, plus keyboard, memory options, voices

The story of the Synclavier stretches back to the early 1970s, when this fabulously expensive dedicated music computer system was hewn out of a high-flown collaboration between research students and the music faculty of Dartmouth College in New Hampshire. Alonso and Jones' original brief—to harness Dartmouth's computer system to control a new digital "FM" synthesizer—grew into a fully integrated synthesis and sequencing system by the time the decision was made to produce and launch an actual product. By the end of the decade, the first Synclavier "digital synth," as it was known, made its brief appearance and about 20 of these units were made.

In 1980, the Synclavier II was released, featuring the company's "partial timbre" system of sound creation, along with the Synclavier's own form of FM synthesis (which has always managed to skate around Yamaha's rigidly policed license to produced "FM"), digital recording and external storage of sounds on disk—all items that were way ahead of their time in terms of being seen on musican-priced pieces of equipment. The only piece of downgrading on the Synclavier II was the keyboard, which is nasty and plasticky.

In 1984, coinciding with a new system (complete with a quality keyboard in the shape of Sequential's Prophet-T8 mechanism), New England Digital reverted to calling their brainchild simply the Synclavier. This component-based flexible system grew and diversified as technology and demand allowed. The Synclavier developed from fairly humble sampling origins—for a long time, the system was only capable of sampling in mono, while instruments at a fraction of the price were gleefully offering stereo sampling in 16-voice polyphony—into a mighty sound and recording environment used by numerous leading composers, notably in the film world. Rock 'n' roll threw up many devoted users, too, including Sting, Geoff Downes and, perhaps most famously, the late, great Frank Zappa (for whom the system became a fortress behind which he could barricade himself from the pressures of the outside world, especially musicians—including, by the end of his life, himself).

Never quite as elegant in design as its great rival the Fairlight, the Synclavier system comprises an external keyboard, monitor and processing and storage units of various shapes and sizes. As disparate as it may look, the concept is to keep music production, from sampling to sound libraries to (re)synthesis to sequencing to post-production for film and video, within a single environment. Specifications are somewhat meaningless, since the system was constantly evolving and being updated, but 64-voice polyphonic sound generation, with 32MB of waveform RAM and a 200-track sequencer, was a standard configuration by the 1990s—well before other companies were producing anything comparable.

The problem with NED and the Synclavier, as with the Fairlight, is that it is far quicker to respond to changes in the market (or to the price of memory or to newly developed applications) on a unit-by-unit basis. In spite of moving into the murky waters of direct-to-disk recording (a term the company trademarked), the Synclavier became too unwieldy for its own good, and NED disintegrated in 1993.

But not for long. Synclavier owners, each of whom invested enough money in the system to buy a house, were most reluctant to let the company abandon their investments. Three Synclavier users purchased all the company assets and set about not only supporting the user base but also developing new software, building new machines and even building new products, such as the brilliant S-Link Macintosh audio file translator.

The Synclavier of 1995 comes in three fundamental guises: A/3200, A/6400 or A/9600, depending upon your basic voice requirement. Whatever the firepower, the system still offers a conglomeration of technologies and techniques ranging from sampling to additive/FM synthesis to hard disk recording and post-production. The whole thing remains fabulously expensive, of course, and relatively unwieldy, but few investors old or new would feel that the much-vaunted rewards of owning such a state-of-the-art system have not been delivered in full.

New England Digital's standoffish treatment of its peers in the music industry was such that few tears were shed when the company came apart at the seams. Happily, though, the new Synclavier Company has a far more communicative approach, and this stance is bound to encourage, rather than frighten off, ownership in the future.

Oberheim 4-Voice
Analog polyphonic synthesizer

THE FAX

Keyboard:	49-note
Programs:	16
External storage:	Cassette interface
Polyphony:	4-voice
Oscillators per voice:	2
Effects:	None
Connections:	L/R outputs, phones, filter footswitch
Dimensions:	1066mm x 290mm x 418mm
Weight:	32kg

THE FIGURES

Chief designer:	Tom Oberheim
Production run:	1975-1979
Approx. units sold:	800
Options:	Programmer, additional SEMs, DS-2A Digital Sequencer, Mini Sequencer
Sounds:	None commercially available
Miscellaneous:	The brass sound on the Weather Report's "Birdland"; rackmount version available from Studio Electronics: 18034 Ventura Blvd., Ste. 169; Encino, CA 91316
Orig. price (1975):	$5690 (£3737)
Price in 1996:	$1200 (£1600)

It's 1975 and the charts are full of the Eagles and the Doobie Brothers. The word "synthesizer" is rarely uttered by musicians, and when it is, it's in reference to either a Minimoog or an ARP Odyssey. A synthesizer is still essentially a lead instrument or a gadget used to supply sound effects. Monophony still rules the audio waves.

In 1975, Oberheim was just emerging as a manufacturer of instruments, rather than pedals and doodads like digital (yes, digital!) sequencers. The company's first instrument was a monophonic synthesizer module, the Synthesizer Expander Module, or SEM as it became known, originally built to be used in conjunction with someone else's instrument (e.g., an ARP or a Moog). Although polyphony at this time was accepted as the domain of pianos, organs and string machines, every manufacturer was desperate to crack the problem of polyphonizing the synthesizer. Oberheim's answer was astoundingly simple: box up a bunch of SEMs. And this is exactly how the 4-Voice and its big brother, the 8-Voice, were put together.

An elegant solution in some respects, but hooking up four or eight self-contained instrument modules and linking them to a digitally scanned keyboard also threw up some major problems, the foremost of which is tuning. In order for a chord to sound remotely acceptable, for example, the tuning of all of the SEMs had to be sympathetic, which is no easy matter when dealing with drift-inclined analog oscillators and relatively coarse control knobs. The result was, and remains, that these instruments are not for the fainthearted or inexperienced. They require constant attention, patience and no small amount of skill.

The reason people bothered then and continue to bother about them now is that, handled correctly, the Oberheim 4-Voice and 8-Voice instruments have a depth and majesty about them that is unique. Those familiar with Weather Report's "Birdland," on which Joe Zawinul employed one of the first of these instruments to roll out of Los Angeles, will no doubt agree.

The 4-Voice is simply four cream-faced monophonic synth modules lashed together in a wooden case covered with black vinyl and wired up. Controls on these self-contained modules comprise two VCOs; a two-pole filter that can operate in highpass, lowpass or bandpass modes; a simple LFO and a pair of ADS envelope generators. If you play a single note on the keyboard, an LED indicates which of the modules you are triggering, allowing you to then twist and tweak its sound into the one you want. In order to have this sound triggered polyphonically, you must recreate your programming setup on each of the other SEMs. A year after the initial release, Oberheim launched a programmer which lets you store 16 setups in memory. (This helps, of course, but the *programmer* is not a foolproof device.)

Each of an SEM's pair of oscillators offers a choice of sawtooth or variable-pulse waveforms, the pulse width variable from 10 percent narrow to 90 percent narrow via a 50 percent "square" shape. Pulse width can be used as a modulation destination in a rotary-controlled contest with oscillator frequency (i.e., pitch). Mod sources include the LFO, which is preset to a smooth, vibrato-inducing triangle wave; the second envelope generator; or an external controller. The envelope generators themselves offer only attack, decay and sustain parameters, with decay effectively doubling up as release. The filter can be switched between its various modes, and there are rotary controls for cutoff frequency and resonance. Again, the filter can be modulated positively or negatively by the LFO, envelope 2 or an external source.

The controls are all large and clearly labeled. Fundamental comprehension is not the problem on one of these instruments.

Although the overall length is 1066mm, the actual keyboard is only four octaves long. A good deal of space is occupied by the 16-channel programmer (originally an optional extra), which houses not only program select buttons but a simplified version of an SEM. The trick is to set up the programmer's controls to conform to those you have been fiddling with on the main panel. Unfortunately, not all the parameters are offered, so you can't always store the exact sound as you'd like. There are no resonance control, bandpass, lowpass or highpass options, for instance.

Once you're set up, your problems are by no means over, either. The process by which you physically commit a sound to memory would take most of this review to explain.

There are various ways in which the SEMs can be harnessed. Most commonly, you assign the instru-

Name: Oberheim Electronics
Head office: 732 Kevin Ct., Oakland, CA 94621; tel: (510) 635-9633; fax: (510) 635-6848
In operation: 1970-1995
Products: Synthesizers, sequencers, pedals, effects, modifications

----

The cross-fertilization of ideas among California musical electronics companies and designers has always been substantial. Of all the names that crop up time and again as having "done some work on" this or that instrument, the foremost is Tom Oberheim.

Tom Oberheim is the ultimate gadget man. The company he founded in 1970 started out producing add-ons rather than complete musical instruments. There was the splendid Music Modulator (a ring modulator that looked like a cross between a lunchbox and homemade bomb), the Phase Shifter and the world's first digital sequencer, produced in 1973. As a one-time ARP agent, Oberheim even produced a modification for the ARP 2600, making it duophonic.

It was at the request of sequencer customers who were looking for ways to enhance the sound-producing part of the synthesis equation, specifically to complement the ARP synths, that Oberheim took its first steps into the musical instrument field with the SEM module. These complete synth modules were later glued together in twos, fours or eights and attached to keyboards to form the mighty Oberheim 2-voice, 4-voice and 8-voice instruments.

Unwieldy and not very practical as far as tuning and operation were concerned, the Oberheim SEM-based keyboards nevertheless delivered a rich, warm and interesting range of polyphonic sounds. Many feel that the early Oberheims, from the 4-voice and 8-voice through to the OB-X and OB-8, best define the phrase "analog synthesizer."

Oberheim's purple patch lasted a decade, from the mid-1970s into the '80s. During this time, the OB sound was de rigeur in the burgeoning L.A. scene of Toto and Michael McDonald, as it was in the emerging Prince camp in Minneapolis.

This period of many high-profile users also saw a great deal of behind-the-scenes work (for which Oberheim is rarely credited) on sequencers, cassette interfaces, guitar synthesis and the establishment of MIDI.

As did MIDI's co-shaker and mover, Sequential, Oberheim ran into trouble in the mid-1980s, partly through underfunding and partly due to the DX7, which at least temporarily rendered the sales of analog synthesizers—with which Oberheim resolutely persisted—almost impossible.

In 1985, Oberheim became ECC Oberheim as part of a rescue package put together by Tom Oberheim's ex-lawyer. Although the next two years brought such innovative products as the Xpander and Matrix-12, Tom Oberheim left and along with him, it seems, went any sense of direction or purpose that the company had.

Since then, Oberheim has stumbled along from rescue bid to rescue bid, at one time becoming part of Hammond Suzuki, with manufacturing in Japan, and more recently becoming a somewhat inappropriate West Coast outpost for the guitar giant Gibson, who must be to synthesizers what the Vatican is to condom manufacturing. This operation is largely built around re-badging Viscount products designed in Italy.

Meanwhile, a bitterly frustrated Tom Oberheim continues to build synthesizers and add-on gadgets (he built a 16-bit upgrade kit for the Akai S900) under the name of Marion Systems.

ment to move sequentially through each SEM in turn. Alternately, you can remain frozen on one for the first note played, then step through the others. You can also split the keyboard. Controls for these various modes of triggering, along with portamento, pitch control and VCF cutoff point maneuvering, lie immediately to the keyboard's left, beside the programmer.

Since you have four separate instruments to work with here, it's hardly surprising that there are four separate outputs; each can be mixed in level and altered in pan position. The "spread" that you can produce is substantially responsible for the instrument's spacious, "big" sound. Brassy tones are perhaps the tour de force here, although the instrument is also responsible for longtime user Lyle Mays' highly distinctive breathy lead sound. More current users include British ravers The Shamen and 808 State, the latter using a 4-Voice for the main riff on "Timebomb Is," off their album *Gorgeous*.

Though this review has concentrated on the 4-Voice version, the 8-Voice instrument is essentially the same, with an additional row of four SEMs glued on the back. If by now you have concluded that controlling the smaller instrument may be problematic, doubling the number of components speaks for itself in terms of potential complexity and hassle.

While hardly common, 4-Voice instruments are not ridiculously rare, as are the 8-Voice versions, especially outside America. Prices have risen in recent years, though it is interesting to note that proportionally they are still nowhere near the original list prices. As for repairs, Oberheim has never been the most reliable of manufacturers, and although a company called Oberheim is currently in existence, its personnel, motivation and ownership have changed several times since the days of the 4-Voice and 8-Voice.

Twenty years down the line, Oberheim (the name now operated by Gibson) went on to produce the OB-Mx, a cream-faced analog synthesizer module highly reminiscent of these early instruments. If you can live with just two SEMs, a modern rackmount MIDI version, the Obierack, can be bought from Studio Electronics of California (see "Miscellaneous").

Oberheim Matrix-12

Analog polyphonic synthesizer

THE FAX

Keyboard:	61-note
Programs:	100 single, 100 multi
External storage:	Cassette interface
Polyphony:	12-voice
Oscillators per voice:	2
Effects:	None
Connections:	2 audio outs, MIDI, trigger input, cassette
Dimensions:	976mm x 515mm x 150mm

Weight:	15kg

THE FIGURES

Chief designer:	Marcus Ryle
Production run:	1985-1987
Options:	Separate voice outputs, FS-7 sustain pedal
Sounds:	Dr. Sound, Walt Whitney
Miscellaneous:	Editor/librarian from Opcode (MIDIMac Patch); service and repairs: Advanced Musical Electronics: 8665 Venice Blvd.; West Los Angeles, CA 90034; tel: (310) 559-3157 or MusicTech Services: 12041 Burbank Blvd.; N. Hollywood, CA 91607; tel: (818) 506-4055; Xpander Users group in the U.S.: tel: (818) 894-9369
Orig. price (1985):	$6399 (£4595)
Price in 1996:	$3000 (£2000)

A thread of quirkiness, of quite deliberate and sometimes irritating idiosyncrasy, seems to run through most Oberheim designs. Not for Oberheim the uniform and corporate march of a Yamaha or even the consistency of a Roland or a Korg. Consistently inconsistent: that's Oberheim.

This doesn't mean that Oberheim products are unreliable, just that the company has always seemed to delight in doing things differently. And few instruments have looked, or indeed sounded, like the Matrix-12.

If that weren't different enough, Oberheim released the Matrix-12's keyboardless partner, the Xpander, first. Even in the fresh-faced salad days of MIDI, an instrument without a keyboard—especially a big, cumbersome instrument without a keyboard, not a cozy 19-inch rack module—was hard to get off the ground. The Xpander didn't exactly flop, but it was not a big seller. The Matrix-12, though a more expensive, double-oscillator design, was clearly a more likely proposition.

The intention with the Matrix-12 was to offer, in a mid-1980s context, an instrument that had the routing flexibility of the giant modular systems of the mid-1970s, wherein almost every parameter could interact using patch cords. The Matrix-12's "patch cords," of course, are hidden in software.

It's an impressive-looking instrument, large to the point of bulkiness, with an exceptionally deep main panel awash with buttons and LEDs, like some sort of space-age board game. But it's not the system that's so radical on the Matrix-12—after all, it's fairly standard subtractive synthesis—so much as the options it offered.

Beknobbed to an extent, the Matrix-12 is navigated with a page system of parameter access and soft buttons. Such a method may now be commonplace, but in 1985, it was new and not a little confusing.

The instrument has 12 fully independent analog voices. Within a few years, what would become known as multitimbralism was also commonplace. Back in 1985, many of us nodded sagely at the prospect of being able to control individual voices on dedicated MIDI channels, but few thought many people would ever want to bother. In truth, the Matrix's system does not have the multitimbral flexibility of an 01/W, but for independent bass, pad and obbligato parts, say, it is still more than sufficient.

There's nothing too frightening about the VCO/VCF/VCA voice architecture. More daunting is the level of choice within each section. Each oscillator can be independently pitched, fine-tuned and set in volume. Page 2 of the oscillator controls provides access to waveforms—triangle, sawtooth or variable pulse—as well as the lag processor for portamento effects, pitch bend and vibrato. VCO2 also offers noise as an additional waveform.

The oscillator pages are reasonably fathomable, but once you get into the filter pages, where a choice of some 15 filter modes and the myriad modulation routings (with no less than five envelope generators per voice, five LFOs and a ramp generator) confront you, then you'll need your wits about you. Oberheim breezily informs you that some 27 modulation sources can be sent out to some 47 modulation destinations.

Filtering is a Matrix-12 specialty, with spectacular choices of one-, two-, three- or four-pole lowpass; one-, two- or three-pole highpass; two- or four-pole bandpass; band reject; phase shift; and several combined filter types. Add in tricks like being able to modulate filter resonance from keyboard dynamics, one of the LFOs, etc., and you can see that this is never going to be a quick or easy instrument to work with, in spite of the plethora of Help pages and a clearly written and organized owner's manual.

Does it sound any good once you have mastered it? Yes, it definitely does. The Matrix-12 is a rich, multifaceted instrument, capable of enormous complexity and fine detail, perfectly suited for progressive noodlings a la Alan Holdsworth, who has loyally used the Matrix-12 and Xpander as a sound source for his Synthaxe guitar. This application as a sound source for a guitar controller makes perfect use of the Matrix-12's multitimbral capability for individual string bending,

sounds, etc. Texture hounds like The Orb also seem to have taken the Matrix-12 into their hearts.

This is a synth with a thousand tricks up its software. It wasn't made in huge numbers, but since it is not for the fainthearted, most people on the lookout for a Matrix-12 should be rewarded in time. Though official production stopped far earlier, a small number of Matrix-12s were made to order by the "new" Oberheim in 1991.

Oberheim Matrix-1000
Analog synthesizer module

THE FAX

Keyboard:	None
Programs:	1000
External storage:	SysEx
Polyphony:	6-voice
Oscillators per voice:	2
Effects:	None
Connections:	Mono audio out, MIDI.
Dimensions:	430mm x 320mm x 42mm
Weight:	4.2kg

THE FIGURES

Chief Designer:	Marcus Ryle
Production run:	1988-1995
Options:	None
Sounds:	MIDIMouse, Sonic Horizon, Key Clique, Angel City, Kid Nepro
Miscellaneous:	Editors include Opcode Patch Factory (Mac), Quinsoft Matrix Editor (PC) and Geerdes 1000 Editor/Manager (Atari ST).
Orig. price (1988):	$599 (£499)
Price in 1996:	$300 (£350)

The good thing about basing an instrument on an old design is that it can never really go out of date. The Matrix-1000 was old even when it was new. Accordingly, it has sold very nicely, thank you, for longer than any previous Oberheim instrument. It has, as has the company, also had a few brushes with death over the years and has even had a paint job from the original black to its "new" Oberheim cream. As of this writing, the Matrix-1000 is still current, though Gibson now operates the Oberheim brand name. Not bad for an eight-year-old!

The Matrix-1000 premise is astoundingly bold, yet astoundingly simple. When I first reviewed the instrument in 1988, I didn't give it a chance. Sure, I thought, I know that while analog is hip, no one can really be bothered to program sounds anymore. But who's going to admit to that by buying what is essentially a preset collection of old synth sounds—even if it is a *massive* collection of old synth sounds? Well, it seems lots of people did, including—I blush to admit—me. Perhaps everyone else came to the conclusion I eventually came round to, namely that the Matrix-1000 is just too useful to ignore at this price.

The Matrix-1000 is an almost totally control-free 1U design. No fancy screen, just a three-digit display, a very slender keypad, a couple of buttons to lock a bank in place and another button to select one of the instrument's operational modes: patch, MIDI channel, fine-tuning, units (we'll get to these in a minute), data dump and external function. Stab away at the select buttons toggles through six LEDs beneath these function names, and you alter parameters using a pair of "+/-" buttons at the end of the keypad.

For a company whose natural inclination is to force-feed its customers a bewildering choice of everything, the Matrix-1000 is restrained almost to the point of abstention. But this six-voice polyphonic module was built to a budget and is none the worse for it, either.

Operated as is (i.e., with no hidden Oberheim Matrix-6 keyboard synth lurking around the corner, nor any waiting Mac or Atari computer with suitable editing software), what you have on the Matrix-1000 is, oddly enough, 1000 preset Oberheim synth patches with which to play. You can shimmy about from one MIDI channel to another, even alter pitch, but that's about your lot. What you do with a Matrix-1000 is sit at your synth or computer and flip through patch after patch after patch until you hear one you like. Then you stop, do your work and move on.

The Matrix-1000 is not multitimbral. It has but a lone, mono audio out. And if you get lost, you really ought to think about another instrument altogether. (Recorder, perhaps, or tin whistle.)

The units function mentioned earlier alludes to Oberheim's hope that you will purchase several Matrix-1000s (or a Matrix-6, the synth with which it shares a soul) and link them together. In "group mode," you can link up to six units together for 36-voice polyphony. The extended functions mode opens the door to unison playing, a key transpose setting and MIDI echo (a delay).

The Matrix-1000 is all about sounds. According to Oberheim's description, there are 195 keyboard patches, 118 strings, 130 woodwind and brass sounds, 239 synths, 119 basses, 74 leads and 125 effects and percussion sounds. There are duplicates, sure. There's the occasional waste of space. But if it's analog you're after, there will be a pretty good approximation of what you want here, no doubt. Lead and bass sounds are not massive, but substantial. Washes are gentle and textural rather than expansive. The doughty few who have snuffled out my 1992 *Back to Bach* album (on EG/Virgin Records) may be interested to hear that "Prelude VI," over which the inestimable Milton McDonald plays his mournful guitar, is pure and unadulterated Matrix-1000.

And speaking of guitar, the instrument's mono mode option will allow a connected MIDI guitar to access individual voices with individual strings.

Before you get lulled into too cozy a feeling, free from the pains of programming possibilities, you can edit the instrument and resave 200 of the patches, using either a Matrix-6 keyboard or dedicated editing software.

Those who investigate editing will find a voice architecture that offers dual oscillators, four-pole low-pass filtering, two VCAs, three envelope generators, two LFOs and two ramp generators per voice. Though it is by no means in Matrix-12 league, the design does allow for some sophisticated modulation routings.

A Matrix-1000 with editing software makes a snappy and cost-effective package, but most users are content to mosey through the presets and get on with the business of making music. From experience, too, I can tell you that you normally either run out of energy or come close enough to your target to stop by about program number 350.

Oberheim OB-1
Analog monophonic synthesizer

THE FAX

Keyboard:	37-note
Programs:	8
External storage:	Cassette interface
Polyphony:	Mono
Oscillators per voice:	2
Effects:	None
Connections:	CV/Gate in & out, VCF pedal, audio input, 2 audio outs, loudness
Dimensions:	700mm x 360mm x 120mm
Weight:	5kg

THE FIGURES

Chief designer:	Tom Oberheim

Production run:	1977-1979
Options:	OB-1 pedal
Sounds:	None commercially available
Orig. price (1977):	$1895 (£1200)
Price in 1996:	$300 (£275)

The OB-1 was the first programmable monophonic synth, blessed with eight patch memories. For that alone, the little Obie deserves its place, but in fact this is also an unusual, interesting-sounding instrument, smartly turned out and very easy to use.

In both audio and features, the OB-1 is not a million miles away from Oberheim's SEM design, used on the company's modular 2-Voice, 4-Voice and 8-voice instruments. Not in any way as gob-smackingly powerful as a Moog, the instrument was designed more as an add-to, like something you'd play alongside a Moog or an ARP. In fact, one of the OB-1's original purposes was as a sound source for 360 Systems' Slavedriver guitar interface. (In the 1970s, Oberheim thought of itself as more of an accessories company than an instrument builder.)

Two VCOs can play through a five-octave range, calibrated in semitones. A fine-tune control is continually variable through an octave. Alongside these on the VCO panel is Oberheim's curious but effective method of waveform selection, comprising a "pulse type/saw type" switch and rotary-controlled waveform shaper that ranges either from square to narrow pulse or from triangle to sawtooth. Both VCOs have this facility, and in the middle of their respective panels, is a sync switch for lashing the oscillators together. The VCO panel wraps up with a sub-oscillator option that can add in a subharmonic square wave to the signal flowing out to the filter. There is no oscillator balance control as such, just a -3 dB (one-half volume) cut option on each oscillator. Cross-mod, for frequency modulation by VCO2, is available as a simple switch on VCO1.

Filtering is switchable two-pole or four-pole, with frequency cutoff and resonance controls, and the filter cutoff can be driven by either the LFO or the ADSR envelope generator. Keyboard tracking is available, though it's simply on or off. The VCF has its own dedicated ADSR envelope generator. A separate set of controls services the VCA.

At the top left-hand side of the control panel are eight program memory buttons, plus a manual mode button. Typically large, Oberheim control knobs govern an LFO delay factor and LFO rate. A three-position switch gives you the choice of square, sine or sample-and-hold LFO waveforms.

Under the panel heading of "keyboard," come a portamento knob (governing amount), an octave transpose switch and a VCF control that lets you manually vary the VCF cutoff point. A flipper-type pitch bend control can bend VCO2 or both oscillators up or down in narrow or broad ranges. The same flipper activates LFO modulation and, curiously enough, noise.

Without going overboard, you should be able to drum up most of the classic analog synth sounds or sound effects. The sync option gives you plenty of intensity, rather than in-your-face power, and cross-mod introduces nice, unpredictable, metallic or "belly" overtones. Good filter options plus noise and portamento complete what can only be described as a full package of programming parameters. And here's the killer punch of the OB-1: You can set up and store your creations—something that very few genuine vintage monophonics allow you to do.

Though it was quite successful in its day, OB-1s are hardly plentiful. They don't command high prices, but you'd be lucky, in both senses, to find one.

Oberheim OB-8 Analog polyphonic synthesizer

THE FAX

Keyboard:	61-note
Programs:	120 single, 24 multi
External storage:	Cassette interface
Polyphony:	8-voice
Oscillators per voice:	2
Effects:	None
Connections:	Stereo audio, MIDI (from software revision B onwards), computer interface, arpeggiator clock in, pedals, program advance
Dimensions:	1016mm x 508mm x 152mm
Weight:	20kg

THE FIGURES

Chief designer:	Tom Oberheim
Production run:	1983-1985
Options:	MIDI, on early models
Sounds:	In 1985, shortly before the corporate balloon went up, Oberheim launched an international OB-8 Patch Hunt, which culminated in the appearance of a 120-program "best of" data cassette.
Miscellaneous:	An OB-8's software revision is revealed by the programmer's LEDs if you press Page Two twice, keep it pressed down and press Sync. Service and repairs: Advanced Musical Electronics: 8665 Venice Blvd.; West Los Angeles, CA 90034; tel: (310) 559-3157 or MusicTech Services: 12041 Burbank Blvd.; N. Hollywood, CA 91607; tel: (818) 506-4055
Orig. price (1983):	$4545 (£4418)
Price in 1996:	$800 (£800)

Oberheim's OB Series instruments, including the OB-X, OB-Xa and OB-SX were, if not the foundations, certainly the walls on which the company was built. This was Oberheim's high spot, its heyday. And the OB-8 was the last of the series.

OB synths all have a certain warmth and richness, and although Tom Oberheim himself has gone on record as saying he feels that the OB-8 is "too perfect" (well!) and lacks the grit of the earlier models, this is still a very human-sounding instrument. These synths were all embraced by the R&B and dance merchants. The block-chords synth riff on Van Halen's "Jump" (the keyboardist's equivalent to the guitarist's "Stairway to Heaven") is OB-Xa, and the main synth part on Prince's "1999" is OB-8. Need we say more? Okay. Definitely groove machines.

The OB-8 has two VCOs per voice, each with sawtooth, pulse and triangle waveforms. Oscillators can be tuned separately and then shackled together in hard sync for searing, hollow lead line sounds. The OB-8 departs somewhat from the earlier OB designs in its filter section, offering a choice of two-pole or the more drastic four-pole filter slopes. An ADSR envelope generator is reserved for the filter. The filter is certainly precise, which probably accounts for Tom Oberheim's slight retrospective misgivings on the instrument.

LFO modulation can be in triangle, square, positive or negative ramp or sample-and-hold waveshapes and can be used to modulate VCO frequency or pulse width, the VCF cutoff frequency or the VCA. Deeper into the programming pages, you'll find additional LFO functions for changing the LFO sweep to half-steps and "unsyncing" the LFO for out-of-phase effects.

The LFO can also effectively track the keyboard and thus speed up as you play higher and higher. Portamento options of smooth or quantized travel and even polyphonic portamento are also found here. Plenty of neat tricks and a taste of things to come, when Oberheim went fully modulation-crazy on the Matrix-12 and the Xpander.

Here on the OB-8, Oberheim (rightly) felt that such in-depth features could frighten off the prospective programmer and so hid these advanced features in a "Page 2" mode. This mode simply activates a second set of programming parameters under the control of the regular panel knobs and switches once you double-press the Page 2/Chord button. The nervous could then, and probably most often did, avoid the heavy programming stuff and just get on with the playing. The Page 2 concept caught on to such an extent that it somewhat rebounded on Oberheim, which subsequently had to offer a new front-panel screen which signposted these secondary, hidden functions. Oberheim charged $150 for this "upgrade,"

says synth guru and OB-8 owner Craig Anderton, who decided to forgo the charge in favor of memorizing the commands. Now, he says, not a little bemused, he has a more collectible unit because of it.

The OB-8 came out on the cusp of MIDI—just before it, in fact—and so MIDI was offered as a retrofit; it became standard from software revision B onwards. It was obviously a bit of a rush job, since even the official MIDI version can only communicate on channels 1-9, with just program, program dump and lever information being transmitted (in addition to note data, of course). A ray of sunshine here is that in split mode, two sounds will send out on separate channels.

Patches come in either single or doubled/layered mode, with internal storage for 120 of the former and 24 of the latter. A cassette interface was the original method of external patch storage, though the MIDI version does allow patch data to be dumped and loaded also.

The OB-8 represents a good blend of a player's and a programmer's instrument. The flipper-type pitch and mod wheel isn't to everyone's liking, true, but the keyboard is firm and the sounds feel playable. And there's a highly groovy arpeggiator that can be clocked externally (via arpeggiator clock input jack, thus probably not directly via MIDI) if need be.

Producer Steve Levine, who first shot to fame with Culture Club's initial success, was a confirmed OB-8 user in the mid-1980s, feeling that the instrument exemplified, to us Brits at least, the archetypal "L.A. sound"—glossy, expansive and expensive. More recently, Italian super-remix team the Rappino Brothers use the OB-8 as a mainstay purveyor of analog pads and gated rhythm synth parts.

The OB-8 was the hub of Oberheim's "System," comprising the OB-8 keyboard, DMX drum machine and DSX sequencer. It was quite the system to have for a brief period, until MIDI arrived and blew the need for such restricted practices to smithereens. You don't buy Oberheim synths for precision accuracy and reliability, but the OB-8 was by far the most stable of the OB range and, when it did go out, the easiest to service.

Octave-Plateau Voyetra Eight
Digital/analog polyphonic synthesizer

THE FAX

Keyboard:	61-note (VPK-5)
Programs:	100
External storage:	Cassette interface
Polyphony:	8-voice
Oscillators per voice:	2
Effects:	Arpeggiator

Connections:	Stereo audio ¼"/XLR, pedals, CV and gate in & out, clock, MIDI
Dimensions:	483mm x 133mm x 305mm (VPK-5: 1003mm x 89mm x 230mm)
Weight:	16.8kg (VPK-5: 12.2kg)
Voyetra Technologies:	5 Odell Plaza; Yonkers, NY 10701-1406; tel: (914) 966-0600; fax: 914-966-1102

THE FIGURES

Chief designer:	Carmine J. Bonanno
Production run:	1983-86
Approx. units sold:	No figures available
Options:	n/a
Sounds:	None commercially available
Miscellaneous:	One of the first "modular" designs; service and repair from DoubleTake Music in New York: tel: (212) 685-7900; keyboard repairs from Achive Sound: tel: (610) 559-7605
Orig. price (1983):	$5590 (£4500)
Price in 1996:	No prices available

The company known as Cat, Octave, Octave-Plateau and Voyetra has had an interesting run. Voyetra Technologies is now a leading software and OEM company in the multimedia industry, but the company began back in 1975, with the aim of producing low-cost analog synthesizers, most notably the Cat.

The Cat had an all-too-familiar look about it, as far as ARP was concerned, and with suits and fur flying, the Cat was only a short-lived success. Undaunted, and this time protected by a U.S. patent, the company dove headlong into the future with an early computer-controlled modular design, the Voyetra Eight.

Like so many pioneering instruments, the Voyetra Eight was important not so much for its own accomplishments as for the doors that it opened. Arriving on the cusp of MIDI, the Voyetra Eight eventually implemented the standard, but not without a good deal of kicking and screaming—especially on the subject of MIDI's physical manifestation in the 5-pin DIN plug, to which the company resolutely objected, preferring, and indeed using, the more professional XLR connector.

The Voyetra Eight is an analog synthesizer under digital control. All the oscillators, filters and amplifiers in the module are analog. The envelope generators, LFOs and keyboard information, and needless to say, all the sequencing operations, are digital. All of the above is packaged in a standard 4U rack-mountable box with knobs, and the instrument is designed to be played not solely, but most probably,

by the separate VPK-5 keyboard. (I say not solely because Voyetra went on to produce a MIDI guitar synthesizer in 1985, for which four additional U.S. patents were granted.)

The concept of separate keyboard and voice modules is now commonplace, but in 1983, it was regarded as radical, despite the fact that such a design had been employed on early modular synths of the 1960s and 1970s.

Even though the voice module offers a good many front panel controls, Voyetra's unique way of looking at synthesis makes it unfamiliar viewing. Occupying almost half the panel are "Program Parameter Trimmers," two rows of pear-shaped knobs for sound-tweaking, as opposed to fine-detail editing. The PPTs let you control overall attack and release, LFO rate, glide, filter cutoff, detune and volume.

The main voice parameters lie within the unit's software and are accessed using a multilayered "page" system: Call up a parameter using the 10-digit keypad and pair of LEDs. Nothing so swift as a free-flowing incremental wheel yet. Although programming software was made for Apple II, IBM and Commodore computers, none seems to be available for present-day environments. Programming, then, is laborious. But remember, this machine was built in 1982.

The synthesis engine comprises VCOs (two per voice), which can choose from four waveforms: sawtooth, triangle, sub-octave square and variable-width pulse. VCOs 1 and 2 can be hard-synched, and VCO1 can bypass the filter module. An early form of FM interplay between the oscillators is even possible. Filtering is four-pole lowpass with cutoff frequency and resonance controls, plus full, half or no keyboard tracking. The filter can be modulated by its own ADSR envelope generator, with variable attack via keyboard velocity and a number of triggering options.

There are two multiwaveform LFOs (with sample-and-hold as one of the waves), which can be assigned to VCO pulse width, filtering, amplifier, etc. The Poly-Mod banks coordinate the Voyetra Eight's extensive modulation routings, allowing pretty much any modulation "patch" to be set up. Sources in this environment include not just the LFOs but also keyboard velocity, keyboard pressure, the VPK-5's joystick and envelope generators. Modulation permutations are a Voyetra Eight specialty.

Arpeggiators go in and out of style as synthesizer fashion accessories. The Voyetra Eight's arpeggiator is quite sophisticated, with its random mode, LFO, external and intriguing keyboard retrigger clocking. There's also a small (1700-event) polyphonic sequencer on which you can overdub and loop.

The Voyetra Eight was a great idea that was slightly ahead of its time and, one suspects, a little underfunded. Concepts such as keyboard/module design, alternative controllers, computer-aided control and the partnership of analog and digital technology have all gone on to mass acceptance and mass-market appeal but under the umbrella of MIDI.

Users must presumably still exist, though the Voyetra Eight is by no means (yet?) a popular act on the retro circuit. Service specialists are few and far between, though there is a rebuild kit available for the Voyetra Eight's Pratt-Read keyboard, which users say is prone to disintegrate somewhat over the years (see "Miscellaneous" for information on repairs).

Voyetra itself has moved on to smaller and obviously more profitable things, but the Voyetra Eight provides a fascinating insight into what and how synthesizer design developed in the MIDI era.

In 1986, Octave-Plateau changed its name to Voyetra Technologies.

OSC OSCar

Digital/analog monophonic synthesizer

THE FAX

Keyboard:	37-note
Programs:	36 (12 programmable/24 preset on pre-MIDI model)
External storage:	Cassette
Polyphony:	2-voice
Oscillators per voice:	2
Effects:	Arpeggiator
Connections:	Mono ¼" jack (configured for headphones also)
Dimensions:	616mm x 110mm x 310mm
Weight:	10kg

THE FIGURES

Chief designer:	Chris Huggett
Production run:	1983-1986
Approx. units sold:	1000 (300 without MIDI, 700 with)
Options:	MIDI retrofit
Sounds:	Data cassette
Miscellaneous:	MIDI retrofit kits are available from Kenton Electronics: 12 Tolworth Rise South; Surbiton, Surrey; KT5 9NN, UK; tel: 181-337-0333; fax: 181-330-1060.
Orig. price (1983):	$1000 (£699) (with MIDI)
Price in 1996:	$800-1000 (£500-600); $500/£300 without MIDI

1983 was the keyboard industry's *annus mirabilis*. The year gave us MIDI, the price-breaking Juno-60 and digital oscillator stability. It gave us Michael Jackson's

Thriller, with dazzling keyboard sounds that influenced a generation of programmers thereafter. Yet into this avariciously forward-looking world entered the OSCar, a British monophonic synth (I ask you) made out of bits of rubber and plastic, with a substantial price tag and a less-than-immediately-obvious operational system. To make matters worse, it was effectively only for sale at a single music store (Rod Argent's) in London. The OSCar's radical design obviously endeared it to some of the more daring and well-heeled sections of the musical community, but as a big seller, it never stood a chance.

The OSCar was made by the Oxford Synthesizer Company, a team that consisted of designer Chris Huggett (a key figure behind the EDP Wasp), his mom and programmer Paul Wiffen. The eye-catching exterior was designed by the same team that produced EDP's swan-song synth, the Gnat.

Physically, clumps of rubber serve as both section dividers and endpieces, giving the OSCar an endearingly industrial look. But this design was expensive in the first instance and continues to add considerably to the task of servicing, since you have to truss the instrument up with rubber bands to prevent it from spilling its guts once you have prized off an endpiece.

Hassles notwithstanding, the importance of the OSCar is its ability to deliver idiosyncratic lead, bass or obbligato sounds with unequaled power and flexibility. You can tweak and store. You can produce custom waveshapes. You can set up and link up and externally clock sequences. You have an arpeggiator. You have fat, Moog-type filtering. And yet, such attributes are offered in digital, mostly MIDI form. (Though perennially lumped in with the Minimoog and friends as one of the great classic "analogs," only the filters on the OSCar are analog; everything else is fully digital.)

Hardly helping basic comprehension, the control panel consists largely of identically shaped and colored knobs that are of a length that tends to obscure their job descriptions unless you are a giraffe. Oscillators 1 and 2 can be click-switched to triangle, sawtooth, square, variable-pulse or pulse-width-modulated waveforms and can be set to a basic pitch range in one of five octaves, together or separately. The pair may be fine-tuned a semitone up or down, also together or separately. Osc 2's detune knob can also be used to set it up in a perfect interval with osc 1, and the master fine-tune knob can then be used as a transposer.

In effect, there are two 12dB/oct filters, which can be used in isolation or combined to produce more powerful 24dB/oct filtering. A parameter called "separation" governs the filter cutoff frequencies, and in bandpass mode, this gives you what David Lynch would undoubtedly call "twin resonant peaks"— i.e., two separate resonances. Filtering modes can be set to bandpass, lowpass or highpass, with control over cut-off frequency and Q (resonance).

In addition to the filter envelope generator (featuring standard ADSR parameters), which can be either normal or inverted, you can set up some excellent repeat effects using the filter envelope triggering. For instance, you can clock the filter envelope using the OSCar's internal clock, with speed governed by the tempo control. (You can do the same with the "VCA" envelope, or indeed clock both at the same time.) If blitzkrieg power is what you want, the filter can be overdriven—an additional function of the master volume control knob.

The LFO offers three basic waveforms—triangle, sawtooth and square—and its six-position control knob also houses three routing options: "env," which utilizes the filter envelope instead of an LFO waveform; "kbd," for a variety of filter tracking effects; and "R," which produces a random sample-and-hold pattern controllable by the LFO's rate control. You can produce delayed vibrato effects using the intro control, and the LFO can be used to modulate both pitch and tone. The VCA has its own ADSR envelope generator, and you have programmable single and multiple triggering.

Although it is quite possible to drive an OSCar sedately along leafy Oxfordshire lanes, choosing a standard waveform and applying some gentle filtering with a fast-attack/mid-release envelope shape, you can also turbocharge your way along the interstate by constructing your own waveforms: combining harmonics, as in additive synthesis, building upon a fundamental pitch in a wide range of combined levels. You can assemble complex, atonal waveforms, albeit through the slightly cumbersome method of using the actual keys on the keyboard as selectors. Such self-created waveforms can be stored for use in later patch programming.

Not in the least surprising for an instrument of this vintage but still rare for a monophonic synth, the OSCar can store patches. OSCar was launched just before MIDI, unfortunately, so at first, the instrument came with 12 programmable memory locations and 24 presets and no MIDI. When OSC hastily rectified the MIDI situation, all 36 memories became user-programmable as well, the only residual nuisance being that, again, the actual keys themselves have to double as program-select buttons.

The OSCar has both a sequencer and an arpeggiator. Sequencer information is stored event by event, using notes and rests. Practice perfects a left-hand/right-hand technique of note and timing input that can be almost real-time. However you do it, seasoned users generally swear by the variety of inspira-

tional rhythms and effects you seem to be able to extract from the instrument. There are 22 sequence locations, plus you can chain sequences (with specific patch changes). Since the OSCar is duophonic, it is quite possible to accompany yourself "live" over the top of a sequence. Editing is concise, as opposed to all-encompassing, and the total storage capacity is 1500 events. (A rest is also an event, don't forget.)

Performance controls include glide (portamento) in several permutations and fiercely spring-loaded pitch and mod wheels, the latter responding to both tone and pitch.

The only real problem on the OSCar is its confusing panel. There are no LEDs, so figuring out many of the multifunction knobs and switches can be tough, or even impossible, on tasks like custom waveform-building, unless you still possess the owner's manual. (Since OSC no longer exists, obtaining spare copies of the manual, or any spare parts for that matter—most notably a MIDI kit—will not be possible.) As production continued, OSC did iron out some of the more irritating wrinkles. For example, from Mk 7 onward, the business of activating each control by turning its knob to the left and right until all the octave lights lit up was replaced by control activation as soon as the knob is merely turned.

A MIDI OSCar is fully 16-channel, allowing patch change, wheels, sequencer and arpeggiator info to be discussed. A little-known fact is that when linked to a regular polyphonic sound source, the OSCar can trigger a MIDI-connected instrument polyphonically, although it in itself remains duophonic, regardless. Although most OSCars sold had MIDI, only 50 or so MIDI kits were installed, which means there must be around 250 non-MIDI models somewhere. Although ex-OSC personnel had previously regarded the Oscar as "un-MIDIable," those resourceful fellows at Kenton Electronics in the UK have now perfected an OSCar MIDI kit.

In its heyday, the OSCar was picked up and used extensively by a number of influential keyboard players, including Billy Currie, who featured the instrument on "Love's Great Adventure," a track on *The Collection*, Ultravox's greatest hits album (the angular, harmonic-laden, linking sequence-type part is copybook OSCar). Jean-Michel Jarre used it extensively on *Industrial Revolutions*, while Stevie Wonder employed it on his less-than-legendary *Skeletons* album. (Apparently Stevie has 120MB of OSCar samples tucked away in his Synclavier library. Then again, what sounds hasn't he got?) In the current ambient/techno world, it's more a question of who *doesn't* use an OSCar, particularly loyal proponents including 808 State and Orbital.

Problems for current or would-be users include

spare parts (knobs, casing, etc.) and memory, since OSCar uses a lithium battery to preserve programs. If you disconnect the board in order to fit a replacement (which you cannot avoid doing every few years), then phutt!—your programs disappear into the ether. The moral here is to either save programs to cassette or dump data over MIDI to a data recorder beforehand. Curiously, the OSCar's casing was not watertight (curious in that how or why was such a discovery made in the first place?), but cases of "rusty" insides have been reported. You may want to check this out on a prospective purchase.

A final tip from the design team advises those on the lookout for an OSCar to search out one with cigarette ash and cat hair in the bottom of its case. These will almost certainly have been hand-built by the chain-smoking, cat-loving Chris Huggett himself. And highly prized by the cognoscenti they are, too.

OSC stopped producing keyboards in 1986.

PPG Wave 2.3 — Digital polyphonic synthesizer

THE FAX

Keyboard:	61-note
Programs:	87 single RAM, 20 multi
External storage:	Cassette interface
Polyphony:	8-voice
Oscillators per voice:	2
Effects:	None
Connections:	Stereo plus separate audio outs, VCF in, pedals, sync in & out, audio in, MIDI
Dimensions:	960mm x 550mm x 150mm
Weight:	23kg

THE FIGURES

Chief designer:	Wolfgang Palm
Production run:	1984-1987
Approx. units sold:	700
Options:	Waveterm sampling station
Sounds:	Via Waveterm
Miscellaneous:	Thomas Dolby is a prominent PPG user, though the main instruments he used on *The Golden Age of Wireless* were the 340 Wave Computer and the 380 Event Generator, limited designs predating the Wave 2.3.
Orig. price (1984):	$8995 (£5175)
Price in 1996:	$800 (£600)

PPG and owners of PPG equipment are a breed apart. It helps, of course, to be German. Or at least have an affinity with things German. Under the stewardship of resident boffin Wolfgang Palm, PPG (Palm Products Germany) produced a succession of highly innovative, creative products in the early 1980s: cross-fertilizing synthesizers and samplers, drafting in computers early on, developing wavetable synthesis sound engines long before American and Japanese companies "invented" the concept, experimenting with virtual instruments like the Realizer a decade before anyone else and much more.

PPG's product range has always been interesting. No, fascinating. But along with this has been a stout resistance to anything that smacked of making life easy for the consumer; a factor that must have contributed to PPG's undoing as a company.

By its very name, we might guess that the PPG Wave 2.3 was prefaced by a 2.2, a 2 and probably a 1. The plain Wave, in fact, started this particular ball rolling in 1980; it was a digital oscillator-sporting instrument, using wavetables and processed by an analog filter and amplifiers. The first production instrument in this PPG line was the Wave 2, a single-oscillator instrument, subsequently replaced by the dual-oscillator 2.2. (Both of these instruments were produced before MIDI.) But of all PPG's Wave keyboards, the most viable and most widely available has been the Wave 2.3.

The thread running through PPG instruments is digital oscillators whose waveforms are chosen from a large wavetable library and subsequently processed and modulated by a number of analog-style filters and envelope generators.

Distinctively styled in bright blue livery and adorned by a double row of large control knobs, an 80-character LCD screen and a keypad, the 2.3 has a velocity- and aftertouch-sensitive keyboard. However, it is light-actioned and highly unsatisfying to play due to an incurable delay.

Though it does have storable patches, much the point of owning or using a 2.3 is to create custom sounds by playing around with the wavetables. There are 30 wavetables, each of which contains 64 sample-based digital waveforms. A classic PPG setup is to access all 64 waves at a time using the "wavetable sweep" mode, so that playing a single note runs through them all in turn. To be slightly more practical, you can select one or more wavetables at a time per oscillator and process the sound through 24dB/oct lowpass filtering with ADSR envelope generator, the amplifier's ADSR envelope generator (there's even a third AD envelope generator on hand, which is used as a simple pitch envelope) and LFO modulation, then set up splits and different tunings.

Where it gets complex is in trying to be specific about a particular set or sequence of waves.

Traditionally, PPG manuals make Roland manuals look like *Dick and Jane*. And even though the screen is a good size for a normal instrument of this vintage, this is not a normal instrument.

The sound of any PPG is necessarily metallic and kind of alienating. But the 2.3 rises to the giddy heights of 12-bit sampling for its wavetables, which does introduce an element of smoothness and production to the proceedings. The 2.3 is also multitimbral (though still only eight-voice polyphonic) and, blessed with MIDI, is capable of use in a MIDI sequencing setup. This is actually quite advisable, since all the PPG keyboards (with the exception of the later PRK controller keyboard) are absolutely fearful to play. Played with anything approaching heavy hands, the whole mechanism wobbles up and down so much as to be almost unplayable.

The 2.3 has its own 8-track sequencer as well, if you're really brave, plus an arpeggiator that is only slightly less impenetrable.

A complete PPG setup might comprise the 2.3, the 72-note weighted PRK keyboard and the Waveterm sampling station—another big blue box with a built-in CRT screen. Waveterms started off life with 8-bit sampling, though by the time of the Waveterm B, they had become 16-bit. "But the Wave 2.3 is only 12-bit," I hear you wail. Yes, but by some fleet-footed piece of mathematical jiggery-pokery, PPG maximized the value of 16-bit input sampling for the 2.3's eventual 12-bit replay. PPG also produced the EVU, which is an extra set of 2.3-style 12-bit/eight-voice polyphonic voices in a box.

As is probably clear (as mud) from this contorted rundown of events, most everything about the PPG is a bit of fudge. It comes down to this: If Palm had Japanese practicality sewn into his designs, he'd now be the hero of the industry. Left to his own devices (a later Palm design became the Waldorf MicroWave), PPG veered off in all sorts of interesting directions and was, in effect, never to return from any of them.

The PPG 2.3 remains a fascinating instrument, if rather a one-trick pony. The potential of wavesequencing, or wavetable synthesis, is undoubted, as was shown to brilliant effect on Korg's Wavestation series. Here on the 2.3, though, the quality of the basic samples is such that everything tends to sound like a tinnier version of the classic D-50 Digital Native Dance patch. Users who have invested time and money in a PPG instrument will probably take issue with this summary—possibly with some justification. Let's just say that this is not an instrument for the occasional user, for whom it will surely be too complex to be worthwhile.

PPG is no longer in business.

Rhodes Chroma

Analog polyphonic synthesizer

THE FAX

Keyboard:	64-note
Programs:	50
External storage:	Cassette interface, 100 programs
Polyphony:	16-voice
Oscillators per voice:	2
Effects:	3-band EQ
Connections:	4 mono audio, two XLR, MIDI
Dimensions:	1000mm x 576mm x 144mm
Weight:	32kg

THE FIGURES

Chief designer:	Philip Dodds
Production run:	1982-1983
Approx. units sold:	3000
Options:	Computer Interface Kit Model 1611
Sounds:	None commercially available
Miscellaneous:	Designer Philip Dodds appeared as a musician in the movie *Close Encounters of the Third Kind*, playing a giant ARP 2500
Orig. price (1982):	$5295 (£3800)
Price in 1996:	$750 (£2000)

Stellar synth company ARP crashed to earth in 1981, midway through the design of this instrument. Both ARP and the Chroma were then picked up by CBS Musical Instruments and branded with the name of Rhodes.

The Chroma looks innocent enough, but it is a complex and intriguing instrument, offering a level of parameter interplay you'd expect only from an earlier, completely modular design coupled with a level of sophistication (velocity sensitivity and a direct computer tie-in) that you'd expect on an instrument five years down the line.

This was never, and indeed still is not, a synth for novices. In the right hands, it is capable of stunning subtlety and richness of texture. In the wrong hands, it'll simply get the user lost and bored.

The Chroma was one of the first synths to implement a form of digital access control (i.e., doing away with panel knobs and switches). It was also way ahead of its time in its ability to interface directly with an Apple IIe computer to run its own sequencing software and patch librarian. And all this before MIDI even entered the picture, though MIDI can be retrofitted at a price.

Part of the reason for the Chroma's fearsome programming reputation is the fundamental freedom you are offered in terms of signal flow; namely, that you can choose from some 16 basic routing configurations to start off with.

The level of flexibility runs through most of the modules: The oscillators can choose from a 1-63 value mix of sawtooth variable pulse waveforms and the filters are switchable between highpass and lowpass; there are 16 modulation sources for oscillator modulation, 16 LFO waveforms... This can be daunting enough at the best of times, but the Chroma makes it worse by failing to name individual parameters on its control panel. Two rows of pressure-sensitive pads double as patch select and parameter select switches, and you must either simply remember that pad number 13, say, governs envelope amount based on key velocity or glue the parameter table to the top of the instrument. The display merely shows numbers.

Idiosyncratic though it is, the Chroma, nonetheless, found many friends in the upper echelons of keyboard life during the early 1980s, most prominently Peter-John Vettesse, who used the instrument extensively during his high-profile stint with Jethro Tull. The Chroma was a newsworthy axe to be seen with due to its sexy link with Apple computers (one of the first planned marriages of computer and keyboard), which spawned dedicated Chroma software for sequencing and patch librarian duties. The Interface Kit opened the door to 16-track sequencing with punch-in/out recording and selective track quantizing—pretty sophisticated for the time. A PC package was also produced. The Chroma was also a bit of a trailblazer in that a keyboardless "expander" was produced (the Chroma Expander), again long before MIDI popularized the whole notion of expanders and modules.

Creditably, the regular keyboarded version makes a very decent stab at keyboard dynamics, a feature that was not high on, or possibly not even *on*, most designers' lists at the time. The action on this quirky 64-note keyboard is pleasantly weighted and, with some 256 velocity levels, sensitive.

Though we have much to thank the Chroma for in terms of computer-aided performance and velocity (the inclusion of velocity levels within MIDI is often credited to Dodds' perseverance on the matter), the Chroma's relevance in the mid-1990s is a little limited. If you can find one that has been programmed by a long-term (and therefore, hopefully, skilled) programmer, it'll turn up a few surprises, and the model still on active duty at Britain's Museum of Synthesizer Technology is a joy.

ARP and Rhodes are no longer in business. See the general listing for service and repairs.

RMI KC-II Keyboard Computer
Digital keyboard

THE FAX

Keyboard:	61-note
Programs:	12 presets
External storage:	Tone cards
Polyphony:	12-voice
Oscillators per voice:	n/a
Effects:	Chorus/vibrato
Connections:	Stereo audio outputs, numerous pedals
Dimensions:	1056mm x 576mm x 220mm
Weight:	45kg
Allen Organ:	PO Box 36; Macungie, PA 18062-0036; tel: (215) 966-2202; fax: (215) 965-3098 (Note, though, that RMI is not a current brand.)

THE FIGURES

Chief designer:	Jerome Markowitz
Production run:	1977-79
Approx. units sold:	Under 100
Options:	Sound data cards
Sounds:	RMI data cards
Miscellaneous:	One of the first sample replay instruments
Orig. price (1977):	$4750 (£3780)
Price in 1996:	n/a

In hard and fast terms, the RMI KC-II Keyboard Computer was another of the synthesizer industry's heroic failures. Very few were made, and a good many of these, one suspects, were loaned or even given to names that RMI felt might benefit the cause. The cause, however, was about ten years too early.

Taking a leaf out of RMI's ad campaign of the time, to answer precisely, "What is the RMI KC-II?" it is easier to start off with what it is not. This is not a synth, nor an organ, nor a piano. In years to come, this colorful instrument, vaguely reminiscent of a Farfisa or Vox organ, would have been called a sample replay or sample+ synthesis digital synth. In 1977, when all eyes and ears were focused on what Moog was going to do next and how we were going to get four-voice polyphony out of a subtractive-synthesis analog machine, the words that RMI was bandying around, like "digital" and "computer," had no significance whatsoever.

The full story of how the RMI KC-II came to be is a long and fascinating one. The potted version, herewith delivered, is that the Allen Organ Company of Pennsylvania, overseers of the RMI (Rocky Mount Instruments) brand name, had been involved in digital sound generation (as in sampling) for its range of church organs as far back as 1971. Although by today's standards, its sampling and encoding techniques are about as closely related to the modern idiom as thrashing wet clothes about on rocks in the river is to the latest computer-controlled washing machine, the Allen Computer Organ products proved

...

popular, and a good number and range of them were made.

Concurrently, RMI scored fair success in the electronic piano market, which was at least related to the synth market, and by the mid-1970s certain enterprising Allen Organ engineers spotted the potential for a marriage. "Why don't we stick the innards of an Allen Computer Organ into the case of an RMI stage piano?" they asked?

First, an RMI KC-1 briefly appeared as a test product in 1974. The KC-1 mainly housed organ samples, though a card slot allowed new sounds to be loaded in externally. Indeed, the KC-II's presets were largely chosen from the types of sounds people had been asking for on the earlier model. These preset sounds were playable in 12-voice polyphony, which was highly unusual at the time, and as on the KC-I, you could load in fresh sounds using data cards posted into a slot on the front panel.

With its bright color scheme and double row of rocker switches, the KC-II looks, for all the world, like a stage organ. There are a dozen presets, spearheaded by an enthusiastic and spirited stereo electronic organ. The organ and bells are rich and classy, and the remainder—bells, pipe organ, Clav, strings, guitar, horn, electric piano, jazz flute and Clav, alto recorder and harpsichord—are all more than passable. (Rereading the preset list, I think we have to be thankful that whoever put this lot together didn't get the job of assembling the General MIDI sound set.)

To the left of the presets is a small bank of tone modifiers, including chorus/vibrato, octave transpose and overall envelope parameters, which can be manipulated in real time using the alarming number of footpedals that come with the KC-II and lie beneath your feet like a row of gin traps.

Pedal control sounds good in theory, because it leaves your hands free for playing. But the KC-II was just too dependent on them for your average clod-hopping rocker. They covered pitch bend, envelope modulation and vibrato, plus a messy, somewhat overhanging sustain and more.

The RMI KC-II is a fascinating instrument, and if found today, will most likely be in working order. You will be amazed at the sound quality, especially of the organs, but you'll need to put in some time to figure out the pedal arrangement (assuming any model found today still has its pedals), plus the various sound-layering and sound-tweaking possibilities. You're fairly unlikely to come across a mint-condition set of sound data cards, but the RMI collection comprised all manner of weird and wonderful noises, from the female vowel "Ah" to waldhorn(?) to recorders to various synth waveforms. New sounds can be loaded in as presets and layered with other

voices, using dedicated envelopes, etc. As I said, the RMI KC-II is a fascinating animal.

So why didn't it sell? A glance upward to the original price (which you can triple to put into true perspective here in the mid-1990s) tells most of the story. The other factor was that people were not ready for digital synthesis in 1977, and by the time they were, some six years later, the RMI division of Allen Organ had been put out to pasture—viewed, it seems, as a bit of a madcap, costly experiment.

Synthesist Roger Powell was tangentially involved with the creation of the instrument and, indeed, used the RMI KC-II, as did Todd Rundgren and other luminaries such as Jean-Michel Jarre. Price limited the KC-II's appeal to the glitterati, though, while no one else could figure it out or afford it. Severe marketing problem, that one.

Roland D-50 — Digital polyphonic synthesizer

THE FAX

Keyboard:	61-note
Programs:	64 single
External storage:	Card
Polyphony:	16-voice
Oscillators per voice:	4 partials
Effects:	Reverb, chorus, EQ
Connections:	Upper/lower audio outs, phones, pedals, MIDI
Dimensions:	974mm x 332mm x 94mm
Weight:	11.4kg

THE FIGURES

Chief designer:	Jimi Yamabata
Production run:	1987-89
Approx. units sold:	200,000
Options:	ROM/RAM data cards, PG 1000 knobs and switches programmer, Musitronics MEX Multimode Expansion board (doubles memory, multitimbralism)
Sounds:	Roland ROM cards, plus PA Decorder, MIDIMouse, Dr. Sound, East-West, Metra, Kid Nepro, Valhalla, Maartists, Voice Crystal, Music Pack
Miscellaneous:	Editor/librarians: Beaverton (Mac), Opcode Patch Factory (Mac), Steinberg Synthworks (ST); books include *D-50 Playing and Programming* by Jon Eiche, *The D-50 Book* by Jeff Burger, *The D-50 Book* from Roland; and *The D-50 Right Now!*, *D-50 Sound Making and Programming*, *D-50: 64 New Sounds* and *D-50: Programming Basses*, all by Dan Walker.
Orig. price (1987):	$1895 (£1445)
Price in 1996:	$650 (£550)

The D-50 was the first big-selling instrument to use what is commonly known as sample+ synthesis design, which is, essentially, subtractive, analog-style processing of sampled waves stored in a large bank of waveform ROM.

In the hands of the D-50, s+s was termed "Linear Arithmetic Synthesis," a system based entirely in software that went on to grace a generation of Roland products, from the seminal pre-General MIDI MT-32 module to the D-70 professional synth. Although LA synthesis is not complex in principle, the D-50 could hardly be accused of being immediate in the hands of the idle programmer—not in the way of, say, the Korg M1, of a similar vintage and not dissimilar style. D-50 users still tend to rely on the presets or invest in some of the squillions of sounds that have been programmed for this classic-of-classics keyboards.

Even years after its release, it's not hard to see why the D-50 was an instant hit. Multitextured sounds like the whirring Digital Native Dance, Breathy Chiffer, Gritttar and Fantasia were not just revolutionary sounds of and for their time, but they have also gone on to become part of the currency and language of synth programming.

Physically a low-key instrument with a 2x40 character screen with soft buttons, a sensible number of dedicated buttons and the added pleasures of a joystick, the D-50 may not blind you with science, but it does make quite a performance out of naming and coordinating constituent parts of its sound architecture. The smallest unit of currency is a "partial," a sound snippet which can be one of two things: a short PCM sample—chink, chiff, blip, bleep or blur—or a full synthesized waveform. Partials can be combined in one of seven permutations: PCM+PCM, PCM+synth waveform, etc. Thus combined, a sound is then called a "tone." Finally, you can combine two tones in either split or layered formation. The result of all this jiggery-pokery is that most D-50 presets are dual voices which utilize four partials. A quick bit of math will then reveal that the instrument's tally of 32 available partials produces, in fact, no more than eight-voice polyphony at the end of the day. Even in 1987, this was a little on the stingy side. Fortunately, classic D-50 sounds tend to be harmonically rich and complex and lend themselves to being used for specific, generally polyphony-light parts rather than for the sweeping gesture.

Having figured out a tone from a structure and a part from a partial, D-50 programming sticks closely to traditional subtractive analog synthesis lines. Sound modifiers include a Time Variant Filter (or TVF), which can only be used for the synthesized waveforms. You can think of it as a glorified VCF with cutoff frequency, resonance and keyboard follow, along with a plethora of parameters governing modulation amounts (from LFO, the envelope generators and dynamic control from the keyboard). The "Time" part of the name alludes to the filter's dedicated multistage, time- and level-type envelope generator. Equally specific envelope generators can be used for the TVA (amplifier), and these, along with many LFO modulation controls, can be used by all the partials.

Each tone can also make use of its own programmable chorus and EQ settings. Reverb is applied globally to the complete final patch; there are 32 preset types on offer, including halls, chapels, gates, slapback echoes and such. The quoted 24-bit reverb exudes quality, even if reverb tends to be the first thing ditched in a recording situation. In which case, the D-50's 8-bit samples are exposed in all their grainy glory.

What gives the D-50 its character—indeed, what gives most any instrument much of its character—is the first snippet of sound that your ear picks up, and this is where the PCM samples stored in ROM come into play. The 100 or so PCM samples comprise 47 one-shot percussive samples, 27 looped samples and 24 reworked loops of other samples, among which you will find chiffy flute attacks, flailing drums, piano front ends, guitar chinks and more. The synth waveform side of the instrument is designed to fulfill the role of a sound's "body"—something that can also change over time using the extensive envelope generators.

Although capable of producing a massive range of sounds, the D-50 does have a distinctive "eeeow" ring to many of its patches, from pianos to strings to pads. Though you may not ascend to the full heights of detailed programming, you can achieve some quite substantial levels of customization simply by altering the balance between two tones with the joystick.

In performance, the D-50 has a lot going for it. Aside from using keyboard dynamics to control volume, tone and modulation, it has aftertouch—helpfully, slider-controlled—portamento and a neat feature called "chase play," which delays the start of one sound within a dual or split pair of tones.

Let's pause for a couple of observations here. First, although the D-50 outputs are clearly marked "upper" and "lower," most people blithely assume these are just stereo outputs. The reason this is important is that since most sounds actually involve two layered tones, you need to be sure you are not losing half the sound by plugging into the wrong output jack.

The second, and far more worrisome, observation is that although the D-50 keyboard is capable of great bouts of player-initiated expression, it is also one of the most notoriously unreliable instruments Roland ever made in terms of the actual keyboard mechanism. The problem is that notes either fail to trigger at all or jump straight to full 127 MIDI volume. Most often, this is due to dirty key contacts, which, if you feel reasonably brave, you can clean this yourself by taking out each key in turn until you get to the offending note and gently rub said contact with isopropyl alcohol. A tip: After you do this, rub the contact even more gently with a piece of paper. Not sandpaper, just paper. For some reason, a contact that

Roland

Name: Roland

Head Office: 4-16 Dojimahama 1-chome, Kita-ku, Osaka, Japan; tel: 06-345-9779; fax: 06-345-9795

U.S. Distributor: Roland Corporation U.S.: 7200 Dominion Circle, Los Angeles, CA 90040-3696; tel: 213-685-5141; fax: 213-722-0911

UK Distributor: Roland UK Ltd.: Atlantic Close, Swansea Enterprise Park; Swansea, Glamorgan SA7 9EJ; tel: 01792-702701; fax: 01792-310248

Founded: 1972

No. of employees: 1000

Business: Synthesizers, samplers, keyboards, digital audio products, sequencers, digital pianos, guitar synthesizers, drum machines, amplifiers, multimedia equipment, computer plotters

Roland (named after one of King Arthur's knights of the round table—this British legend being one of founder Ikutaru Kakehashi's many keen interests) is the most accessible and perhaps the most interesting of all the big Japanese musical instrument companies.

Mr. Kakehashi began as an engineer for the Acetone organ back in the 1960s. Though a large company to Western eyes, Roland is in fact a tiny company by Japanese standards, merely a fraction of the size of Yamaha or Kawai, which in turn are but a fraction of the size of Matsushita, which manufactures Technics and Panasonic instruments.

Roland's influence far outweighs its size, though. Stemming largely from Mr. Kakehashi's passionate love of producing music and lack of hands-on skill, Roland has championed the cause of electronic products and gadgets that allow nonmusicians (in the dexterous sense) to create music. These include sequencers, drum machines, arpeggiators and most importantly of all, the MIDI standard. A similar "open door" policy has led Roland to push the development of alternative MIDI controllers, most notably guitar synthesizers but also drum pads.

In 1972, Roland was set up primarily as an R&D company. The first products, the TR-77, -55 and -33 drum machines, were co-developed with Pioneer. Soon after came keyboards and the SH series of monophonic synthesizers, then electric pianos, amplifiers (the JC-120, first produced in 1975 and still a wonderful product) and guitar synthesizers (1977). BOSS, a brand-name division of Roland, was set up in 1973, mainly for the production and widespread distribution of effects pedals (so you don't need to be a "Roland dealer" to stock them).

During the 1970s and the first half of the 1980s, Roland aligned itself quite strongly with analog synthesizers, only moving into digital waters, as seemed inevitable, in 1987 with the D-50—not a bad debut, of course.

Even so, Roland was the first to take up the challenge, first posed in America by Sequential and Oberheim, of a universal communications standard, which became MIDI.

General MIDI was another standard that Roland not only helped promote but practically helped itself to, since the first GM product (the Sound Canvas) was actually in production as GM was still in the process of being ratified. This risky piece of jumping the gun has paid handsome dividends and provided sufficient clear water to establish Roland and the Sound Canvas as the de facto standard in the emerging multimedia race.

In the late 1980s, Roland went through a period of rapid expansion, not only adding new factories in Japan but acquiring a 65 percent stake in the Italian firm Siel. (Roland's successful E Series of home keyboards is now produced in Europe. Roland also has numerous joint ventures in countries around the world, including the U.S., Canada, the UK and Scandinavia.) During this period, Roland also acquired organ specialists Rodgers and the rights to the Rhodes name, subsequently producing a range of piano-based synths under that brand. However, it is unclear how long this will continue, since Harold Rhodes now seems to want his name back and is presently on the verge of producing his own electric pianos once more.

Roland spends the highest percentage of its income on R&D, employing an unusual system of independent production teams that develop and nurture their own products and prepare them to manufacture. While this system of "competing" teams keep spirits high and products focused and also keeps an absolute avalanche of products on the starting blocks, it also throws up the odd anomaly wherein sequential Roland products seem to overlap or have blurred technologies because they were designed and produced by different teams. The potential for confusion is exacerbated by Roland's steadfast refusal to produce written owners manuals in an intelligible form, a criticism that has been voiced universally for many years but remains unheeded.

Although Roland has not diversified into bathroom fittings a la Yamaha, Roland DG (Digital Group) has established itself as a world leader in the production of plotters and associated computer design equipment. In general, Roland was quick to ally itself with the computer industry, producing "gray boxes" long before other companies saw any potential in this area of the market. Computer control is, of course, the ultimate "nonmusician's" entry into the world of music, and Roland's efforts in this field are very much in line with its philosophy of making music attainable and obtainable by all.

Like any company, Roland has had its ups and downs, its successes and failures, but the links it maintains in the musical community remain steady and invaluable. Throughout the years, Roland has set great store by hitting the streets with road shows and endorsements (most notably by Elton John, with the RD-1000 piano), plus sponsorship of song and sound contests, magazines and music schools in Japan—small scale endeavors, perhaps, but relevant, effective and totally in the spirit of Roland's charter philosophy to be "the best rather than the biggest."

In 1991, Ikutaru Kakehashi received an honorary Doctorate of Music from Berklee College of Music, an extraordinary achievement for this (essentially) nonmusician and visionary who retired from the presidency in early 1996.

is too clean works—or rather, doesn't—just as if it were too dirty, and rubbing with the paper dulls down the contact to perfection.

The MIDI is well-defined and easily controlled. Splits or combinations can be sent out on different channels. Mono mode is available (good for guitarists), but multitimbralism is limited to two channels. Painstaking programming, mapping two halves of a split tone to separate areas of the keyboard, can squeeze a little extra zoning out of a standard instrument, but if you want actual multitimbralism, you had better buy yourself the Musitronics MEX Multimode Expansion board, which not only multitimbralizes the D-50 but also doubles its internal sound storage capacity. Be warned, though, that the polyphony will of course remain as it was.

Many ROM and RAM cards have been made over the years (there are some good newish ones from Metra Sound) though none are cheap. A more cost-effective method is to store sounds on disk via SysEx. Not clear in the manual is that you must press and hold down the data transfer button until you press Enter, when loading or dumping sounds.

Hazy chiffy and/or "belly" sounds may be the classic types associated with the D-50, but in truth, it is capable of much more. It does some excellent organs, you can program some lush analog strings and the range of moody electric pianos is surprisingly good. The D-50 is not as good for acoustic sounds (notably acoustic piano) as we have come to expect from sample-based synths, but the range of pad sounds is still as good as they come.

There can hardly be an artist who has not used a D-50 in his or her time. It is all over Prince's *Lovesexy*, and Genesis were extensive users, as was Sting around the time of *Dream of the Blue Turtles*. One of Michael Jackson's programmers, Eric Persing, was and remains a senior Roland voicing specialist. And on and on.

The all-important factory presets were programmed by Eric Persing and Adrian Scott. The classic Digital Native Dance came about by accident, via one of the senior Roland PCM engineers, who had a habit of spinning through the current crop of PCM sounds back-to-back on his NEC computer when showing Persing and Scott how the library was coming. One day, a new ROM appeared with a bunch of sequence/loops at the end; this was greeted with great excitement by the programming team. "Oh, no," exclaimed Mr. PCM, much taken aback. "Only a joke." "No, it's amazing. Make more of them!" insisted Persing and Scott. And so Digital Native Dance, and thereafter thousands of wavesequence/loop-type sounds, entered the musical vocabulary.

Roland went on to produce a number of D-50 soundalikes, from the D-5 to the D-10 to the MT-32, etc. And as is so often the case, none has quite the same breadth as the original D-50. Though the D-50 is hopelessly outpaced in terms of polyphony, effects programming, multitimbralism and all the rest of it, many of its classic sounds are still highly sought after and are not, frankly, available anywhere else.

Roland JD-800 Digital polyphonic synthesizer

THE FAX
Keyboard:	61-note
Programs:	64 RAM
External storage:	Card
Polyphony:	24-voice (tones)

Oscillators per voice:	4 tones per patch
Effects:	One multieffects processor
Connections:	Stereo audio (mix/dry), phones, footswitches, MIDI
Dimensions:	1040mm x 420mm x 108mm
Weight:	15kg

THE FIGURES
Chief designer:	Mr. Takahashi & Mr. (Jimi) Yamabata
Production run:	1991-93
Options:	M-256E Data cards
Sounds:	SL-JD80 series waveform cards, Metrasound, Soundsource, Dr. Sound, East-West, Voice Crystal
Miscellaneous:	You can record real-time parameter changes using SysEx.
Orig. price (1991):	$2895 (£1499)
Price in 1996:	$1200 (£900)

Roland tells a story of the perils of responding to "demand": Let's say one person wants a certain instrument. He rings up his local dealer. They haven't got it. He rings another dealer. They don't have it either. In the course of the next few weeks, he rings up dozens of dealers. Stories then filter back to the manufacturer via the dealers that this instrument is being requested, and the manufacturer is left with the totally erroneous impression that everyone wants this particular product.

Roland didn't tell this story about the JD-800, but it kind of fits. Everyone, it seemed to Roland, wanted the return of panel knobs and switches. Fanfare of trumpets...ladies and gentlemen, the JD-800! Er....silence. Then, "What does this do?" "Oh, I don't understand that..."

The JD-800 is a wonderful instrument, but it did not break any sales records. In pure sales terms, it was in fact, a major disappointment for Roland.

On a synth, it all comes down to sound. The JD-800 sounds like it looks: big, impressive, complex, deep, multilayered. It doesn't adhere overtly to some fancy new synthesis method. Loosely, you can call this a sample+ synthesis instrument, since it does pluck starter samples from a pool of waveform ROM (internally or from cards), process them with filters and envelope generators and such and then add a top coat of glossy effects. But the whole is greater than the sum of these parts. Flip through JD-800 presets and, in an instant, you know you are in serious company. This is a synth you can take on a gig by itself. I know—I've done it many times.

With its array of sliders, rakishly angled system and patch controls, firm keyboard and distinctive orange display, the JD-800 is wonderfully tactile. It really makes you want to play and start tweaking. However, you shouldn't do this without first having studied a bit of JD-800 sound construction theory.

A JD-800 patch can be made from up to four "tones" marked A through D, each of which can be thought of as a complete synth in itself, with its own starter PCM wave, filtering, envelope, etc. Before you start tweaking, you need to let the panel know which of the four tones within your current sound you want to adjust. This is done by pressing the "active tone" button followed by one or more of the Tone A-D buttons. The selected tone(s) then blink and off you go.

At the heart of this instrument is a bank of waveform ROM containing 108 preset samples and waves sampled at 44.1kHz. This last fact should not be glossed over, because it is one of the two main reasons why the JD-800 sounds as glisteningly fresh and clear as it does. The other is the fact that the JD-800 has separate microprocessors for its synthesizer section and keyboard scanning. This makes the JD lightning-fast in touch and response and makes it feel as immediate and controllable as early synths, which were not weighed down with overloaded processing. Roland was roundly, and perhaps rightly, criticized for its sluggish keyboards (notably on the D-50 and D-70), and the JD, in the words of one Roland programmer, was very much the "D-50 done right."

In comparison to some s+s instruments that offer hundreds of starting-off points, the JD-800 is not over-endowed. Yet this collection of sine, triangle, square, pulse and noise waveforms, plus fully looped instrument samples and sundry front-end attacks covers the ground more than adequately. The reason, as ever, is simply that the programming team made good choices. And for this, we have to thank Eric Persing in Los Angeles, who not only produced the waveform ROM but also programmed the stunning factory presets. Persing consciously honed in on classic synthesizer sounds as opposed to "natural" sounds, offering, for instance, a whole range of sawtooth waves culled from illustrious synths of the past rather than just "a sawtooth wave."

Within each tone, your chosen PCM wave appears in what the JD calls the waveform generator. Other controls here include fine and coarse tuning, random pitch, key follow (with which you can stabilize pitch over the whole keyboard range, if you like), aftertouch and pitch bend controls, and LFO1 & 2 modulation amounts. Above the waveform generator is a complete pitch envelope section featuring Roland's time- and level-based envelope generators as well as velocity, time and key follow amount sliders. Bear in mind that this is simply the "oscillator" section of one of the instrument's four possible tones. In particular, it is the cross-referencing of so many parameters to velocity and aftertouch that makes the JD such an expressive instrument to play.

The filter offers not just resonant lowpass filtering, but highpass and bandpass, with modulation from LFOs or the dedicated six-stage envelope generator. What is so impressive here is that you can see as well as hear how different filtering configurations affect your sound. And the JD does not simply rehash the tools of yesteryear; it's brilliant to be able to control aftertouch from a slider or to envelop a modern sample with bandpass filtering. The blend of technologies is both seamless and wondrous.

With multistage envelope generators for the amplifier and multiwaveform LFOs (two of them), the JD would seem to offer every parameter at your fingertips. Well, not entirely, as it happens. There's no maneuverable pulse width, for example, and no sync between "oscillators," so this is not entirely an old-style synth in modern clothes. But the chance to layer up to four tones in a single patch should be compensation enough for most.

A few caveats: The maximum polyphony is 24-voice, but a voice may not be what you think it is. A patch employing all four tones (A-D) will in fact be six-voice. Users also frequently whine about the JD-800's multitimbralism, which is a one-at-a-time configuration only and capable of playing only six parts at that. True, multitimbralism is not the JD's best feature, but what it does do, bearing in mind restrictions on polyphony, it does very well. For instance, you can program a different amount of reverb or chorus on each part.

This works well with the JD's excellent range of drum sounds. Though one drum map of sounds exists internally, the JD's best drum performances come off Roland PCM cards that slot in, alongside new program cards, at the back. Most are taken from the Roland S-series sample library and feature eerily accurate TR-909 and TR-808 samples. Overall, the drum sounds are live, sibilant and inspiring.

On a single sound, you can trowel on no less than seven simultaneous effects, ranging from reverbs to delays to chorus, distortion and spectrum enhancer, most, though not all of them, editable in terms of speed, depth or size. The effects section of the JD is not under slider control, but you can chop and change the order of effects (do you want reverbed chorus or chorused reverb?), which is rare, and the effects are ultra high quality.

Though it seems almost sacrilegious to talk in terms of presets on an instrument like this, in designing the presets (all wholly overwritable, of course, though it's a fair bet most second-hand models will still have the factory settings intact), the Roland programmers outdid themselves. Look out for Syzygy, a wild amalgam of post-nuclear bangs and swooshes; Crystal Rhodes, an ice-castle electric piano that Steve Hackett fans may be interested to learn was used as the sole backing on "A Blue Part of Town" (a one-take improvisation, incidentally) from his *Blues With a Feeling* album; the searing Wailing Guitar (the ultimate synth guitar patch) and the translucent Spun Glass. If you are not capable of creating sounds from scratch, the JD system permits even the idle noodler to change presets by substituting new PCM samples on the waveform generator or altering the balance between four tones or going crazy with effects and coming up with plenty of original patches. You don't have to be a MIDI geek to have fun on a JD-800.

Speaking of MIDI, the spec is generally good, though with one or two curious features. Each patch can be programmed with its own MIDI channel, which is useful, and most sliders kick out SysEx, so you can record timbral changes into a sequencer in real time and have them play back. SysEx fairly devours data, and if you embark on overly ambitious feats of programming, you'll quickly land yourself in a SysEx traffic jam. MIDI controller messages would have been less greedy on the processing, but there we are. Also, Local Off doesn't just disable the keyboard; it also disables the ability to change patches on the control panel. This is surprisingly annoying.

The JD-800 is unreservedly one of the great synths of the modern age. Flawed, to be true, but then so are the Minimoog, Prophet-5, et al. Be careful of brightness, though. The JD can take your head off on some patches, and you'll do well to find and make use of the global EQ feature when you are playing live.

Playing around with the panel sliders live is great fun, of course. Handily, the status of each of the four tone buttons is automatically stored within the patch data. Live, then, you can simply press the "layer active" button and your predestined choice of active tone will be available. Whenever you do nudge a slider, the value is not simply added or subtracted but rather goes instantly to an absolute value determined by slider position.

The JD-800 appeared on the crest of retro fever, when everyone wanted more than vintage sounds and features—they wanted vintage instruments. Now, with more perspective and fewer vintage instruments around to buy, the JD-800 is finding its way into sessions alongside the standard setup of Rhodes, Minimoog and Clavi. (Scant compensation for Roland, one suspects.)

Keen Roland observers may have idly pondered the question of the JD-800's name. Initially Roland was to call this the JP-800, the JP for Jupiter, a name Roland had good fortune with in the past. Unfortunately for Roland, Sanyo had, in the meantime, copyrighted the names of all of the planets and that, sadly, was that. D, with its connotations of "D-50," was deemed the next-best letter.

Roland Juno-60
Analog polyphonic synthesizer

THE FAX

Keyboard:	61-note
Programs:	56
External storage:	Cassette Interface
Polyphony:	6-voice
Oscillators per voice:	1, plus sub-oscillator
Effects:	2 choruses, arpeggiator
Connections:	Mono/stereo, phones, VCF control jack, pedal hold, patch shift, arpeggio clock in, data load/save, DCB
Dimensions:	1060mm x 378mm x 113mm
Weight:	12kg

THE FIGURES

Chief designer:	Hideki Izuchi
Production run:	1982-1983
Approx. units sold:	30,000
Options:	CB-Juno Carrying case, KS-2 stand, OP-8 CV Interface, MD-8 DCB-MIDI Interface
Sounds:	Roland program data cassette; cassettes from Kid Nepro, Walt Whitney
Miscellaneous:	MIDI kits available from Analogics: (212) 466-6911 and Encore Electronics: (510) 820-7551 in the U.S.; Miditec (807) 345-6434 in Canada; Kenton Electronics: 0181-974-2475 in UK.
Orig. price (1982):	$895 (£800)
Price in 1996:	$300-400 (£300-450)

In 1982, the words "digital" and "synthesizer" were only juxtaposed by people wearing thick spectacles in university electronic-music labs, and "sampling" was still something you did with certain sections of the public or real ale. The cost of a decent polysynth (as they were then known) from a serious company like Oberheim or Sequential Circuits was several thousand dollars. Sure, the Japanese were making clever instruments like the Jupiter-8 and the CS80, but many still viewed them as cheap, harsh-sounding substitutes for the real thing. All synths were unstable, and programmability—being able to actually store patches—was eagerly sought after and by no means yet standard.

Then out came the Juno-6—a spanking new polyphonic synth with digitally controlled oscillators (wording that caused considerable confusion) for under a grand! It was an instant success. But by the summer, Roland had the Juno-60: an identical synth, marginally more expensive, but with memories. Juno-6 owners were understandably miffed, but it didn't stop the Juno-60 from becoming a rip-snorting success. For an entire generation of piano and organ players whose new instrument aspirations were firmly backstopped at a monophonic synth or a synth/string machine, the arrival of the Juno-60 unlocked the door to an uncharted world of polyphonic synthesis.

The Juno-60 was affordable. It was stable, for heaven's sake, with digitally controlled oscillators. It even seemed understandable. And it also had this curious gaping hole at the back called DCB, with which you could hook it up to all manner of other exciting Roland goodies, like other synths and sequencers. Above all, the sounds "out of the box" were big, interesting, rich and powerful.

This last fact was and still is quite surprising, because there is only one oscillator per voice on board, and perceived wisdom says that you need two or even three oscillators per voice to produce sounds that really say something. But on the Juno-60, only a square-wave sub-oscillator is around to lend a hand in this respect

The control panel is the model of self-evidence. Every parameter section has its own little space which follows the general signal path, running from oscillator to filter to envelope generator. Though still an analog instrument, the oscillators are DCOs, which basically means they don't drift out of tune. The DCO panel features push-button-selected sawtooth and/or variable-pulse waveforms, with a pulse width modulation slider and LFO manual/env routing switch alongside. A third push-button activates the sub-oscillator (one octave below, square-wave), and this signal can be added at any volume courtesy of its own dedicated slider. You can also add white noise to the sound.

Filtering comes in two basic modes: a simple highpass filter—a notched slider operating at three set frequencies of 350Hz, 1kHz and 5kHz—and a lowpass filter with cutoff frequency and resonance sliders. Three sliders select filter control: from the envelope generator (in positive or negative inversions), from the LFO or from keyboard follow (for setting up sounds that get less bright the higher you play, etc.). The filter can be set to self-oscillate, producing the spooky, spacey, atonal noises that were featured on some of the Bank 7 patches on the factory data cassette. The VCA can either be shaped by the ADSR envelope generator or set to a preset gate (full on or off) as determined by the level slider. There's just the one envelope generator, with attack, decay, sustain and release sliders.

For LFO modulation, there are rate and delay time sliders and an auto/manual switch, so that modulation will start either when the set delay time has passed or when, in the manual position, you press the LFO trigger button on the performance panel. All of these parameters are controllable in real time: Move a slider, and you'll hear the effect of that move immediately. Two types of chorus can also be added to a patch: one stronger and one weaker. These can even be combined (press both buttons at once) for a fairly convincing, whinnying, fast-Leslie effect.

If a Juno-60 has a definable, recognizable sound, it is one of earthy richness. The Juno excels at two types of sound in particular: classic synth strings (the sort of patches that fill up space and contain enough movement to be interesting without being obtrusive) and punchy synth basses, ranging from substantial, muted sub-bass types to edgy, resonant tones perfect for burbling through a rave or techno track. Of course, this is not the whole story. The Juno can produce some wonderful, if simple, sound effects, like muted bells, wind noises and a whole plethora of whooshes and whizzes.

The Juno's best "effect" is probably the arpeggiator, operating in a variety of modes (up, down, up and down) over a maximum of three octaves, with speed controllable. The hold button alongside is ideal for setting up an arpeggio groove and changing chords at will while the groove continues. The arpeggiator can also be clocked by an external device, like a drum machine or sequencer, via the arpeggio in jack. This is strictly a trigger pulse (+2.5V or more) not a MIDI clock. For anyone who doesn't play keyboards too well, the arpeggiator will provide hours of brilliant fun and inspiration.

The performance controls include spring-loaded pitch bend (which you can select to drag the cutoff point of the VCF along with it) an LFO trigger button and a small octave transposer spanning three octaves.

The Juno-60 came out shortly before MIDI but at a time when most companies, especially Roland, were looking at digital interfaces for connecting synth to synth or synth to sequencer. Roland's pre-MIDI answer was the Digital Communication Bus (DCB), a multipin connector supported by Roland's MSQ-700 and JSQ-60 sequencers and, via the OC-8 kit, the Jupiter-8. The optional OP-8 VC Interface kit was also produced to allow communication with Roland's classic MC-4 Microcomposer. Of course, when MIDI came along only a year after the Juno's release, Roland had to scramble to produce a DCB-to-MIDI box, the MD-8. Though this bulky standalone box does give you full 16-channel access, users are far better served by an actual MIDI kit inserted into the instrument.

The Juno does not excel at bells or gongs or complex patches that need cross-mod or ring mod parameters and two oscillators per voice, and there are no portamento or unison parameters. You must also remember that the envelope generator is shared between the VCA and VCF. However, analog synthesis has rarely been made so easy; indeed, the Juno is a first-class instrument on which to learn about subtractive synthesis, because it is almost impossible to get lost. Data can still be lost or accidentally erased, though, in which case you will have to find one of the original program data cassettes.

In its first flush of youth, the Juno-60 was snapped up by a whole host of players for whom the concept of owning a polyphonic synth had previously been but a dream (among whom I number myself). "Name" users were not particularly visible at the time, because name users could afford seemingly more glamorous instruments like the Jupiter-8 (although Howard Jones was keen on the Juno-60 early in his career).

With the analog revival, however, a stream of bands and players have rediscovered the instrument, from such stalwarts as Vince Clarke ("It is really special") to The Beloved's Jon March ("My favorite") to myself: I wheeled the Juno out on the Anderson, Bruford, Wakeman and Howe tours in 1990 and have not looked back since. Finally, in an era when Roland is rightly slammed for producing unreadably complex owners manuals, the Juno-60 also deserves praise for its concise, helpful and "musicianly" manual. See, Roland, you used to be able to do it!

Roland Juno-106
Analog polyphonic synthesizer

Michael Mendelson

THE FAX

Keyboard:	61-note
Programs:	128 single
External storage:	Cassette interface
Polyphony:	6-voice
Oscillators per voice:	1, plus sub-oscillator
Effects:	2 chorus,
Connections:	Mono/stereo, phones, MIDI, cassette load and save, pitch shift, hold
Dimensions:	992mm x 120mm x 320mm
Weight:	10kg

THE FIGURES

Production run:	1984-86
Approx. units sold:	40,000
Options:	AB-1 resin-molded case
Sounds:	Roland program data cassette
Miscellaneous:	Computers & Music Editor (PC), Opcode Patch Factory (Mac)
Orig. price (1984):	$1095 (£880)
Price in 1996:	$400 (£350)

In keeping with so many Roland instruments, the Juno-106 has seesawed its way through life—appearing first as a desirable "MIDI Juno-60," before more detailed comparisons revealed the 106's sound to be rather thinner than its mentor's. Though it sold in large quantities during the 1980s—indeed Roland president Mr. Kakehachi proclaimed this the company's biggest selling synth (before the D-50 came along, of course)—it's only in the mid-1990s that classic status seems to have been conferred. Certainly in America, as of writing here in 1996, the 106 is one the most sought after of the readily available vintage synths.

The basic voice architecture of the Juno-106 is very similar to both the Juno-60 and the JX-3P, with six stable DCOs configurable in either sawtooth or variable pulse waveforms supported by an audio square-wave sub-oscillator, plus noise, all slider controlled in terms of volume. A useful improvement from the Juno-60 design is the oscillator panel's pitch range selector (16', 8', 4'). On the J-60, pitch is handled by a performance panel "octave" switch. There's also portamento, with its own on/off switch and rate control.

On the downside, the Juno-106 shaves off one or two Juno-60 features, most notably the arpeggiator, which, ironically, is a tool whose storming comeback seems to have coincided with the 106's. There is no "hold" button, and neither, for some curious reason, is there envelope generator control over the pulse width, both of which were features on the Juno-60.

This is a bright and cheerful instrument with plenty of large, hands-on switches and sliders, making it extremely easy to understand and program. Even the MIDI has features under dedicated button control (channel selection via the 16 program buttons), plus you can choose to transmit or receive just keyboard information, keyboard + bender and program change, or "all," thanks to the three-position MIDI function switch at the rear. Simple, direct and useful. In "all" mode, the Juno-106 can send or receive SysEx for most of its programming parameters, including its famously smooth chorus. SysEx might be a data-heavy method, but at least it does give you the opportunity to record real-time changes within a sequence.

The Juno-106 excels at much the same type of sounds as the Juno-60; a little thinner, perhaps, but still excellent across a range of sounds from twangy, rubbery basses and organs to analog synth string washes to attacky vamping synth patches.

A liberal sprinkling of Juno-106 can be heard on George Michael's "I Want Your Sex," where the 106 not only provides the warbling synth tone but also the bass and the "gated synth" as well.

In the 1990s, this instrument has also begun to find favor with the likes of DNA, Bass-o-Matic and Incognito, placing it high on the must-have list of gear within the dance scene.

Roland Jupiter-8
Analog polyphonic synthesizer

THE FAX

Keyboard:	61-note
Programs:	64 single, 8 combination
External storage:	Cassette interface
Polyphony:	8-voice
Oscillators per voice:	2
Effects:	Arpeggiator
Connections:	3 mono ¼" jacks, 2 XLRs
Dimensions:	1063mm x 120mm x 485mm
Weight:	21.5kg

THE FIGURES

Chief designer:	Mr. (Jimi) Yamabata
Production run:	1981-84
Approx. units sold:	2000
Options:	KS-20 stand, pedals, OC-8 Interface
Sounds:	Walt Whitney
Miscellaneous:	MIDI Kit specialists include: Analogics: 5261 Maple Ave. E.; Geneva, OH 44041; tel: (216) 466-6911; Encore Electronics: 30 Glenhill Ct.; Danville, CA 94526; tel: (510) 820-7551; Miditec: 423 Darwin Crescent; Thunder Bay, Ontario, P7B 5W5; Canada; tel: (807) 345-6434; Kenton Electronics: 12, Tolworth Rise South; Surbiton, Surrey KT5 9NN UK; tel: 0181-337-0333.
Orig. price (1981):	$5295 (£3999)
Price in 1996:	$1500 (£1000)

By 1981, the custom of slaving up two or more synthesizers in order to produce big new sounds was relatively commonplace among the serious synth fraternity. It was not a happy sight, though, and manufacturers were well aware of the interest in—and, they hoped, benefits of—finding some way to streamline and standardize such capers. Which, of course, they did, with MIDI.

But the Jupiter-8 was on the drawing board just a bit too early. In 1981, the best companies could drum up was an interface not for cross-manufacturer collaboration but for intracompany communication. Launched in the early summer of 1981, the Jupiter-8 arrived on the cusp even of this development, Roland's pre-MIDI digital interface DCB (Digital Communication Bus) didn't find its way onto an instrument until the Juno-60 the following year.

This, in itself, did not prove too much of a drawback for the Jupiter-8. It was, and remains, a purveyor of almost unfeasibly large and weighty sounds. Who needs to connect up synths if one of them sounds like this?

Roland's design philosophy behind the Jupiter-8 was to offer depth, from basic sound to performance. Small wonder, then, that this heavyweight synth was used on such heavyweight sessions as Michael Jackson's *Thriller* and has remained a firm favorite on the recording circuit more or less ever since.

But it was not all smooth sailing; the Jupiter-8's early days were riddled with problems. The first models were notoriously unstable (prompting Roland to upgrade its microprocessors from 12 bit to 14 bit, which also sped up the auto tuning time). Then, the instrument had to be retrofitted with a Roland OC-8 interface in order to bring the instrument into line with DCB. (The OC-8 also lets you tap into MC4 via another interface, the OP-8.) And after all this palaver, you had to use yet another interface, the MD-8, in order to tap into MIDI when "Em One Dee One" arrived on the scene a few years later. Purists of the Vince Clarke variety, who persist in resisting MIDI anyway, may well fancy tracking down some of these ancient connectors (the MC4 Microcomposer, an early sequencer, is still decidedly hip, I'll admit), but for the vast majority of sensible people looking to try their hands at a Jupiter-8, the moral of the story is surely to get your Jupiter-8 MIDI-ed direct. A direct retrofit may also get round the fairly major MD-8 bummer of limited data transfer—as in no modulation or pitch bend.

In spite of such substantial teething problems, the JP-8's range of unbeatable synth/brass patches quickly established it as the only real rival to Yamaha's CS-80, the previous undisputed world champion in the heavyweight division. With 16 oscillators available between VCOs 1 and 2, sounds can be both split and layered for, if you like, a pair of four-voice poly, double-oscillator sounds. VCO1 offers a choice of sawtooth, triangle, pulse or square waveforms, while VCO2 adds noise as a sound source. Cross-modulation between the oscillators, which produces complex, ring modulation-type sounds, is slider-controlled from VCO1's panel. Oscillators can be hard-synced, detuned or given completely independent pitches.

The main filters are lowpass and switchable from 24dB/oct to 12dB/oct, with the choice to shape them by one of the two envelope generators in positive or negative polarities. There is, as was often the case on early Roland synths, a separate, single-slider highpass filter. The envelope generators themselves are configured in standard ADSR form, also offering Key Follow control so that the envelope of a sound (essentially, its decay) can be tailored appropriately as its pitch changes over the keyboard range. The LFO has three waveforms, plus polyphonic sample-and-hold and delay.

Colored similarly to the Jupiter-6 that followed it, the JP-8 has a control panel that's divided horizontally between programming controls and management controls. There's a small central screen that keeps you abreast of both upper and lower patch numbers (an impressive 64 single patches can be stored). More impressive still, for the time, there are an additional eight "patch presets," in which you can store split/"Dual" combinations. Further modes of playing include Solo, which allows you to perform as on a monophonic instrument, and Unison, which lumps all 16 oscillators together for a truly mammoth display of oscillator power.

Although subtractive synthesis was never quite the doddle that people would have you believe it was back in these early days, the JP-8's control panel is labeled so clearly and cleanly that a way out of trouble is rarely far away.

Nowadays, you'd have to be a brave soul to want to take a Jupiter-8 out on a gig, but in its day it was considered a major performance instrument. The left-hand panel below the keyboard is awash with switches and controllers, giving you independent slider control over levels of VCO1, VCO2 and VCF (cutoff point maneuvering); VCO/VCF modulation and (polyphonic) portamento times. Real-time LFO activation is via a white oblong touchpad.

Arpeggiators have gone in and out of fashion as many times as the miniskirt. Should you be reading this in an arpeggiator-friendly time, then you'll be especially pleased to learn of the JP-8's powerful yet simple arpeggiator, which can be clocked externally using a variety of pulse options. The arpeggiator can work over the bottom two octaves, leaving you free to play in right hand, and can operate in up, down, up and down and random modes over a one- to four-octave range.

Although many people subsequently took to Roland's MKS-80 as a MIDI-ed, modular version of the JP-8—indeed, Greg Phillinganes takes a brace of

them out with Michael Jackson to recreate the JP-8 sounds used on older material—the immediacy of the JP-8 cannot be recreated in this or any other way. Many's the programmer who swears by their Jupiter-8 simply because they can twiddle a knob and achieve pretty well in seconds exactly the effect or texture that they're looking for. As a studio synth, the Jupiter-8 provides not just power but a timbral richness and substance sadly still missing from most of today's digital darlings.

Provided you don't have to cart it around too much, a Jupiter-8 that survived to this day should be a relatively safe bet (though it has to be said that reliability was never the JP-8's best point). For extended use, even within the confines of a studio, a MIDI conversion makes a lot of sense, not in the least because you can then save patch data via SysEx, which circumvents the nightmarish cassette interface.

Roland later brought out the Jupiter-8a, which not only had DCB as standard but also gave you the option of an alterable split point (the split point is otherwise set to two octaves left/three right). In time, the MKS-80 module also appeared, a sort of blend of the Jupiter-8 and its younger cousin, the Jupiter-6, in module form. The MKS-80 is itself a sought-after instrument now (and rightly so), but the Jupiter-8, with its hands-on controls and rich oscillator power, is perhaps the more classy, classic instrument to which to aspire.

Roland JX-3P Analog polyphonic synthesizer

THE FAX

Keyboard:	62-note
Programs:	32 RAM, 32 ROM
External storage:	Cassette interface
Polyphony:	6-voice
Oscillators per voice:	2
Effects:	Chorus
Connections:	Stereo audio, phones, hold, seq trig in, tape, MIDI
Dimensions:	244mm x 172mm x 45mm
Weight:	1.4kg

THE FIGURES

Chief designer:	Mr. Matsui
Production run:	1983-1985
Options:	PG-200 programmer, KS-2 stand, CB-JX leatherette case

Sounds:	Kid Nepro
Miscellaneous:	This was a favored weapon of Prefab Sprout and Thomas Dolby circa 1985.
Orig. price (1983):	$1395 (£1075)
Price in 1996:	$225 ($275 with programmer)

Synths released in 1983 didn't just have their own teething problems to sort out; they all had to confront the burning issue of the day: MIDI. The JX-3P was the first full MIDI instrument from Roland—one of MIDI's prime motivators.

As if this introduction wasn't enough, Roland also chose the JX-3P to see how people would react to sweeping control panels free of knobs and switches, using digital access control instead. So as to ease customers into this new and less expensive form of control, Roland provided the option of a separate programmer (the PG-200). Those who absolutely must have knobs and switches should therefore pay a little extra to get it. (Options: Roland likes options.)

The JX-3P followed hard on the heels of the highly successful Juno-60, although it sprang from a different section of the company: Roland Electronics. (Roland occasionally uses the unusual technique of employing "rival" design teams within the company, a factor that may well encourage the troops but has also been responsible for inconsistencies and overlaps between certain Roland products over the years.) Anyway, at the time the JX3P was a good step up: dual oscillators instead of the J-60's single, a handy little playsequencer, slightly more advanced programming features like cross-modulation, a ring modulator and, of course, MIDI. For a price only slightly higher than that of the J-60, the JX-3P was an attractive proposition, and it sold well.

Each of the two digitally controlled (and thus more stable) oscillators can choose from three waveforms and three octave pitches. They can be detuned, cross-modulated or independently modulated by the LFO or envelope generator, which makes for an excellent start.

The lowpass filter has cutoff frequency and resonance controls, plus envelope amount. No dedicated EG here—the filter can vary its amount of modulation by the envelope generator and even switch polarity, but one envelope generator has to service both filter and amplifier. Filter cutoff can be modulated by the LFO and has variable keyboard tracking.

The EG itself has ADSR parameters and can modulate the amplifier, as with the filter, in positive or negative shapes. The amplifier's gate position goes some way toward overcoming the shared envelope generator.

This is all very neat and tidy. The JX-3P is by no means an advanced analog synthesizer, but in parameter terms, it is quick to get around and encourag-

ing to listen to while you do. Actually, I should qualify that statement to say that *with a PG-200 in tow*, it is quick to get around. Operating in edit mode without the programmer is frustrating because there's no screen and your only clues as to current parameter values are the LEDs. Not only that, but the graphic of a PG-200 stenciled onto the control panel will forever remind you of how much easier it would be if only you had dedicated knobs and switches with which to work. Clever stuff.

Unusually, the sequencer records in step time only, though it is polyphonic, and it has just a 128-note capacity. Provided all you want to do is program up a few pulses or stabs, it's fine. The sequencer is quite fast to use—input notes first, then add the rhythm information—and it can be clocked externally. You can also dump sequences to tape.

Although there is no screen and so no patch names grinning at you, Roland included 32 presets that (according to the manual, at any rate) mimic a whole range of useful tones. Presets include a number of organs, strings, electric pianos and Clavinets, plus one or two "synthy" tones with descriptive names like Fat Fifth, Juicy Funk and Sync Sweep. For home-grown tones, 32 additional memory locations await. As an imitator, the JX-3P inclines towards the thin and one-paced, but let it loose in the free world of "synth," and the cross-mod features and typically warm Roland chorus can drum up interesting mood sounds in a trice.

Though it isn't an earth-shattering instrument in any way, people have grown very fond of the JX-3P. Paddy MacAloon of Prefab Sprout says that this was his main writing instrument in the mid-1980s. "I'm trying to be Picasso with a JX-3P," he said, mysteriously, at the time. MacAloon cohort Thomas Dolby has also been a keen exponent, and you can hear a classic JX-3P patch playing the heavy-sustain, fluted lead line on his "I Live in a Suitcase."

To cover all possible bases, Roland also produced the MKS-30, a full modular version of the JX-3P, which can also make use of the PG-200. In fact, the MKS-30 is marginally more sophisticated in that it responds to velocity (which the JX-3P doesn't) and has 64 memories, all RAM, plus room for another 64 on cartridge. (The JX-3P has no cartridge slot and can only store sound and sequence data externally via the dreaded cassette interface. No SysEx dumping, I'm afraid.) JX-3P owners can peg back a couple of points, because the MKS-30 doesn't have a sequencer. Star U.S. programmer Eric Persing cut his teeth on the JX-3P, producing data cassettes and patch charts for Goodman Music in Los Angeles before he was snapped up by Roland itself.

Bearing in mind the release date, the MIDI spec

isn't too bad, and the instrument does respond to Program Changes. Rather more restricting is the choice you have to make between PG-200 operation and MIDI, by means of a rear-panel switch. But all in all, this remains a friendly analog synth and one made in sufficient quantities for the second-hand market to be balanced evenly between supply and demand.

Roland MC-202 MicroComposer
Analog synth/sequencer

THE FAX

Keyboard:	32-note (pads)
Programs:	None
External storage:	Cassette interface
Polyphony:	Mono
Oscillators per voice:	1 (plus sub-oscillator)
Effects:	None
Connections:	Mono audio, phones, CV and gate in and out
Dimensions:	343mm x 204mm x 55mm
Weight:	1.35kg

THE FIGURES

Chief designer:	Unknown
Production run:	1983-1984
Approx. units sold:	4000
Options:	Connection cord, demo tape, batteries
Sounds:	n/a
Miscellaneous:	Roland's worst-selling instrument ever
Orig. price (1983):	No U.S. price (£160)
Price in 1996:	$350 (£250)

Welcome to one of the hippest instruments of the 1990s, which was in fact Roland's worst-selling instrument in the 1980s. This was not the first time that Roland produced an instrument that everyone wanted—in retrospect. But the MC-202 hit the high spot at both ends: spectacularly unsuccessful upon release; devoured, lauded and avidly collected a decade later.

"MicroComposer" was Roland's fancy name for a sequencer, a type of instrument that had been something of a Roland specialty since the days of the MC-8 and MC-4 back in 1978. The MC-202 nods in the direction of both the MC-4 and Roland's SH-101 mono synth as an all-in-one sequencer and sound

source. If only the Roland marketing people had thought of the word "workstation," it all might have ended very differently.

Now, such a concept seems like a great idea. In 1983, on the eve of MIDI, when the world had ears only for polyphony, the MC-202, with its restrained monophonic synth section and quite fiddly sequencer section, was not what the doctor ordered at all.

A chunky, interesting-looking unit with a pad-type keyboard (on which you input but hardly play), display screen (a rarity) and SH-101-type sliders and buttons controlling the synth section, the MC-202's major problem was identifying itself and its target audience. Viewed as a sequencer with a built-in sound source, the MC is capable of storing some 2600 notes across two channels. The input methods seem primitive by modern standards, but via either "playing" the little key pads in real time, accompanied by a metronome; "tap" input (notes first, tap out the rhythm afterwards); or full step-time input, complete with dotted rhythms and rests (claimed at the time to be a first on a digital sequencer), the MC-202 covers pretty much all eventualities and skill levels. All except the real-time input method are a trifle button-heavy, though, and this perception of complexity was a big turnoff back in 1983.

Expression can be added using features such as portamento and accents, again rudimentary compared to the sophistication of modern sequencers but capable of turning in passages and lines of rare groove value and subtlety.

The beauty of the MC-202 is that you also have a made-to-measure sound source and a good one at that. Though it's only a single-oscillator-plus-sub-oscillator design, as on the SH-101, you can build up a fairly substantial sound, because the pulse wave, sawtooth wave and sub-oscillator each have their own slider volume controls. Pulse width can be modulated by the LFO or the ADSR envelope generator or set manually; the sine wave LFO has simple rate and delay control and the filter, though resonant and capable of being modulated by the LFO or the envelope generator, has to conform to the shape of the amplifier unless the amp is in its gate position. Keyboard tracking is free-flowing and slider-controlled.

All-in-one it might be, but the MC-202 is also well-equipped for the outside world. In 1983, however, the outside world mainly comprised a host of rhythm-based instruments like Roland's TR-606 Drumatix and its now-fabled TB-303 Bassline. The MC-202's dual-channel sequencer is designed so that you can trigger one track with, say, the internal voice and the second with an SH-101 synth or perhaps a TB-303. (Speaking of which, resourceful users are now beginning to realize that an MC-202 can emulate the far more expensive TB-303 pretty successfully, especially if you sprinkle a sequence with enough accents and portamento.)

The CV and gate outputs are not wholly foolproof in their speed and range. Modifications are quite commonly carried out to bypass the sequencer stage of the instrument. In terms of straight clocking, the MC-202 has the pre-MIDI lookalike Sync 24 input and a pair of Sync 24 outputs. Many a MIDI converter will be able to convert this into or out of MIDI.

An interesting, useful device, compact and very well constructed, the MC-202 is keenly sought after.

Roland MKS-80
Analog polyphonic synthesizer

THE FAX

Keyboard:	None
Programs:	64 single RAM, 64 multi RAM
External storage:	M-64C cartridge
Polyphony:	8-voice
Oscillators per voice:	2
Effects:	None
Connections:	Upper/lower audio (¼" and XLR) programmer out, MIDI
Dimensions:	480mm x 88mm x 400mm
Weight:	8kg

THE FIGURES

Chief designers:	Keiji Akamatsu, Hiroshi Ueno
Production run:	1984-1988
Approx. units sold:	5000
Options:	MPG-80 Super Jupiter programmer, M-64C memory cartridges
Sounds:	Livewire (ST, Mac, PC disks), Key Clique Super Jupiter Library (ST)
Miscellaneous:	Editor/librarians: Roland Super Jupiter Editor (PC), Eidco Super Jupiter Sec (ST), Opcode Patch Factory (Mac)
Orig. price (1984):	$2495 (£2200)
Price in 1996:	$1000 (£1500)

The MKS-80 was sought after long before the retro revolution. On release, this modular reworking of the Jupiter-8 and Jupiter-6 represented the peak of analog synthesis in module form, and it has never really been out of favor since. The MKS-80 is a perennial hard-to-find on the second-hand market.

Similar to the Jupiter keyboards in voice architecture, though with improved filter chips and a regular—as opposed to "early"—MIDI spec, this is a dual-oscillator synth offering sawtooth, square, triangle and variable-pulse waveforms, plus noise; with cross-modulation in tow, it is capable not just of warm, bland analog sounds but richly textured, harmonic-laden tones as well. The new resonant filters also give the MKS real edge and bite. Both lowpass and highpass filtering are available, lowpass complete with a dedicated ADSR envelope generator on tap.

There's one multiwaveform LFO for pitch, tone or volume modulation, and one triangle wave-only LFO dedicated to controllers—mod wheel or aftertouch. This is an elegant solution to an age-old problem of single LFOs, where a single setting has to cover all eventualities within a patch. Sounds could not be dynamically controlled on the Jupiter keyboards, but here you have modulation by both velocity and aftertouch.

Patches can either be single, at eight-voice polyphony, or dual or split at four-voice poly. For split sounds, there are even two modes to choose from, depending upon whether the controlling keyboard is sending out on one or two separate MIDI channels.

Although the front panel has patch and bank push-buttons, dedicated sliders for volume and velocity, a small screen and a button for MIDI modes—in other words, it's busy for a module—serious programmers have to use either a software editor (Roland made one for the PC, in which you can store up to 1280 patches per library) or the dedicated MPG-80 Programmer, (a flat box with knobs and sliders).

The unit itself can store 64 single sounds and 64 combination sounds, called "patch preset pairs"; the M-64C cartridge houses an additional 128 of each. The MKS-80's range of sounds is vast. Classic analog sweeps and swoops are complemented by ultra-big unison basses (in unison mode, the oscillators automatically detune slightly) and synth string and brass sounds, and the instrument has a surprising aptitude for complex, metallic noises.

Appearing when it did, the MKS-80 was staring down the barrel of Yamaha's DX7, which was replete with the most "realistic" sounds anyone had ever heard on a commercial synth and was already a massive seller. Eric Persing and Dan de Souza, brought in to voice the MKS-80, felt compelled to try and match the DX7, angling the factory programs towards such natural acoustic instrument facsimiles. This is a shame, in a way, because the MKS-80's strong points do not lie in this direction. The MKS-80 is best used as a real synthesizer: free to sizzle and pop as only electronic instruments can. The two sound cartridges subsequently produced by the programming team for the MKS-80 reflect the instrument's potential far better and are worth looking out for.

The MKS-80's three MIDI modes include Mono, giving the instrument potential for MIDI guitarists. I noted some years ago that Steve Howe kept an MKS-

80 in the bottom of his rack. Noting also that he never seemed to use it, I made him an offer for the unit. His reply was simply a withering look. MKS-80 owners tend to hang onto their charges.

Roland MT-32 Sound module

THE FAX

Keyboard:	None
Programs:	128
External storage:	SysEx
Polyphony:	32-partial
Oscillators per voice:	4 partials
Effects:	Reverb
Connections:	Stereo audio, MIDI
Dimensions:	305mm x 200mm x 60mm
Weight:	2.6kg

THE FIGURES

Chief designer:	Ikutaru Kakeshashi
Production run:	1987-1989
Approx. units sold:	100,000+
Options:	Real World Interfaces produces upgrade kits (battery-backed RAM, additional drum kits/reverbs, individual voice outputs)
Sounds:	Soundsource, Blue Ridge, Dr. T's, Livewire
Miscellaneous:	Editors: Dr. T's MT-32 Editor (ST, PC, Mac), Steinberg D Series Synthworks (ST), Big Noise MT/CM-32 Editor (PC), Imagine MT-32 (PC), MIDIMouse MT-32 Capture (ST), Tigress Designs Patchbox 32 (ST), Blue Ridge (Comm 64).; books: *Using the MT-32* by Bob O'Donnell, *The Roland MT-32* by Terry Griffey
Orig. price (1987):	$695 (£450)
Price in 1996:	$225 (£175)

The MT-32 served as the blueprint for General MIDI, and though "designed" by a veritable phalanx of Roland engineers, it was very much the brainchild of Roland president Ikutaru Kakehashi.

Released in 1987, the MT-32 appeared as a miracle of multitimbralism and musicality: a box full of multitimbral D-50 sounds and TR-626 drum sounds at the price of a combo amp. Although the concept of desktop music had not at the time been invented, much less explored, the MT-32 was quickly embraced not just by the musical fraternity but also by the education market and the computer musician, plus the fledgling multimedia industry. The MT-32 was also the first synthesizer to gain major acceptance within the games market, and long after the actual instrument's departure, "MT-32" mode remains a commonly seen specification for games/multimedia devices.

Why? A mixture of price and performance, real-

ly. With the MT-32, Roland analyzed just what it was that "nonmusician musicians" needed and gave it to them at a price they couldn't afford to turn down. No more, no less.

Sound engine-wise, the inspiration for the MT-32 was the D-50, released in the same year: a bank of samples and digital waveforms processed by analog-style parameters. However, it was never touted as a multitimbral D-50 module. The MT-32's target audience of schools, Roland HP Piano owners (to whom this was sold as an expander) and emerging computer musicians were only very marginally interested in programmability—at first merely a distant option on the MT-32.

Sounds are corralled into 17 Sound Groups (Bass, Wind, Percussion, etc.), with an immediate choice of 128 sounds in all (note the magic number, later adopted by General MIDI). Though sounds are frequently 8-bit and not surprisingly a bit noisy, there's an underlying quality and cohesiveness that made the MT-32 impressive to listen to. "All this is coming from that?" was the common response to hearing a complete demo handled by a lone MT-32. In 1987, the idea that any one single unit could house good-quality drum sounds as well as a decent piano, strings, brass and more suggested a price tag with an additional zero on the end of it. Stars among the presets include the richly resonant Taiko in the percussion group and Koto and Shakuhachi in the special group, plus old D-50 favorites like Fantasy, Echo Bell and Atmosphere in the two synth groups.

On the front panel, aside from the display and sundry buttons for volume, sound and sound group, is a set of six "part" buttons numbered 1-5, plus Rhythm. Each part comes preassigned with its own MIDI channel and then you can choose from any of the 128 internal sounds. Part 1 defaults to MIDI channel 2, Part 2 to 3, etc. Drums default to MIDI channel 10, another Roland standard later adopted by General MIDI.

Operating the MT-32 in simple "choose a sound and play" mode from a sequencer couldn't be much easier: Press Rhythm for a drum sound/part. Press one of the other part buttons and choose a sound for all the rest. Multitimbrality, though, is nine-part, including drums. (GM did manage to up the stakes on this score.)

As with all Roland instruments based on LA synthesis, polyphony is at the mercy of the partials. If all sounds used employed only one partial—a highly unlikely situation, frankly—then you'd have 32-voice polyphony to play with. A more likely polyphony count is 16-voice. The MT-32's preset timbre map tells you exactly how many partials each sound uses. The MT-32 does have a partial reserve feature, though, which lets you reserve and preserve required polyphony on selected parts. An overflow function also lets unused slices of polyphony become available to other sounds, should the need arise.

The MT-32 was designed as a playback unit; it was not really meant for detailed editing by the end user. Such was its immediate success, however, that the *bête noire* of all manufacturers (editing is always demanded but rarely used, it seems) soon raised its head.

Ways to edit an MT-32 include a D-50 programmer or special editing software. Edited sounds can be stored in 64 internal memories, though only temporarily: On power down, they're gone. Long-term storage must be external via SysEx, unless you can find a unit that has a (non-Roland) battery-backed RAM upgrade.

The MT-32 was one of the key pieces in Roland's ISM (Intelligent System of Music), a music education concept comprising Roland HP pianos, Roland PR sequencers and MT-32 sound generation. A good deal of custom software was written for this format in terms of music-minus-one files, ear-training packages and complete classical and jazz orchestrations.

The MT-32 also inspired and spearheaded the GM revolution, and Roland's experience with the MT-32 clearly enabled the company to catch the rest of the industry on the hop with its Sound Canvas (the first GM instrument, which appeared within minutes of GM being ratified). The MT-32's post-GM viability is limited, though, because GM has gone on to offer so much more in terms of parts, effects, sounds and compatibilities. Not a sufficient amount of time has elapsed for the MT-32 to become collectible, either. A milestone instrument, all the same.

Roland RD-1000 Digital piano

THE FAX

Keyboard:	88-note
Programs:	8 tones (56 memory locations)
External storage:	M-16C cartridge
Polyphony:	16-voice
Oscillators per voice:	n/a
Effects:	Chorus, tremolo, EQ
Connections:	Stereo XLR audio outputs, phones, pedals, MIDI
Dimensions:	1352mm x 557mm x 154mm
Weight:	43.5kg

THE FIGURES

Chief designer:	Mr. Miki
Production run:	1986-1990

Options:	KS-11 Keyboard Stand, carrying case, pedal case, keyboard stand case
Sounds:	None commercially available
Miscellaneous:	Elton John was a big endorsee for a number of years.
Orig. price (1986):	$3900 (£2587)
Price in 1996:	$1,500 (£1200)

For a long time, Elton John played an RD-1000. This simple, powerful fact kept the RD flame alive far longer than Roland continued to produce the instrument, in fact, so one has to presume that the reflected glory on Roland as a whole must have been adequate compensation.

The RD-1000 was launched alongside its modular partner the MKS-20 and home keyboard equivalent the HP-5500, all proud recipients of Roland's then-latest word on piano sampling technology, SAS—Structured Adaptive Synthesis (really more like additive synthesis than sampling as we now know it), pioneered by one Mr. Miki at Roland HQ in Japan.

The RD-1000 is a fully professional stage piano with a thunderingly good, masculine keyboard action and a range of editable and storable piano tones, built-in effects and a reasonable MIDI spec. This large, impressive-looking instrument, with a distinctive pedal arrangement, is basically foolproof to operate. Out-of-the-box tones comprise three acoustic pianos, harpsichord, clavi, vibraphone and two electric pianos. Unashamedly slanted towards rock rather than classical playing, the acoustic tones are all on the bright and cutting side, though you can tone them down a bit using the built-in three-band EQ (100Hz bass, 10kHz treble and 400Hz-4kHz sweepable mid with Q). The harpsi and clavi are both good vamping tones, and the electric pianos, especially with the aid of chorus (analog), are as moody as they come. Both EQ and the actual effects parameters like chorus and tremolo settings can be stored in 56 memories. EQ alone can change tones beyond all recognition, so this is a genuinely useful proposition. In fact, you may even eat up all 56 memories, in which case you can download onto an M-16C cartridge, if you like.

RD-1000 tones are not samples as such but synthesized creations, painstakingly and lovingly created by Roland programmers in Japan. It is said that many programmers were assigned the task of single voices, some of which took more than a year to perfect. SAS is clearly an ingenious, though hardly quick, method of sound manipulation.

The MIDI allows you to set independent transmit and receive channels, control a full complement of 128 Program Changes on external instruments, control external volumes and assign footpedals to numerous MIDI control functions. On the downside, there is no provision for keyboard splitting with an external sound source, nor is there a pitch or mod wheel.

The MKS-20 is pretty much an exact modular equivalent except that it adds an octave shift feature. In fact, with plenty of dedicated panel controls, the MKS-20 is far less mystifying than most modern modules.

The weighted wooden keyboard action on the RD-1000 didn't last long. A year later, Roland launched its S keyboard action, utilizing a compressed, rather than extended, spring and a special rotary oil damper to smooth out the rebound of the keys. This new keyboard action eventually found its way onto the subsequent RD-200 and RD-300, which were rereleased as the RD-250S and RD-300S. Both pianos bear a close resemblance to the RD-1000, the prime difference being keyboard length.

Of all the RD stage pianos, the RD-1000 is clearly the most sophisticated, with its editability and memories, but the RD-300S still offers 88-note weighted keyboard control over these high-quality piano voices. The MKS-20, though unrivaled and highly sought after at the time, was temporarily overshadowed not only by Roland's P330 but by the P55, launched in 1993. But it is to the MKS-20 that players seem to return, in part due, one feels, to its analog chorus rather than the digital version on the 330 and 55. Not Fat Reg, though. The last I saw of him, he was grinning out of a Technics poster, endorsing the latest PX piano. Then again, Yamaha was claiming him as an avid user the year before. Loyalty, shmoyalty, eh?

Roland SC-55 Sound Canvas
General MIDI module

THE FAX

Keyboard:	n/a
Programs:	317
External storage:	SysEx
Polyphony:	24-voice
Oscillators per voice:	2 partials
Effects:	Reverb, chorus
Connections:	RCA audio out and in, MIDI phones
Dimensions:	218mm x 233mm x 44mm
Weight:	1.4kg

THE FIGURES

Chief designer:	Mr. (Jimi) Yamabata
Production run:	1991-93 (subsequently replaced by Mk 2)
Approx. units sold:	100,000+

Options:	RAD-50 rackmount adapter, pedals and footswitches
Miscellaneous:	Editors include Newtronic Soundmaster SC-55, Hands on Soundcanvas Editor (ST), Musiccator GS, Dan McKee WinCanvas (PC).
Orig. price (1991):	$795 (£649)
Price in (1996):	$300 (£250)

It was the Winter NAMM show in California, January 1991. Roland had a presentation to make, to which a select few battle-hardened journalists and software developers had been invited. As this motley crew lounged about in front of the darkened stage area waiting for the show to begin, a flutter went through the Roland ranks, from senior management to local reps. "They've ratified it." "It's through." I recall thinking that Roland employees must all have joined some fringe religion or something—such was their obvious and unbridled excitement about something that none of the assembled audience seemed to have any make of whatsoever.

And so the show, and the revelations, began. Ladies and gentleman: General MIDI and the first product to meet the new standard, the Roland Sound Canvas. Yes, the call was as close as that. A legion of GM modules have by now followed in the wake of the Sound Canvas, but Roland was at the head of the pack, and to Roland have gone the spoils.

Sound Canvas, of itself, became a standard, not just because of the GS logo, representing as it does a sort of supercharged version of General MIDI. Roland's position might have been taken by a masterful piece of timing and extraordinary courage, but it held because Sound Canvas products are extremely well thought out and do the job of providing sounds that knit better than anyone else's, whether it be for multimedia, commercial GM songfile playback or plain user sequencing.

In 1991, the plain SC-55 (which an SC-55 Mk 2 subsequently replaced) was initially viewed as a miracle of modern engineering. This modest module the size of a midi (as in hi-fi) component came packed with more than 300 LA synthesis (D-50, et al.) and RS PCM tones, drum kits, sound effects, "effects effects" such as reverbs and chorus, a pleasant and for the most part idiot-proof user interface and even—another master stroke—a TV-style remote control so you can carry out most day-to-day adjustments from the comfort of your studio rocker. Goodbye to neck pains from twisting and swiveling in front of an LCD and prodding away at pinprick pushbuttons!

The Sound Canvas is not one of those half-hearted, "Yes, we have a GM mode," instruments. This instrument is specially built for General MIDI.

All its sounds and drum kits can be accessed in GM mode, the additional (to GM's standard 128) tones accessed via the dreaded MIDI Bank Select (dreaded in that no one seems to agree on precisely how you access it).

GM playback is as foolproof as it gets, thanks to the sensible amount (and functions) of panel buttons and a particularly helpful and readable display. You can see level metering of eight parts at a time bouncing up and down or select Peak Hold metering, pans, effects settings, MIDI channel assignments, etc. Most of these can be tweaked using the remote, which was also designed to control the Sound Canvas' partner, the SB-55 Sound Brush MIDI File Player, as well.

This being the world's first GM/GS module, the polyphony is bang-on at 24-voice. As ever, though, you need to keep an eye on the types of tones employed, since some use two sound components (called partials) per voice and chop the polyphony in half. Polyphony can also come under threat if you mute one of its 16 parts via SysEx, because Note On data is still recognized (muting parts from the front panel does not cause the same problem).

The GS format works on a system of "Capital Tones," which number the standard GM 128 and are augmented by a number of Variations. In addition, the SC-55 can be switched into MT-32 (the earlier Roland module that inspired GM in the first place) mode, so that sequences created using this classic module can be played back without having to reassign. There is even a special MT-32 drum mode conforming to the MT-32 drum map. Drum-wise, there are no less than nine actual kits, including some understandably authentic TR-808 sounds.

Effects comprise eight reverbs, a few somewhat cursory delays and eight chorus settings. Not only is there part send level control over reverb and chorus, but you can, if so inclined, control individual drum sound effects within a drum set using Non-Registered Parameters. NRPs can also be employed to set up sound editing on the fly. Although this is distinct from actual real-time editing (i.e., as a performance control), it does mean that sounds can be reprogrammed in the middle of a sequence. Complete sound-to-part-to-MIDI channel assignments remain once the Sound Canvas is switched off, but there is no provision for storing any more than this current set.

The Sound Canvas functions perfectly well as a simple synth expander, too. Editing is possible in simple tweaking fashion. You can alter vibrato settings, the basic envelope, filter cutoff and resonance. Editing from the front panel is more of a hassle than it's worth, probably, but a number of editors are available (see "Miscellaneous"). An edited sound will remain in memory unless (or until) you re-initialize. The thing to be aware of when editing is that you are only editing the part—the slot in which a sound has been put—so if you alter a part's envelope and filter setting and then decide that your song would be better served by another sound altogether, the replacement sound will still be subject to the previous sound's edits. (Understandable, but a bit of a pain.) Another feature, excellent for keyboard playing operation, allows you to double up sounds on a MIDI channel in order to produce bigger, fatter layered patches. With the second MIDI In (mounted on the front panel) and part mute function, you can selectively switch out parts within a sequence and have a go at them yourself in a "music-minus-one" style.

These bonus usages notwithstanding, the Sound Canvas has become the de facto standard for software developers, MIDI File composers, presentation developers and anyone else working in a "sound" capacity with a third party who needs a point of reference—ironically enough, seeing that GM itself was supposed to open the doors so that it wouldn't matter what unit you worked on, provided it was GM.

Many people—especially the competition, and those who think they're "in the know"—like to criticize Sound Canvas as offering fairly unspectacular sounds. Just play the violin sound, they crow; it's thin and uninteresting. Quite possibly, but who "just plays" the violin sound? The Sound Canvas is designed for ensemble playback. Its sounds may not stack up to the latest Korg or Yamaha or even Roland in individual terms, but its sounds blend effortlessly and musically. Even viewed on a singular basis, Sound Canvas' acoustic guitars are rich and lively, the pianos more than acceptable and some of the less obvious "hidden" variation tones, like Hawaiian guitar (which makes an excellent pedal steel, incidentally), are extremely useful.

There was some early, justified, criticism regarding aliasing at the decay stage of many sounds that was rather too noticeable, and curing this was the main motivation behind the SC-55 Mk 2. Aside from its improved audio quality, the Mk 2 also offers a useful direct computer interface to both Mac or PC, which had been one of the few advantages, aside from cost, that subsequent GM modules from Yamaha and Korg had going for them.

It's far too early to talk in terms of collectability, since the SC-55 Mk 2 is barely cold and a legion of replacements at varying price points are still current. But if you want to know where this particular strand of synthesizer life started out, it started here. A key product.

Roland SH-101
Analog monophonic synthesizer

THE FAX

Keyboard:	32-note
Programs:	None
External storage:	None
Polyphony:	Mono
Oscillators per voice:	1
Effects:	Arpeggiator
Connections:	Mono audio, phones, CV and gate in and out, hold, ext clock input
Dimensions:	570mm x 80mm x 311mm
Weight:	4.1kg

THE FIGURES

Chief designer:	Unknown
Production run:	1982-1984
Approx. units sold:	50,000
Options:	SC-101 soft case (MG-1 Modulation Grip was standard)
Sounds:	n/a
Miscellaneous:	SH-101s came in a range of colors: red, blue and gray.
Orig. price (1982):	$495 (£249)
Price in 1996:	$300 (£150)

By 1982, MIDI was on the horizon, if not yet drilled into the backs, of synthesizers. Polyphonic synthesis represented the future, and almost inevitably, digital polyphonic synthesis at that. Though at the forefront of these new products, Roland was a company that still had faith in analog sound generation, and it couldn't resist one final crack at an analog, monophonic synth. This was it.

Analog and monophonic it might have been, but the SH-101 was a far cry from the System 100 modules of the previous decade. The SH-101 was designed as a mono for the 1980s: fast, flexible and fluid. Gone were the million routing permutations, the endless alternatives. Instead, immediate access to strong and punchy sounds and controllers in place of sound-generating parameters.

You can take in the entire instrument in the most cursory glance at the control panel: single-oscillator design (though with support from a sub-oscillator), resonant lowpass filter, four-segment envelope generator shared between filter and amplifier and multi-waveform LFO.

A glance at this lot would lead you to expect a thinnish, limited set of tones, but you'd be wrong. The SH-101 is a surprisingly kicky little synth, whose range of bass sounds has endured to the present day.

Each segment of the audio chain has its own section on the control panel, making this a very easy instrument to understand. The VCO panel has a click-stopped pitch range knob (16' to 2'), a pulse width amount control, a modulation amount slider, a pulse width slider and a pulse width modulation source switch: envelope, manual or LFO. You may wonder for a second where the oscillator waveforms are; they're next door on the Source Mixer panel. Here, simple sliders control the volume of a pulse wave, a sawtooth, a sub-oscillator and noise. Aha! So that's why this single-oscillator instrument can sound so thick and full. Unlike most synths, where you are forced to choose one from a group of waveforms, here you can build up a composite of waves.

The lowpass filter has cutoff frequency and resonance sliders (the filter can self-oscillate), along with an envelope amount slider, modulation amount slider and keyboard (follow) sliders. Slider operation over these parameters makes for very expressive and sophisticated, yet completely idiot-proof, programming. The SH-101's user interface is absolutely copy book. The VCA segment can be shaped by the envelope generator or switched to a gated (on or off) output. The envelope generator has standard ADSR parameters, and the gate trigger select switch can be set to gate+trigger, gate or LFO.

On the modulator panel is a choice of sine, square, random or noise waveforms, plus a speed slider with handy LED above so you can see the current LFO rate blinking away at you.

In a way, it's a shame there are no program memories, because this is such an intuitive and handy little synth. Then again, setting up sounds is direct and simple. Being able to mix waveforms and noise in almost additive style is also great fun. You'll always come up with something that sounds good and is slightly different.

In place of programmability are a small digital sequencer and an arpeggiator, both of which have control buttons just above the keyboard. Neither is exactly comprehensive: a 100-step sequencer and up, down, up and down arpeggiator, both under LFO clock rule. Thanks to a hold feature, you can set up a sequence or a piece of arpeggio-ing and transpose the part at will using the keyboard or the octave transpose switch. Like the rest of the instrument, this is immediate and fun and sounds great.

Real-time control is the SH-101's forte. Not only is there a natty little add-on handle and strap, so you can swing the instrument around your neck and get down with the boys up front (the add-on MGS-1 houses a pitch wheel and lets you initiate modulation with your thumb), but on a small panel beside the main pitch wheel-cum-mod lever, two sliders let you mix progressive amounts of pitch or tone modulation. Portamento, operating in a choice of modes (automatic or single-trigger—i.e., legato playing only), completes this powerhouse of control and effects.

Though the SH-101 just missed MIDI, there are CV and gate ins and outs, which, along with the audio output, phones and external clock input, are placed on a small ledge at the back of the control panel. Such a design means you don't have to squint over the edge of the instrument to find a desired input or output. Why didn't all synths take up this solution? We can but wonder.

There's an external clock input, but the LFO clock does not send out, so you won't be able to have the SH-101 as the master in a setup using hip SH-101 arpeggiator grooves. It is quite possible to MIDI an SH-101, which may be sensible if you want full access to the outside world, even if the average MIDI kit will probably cost about as much as the instrument itself.

The innards of the SH-101 are to be found in Roland's MC-202 Microcomposer, the darling of the rave scene in the 1990s. With its precise and whistly filter, simple controls and creative waveform build-up, the SH-101 is a great synth to have around for bass or arpeggio effects. If you can't get a great sound within minutes, you either need a break or a new job.

Roland TB-303 Bassline
Bass synthesizer/sequencer

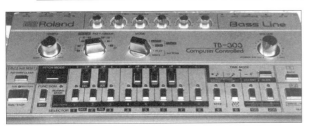

THE FAX

Keyboard:	12-note (pads)
Programs:	None
External storage:	None
Polyphony:	Mono
Oscillators per voice:	1
Effects:	None
Connections:	Mono audio, phones, CV and gate outs, Sync 24 in, mix in
Dimensions:	300mm x 150mm x 55mm
Weight:	1kg

THE FIGURES

Chief designer:	Mr. Muroi
Production run:	1982-1984

Options:	None
Sounds:	n/a
Miscellaneous:	The TB-303 became the darling of the dance scene in the 1990s.
Orig. price (1982):	$395 (£290)
Price in 1996:	$750 (£450)

The dread of any reviewer is to annihilate a product that goes on to become a classic or praise to the hilt something that becomes commonly acknowledged as a turkey. You don't mind sticking your neck out, but if your lead is totally ignored or totally at variance with everyone else's opinion, it's...well, disquieting. I reviewed the TB-303 in the British music newspaper *Sounds* so long ago that I honestly couldn't remember what I'd thought of the TB-303 at the time.

Sounds was a robust publication, much given to running earthy reviews. Please don't say I lambasted this oddball bass synth-cum-sequencer that is now impenetrably and universally revered! After much leafing through files, I come across some yellowed pages of *Sounds* (in 1981, my reviews were written in longhand, never mind a computer, so "filing" involved cutting out press clippings). Phew! Top marks in all departments.

The TB-303 came out of nowhere and went nowhere for the next ten years. There was no bass synth market as such in the early 1980s, and the Bassline was simply an idea that Roland ran up the flagpole. Released alongside the TB-303 was the TR-606 Drumatix drum machine; both were silver boxes the size of cigarette cartons, simple to look at but a hassle to program. In 1984, I took a Drumatix in place of a session fee and promptly lent it to Jethro Tull drummer Barriemore Barlow, who fell in love with it, and hell, he's still got it!

The TB-303 I was not tempted to buy, however, since I liked synth bass playing, and synth bass *programming* is what the TB-303 is all about.

The concept is one machine with two tasks: bass sounds and a mini-sequencer for playing those sounds. Once a part is programmed, you connect the unit up to a drum machine or sync it to tape, and all your bass-playing troubles are over. That was the concept, anyway.

With a sleek brushed-chrome finish and small but workable knobs and switches, the TB-303 has sound-generating controls running along the top and sequencing controls along the bottom.

You input a line using the octave's worth of "keys," each complete with LED and note name. You can transpose up or down an octave, so you effectively have three octaves' worth of range with which to play.

There are seven tracks or channels on the

sequencer, each of which can store a maximum of 64 bars of music; they can play in isolation or run on one after the other. Although you can record a sequence in real time, the limited keyboard and lack of quantization almost guarantee that what you'll get will be of dubious value. The method that provides the best results is also the most complicated, involving inputting notes first without worrying about duration or rhythm, then going back and inserting the sustain/duration/rest information.

In Japan, the Bassline was voted the year's most difficult instrument to use in its launch year of 1982; even on a one-to-ten scale of complexity, the TB-303 is really only a fighting four. There are very limited functions here; once you have grasped how to add up sixteenth beats or input an accent or a slide, that's about it. Acid programmers may well prefer thrashing about and taking what comes, but you can be precise on a TB-303 if the mood takes you. A third option, tapping in a rhythm to your note-only sequence, is sometimes a reasonable compromise.

The accent and slide buttons clinch the TB-303's worth. Even input randomly (some would say, especially input randomly), they just inject a sequence of notes with instant groove and bounce.

Sound has something to do with it, of course, and the TB-303's sound generator is viewed by those that know as the apotheosis of squelchy, flicky, squeaky synth bass. Controls are minimal: You have either a sawtooth or square-wave oscillator; a razor-sharp lowpass resonant filter with cutoff, resonance, and envelope generator modulation amount controls and a lone decay control (as much of the envelope generator as you see).

There are no memories here. You simply set up a sound, play and move on. It is quite sobering to play around with a TB-303 and achieve so many powerful, meaningful tones, armed with so little. The tuning knob is coarsely calibrated, too, so you are not restricted to bass register tones. You'd never call the TB-303 a lead synth, but it can turn in an infectious arpeggio or "gate effect" line, no problem. The sound-generating aspect of the TB-303 is dead easy and dead effective.

The TB-303 was not massively popular when it was new. Because it was different, and rather intriguing, it caused a brief stir and then quickly fell away in the wake of a far more exciting concept: MIDI. Perhaps if the TB-303 had come out a year or so later with MIDI, things would have been different. The subsequent dissatisfaction with digital sounds and MIDI blandness has rekindled interest in the TB-303—thanks mainly to groups like Orbital and The Shamen in the early 1990s—and the unit, as of this writing, is almost unobtainable.

Though Roland itself has gone on record as saying it will not rerelease the TB-303—citing as its main reason that the parts are no longer available— other manufacturers have willingly taken up the challenge. In England, two dedicated bass synths— the Deep Bass Nine and Novation's BassStation— both advertise TB-303 modes and sounds as principle features.

As fashion moves on, it seems likely that high prices will fade (one TB-303 fetched £500 [$800] in July, 1995, at the VEMIA vintage synth auction in the UK), but the TB-303 remains a unique instrument, and its uniqueness is somewhat of a hedge against deflation.

Roland U-20 Polyphonic synthesizer

THE FAX

Keyboard:	61-note
Programs:	128 single RAM, 64 multi
External storage:	Card
Polyphony:	30-voice
Oscillators per voice:	2 (tones)
Effects:	Reverb, delay, chorus, arpeggiator
Connections:	Stereo audio (dry/mix), MIDI

THE FIGURES

Chief designer:	Unknown
Production run:	1989-1991
Options:	Footpedal, PCM sound cards
Sounds:	Accepts Roland U110 card library
Miscellaneous:	The U-20's velocity-switched electric guitar was used on Stevie Wonder's "Jungle Fever."
Orig. price (1989):	$1795 (£1050)
Price in 1996:	$650 (£450)

Some instruments make headlines and are widely talked about but don't actually sell very well. Others quietly get on with their job, remaining popular and useful long after the marketing budget has run dry. The U-20 falls into the latter camp.

This stylish multitimbral keyboard, based on PCM samples, is in many respects an upgraded version of the U-110 module. The U-110 is another "quiet one," extremely handy as a supplier of filler sounds in a multitimbral studio setting but a little noisy; also, editing is very broad, and it only came in module form. The U-20, along with its modular partner the U-220, answered most of these criticisms and then went on from there.

The hierarchy of the U-20 starts with PCM sample-based sounds called "tones," which can be edited using a number of broad editing parameters. In order to solve the U-110's problem, which is when you edit a tone you are editing a location rather than a sound (which can throw a large spanner in the works when it comes to rejigging and relocating multi memories), the U-20 introduced a mid-level editing stage called the "timbre." Essentially customized tones, timbres themselves are stored in the multitimbral patches.

The three main areas of editing are level, pitch and vibrato. Level controls tone volume, velocity, aftertouch sensitivity and full ADSR envelope generating. Pitch governs a tone's basic tuning as well as keyboard, pitch bend and pitch modulation. Vibrato controls set LFO waveform, rate and depth and modulation amount.

The key to the U-20's popularity is really the quality of its PCM samples. As a PCM sample playback instrument, it is definitely happiest on natural instrument tones—the pianos are particularly warm and satisfying, as are the strings—and the velocity-switched electric guitar 1 was used unmistakably on Lisa Lisa & Cult Jam's 1991 album *Let the Beat Hit 'Em* and Stevie Wonder's "Jungle Fever."

Sound quality and controllability are what make the U-20 a spectacular producer of drum parts. There are four Rhythm Sets, which are multi-instrument drum kits accessible beyond the U-20's six-part tone multitimbralism. Yet you are not forced to use what Roland considers to be drum sounds. One of the regular pitched tones can also be used as a drum or percussion voice, an option that opens up endless percussive possibilities.

You also have many of the same controls over individual drum sounds as over a regular tone—level, pitch and vibrato. In other words, you can apply some random pitch modulation to, say, a tambourine, which lets you do a pretty fair impression of what a real percussion player naturally delivers through different strengths of hits and shakes. Who needs physical modeling, eh?

The U-20 has limited but good-quality internal reverbs and chorus. Reverb comes in varying types and sizes (rooms, halls, a gate, a couple of delays), and chorus comes in several strengths and speeds, including flanging. Reverb and chorus are completely separate items and can be applied to the final patch in either parallel or series. Parts can be routed individually through the effects.

The U-20 is well endowed with nice little touches. These range from a pair of assignable panel sliders, whose function can be stored within an individual patch, to an arpeggiator (only clockable internally, though) to a handy chord function whereby you can store and recall chords with either a pair of panel buttons or the keyboard. Far from being some kind of home keyboard throwback, this is an excellent little writing aid, because it allows you to be able to play chord progressions into a sequencer more adeptly than your own physical technique would normally allow.

Many of the U-20 sounds went on to become the staple diet of Roland's world-class Sound Canvas GM module. As with sounds on the Sound Canvas, U-20 sounds knit very well. The U-20 is a powerful workhorse of a keyboard. The lack of filtering—never mind resonant filtering—places it firmly in the acoustic instrument playback camp, but if you have a software sequencer, the U-20's pleasant keyboard and stylish natural sounds, plus one or two handy extras, may endear itself to you, as it has to many a songwriter.

RSF Kobol — Analog monophonic synthesizer

THE FAX

Keyboard:	44-note
Programs:	16 RAM
External storage:	None
Polyphony:	Mono
Oscillators per voice:	2
Effects:	None
Connections:	Mono audio, line out, footpedal jacks, keyboard out, gate in and out
Dimensions:	720mm x 440mm x 200mm
Weight:	5kg

THE FIGURES

Chief designer:	Rubin Fernandez
Production run:	1980-1983
Approx. units sold:	500
Options:	None
Sounds:	None commercially available
Miscellaneous:	Used on the soundtrack to *The Last Emperor*
Orig. price (1980):	n/a (£780)
Price in 1996:	$800 (£450)

If the Kobol had been made by Oberheim or Moog or Roland, it would have been a well-known instrument. However, it was made in France by RSF, a company whose international penetration was enthusiastic but limited.

Yet the Kobol has endured in minds, and indeed collections, of enthusiasts all over the world, not only as France's most notable contribution to synth manufacturing since the Ondes Martinot but also as a solid, interesting-sounding monophonic synth sporting the all-too-rare feature of program memories.

The Kobol doesn't look dissimilar to the Minimoog, encased in wood and with a control panel that rises up sharply from the back of its 3½-octave keyboard. Most interesting, perhaps, is the oscillator panel, which has two independent VCOs that can cover a four-octave pitch range, delivering triangle, rampe (sawtooth), rampe doublee, carre (square) and pulse waves.

But instead of being in set positions, each oscillator glides through the spectrum, providing over 40 variations, or mixes, of waveform. This is an innovative concept, with only Moog's Multimoog offering something along these lines, though in a more limited fashion, a few years earlier.

The basic tone is rich and especially fruity in the lower registers. Filtering is 24dB/oct lowpass with cutoff frequency and resonance, plus its own ADS envelope generator. The amplifier too has an ADS envelope generator and a bypass switch for continuous sustain. The calibration is fairly coarse on the envelope generators, and you will no doubt have spotted the lack of a dedicated release parameter. The lone LFO has two waveforms (sine and square), along with a speed control.

The Kobol's modulation and processing parameters may not live up to the instrument's excellent start on the oscillators, but it comes back strongly with 16 program memories. A row of nine push-buttons function as memory selects, and programming involves simply finding a sound and then holding down Record and one of the program buttons until the button's LED stops flashing.

Less idiot-proof is the Kobol's sequencer, which operates on a system of individual note input into each of the program memory locations. In order to program a sequence of changing notes, you have to record the first note into the first location, stop and alter the pitch using the VCO frequency knobs, then record your second note, and so on. The payoff, perhaps, is that each note of a sequence can use not only a different pitch but a different sound. Since the maximum storage is 16 notes, the Kobol sequencer is strictly for riff or effects usage. I'm not aware of the Kobol being used extensively in the dance scene, but this intriguing concept, plus its relatively open-minded keyboard and gate ins and outs, should allow you to interface adequately with the modern world.

Performance controls on the instrument itself include pitch and mod wheels, plus a special VCF knob that alters cutoff position.

RSF went on to make a memoryless expander version of the Kobol and even a limited number of polyphonic Kobols (called PolyKobols). In spite of a few loyal Euros who latched onto this instrument at the time—notably Monsieur Jean-Michel Jarre, not surprisingly, though Hans Zimmer is also said to have used Kobols on his soundtrack to *The Last Emperor*—

neither the Kobol nor its designer nor RSF set the world alight with this instrument. A hip instrument to own, though, and rare.

RSF is no longer in the business of producing synthesizers.

Sequential Circuits Pro One
Analog monophonic synthesizer

THE FAX
Keyboard:	37-note
Programs:	none
External storage:	none
Polyphony:	mono
Oscillators per voice:	2
Effects:	arpeggiator, sequencer
Connections:	Mono audio out, CV and gate jacks

THE FIGURES
Chief designer:	Dave Smith
Production run:	1981-84
Approx. units sold:	10,000
Options:	none
Sounds:	n/a
Miscellaneous:	Servicing and repair: Wine Country Productions: 1572 Park Crest Ct. #505; San Jose, CA 95118; tel: (408) 265-2008; Musician's Service Center: 998 S. 2nd St., San Jose, CA 95112; tel: (408) 286-4861; Analogics: 5261 Maple Ave. E.; Geneva, OH 44041; tel: (216) 466-6911
Orig. price (1981):	$995 (£470)
Price in 1996:	$400 (£250)

It was twilight time for the monophonic synth in 1981. The Pro One was one of the last major monophonic releases produced, ironically, by the company whose world-class Prophet-5 was largely responsible for the demise of this product category. 1981 was also the year Vince Clarke left Depeche Mode to form Yazoo, with whom he scored the massive hit "Only You" a year later—a track primarily recorded using a Pro One.

Sequential used the same basic voice electronics on the Pro One as on the Prophet-5. In looks, the Pro One has a fairly distinctive "Prophety" feel.

There are two VCOs with sawtooth and variable pulse waveforms (osc B also has triangle) which can be independently and continuously pitched through one octave. Both have a range of four octaves, and they can be hard-synched for those classic, regurgitatingly screaming lead sounds. Osc B can also be used as an audio signal or as a sub audio LFO. A small mixing panel balances the oscillators and either noise or the signal from an external source. The heart of any synth lies in its oscillators, and the Pro One was a strong and gutsy performer. Without recourse to detuning or excessive pulse width modulation, the instrument sounds full and fat.

Filtering is the next most vital ingredient, and the

SEQUENTiAL

Name: Sequential Circuits
In operation: 1974-1987
Business: Synthesizers, samplers, drum machines, sequencers, software

Sequential Circuits, or just plain Sequential as it became, is one of the great names associated with modern synthesizers, equally as important as Moog or ARP, and sadly, like those fellow pioneers, no longer in business.

The company was formed in 1974 by Dave Smith, then a young guitarist with a keen interest in electronics. Dave's first enterprise was an inexpensive analog sequencer called the Model 600. The Model 600 was sold to Dave's friends and a few other people. A year or so later, armed with the new cost-effective SSM chips, Smith had the idea (which he figured everyone else would, too) of building a "programmable" synthesizer, one with full patch memories. An idea was one thing but funds were another, and Sequential drafted Dave Rossum from E-mu to work on the project in return for royalties.

The Prophet-5 was shown at the 1978 Winter NAMM show and caused an immediate sensation. Orders flooded in, though at the time Sequential had just two employees.

In a way, Sequential never quite recovered from this crash-bang start in life. It took far longer than planned to build a follow-up instrument (the Prophet-10), and even then the instrument was riddled with problems. Throughout Sequential's brief though distinguished career, it always fought a rearguard action in terms of filling orders or meeting announced release deadlines. In retrospect, it was a classic case of too much success, too quickly, combined with drastic underfunding.

However, along the way, Sequential and Dave Smith generated the notion of MIDI and then did much of the early work on its development. Sequential's Prophet-600 was the first MIDI keyboard.

In 1983, Sequential launched the Prophet T-8, another high-class synth in the mold of the Prophet-5. But the investments that Sequential made in this instrument, especially in its weighted wooden keyboard, coupled with the two years of work between announcement and delivery,

could not hope to be recouped from the 800 people who bought the T-8. (A good design nonetheless, the T-8 keyboard was later snapped up by NED for the Synclavier.)

While the MIDI spec was being finalized, Smith argued for (and got) what was then regarded as a bit of a brainstorm, namely "Mode 4" and the concept of multitimbrality. At the time, no one was thinking in terms of a single instrument being able to provide a simultaneous, multi-instrument collection of sounds, but the subsequent explosion of low-cost sequencing packages for personal computers proved his point within a couple of years. Sequential's MultiTrak has the honor of being the first multitimbral instrument, even if its ability was strictly a result of simultaneous monophonic patches.

Ironically, the emergence of software sequencers, which so neatly justified Sequential's insistence on Mode 4, was also partly responsible for the downfall of the company. In the mid-'80s, Sequential embarked on a disastrous shift in focus towards entry-level products and even a software sequencer of its own, based on the Commodore 64. A great idea, just ten years too early. Sequential realized its user base was horrified by this downgrading and managed to bring instruments like the VS digital synth and the Prophet-2000 to market, but the company was already mortally wounded, and it was only a matter of time before the chronic cash-flow difficulties spelled the end.

Sequential's final days were bizarre. By the end of 1987, it wasn't so much a question of whether the company would survive but simply who, if anyone, would come to its rescue. Yamaha was the temporary knight in shining armor, with Sequential going into bankruptcy in order to facilitate the maneuverings. And then...nothing. Yamaha and Sequential "teamed up" for just over a year, during which no products appeared under the Sequential banner nor, seemingly, did any Yamaha product with direct Sequential involvement. When this stalemate ended, Yamaha let go the remnants of the Sequential R&D team, and Korg swooped in and offered them all jobs the very next day. This partnership has produced not only the Wavestation series of products but also the OASYS sound modeling instrument, as well as much valuable voicing and programming work. Dave Smith has come and gone as a paid Korg employee and is currently heading up his own design consultancy.

Pro One's four-pole 24dB/oct lowpass Curtis filter (as later found on the Prophet-5) provides the instrument with its cutting edge. The filter panel comprises cut-off frequency and resonance controls, plus a dedicated ADSR envelope generator and envelope amount and keyboard amount (follow) controls.

Underneath the osc B panel are the LFO controls of frequency, plus a choice of three waveshapes: ramp, triangle and square. The LFO not only serves as a clock source for modulation but also controls the speed of two rare features for a monophonic: the sequencer and the arpeggiator.

On the modulation panel itself, life can be further breathed into sounds by using one of a choice of filter envelope, oscillator B or LFO as mod source (each with its own amount slider) and routing these,

in turn, to one of a number of destinations: osc A frequency or pulse width or osc B frequency or pulse width. Modulation can occur automatically or can be initiated simply by moving the mod wheel. Portamento can be introduced either permanently or just when notes are played legato. Two wheels control pitch bend and mod effects..

The sequencer operates in step time only and is a two-channel affair with 40-note maximum storage. In 1981, sequencing was only thought of as the stringing together of a number of notes sequentially, with deviations from strict timings inserted after the event if at all. On the Pro One, you play your series of notes into the sequencer one by one, "rests" are inserted simply by toggling back and forth between record and play modes. You can transpose sequences and control speed via the LFO clock. Sequences can also be clocked externally using the CV and Gate inputs. The arpeggiator will arpeggiate any chord you hold down, with speed under the control of the LFO clock. Arpeggiator modes comprise up or up down.

Imagine a monophonic Prophet-5, and you're not far off from a Pro One. It is a versatile instrument, full and rich thanks to its dual oscillator design, but also capable of great subtlety. Vince Clarke claimed that pretty much everything on "Only You" was Pro One, from bass to bass drum (using self-oscillating filter only) to strings to effects.

There were some early reliability problems with the keyboard, to the extent that on later models an entirely different keyboard was used. The Pro One came out long before MIDI, but a MIDI kit is quite feasible from a MIDI specialist.

Pro Ones sold in respectable quantities, becoming, in fact, Sequential's best-selling instrument in pure number terms, but not that many were sold in the UK. Because it was a comparatively late model mono, the Pro One doesn't have anything like the collectability of an early Moog or ARP, but wise owls who just want a good (and still genuinely vintage, too) mono can pick up a bargain in this instrument. Sequential (Circuits) ceased trading in 1988.

Sequential Circuits Prophet T-8

Analog polyphonic synthesizer

THE FAX

Keyboard:	76-note
Programs:	128 single
External storage:	Cassette interface
Polyphony:	8-voice
Oscillators per voice:	2
Effects:	None
Connections:	Stereo audio, MIDI
Dimensions:	1152mm x 504mm x 109mm
Weight:	27kg

THE FIGURES

Chief designer:	Steve Salani
Production run:	1983-85
Approx. units sold:	800
Options:	Poly mode, plus MIDI clocking of sequencer
Sounds:	Kid Nepro
Miscellaneous:	Service and repair: Wine Country Productions (David Sesnak of WCP is a former Sequential employee and designer of the T-8 keyboard): 1572 Park Crest Ct. #505; San Jose, CA 95118;

tel: (408) 265-2008; Musician's Service Center: 998 S. 2nd St.; San Jose, CA 95112; tel: (408) 286-4861; Analogics: 5261 Maple Ave. E.; Geneva, OH 44041; tel: (216) 466-6911

Orig. price (1983):	$5895 (£4500)
Price in 1996:	$1400 (£900)

- -

The Prophet-5 installed Sequential as the perceived leader in the field of no-holds-barred, professional synthesizers. Replacing the Prophet-5 was always going to be a nightmare for the company.

Sequential made a very creditable attempt. The Prophet T-8 retained and built upon many of the features and capabilities of the Prophet-5, so that upgrading users would not feel alienated. Yet with its super-duper, 76-note, weighted-action keyboard, MIDI and sequencer, the T-8 was a million miles away in terms of feel and application. On paper, the T-8 should have sold by the thousands.

So what went wrong? Mistake number one was that Sequential announced the T-8 almost two years before they were able to deliver. To even come close to expectations after that would have been a miracle. Then there were performance problems: This is a highly sophisticated instrument, and being temperamental goes with the territory. Then there's the price: At around $6000, this was destined for top players only. Finally, as so often happens in synth design, the company got fooled, plain and simple. In a 1985 interview, Sequential boss Dave Smith admitted that the T-8 was "one of those instruments that we always heard people wanted. So we went ahead and did it. And then a lot of people decided they didn't want that after all." The problem was that Sequential spent a huge amount of time and money on the T-8, but customers, fashion and applications change. It's a fickle business.

With a dual-oscillator design like the Prophet-5, the T-8's eight-voice polyphony was impressive even for 1983. With its clearly compartmentalized front panel, working your way around the instrument is straightforward, even with the addition of MIDI, program layering and sequencer controls.

Oscillators A & B feature sawtooth, triangle and variable-pulse waveforms; oscillator B can operate in low frequency form as well. A small mixing panel blends the signal from the two oscillators along with noise. The 24dB/oct lowpass filter panel has resonance and cutoff frequency controls, plus envelope amount, governing the intensity of the filter's own ADSR envelope generator contouring, as well as keyboard tracking. In fact, both the filter and amplifier EGs go on to offer a second release stage, something that helps in the creation of naturally fading acoustic piano sounds.

Modulation systems comprise a multiwaveshape

LFO, the famous Prophet-5 poly-mod (whereby the filter envelope generator or oscillator B can be used to interact with oscillator A or B or their pulse width or the filter cutoff point), and pressure-mod, for keyboard pressure as a mod source. Destinations include pulse width of the oscillators, filter cutoff point, LFO amount, etc. A velocity-sensitivity panel separately controls the keyboard's initial dynamics over a sound.

The T-8 has 128 programs on board and can be called up in single or split/layered modes (the latter, of course, cuts the polyphony in half). Sounds can be funneled into unison, you can latch a chord (i.e., set up a chord to be played subsequently by one finger—great for fast brass stab lines), and there is also polyphonic portamento.

The T-8's sequencer is a basic scratchpad device offering 670 notes of storage over eight channels. Speed is variable, but there's no transposition. External clocking of the sequencer was only offered on Rev 3.8.

The T-8's specially designed keyboard proved a mixed blessing from Sequential's perspective. It was complicated to perfect, with its long pivot keys and special inks working in conjunction with each individual key's optical velocity sensor, but it did offer its users enormous depth of control. In fact, the Synclavier used a T-8 keyboard as standard for many years.

The T-8 never really fulfilled its potential. Pros used it quite a lot in the mid-1980s, but then it went completely out of fashion. The 1990s have seen some resurgence of interest, but a lot of people are frightened by the T-8. It's just a bit too big, too unmanageable-looking. With so few units made, though, it has obvious collectability value.

Sequential (Circuits) ceased trading in 1988.

Sequential Circuits Prophet VS
Digital/analog polyphonic synthesizer

THE FAX
Keyboard:	61-note
Programs:	100 single
External storage:	Cartridge
Polyphony:	8-voice
Oscillators per voice:	4
Effects:	Arpeggiator, chorus
Connections:	Stereo audio, MIDI, phones

Dimensions:	967mm x 400mm x 105mm
Weight:	16.3kg

THE FIGURES
Chief designers:	Joshua Jeffe, Chris Meyer
Production run:	1986-87
Approx. units sold:	3000
Options:	RAM cartridges, footswitches
Sounds:	Dr. Sound, Walt Whitney
Miscellaneous:	VS Wavewrangler editor/librarian from Interval Music (Mac); Patch librarian from Opcode; service and repairs: Wine Country Productions: 1572 Park Crest Ct. #505; San Jose, CA 95118; tel: (408) 265-2008; Musician's Service Center: 998 S. 2nd St.; San Jose, CA 95112; tel: (408) 286-4861; Analogics: 5261 Maple Ave. E.; Geneva, OH 44041; tel: (216) 466-6911
Orig. price (1986):	$2995 (£1895)
Price in 1996:	$1200 (£800)

In little more than ten years, the Sequential team in California came up with, developed and pushed through so many wonderful concepts and technologies—the use of microprocessors, MIDI, multitimbralism and wavesequencing, to mention just a few—that it seems criminal that the company could not survive on its own.

Chris Meyer is credited with the kernel of the idea that became the Prophet VS. The fundamental difference between this and almost all previous synths, with the exception of the PPG models in Germany, was that on the Prophet VS, waveforms are not static but move, change, evolve.

This concept went on to find wider acclaim under the auspices of Yamaha (SY-35) and Korg (Wavestation), two companies who had (and in the case of Korg, still have) a working relationship with the heart of the old Sequential company in California.

But you heard it here first, on the Prophet VS.

A substantial instrument (at the time viewed as somewhat intimidating) the VS's complexity isn't the type that insists you know exactly what you're doing in order to produce plenty of interesting and valid sounds. (Unlike a PPG, in other words, which is equally complex but demands a serious level of commitment in order to get much past the on switch.) The mysterious "Vector Synthesis" tag attached to the VS can be thought of as merely noodling around with the relative balance between four waveforms using an X/Y axis joystick. There are also plenty of familiar subtractive synthesis parameters to latch onto.

At the heart of the VS is a bank of some 96 preset digital waveforms, many of which were created, according to voicing specialist John Bowen, in an almost random, grab bag fashion. But such a concept of numerous starter waves was something that had only been glimpsed at before, on instruments like the DW-6000 and DW-8000 from Korg. It was inspirational. In addition to the 96 ROM waves, the VS can store 32 user-created waves, created by the fun method of mixing and matching with the joystick. Although what is going on may be advanced, it is quite possible simply to play around with this "vectoring," hit on a combination that sounds good and then store it away for safekeeping. No knowledge, as such, is required. You can even generate random programs; instructions are given in the owners manual.

After a blend of waveforms has been chosen, the VS starts to behave more like a normal analog-type synth, with four-pole analog filters, rate- and level-type envelope generators, multiwaveform LFOs and extensive modulation routings and permutations.

I say "more like" because the VS's interpretation of standard subtractive synthesis parameters is often a heady concoction. Rate and level type envelope generators are never the easiest to work with, and the VS even allows you to loop individual EG segments. Well, yes, but who does this in real life? The VS's 32-character display screen was more than respectable in 1986, but even this is wholly inadequate for such in-depth, complex-to-grasp programming.

Modulation from two LFOs, keyboard pressure, velocity, the filter envelope or the mod wheel can be applied to pitch, tone, vibrato, volume, pan and even chorus rate and depth, again making the VS a highly versatile instrument for someone with patience.

Someone with less patience can simply fire up the VS's superb arpeggiator. No plain vanilla "up, down, up and down" merchant, this. Here, you can insert rests, reverse, randomize, repeat certain notes, program splits, even work polyphonically and clock to MIDI. The version on the VS is commonly accepted as the bee's knees of arpeggiators.

Further performance features of note include polyphonic glide, unison and a program layering capability that allows you to stack up a couple of sounds with a delay or a detune factor.

In its heyday, the VS made some high-profile friends like Nik Kershaw, on the crest of his own particular wave at the time, who was a committed user. David Sylvian, a committed Sequentialite at the best of times, featured VS heavily during the time of *Gone to Earth*. And British jazz saxophonist Courtney Pine was introduced to the Wavestation only after extensive experience on a VS. Top American session player Alan Pasqua continued to use his VS Rack long into the 1990s.

It was unfortunate for the VS that during its day Sequential was not enjoying the best of health as a company. The public needed careful and constant education with a new concept like the VS, and funds for this just weren't available at the time.

In the main, people had to discover the VS for themselves, which they did, in reasonable quantities. This is a much-loved instrument by those who have bothered to make the investment of time to fathom out its deeper features. The Korg Wavestation may have superseded it, being more stable and slightly more amenable to comprehension, but the VS is unique and definitely the instrument for the purist.

Sequential (Circuits) ceased trading in 1988.

Sequential Circuits Prophet-5
Analog polyphonic synthesizer

THE FAX

Keyboard:	61-note
Programs:	40 (later 120)
External storage:	Cassette interface
Polyphony:	5-voice
Oscillators per voice:	2
Effects:	None
Connections:	Mono audio, CV in (amp & filter), gate in/out, digital/analog interface
Dimensions:	888mm x 384mm x 240mm
Weight:	17kg

THE FIGURES

Chief designers:	Dave Smith, John Bowen
Production run:	1978-1984
Approx. units sold:	8000
Options:	Poly-Sequencer Model 1005, Analog Interface Box Model 842
Sounds:	Data cassettes and sheets from Kid Nepro, Dr. Sound
Miscellaneous:	Service and repair: Wine Country Productions: 1572 Park Crest Ct. #505; San Jose, CA 95118; tel: (408) 265-2008; Musician's Service Center: 998 S. 2nd St.; San Jose, CA 95112; tel: (408) 286-4861; Analogics: 5261 Maple Ave E.; Geneva, OH 44041; tel: (216) 466-6911. You can hear a Prophet-5 in action on Microsoft's *Musical Instruments* CD-ROM.
Orig. price (1978):	$4495 (£2845)
Price in 1996:	$750-2000 (£700-1500): depends on condition, Rev, MIDI, etc.

- -

The Prophet-5 was the world's first sexy synthesizer. It looked sexy, it sounded sexy. Before the Prophet-5, synths had always looked complicated. Design, if companies ever took up the issue, was based upon practicality or an appeal to the gadget freak. Then along comes this instrument out of nowhere, from a company most people had never heard of, looking for all the world like it stepped out of a Bang & Olufson catalog. Nice wood, ultra-smooth panel hardware.

Whoa, and it sounds killer too? With memories? Who cares what it costs, gimme one.

Also, at the time of its launch at the Winter NAMM show in 1978, the Prophet-5's competition included such inspired items as the Jeremy Lord Skywave, the Keynote Scorpion and the fearsome Polymoog.

This was a watershed in synth design. Microprocessors, allowing all parameter values to be stored in memory cost effectively, had hitherto never been employed—indeed, designer Dave Smith was amazed that no one beat him to the punch—so both the internal and external sophistication of the Prophet-5 took the keyboard world by storm. Orders were amassed at the NAMM show, and for the next ten years, Sequential Circuits, thrust onto center stage overnight, was viewed as the company to beat, the team on the cutting edge.

The Prophet-5 story actually began a few years earlier when Dave Smith, a young bass-playing designer of electronic sequencers and programmers, met another young bass player by the name of John Bowen, who was working for Norlin at the time, demonstrating and selling Moog synthesizers. Bowen was always being asked by customers for add-ons, and when he ran into Smith and his collection of doodads, he offered to help Smith sell some of his units, on a strictly "I'll help out in return for bits of gear" basis.

Smith saw himself and Sequential as a peripherals company, rather in the same mold as Oberheim in the early days. But constant gentle pressure from clients who liked Smith's Model 700 Programmer and wondered why something like this couldn't grow into an instrument, along with, more significantly, the appearance some six months ahead of schedule of new, cost-effective SSM chips, persuaded Smith to go for it and build an instrument.

Bowen sketched out a front panel with the sort of features he wanted to see on a synth, such as sync and a flexible, polyphonic modulation system (this would become the poly-mod section, with the resulting polyphonic oscillator-sweep sound becoming very much the instrument's sonic calling card), and Smith launched headlong into the design, completing a basic model in a matter of months.

Initially, the instrument was called the Model 1000. But none other than Rick Wakeman, who was an endorsee of Sequential sequencers at the time, said, "No, you've got to give it a name." So a naming contest ensued, and out of all the wizardry, sword and sorcery names that were bandied about (it almost became the Seer), the name Prophet was selected.

Why "-5"? As in, why five voices? Aside from some degree of logic, in that a hand has five fingers, the real reason is simply that Dave Smith wanted to be dif-ferent. The few polyphonic synths around, such as the Oberheim SEM-based instruments, always had even numbers. Five seemed like a suitably different choice.

At this time, Sequential was a minuscule company. Even Bowen, who was by now heavily involved, programming the initial (classic) batch of 40 programs, still wasn't on the payroll, preferring to pursue his dream of becoming a rock star with the Neilsen Pearson Band (three albums on Epic and Capitol Records). As such, help was frequently needed from the outside. Dave Rossum of E-mu is perhaps the most famous Prophet-5 "assistant" who carried out work on the oscillators and the keyboard. Smith wasn't in a position to pay for any of this, of course, so E-mu negotiated a royalty deal. This worked fine at first, but after a few years, the checks became irksome and "an issue," so they stopped coming, and Smith and Rossum, who'd always eyed each other suspiciously from opposite ends of the California synth-design scene, ended up in court.

The first Prophet-5s, built to fulfill the swollen order books from the 1978 NAMM show, were the Rev 1 models, which numbered around 200. On these instruments, moving into edit mode required hitting two buttons in order to ready the instrument for tweaking. "Why not just let the motion of turning a knob put it into edit?" said one Tom Rhea. "Oh, yeah," came the response. And so it was, from Rev 2 onward.

Some 1300 Rev 2s were built until 1980, when the bulk of the Prophet-5s were made. The Rev 3s are substantially different from the earlier models, since by that time the Curtis chip was available and used, being deemed more stable and more reliable than the SSMs. This was all fine, but it made nonsense of Bowen's 40 classic programs, since the envelopes were now at different speeds and the whole sound of the instrument was cleaner and lighter. The presets were reprogrammed (also by Bowen), but the debate over which is the better instrument has continued through the years. Rev 3s are definitely more stable, anyway.

The Prophet-5 is a two-oscillator design, with each oscillator offering sawtooth and variable pulse waveforms, tunable independently and featuring the all-important sync option. Filtering is a gutsy 24dB/oct lowpass with resonance; the filter can be shaped by its own ADSR envelope generator and has the option of tracking the keyboard (by pressing a button).

Much of the Prophet's charm, and certainly its character, can be traced back to the poly-mod section, where interplay between the oscillators and the filter (envelope) is set up. The LFO comes in three waveshapes, is fully speed-variable and can be pointed in the direction of either or both oscillators, the pulse width or the filter cutoff frequency. Portamento is available, and you can switch instantly into unison mode for all-oscillator power sounds.

Looking at a Prophet-5's front panel, the instrument seems straightforward to the point of simplicity. Not difficult to program, but definitely not a doddle (poly-mod's often surprising results see to that), the Prophet-5 has been used most extensively for lush washes, textural sounds (Phil Collins on practically everything, The Cars, Japan...) and, as mentioned, the classic polyphonic sweep. Prophet-5s can also do a nice line in bells and atonal noises and are by no means substandard for synth brass patches, both soft and hard. The presets are still wonderfully evocative of the early 1980s "L.A. sound." A versatile instrument, in other words.

Versatile, then, but how reliable and how relevant in the 1990s? If you have a Prophet-5, you don't need some geek in a book telling you how useful it is. This you know, and you've obviously balanced that against the inherent maintenance problems involved in owning one of these classic synths. A Prophet-5 needs care, like a classic sports car.

The other decision for modern users to make regards MIDI. The Prophet-5 was produced long before MIDI, and a retrofit is only regarded as feasible on Rev 3.2 or later. Even with MIDI, the Prophet-5 does not possess a touch-sensitive keyboard, though, so it will probably never feel or behave like a modern instrument. If you want the Prophet sound in a modern MIDI environment (with velocity and aftertouch response), Studio Electronics' P-Five rackmount instrument/equivalent may be the wiser choice.

The Prophet-10, a double helping of Prophet-5, was on the schedule at the same time, though it took far longer to get out and even longer than that (some say never) to get right. Some eight Prophet-10s were built into Prophet-5 casings (two of which synthesist Pat Gleeson bought), but heat problems made the design unworkable. Eventually the double-manual Prophet-10, with its massive, almost double-space casing, was released, complete with one of Sequential's polyphonic sequencers built in. Though Geoff Downes was a loyal Prophet-10 user for a number of years, only a few hundred units were built, and the problem of heat buildup dogged the instrument for most of its life.

Sequential (Circuits) ceased trading in 1988.

Sequential Circuits Prophet-600
Analog polyphonic synthesizer

THE FAX

Keyboard:	61-note
Programs:	100 single
External storage:	Cassette interface

Polyphony:	6-voice
Oscillators per voice:	2
Effects:	Arpeggiator
Connections:	Mono audio, filter CV in, footswitch, MIDI
Dimensions:	850mm x 370mm x 240mm
Weight:	15kg

THE FIGURES

Chief designers:	Dave Smith, John Bowen
Production run:	1983-85
Approx. units sold:	5000
Options:	Model 840 Voltage Pedal (for filter input)
Sounds:	Deep Magic, Walt Whitney
Miscellaneous:	The world's first MIDI synthesizer; service and repair: Wine Country Productions: 1572 Park Crest Ct. #505; San Jose, CA 95118; tel: (408) 265-2008; Musician's Service Center: 998 S. 2nd St.; San Jose, CA 95112; tel: (408) 286-4861; Analogics: 5261 Maple Ave E.; Geneva, OH 44041; tel: (216) 466-6911
Orig. price (1983):	$1995 (£1650)
Price in 1996:	$500 (£400)

This was the world's first MIDI synth. Considering what MIDI has become, you'd be forgiven for thinking the 600's release must have been some momentous occasion. But you'd also be wrong. The Prophet-600 snuck out days before the end of 1992, essentially in response to Korg's Polysix, which, having broken the $2000 barrier, was tearing up sales throughout the world.

Much of the pioneering work on MIDI had been done by Sequential's own Dave Smith. In Smith's mind, MIDI was primarily designed to hook up two or more keyboard synths and play them together. Though multitimbralism was a feature Smith lobbied hard for, fueled, no doubt, by Sequential's concurrent development of the MultiTrak and Six-Trak, the Prophet-600 is a relatively straight-ahead two-oscillator synth, in a similar mold to the Prophet-5 but with enough nips and tucks to bring the price down to a fighting $1995.

In hindsight, it is tempting to trace the eventual decline of Sequential Circuits to the Prophet-600. Hitherto, Sequential products had been expensive, uncompromising, keenly sought after and by no means available to all. (Exclusive? You bet.) The Prophet-600 marked the beginning of Sequential's courtship with street-level, mass-market instruments and even—heaven forbid—inexpensive music software. Such a network of roads always looked inappropriate for this intrinsically pro muso-oriented, classy, quirky California company, and, indeed,

Sequential never looked very comfortable traveling down any of them. If only they could have seen those signs reading "Chapter 13—10 Miles"!

I clearly recall my disappointment upon first seeing this instrument. The panel hardware is noticeably pared down, with membrane switches that constantly mistrigger in place of the Prophet-5's Rolls Royce-feel buttons. The sound, too, is reminiscent of a Prophet-5 but lacking the smoothness and texture. Software envelopes, as found on the Prophet-600, are possibly much to blame for this.

Of course, the instrument is not by any means all gloom and doom. The layout is still clean and uncluttered and helpfully sectioned off into oscillator, filter, envelope generator and poly-mod areas. Each oscillator can choose from sawtooth, triangle and variable-pulse waveforms and can be varied in pitch over a four-octave range. Oscillator B has a fine-tuning control, and the oscillators can be forcibly married using sync.

The VCF, VCA and poly-mod parameters are basically unchanged from the Prophet-5, with the small enhancement of "half" keyboard tracking (instead of just on or off); also, the oscillator A pulse width option has been removed from the list of poly-mod destinations, as has the mono mod section altogether.

While it's true that none of these losses drastically affect the instrument's ability to produce good, solid, basic patches, they do impinge on the weirdness factor—something that was, after all, much of the appeal of this line of instruments at the time.

The Prophet-600 has a small sequencer: real-time recording only but a choice of two tracks. You cannot clock the sequencer externally. Slightly more useful features include the arpeggiator, a chord memory facility (also seen on the T-8) and good polyphonic portamento.

To talk of the Prophet-600's MIDI spec in any critical sense would be churlish beyond belief, but while you do have basic MIDI communication, it is just that: basic. By 1985, the MIDI spec had been upgraded to include modes 1 and 3 and full 16-channel assignment, transmitting Program Change plus mod and pitch wheel data.

The Prophet-600's best line is probably in moody synth strings and pads. Full 12-oscillator unison mode enables it to pump out some tasty lead sounds, too, as does the sync feature.

Not especially reliable in its day, and not highly collectible now, the Prophet is still a landmark instrument as MIDI Synth Number One. Nothing can ever change that.

Sequential (Circuits) ceased trading in 1988.

Vox Continental Organ

THE FAX

Keyboard:	49-note
Programs:	7
External storage:	None
Polyphony:	Full
Oscillators per voice:	n/a
Effects:	Vibrato
Connections:	Mono audio

THE FIGURES

Chief designer:	Ken McDonnell
Production run:	1960-1971
Approx. units sold:	10,000
Options:	A wide variety of components were used during the production run. Some units were made in the UK, others in Italy. Tone and performance may vary considerably.
Sounds:	n/a
Miscellaneous:	This is the sound of The Doors' "Light My Fire," The Animals' "House of the Rising Sun" and many others.
Orig. price (1960):	$250 (£100)
Price in 1996:	$300-1000 (£400-750): instruments in good condition are very rare

Like royal wedding memorabilia, traces of the once-ubiquitous Vox Continental are now very hard to find. The British company Vox produced a range of combo organs for the burgeoning beat market in the 1960s, of which the Continental has come to be considered the high point. The brash, voguish Continental came with a sound that sliced through the clattery drum and tinny guitar sounds of the day and was highly maneuverable compared to the ponderous dead weight of a Hammond. Dead easy to play, too, and not even particularly expensive, the Continental became an instant hit not only among British popsters at the time, such as the Dave Clark Five and The Animals but also within the artier confines of The Doors; Ray Manzarek's organ "sound" was pure Vox Continental.

Vox's stock in trade was amplifiers, and the company's AC30 amp was the staple diet of '60s guitarists. In the '60s, keyboard players were either organists or pianists, and for organists, Vox produced a range of portable, "transistorized" organs ranging from the Continental to the double-manual Super Continental to the equally famous, though not as sought after, Vox Jaguar.

Unlike its great rival, the Farfisa Compact, the Vox Continental has drawbars, although the tones pumped out by its screeching transistors are not dissimilar to the Farfisa's. The Continental's drawbars are similar to a Hammond's, offering footages at 16', 8', 4', 2-2/3', 2', 1-3/5' and 1'. Only the the 1-1/3 pitch is missing, for some reason. Somewhat defeating the point of drawbars, the four higher registers all come under single-drawbar control. Vibrato is the sole effect (preset and highly distinctive). The Continental is also fully polyphonic, 12 tone generators cleverly dividing the three-octave keyboard range.

Also unlike the Compact, with its conservative folding legs, the Continental's eye-catching, tubular-steel Z frame gives the instrument an unmistakable, space-age look. Reverse-color keys (wooden) complete the zany, televisual design.

Replacing the instrument's germanium (pre-silicon) transistors, which most, though not all, of the instruments employed, is one of the most likely problems modern-day users will encounter. On the other hand, tuning problems, in which the Continental always delighted even when new, may simply be a matter of bias adjustment. Another problem is sticking keys, for which the immediate cure is simply to pull them back up as quickly as possible (or as Internet denizen and Continental owner Frank Fuda recommends, use a simple piece of elastic). Continentals "weren't meant to be in this world for a long time," observed Ray Manzarek in a 1991 *Keyboard* interview. Indeed, Manzarek reportedly owned half a dozen of them, all of which eventually "died."

This situation accounts for both the comparative rarity of Continentals and the wide disparity of second-hand prices. Junk shops may sell a unit for a couple hundred, but for a unit in good condition, you may well have to pay two or three times this amount.

The appeal of a Vox Continental is not so much timeless as precisely timed: In keyboard terms, this is "the sound of the '60s."

Vox is no longer an independent business; the name was acquired by Korg UK in the 1980s.

Waldorf MicroWave
Digital polyphonic synthesizer

THE FAX

Keyboard:	None
Programs:	64 single, 64 multi
External storage:	Card
Polyphony:	8-voice
Oscillators per voice:	2
Effects:	None
Connections:	Stereo audio plus four separate outputs, MIDI

Dimensions:	750mm x 320mm x 84mm
Waldorf Electronics c/o TSI GmbH:	Neustrasse 9-12; D-53498 Waldorf, Germany; tel: 02636-7001; fax: 023636-7935
Waldorf Electronics c/o GSF:	tel: (310) 452-6216; fax (310) 452-3886
Waldorf Electronics c/o Turnkey:	114-116 Charring Cross Rd.; London WC2H ODT.; tel: 0171-379-5148; fax: 0171-379-0093

THE FIGURES

Chief designer:	Wolfgang Palm
Production run:	1989-1995 (replaced by the MicroWave 2)
Approx. units sold:	No figures available
Options:	University Edition (different temperaments)
Sounds:	Waldorf Signature Series Soundsets (Claudius Brüse, Dirk Fabritius, Rob Papen, Mike Rosen, Wolfam Franke, Moebius 1, Geoffrey Ryle), plus PPG Wave, Bass, Wavepool, also: East-West, Voice Crystal, Metra Sound
Miscellaneous:	Editor: Geerdes MicroWave (ST); Waldorf on the Web: http://www.waldorf-gmbh.de
Orig. price (1989):	$1495 (£1249)
Price in 1996:	$750 (£700)

There is something very appealing about the Waldorf MicroWave, even if these ears cannot tell you precisely what it is.

By any normal logic, this wavetable synth from none other than the illustrious Wolfgang Palm, formerly of PPG, would have sold to the 500 diehard techno bands in and around Frankfurt and that would have been that.

But the MicroWave has not only transcended Northern Germany, seeping into the rest of Europe and on into the U.S., but has done so over a period of some five or six years (to date) and now has even spawned a Mark Two.

Conventional behavior is not for the MicroWave. This dark blue module with distinctive blood red increment knob looks like no other, and the sounds—at the same time grungy, clangorous, industrial and supremely techno—could only have come from the stable that once brought you those grungy, clangorous, industrial pre-techno noises from the PPG Wave series. Indeed, most of the MicroWave's tally of 32 wavetables—banks of waveforms that fire up the oscillators—were lifted straight out of the Wave 2.3.

As on the 2.3, the oscillators have the ability to step through, in a mind-bending variety of ways, a series of waveforms to produce a multifaceted sound that is always on the move. A dual-oscillator design, the only minor restriction here is that the oscillators must choose waves from the same wavetable. Each oscillator can, on the other hand, dive into that self-same wavetable at different points and for different amounts of time.

Having chosen one (or all, as in wavetable sweep) of the waves as a starting point and having decided whether a wavetable is traversed smoothly or in steps (the latter option providing the MicroWave with much of its distinctive graininess), programming begins to look more normal. The oscillators can be coarsely and finely tuned and broadly balanced in relative volume (0-7 increments). There are three envelope generators, the most impressive used for moving through the wavetable, which is eight-stage and time- and level-type and offers you the chance to loop adjacent segments. The EGs can run positively or negatively per individual oscillator, which makes for some pretty dramatic crossover sweeps.

Filtering is steep four-pole lowpass with resonance that can be shaped using an ADSR-plus-delay envelope generator. There are also two LFOs. (All of this is per voice, of course.)

For a module, the MicroWave is at least feasible to program—far more so than a Wave two-point-anything ever was. Some quick edit parameters let you view and tweak a single screen full of "most likely" parameters. A device called "link" lets you twin oscillator 2's modulation configuration with the one you have set up on oscillator 1. Also provided are Macros—modulation and envelope templates that provide instant access to a particular effect or the envelope of a particular instrument type.

The MicroWave is multitimbral up to its maximum of eight voices, with each multitimbral part capable of being triggered on its own MIDI channel with volume, range, transposition, etc. intact. A clue to the MicroWave's intended purpose for bass and arpeggio lines can be found in its four separate outputs in addition to the stereo pair, which are monophonic.

Upgrades have followed the MicroWave throughout its career. Version 1.2 introduced sophisticated, real-time pure harmonic tuning, a system that analyzes a chord and can then output it in pure tuning. This is a unique, if not widely sought after, facility. SysEx control over just about any parameter in both single and multi patches was also introduced at this time. This real-time/recordable tweaking capability is manna for the techno boys, even if SysEx is invariably data-hungry.

Version 2.0, released in 1995, doubles the number of internal wavetables to 64 and makes some enhancements to the LFOs (both now offering a sample-and-hold waveshape). Version 2.0's new two-speed SysEx mode, plus embryonic implementation of MIDI Clock synchronization, also panders to this instrument's penchant for ravey dance floor activity.

With no internal effects, very limited polyphony, no GM drum kits and only very modest factory presets (though along with version 2.0 come three new sets of improved patches that can be loaded via SysEx), the MicroWave is almost the antithesis of modern synth design. And yet it sold and continues to sell. Interesting.

Wurlitzer EP200 — Electric piano

THE FAX

Keyboard:	64-note
Programs:	None
External storage:	None
Polyphony:	Full
Oscillators per voice:	n/a
Effects:	Tremolo, built-in amplification
Connections:	Mono audio
Dimensions:	960mm x 170mm x 432mm
Weight:	25kg
The Wurlitzer Co.:	422 Wards Corner Rd.; Loveland, OH 45140; tel: (513) 576-4601; fax: (513) 576-4636

THE FIGURES

Chief designer:	Unknown
Production run:	1968-1981 (but the earliest models were made in 1954)
Approx. units sold:	100,000
Options:	Models 210, 203 (Spinet); Models 206, 214, 215 (Classroom: no tremolo but with a headphones socket); Model 207 (Teachers); colors: red (rare), olive green, cream and black
Sounds:	n/a
Miscellaneous:	Original EP100 design released in 1954. Service and repair: Numerous Complaints Music: 1537-B Howell Mill Rd.; Atlanta, GA 30318; tel: (404) 351-4422; fax: (404) 351-4442
Orig. price (1968):	$995 (£650)
Price in 1996:	$500 (£400): Wurlies can still be found for $200 in junk shops but will almost certainly need a severe overhaul. Prices are for a reconditioned model.

I'm speaking purely personally, you understand, but nothing for me exemplifies the 1970s quite like a Wurlitzer electric piano. I'm clearly not alone, since, in the 1990s, a whole generation of '70s-fueled outfits, from Jellyfish to Lenny Kravitz, have gone on to enjoy the Wurlie's distinctively hollow and clunky piano sound.

If character is what you're after, then you're on to something here. From the tip of its odd-length keyboard to its tone generation, the Wurlie is all about character.

The first Wurlitzer electric pianos were produced in the 1950s, first breathing life as the EP100 (plus a range of "100 series" variables) and then re-emerging as the physically revamped EP200, which was launched upon an eager (if completely stoned) public at the back end of the '60s. Produced in a range of colors, from red to beige to green, the EP200 was a great success.

The EP200 employs a light but nonetheless genuine hammer action, the hammers hitting metal reeds. The system was designed not to go out of tune, though the instrument surely does, and you have to dab on or scrape off bits of solder in order to affect a cure. Tremolo is the only tone-altering proposition, with speed alterable, unlike on the Rhodes Stage 73, pretty much the only serious alternative for pro players until the arrival of digital instruments (which squashed them both). The Wurlitzer has a small built-in amplification system that gave the instrument an edge, even if only for bedroom practice. Very early models, in the 100 series, employed tube amplification—something that will probably be the audio icing on the serious collector's cake. Later models used solid-state circuitry. The other gain over its old sparring partner is the sound. Only a total moron is going to pretend that the sounds of either the Wurlie or the Fender Rhodes bear anything more than a passing resemblance to that of an acoustic piano. But the Wurlitzer's tone, comparatively cutting and edgy as it is, was far more likely to be heard in most band contexts.

More likely to be heard, but there's not much room to stretch out on the instrument's measly 64-note (was someone drunk?) keyboard. With this in mind, don't expect too much out of the bottom end (most of it ain't there at all, and what is there is quite lightweight), and up at the top the sound quickly wimps out. The Wurlitzer's prime range is an octave-and-a-half either side of middle C. (This area is punchy already, but if you want to tighten it up a little in a recording situation, try some compression.)

As with so many companies at the time, Wurlitzer thought nothing of releasing a vast number of variations on this one basic design—not just color variables either, but different amplifications, stylings and applications (see above). However, the sound of a Wurlitzer electric piano is a fairly constant entity, and if purists and collectors may still hound down a particular vintage and hue, a Wurlie (if hunted down at all) should be hunted down in order to be played. Compared to modern instruments, the action gives you a rough ride (it's shallow, and on most instruments you'll find, it's about as smooth and even as corrugated iron), and the sound is basically unalterable and instantly recognizable.

In its initial heyday, the Wurlie was employed by such varied players as Joe Zawinul and Supertramp's Richard Davies, the latter stamping this sound (generally vamped in repetitive eighth-note chords) indeli-

bly on the band as a whole.

Price played a large part in the instrument's original success, and second-hand prices, though firm and on the upward swing, still make the instrument accessible to most players.

Wurlies were never expensive, nor did they look it. Frankly, they look pretty plasticky, and they're not exactly built to last. I've seen Wurlies in some fairly desperate conditions (cigarette burns are de rigeur), but a decent pair of eyes and half a brain will tell you whether a potential purchase merits the top sticker price. Because so many were sold—albeit long, long ago—parts and repairs are not generally a problem.

If it's the sound you're after and you're happy to leave the actual instrument behind, the basic Wurlie sound is almost as widely copied as that of a Clavinet. To these ears, the best current rendition can be found on the Korg X-series synths and modules. The sample Korg uses is, in fact, largely a clarinet (yes, the long, blown thing). Odd, but true.

As for Wurlitzer itself in the 1990s, this American blast from the past (maker of classic jukeboxes and theater organs, of course) has undergone something of a resurrection, producing not only a range of digital pianos but also home keyboards.

Cheap to buy and relatively cheap to run, the old Wurlie electric piano still has a place in today's music (a MIDI retrofit is possible, but it would be a bit like turbocharging a Ford Model T), especially for those who weren't users the first time around. However, endless subjection to Supertramp's "Dreamer" on the radio during a succession of U.S. tours back in the '70s has seen to it that the Wurlie will continue to be viewed only from a distance by your author, even if legions of 1990s touring outfits, from Pearl Jam to Pink Floyd, think otherwise.

Yamaha CP80 Electric grand piano

THE FAX

Keyboard:	88-note
Programs:	n/a
External storage:	n/a
Polyphony:	full
Oscillators per voice:	n/a
Effects:	Tremolo, 3-band tone controls, brilliance
Connections:	stereo audio outs (jack or XLR), effects in/out

THE FIGURES

Production run:	1978-1988
Options:	none
Sounds:	n/a
Orig. price (1978):	$8000 (£4999)
Price in 1996:	$1000 (£750)

The CP80 was launched in 1978, just as punk was dragging itself out of the gutter and into that black hole called "fashion statement." Almost innocuously, Yamaha launched the look that was to outlast not only punk, but also two or three forms of synthesis, plus the siege of MIDI and even now is the preferred attire for legions of gigging pianists. The CP80 looks like, and indeed is, a real piano, with real strings and hammers. It has, like its customers back in 1978, simply been electrified.

The CP80 cuts an imposing figure onstage. To be seen seated behind a CP80 is to say, "I am a player. I am not some wally who triggers samples. This is a musical instrument, and I am a proper musician." You see, you have to do all the work on a CP80. It is not the recommended weapon for bluffers. There are no frilly, silly sounds to dial up. No MIDI input with which you can be triggered by a sequencer. Nothing much in the way of (internal) effects to enhance, or perhaps disguise, your playing. This is a piano, and either you can play one or you can't.

Prior to the launch of the CP80, players had two options when it came to purveying the art of the piano onstage: an electronic sound could be fudged (and I choose the word deliberately) by one of a plethora of mainly Italian and invariably horrible electronic pianos, or a regular steam joanna could somehow be miked up. Both options were fairly miserable.

The CP80's solution was to couple the sound and feel of a real acoustic with ready-to-go electronics, allowing you to just plug in and play. This author first took the stage with a CP80 on a John Miles tour in 1979, and, boy, did I feel like a king. There was nothing else around that sounded, felt or looked as good. Those babies were hardly cheap and definitely not lightweight. But record companies were quite happy to stump up for something that splendid-looking, and its Houdini-like feat of collapsing into a pair of luggable flight cases even endeared it to the road crew.

Set up, the CP80 may not have quite the luster and sheen of a concert Bosendorfer, but its mini-grand design does have presence. The casing is tough, quite tough enough to deposit a synth and sequencer on its flat top. Metal legs screw in; a sustain pedal connects to the underneath via a metal rod and is (sort of) kept in place using chains that clip onto the front legs.

This is an electroacoustic instrument. You can hear something when it's unplugged, because hammers are actually hitting strings. But there is no soundboard, so unamplified, the instrument sounds like it is being played several streets away—just barely audible. However, switch it on, plug it in via the professional XLR outs and presto: a pre-miked, ready-to-go acoustic piano, with volume, tremolo (depth and speed), three-band EQ and brilliance controls. Overall, the sound is good. In a band context, you would still be hard-pressed to tell this from an acoustic. Only the bottom octave reveals its true nature with a tell-tale thunk, due to the excessively short and fat strings Yamaha had to use in order to shoehorn the instrument into a sensibly sized casing.

Despite Yamaha's Humid-a-Seal pin block, with which the strings are attached, the CP80 needs regular and proper tuning. And a piano is not like a guitar, which can be coerced into a state of concert readiness by anyone who can read a tuner. People spend years learning the mathematical and musical conundrum that is the art of piano tuning. Having said this, it is probably fair to say that any old tosser with a tuner should be able to fix a single note that has gone off its trolley, and, as mentioned, the bottom octave is effectively untunable anyway.

The action is not like an acoustic piano, as every new Tom, Dick and Harry digital would have you believe these days, it *is* that of an acoustic piano. Not an especially smooth one, mind you, but the feel of the sound being produced and changing because something is actually hitting something else is unmistakable (and as yet unrecreatable, if we're all being dead honest). The CP80 may never have made the prettiest noises nor felt the most comfortable, but it did, and still does, feel real.

From 1978 to 1983, the CP80 was in an almost unassailable position. By the mid-1980s, the development of MIDI and the growth of sparkling, sample-based sound design changed the picture somewhat. The perceived value of instruments that could trigger a whole multitude of sounds and sound modules took precedence. The CP80's day looked like it was over. Some plucky fellows offered MIDI kits for the piano, but prices and interest dropped alarmingly, to the point where CP80s could be seen gathering dust at the back of storage cages but were rarely spotted elsewhere.

There was a small blip of revived interest in 1986, when Yamaha released a built-in MIDI version, the CP80M, which featured a full seven-band graphic equalizer. An upright model, the CP60M, was launched the same year, featuring pretty much the CP80M spec—tremolo, graphic, etc.—and also offering a modicum more in the way of MIDI keyboard assigning (you can send out over a specific range). But the CP60M never enjoyed anything approaching the

YAMAHA

Name:	Yamaha Corporation
Head Office:	Urakucho-Denki Building; 7/1 1-chome, Yuracho Chiyodi-ku; Tokyo 100, Japan
U.S. Distributor:	Yamaha Corp.: PO Box 6600; Buena Park, CA 90620; tel: (714) 522-7011
UK Distributor:	Yamaha Kemble: Sherbourne Drive, Tilbrook, Milton Keynes, MK7 8BL; tel: 01908-366700
Founded:	1887
No. of employees:	Approx. 11,000
Business:	Acoustic and electric musical instruments, semiconductors and related materials, industrial robots, hi-fi equipment, sporting goods; also has its own retail stores

Yamaha is the biggest dedicated musical instrument company in the world, with its corporate fingers in pies ranging from chip manufacture to retail, producing products both acoustic and electric, hardware and software, professional and amateur, and everything in between. If a device can be used for making, processing, storing or outputting musical noises, chances are Yamaha makes one.

The company was founded in 1887 by Torakusu Yamaha. Yamaha had built up something of a reputation as a "Mr. Fixit" in his sleepy backwater town of Hammamatsu. One day, he was called into Hammamatsu primary school to repair an American-made reed organ. While taking it apart, Yamaha carefully noted how it was made and figured he could make one himself. Indeed he could, and did, making tools and parts out of anything he could find. Flush with this success, Yamaha formed the Yamaha Organ Manufacturing Company, which happily coincided with the opening of the Hammamatsu railway, turning this once-sleepy town into a bustling business center for the entire region.

Within ten years, Yamaha's organ business proved its worth and a new parent company, Nippon Gakki, was incorporated in 1897, with Torakusu Yamaha as president. Trips to the United States were undertaken to study piano-building techniques, and by 1902 the first Yamaha grand pianos were built and took the Honorary Grand Prize at the St. Louis World Expo two years later.

Yamaha understood the power of diversification, and in the years before World War I, the company began to manufacture a broad range of instruments. Sadly though, with his company poised on the edge of full international recognition, Yamaha contracted an incurable illness during the war years and died in 1916.

The postwar period, along with the Depression, a major fire that destroyed Yamaha's new plant in Nakazawa, the 1923 Kanto earthquake and an all-out strike at the factory in 1926, almost saw the end of Nippon Gakki. A new leader was sought, and in 1927, Kaichi Kawakami became president, founding a family dynasty that remained at the helm until 1992.

After the inevitable upheaval of World War II, during which Yamaha produced aircraft propellers, the company was quick to resume hostilities with the musical instrument business in 1946, bouncing back not only in instrument manufacture but in retailing. Yamaha's first "musical instrument palace" was opened in the chic Ginza area of Tokyo in 1951. During this period, Yamaha also diversified beyond the music market into motorcycles (in 1955) and from there into leisure and sports equipment.

Although these two "halves" of Yamaha came to be, and remain, under separate control, they are united by the company's overall passion for leisure activities, since it believes that music is a leisure activity in the same way as skiing or golf. Though Yamaha makes professional instruments, the company's efforts are steered towards music as a pastime for the many as opposed to an occupation for the few. The Yamaha Music Foundation was established in 1966 to promote interest in music; and the World Popular Song Festival, created in 1970, was held at Yamaha's own Tsumagoi sports and leisure complex.

Yamaha was one of the first companies to move headlong into home keyboards and is presently a keen proponent of home computer-based desktop music. There are also now some 10,000 Yamaha Music Schools in more than 30 countries around the world.

As with many Japanese businesses, Yamaha's great strength is its ability to plan long-term. In 1971, a call from Stanford University's Office of Technology Licensing Department to young Yamaha engineer Mr. Ichimura led to Mr. Ichimura's visit with electronic music composer John Chowning. Chowning demonstrated to Ichimura the possibilities afforded by his experiments with FM synthesis. American companies all said, "Thanks, but no thanks" to Chowning, but Yamaha saw the technology's potential and spent the next ten years developing FM synthesis into the watershed DX7, which sold 160,000 units and changed the face of the synthesizer world forever.

The Kawakami dynasty has run Yamaha with a rod of iron. In turn, Yamaha has a worldwide reputation for scrupulously honest, if merciless, business dealings. Flushed with the success of the DX7 and its many offspring, Yamaha set out on the acquisition trail in the 1980s, purchasing stock in Korg, buying the ailing Sequential Circuits outright and also grabbing British drum company Premier. However, the plans for world domination, coming on the heels of Nippon Gakki's name change (back) to Yamaha Corporation, have generally backfired. Most of Yamaha's acquisitions and expansions around the globe were withdrawn or sold off by the end of the decade.

The downturn in the keyboard market in the 1990s has hit Yamaha very hard, coming as it did while the company was "in between technologies." With FM now only viable (though admittedly, profitably so) in the sound card/chipset market, physical modeling is being lined up as Yamaha's chosen weapon for the 21st century, and indeed similarities between the first generation of FM instruments (GS1 and 2, CE25) and water-testing physical modeling instruments like the VL1 are obvious.

Whatever the current trends in synthesis, Yamaha's long-term planning and breadth of products seem certain to keep the company in its number-one position for many years to come.

success of the CP80. In fact, come to think of it, the only models I've ever seen were in Yamaha's own swanky music store in downtown Tokyo. The CP70 is a sister act to the CP80, offering almost the same features (less in terms of EQ and processing) and with a shorter scale, 73-note keyboard.

In the same way that the dominance of digital in the synth market has taken a hefty knock in the '90s, digital pianos are by no means everyone's cup of tea nowadays. Aside from considerations of the inevitable (to a degree) fossilization of sound, there is polyphony to consider, plus, of course, looks.

This has added up to a revival of both interest and prices for the CP80 in recent years. Increasingly, it seems, you see CP80s on TV, at gigs, in rehearsal studios, in theaters and so forth. Why? Because this lovable old workhorse just gets on with the job of providing amplified acoustic piano sounds and looks and feels—and to an extent, still sounds—rather more authoritative and professional than its dinky digital cousins.

In the main, these pianos are extremely reliable, and sufficient numbers were sold around the world for spares and repairs to be no problem.

Yamaha CS80 — Analog polyphonic synthesizer

THE FAX

Keyboard:	61-note
Programs:	22 (plus 2 user programs)
External storage:	None
Polyphony:	8-voice
Oscillators per voice:	2
Effects:	Tremolo, chorus
Connections:	Stereo audio, phones, expression-wah pedal in
Dimensions:	1205mm x 304mm x 702mm
Weight:	100kg

THE FIGURES

Production run:	1978-1980
Approx. units sold:	2000
Options:	Standard accessories include hard cover, music rest, foot controller, footpedal, detachable castors and a tube of Yamaha key cleaner cream!
Sounds:	None commercially available
Miscellaneous:	One of Stevie Wonder's reputed four CS80s can be found and played at the Museum of Synthesizer Technology in Britain.
Orig. price (1978):	$6900 (£4950)
Price in 1996:	$1000 (£800)

Everything about the CS80 reeks of extravagance. It's not just big, it's overbearing, not heavy so much as leaden. Its keyboard is not just aftertouch-sensitive, it's polyphonically aftertouch-sensitive. CS80 sounds are not just fat, they're massive.

This brightly colored analog was launched in 1978 alongside the Prophet-5. Like the Prophet-5, the CS80 uses microprocessor technology, but whereas Sequential designed the Prophet-5 from the ground up, offering streamlined programming and sophisti-

cated synthesis programming features, Yamaha essentially strapped this newfangled technology onto a home organ.

The Prophet-5 devoured column inches in 1978, whereas the CS80, smacking of yesterday's news, was largely overlooked. Yamaha knew what it was doing, though. By the end of the decade the CS80 was widely acknowledged as *the* instrument for organ or piano players getting into synthesis, players who were not particularly fussed about programming and storing a sound for eternity but wanted good levels of expression and real-time control. "Polyphonic, playable, portable instruments conceived for live performances," ran Yamaha's promotional blurb for the CS80 and its younger brothers, the CS60 and C50. The portable aspect might only have applied to gorillas, but the rest paints an accurate picture of the CS80 customer in 1978.

Popular at the time without ever being fashionable, the CS80's weight, unreliability, limited programmability and chronic lack of MIDI meant that by the end of the 1980s, you could hardly give one away. CS80s could be found cluttering up many a studio storeroom, with the tacit offer of, "If you can physically take it away, you can have it."

Bloodied but unbowed, the CS80 came back with a vengeance in the 1990s. Mods have been developed to compensate for some of its foibles. Indeed, some of its foibles have now come to be viewed as distinct advantages.

The thread that runs throughout is the CS80's distinctive, cutting, ripping sound. Few synths have ever sounded this big. The CS80 is a dual-oscillator synth, with each offering variable pulse or sawtooth waveforms, plus noise. There are independent high-pass and lowpass filters, each with resonance and filter cutoff sliders, though they share ADR and initial level and attack level envelope generators.

Much of the praise for the CS80's range of raw and raucous sounds is due to the ring modulator, which has its own mini envelope generators, plus speed, depth and modulation controls. (Bon Jovi's David Bryan used this CS80 feature to good effect at the start of "Dry Country" on the *Keep the Faith* album.) Ring mod needn't just be used for weird, clangorous sounds, though; it is also good for more subtle effects, like adding some shimmer to string patches. Meanwhile, LFO parameters include routing to VCO/VCA/VCF and a choice of five waveforms, plus the option of external control.

This is an eight-voice instrument, but as a glance at the mirror-image panels shows us, the CS80 really operates as two independent four-voice instruments, and indeed, two independent sounds can be layered.

The instrument comes with 22 presets, accessed

via huge and brightly colored rocker switches (so designed as to allay the fear of synthesizers among the organ fraternity, presumably). They're not great but they're serviceable.

Part of the CS80's revived appeal is because it is almost the antithesis of the cloney, preset-laden workstations and sample replay machines of the 1990s. Armed with a forest of panel switches and sliders and a brilliant selection of performance features, the CS80 just begs to be mucked around with, to be tweaked, customized and maneuvered on the fly. Incredibly, for a synth of this vintage, the keyboard is semi-weighted and sensitive to both initial pressure and aftertouch, with control over pitch, vibrato, brightness and volume (though aftertouch response is stiff to the point of being another gorillas-only feature). Equally impressive, aftertouch is polyphonic—it can respond to added pressure on just one note played within a chord. You just set up the particular response you want on the small Touch Response panel.

There are also footswitches for the polyphonic portamento/glissando and sustain, and you can even use a standard expression pedal to activate a wah-wah effect (sweeping the filter cutoff position). The CS80 also offers a form of keyboard scaling at your disposal, which is excellent for adding some cut, perhaps to a bass line, or conversely for preventing the instrument from slicing through people's eardrums on a lead solo up at the top end.

Perhaps the prime feature, though, is the ribbon controller, which, though primarily designed for pitch bending, can also be used by the nimble-fingered for producing finger vibrato or trills. The trick, according to longtime CS80 player Jonn Savannah (currently with Squeeze, though not with CS80 in tow), is to use your little finger as a starting point and slide up to a pitch with your first finger or just play trills. Stevie Wonder reportedly wore out his pitch ribbon.

Programming on a CS80 is a real laugh, because in order to store custom sounds, you have to recreate the panel settings on minuscule sliders hidden under a little trapdoor alongside the preset buttons. Understandably, this is something of a hit-or-miss affair. You can set up four custom sounds here and program two more in real time on the main panel.

The CS80 is perhaps most famous for its range of powerhouse brass sounds (where the chance to add noise to a sound comes into its own)—definitely worth sampling if you can't run to a CS80 itself—but this is by no means all it is good for. The direct and simple way in which ring modulation is offered and the speed with which you can lunge at the filter cutoff and resonance make it a wonderful instrument for instant, expressive (if occasionally "synthy") sounds— just the thing to liven up one of those clinically "per-

fect" digital keyboard tracks.

Tuning instability remains the CS80's worst fault. Once tuned, and left *in situ*, the CS80 can hold its tuning for reasonable lengths of time, so the instrument is definitely best kept in the studio rather than dragged out on the road. The other reason the CS80 is probably best left in the studio is its inordinate weight, even if Yamaha did make some concessions by providing four removable casters that can be used for wheeling it around.

Used, but both hated and loved, in its heyday by most major keyboardists, including Michael McDonald, Vangelis, Stevie Wonder and Herbie Hancock, the CS80 was also prominently featured on Peter Gabriel's *So* album. Today, CS80s are in relatively short supply and second-hand models only rarely appear. People who now recognize their value seem most reluctant to part with them.

The CS60 is effectively half a CS80, still eight-voice polyphonic but with a pretty dire selection of just 12 presets and only the one programmable panel. The CS50 is a four-voice, 49-key version with no memories. The frequency ranges of both the CS60 and the CS50 only go up to 4kHz, as opposed to the CS80's 8kHz, which probably accounts for the smaller models' lack of zing.

Yamaha Disklavier Series
MIDI player piano series

THE FAX

Keyboard:	88-note
Programs:	1
External storage:	Disk drive
Polyphony:	Full audio (16 simultaneous over MIDI)
Oscillators per voice:	n/a
Effects:	None
Connections:	MIDI In, Out, footswitch, phones

THE FIGURES

Production run:	1986-present
Options:	FC-4 or FC-5 footswitches
Sounds:	PianoSoft song library
Miscellaneous:	In 1995, Gershwin piano rolls (that the composer recorded between 1916 and 1926) were released in Disklavier format, having been transported via the unique Pianola "fingering" contraption, which actually plays the keys of any keyboard positioned next to it.

Orig. price (1986): No U.S. price (£5999)
Price in 1996: No U.S. price (no UK price)

Japan loves gadgets. Any visitor to Japan will marvel at the country's level of gadgetry, whether it be actual products in the shops, in manufacture or in hotels. Some gadgets travel, some are destined only for the domestic market.

I came across my first Disklavier, tucked away in a corner of Yamaha's own high-tech music store in downtown Tokyo, on a visit in 1986. At the time. Yamaha was uncertain if this supreme musical gadget, essentially a MIDI-controlled player piano, had any future overseas. But like that other great (and initially deemed unexportable) concept, karaoke, the Disklavier has made slow and steady progress into the rest of the world's consciousness. Not that Yamaha hasn't also spent billions promoting it, mind you.

The notion of a MIDI-controlled player piano seems thoroughly preposterous until you play one. Only then, as you feel the response of a genuine acoustic piano under your fingers kicking out MIDI and experience the wonder of being able to hear and see MIDI sequences played back via hammers and strings, can anyone be expected to see why Yamaha saw fit to revive the centuries-old concept of automated musical instruments.

Although there is now a large and ever-expanding range of Disklaviers, under the bonnet, one Disklavier is much like another. The MX upright is based on Yamaha's U series of acoustic pianos, complete with ebony and slip-resistant Yamaha-developed Ivorite on their 88-note keyboards; the DC and DG grands follow the popular G series and high-end Conservatory series. A Disklavier plays exactly as if it were a regular acoustic piano.

As on Yamaha's MIDI Grand, the use of fiber optics allows the most subtle note and expression information to be turned into MIDI data and sent out via the MIDI Out. The difference here, though, is that such information can also be pumped in via the MIDI In and specially designed motors beneath the keys. Beneath each hammer lies a solenoid unit with a tongue that has no mechanical resistance and is therefore undetectable to the touch when you play. To prevent retriggering, Yamaha has constructed special deerskin-backed shock absorbers so the hammers won't bounce back onto the strings. Controls blend in but are still clearly visible on the MX range, while on the grand pianos, a "control wagon" trundles alongside the piano, connected via a single umbilical cord.

The MX100A's control panel, located just below the lip of the lid, is comprised of a DS/DD disk drive, a 16x2 dot-matrix LCD and a two-digit LED, followed by a collection of sequencer controls—stop/pause, repeat, record, volume, tempo, transpose, metronome, and L/R part cancel.

Watching the actual keys of the keyboard moving up and down as your tune is played back before your eyes is a miraculous sight. On the upright MX models, the sequencer is more suited to scratchpad work, but the later grand models offer slightly more control, such as punch-in and overdub recording and note editing, as well as song search, delete, copy and chain play on playback.

In spite of the high specifications and the wonderful potential for pro musicians to be able to sit down at such an instrument and both record and play back their performance, it is sad to report that the main resting place for most Disklaviers is in the living room, bedecked with family photos and played only by the internal motors, at the mercy of Yamaha's PianoSoft library. However, it seems fairly obvious that Yamaha intended this to be the market from the beginning, since there is no internal amplification. If you want to amplify a Disklavier, you have to mike it up just like an acoustic piano.

The disk drive can hold a considerable amount of music at any one time, and you can either program a complete selection of music to play through or use the remote control to dial up a particular piece when you want it.

As an instrument for use in hotels or bars, the Disklavier provides the best of both worlds: When you want—and can afford—a real player, then you have a "real" piano; when you don't, you can slip in a PianoSoft disk and let the Disklavier play itself.

For rock, pop or film composers, the Disklavier solves one of the few remaining limitations of living in the MIDI world: namely, that a genuine acoustic piano part generally still has to be played. There are slight delays inherent in the system, so the instrument adds a 500ms delay buffer before MIDI data goes out.

The Disklavier continues to gain followers, and Yamaha continues to support the concept. In 1991, Yamaha even produced a wildly wacky, solid birch instrument (see photo) reminiscent of a Henry Moore sculpture for Tetsuya Komuro (keyboardist with the Japanese group TMN).

Yamaha's great strength is its ability to think and plan long term. In ten years, the Disklavier has blossomed from a lone upright model unobtrusively displayed in a Tokyo music store to a full range of instruments and software distributed freely around the world. The PianoSoft library currently includes the Original Artist Collection (Steve Allen, John Jarpin, Chick Corea, Don Grusin, Dick Hyman, Andy LaVerne and Liberace, among many others), the Broadway Collection, the Children's Collection, the Christmas Collection, the Classical Collection,

Contemporary, Country, International, Jazz, Movie & TV Themes, Pops, Sacred, Standards, Accompanist (providing the backing while you—say, the flautist—play over the top) and more, as well as a range of PianoSoft Plus disks that are programmed for use with a Disklavier and an additional tone module.

Yamaha DX7 Digital polyphonic synthesizer

THE FAX

Keyboard:	61-note
Programs:	32 RAM
External storage:	Cartridge
Polyphony:	16-voice
Oscillators per voice:	6 operators
Effects:	None
Connections:	Mono audio, phones, footswitch, foot control, breath control, MIDI
Dimensions:	1018mm x 102mm x 329mm
Weight:	14.2kg

THE FIGURES

Chief designers:	John Chowning (FM), Phil Nishimoto, Hans Yamada, Karl Hirano, Mr. Koike
Production run:	1983-1987
Approx. units sold:	160,000
Options:	BC1 Breath Controller
Sounds:	Yamaha RAM cartridges; also available from Valhalla, PA Decoder, Maartists, Many MIDI, Sound Logic, Sound Source, Soundsations, Metra Sound, Key Clique and many more
Miscellaneous:	Editor/librarians: Opcode 6-Op (Mac), James Chandler Jr. (Mac), Steinberg TX/DX Synthworks (ST), Dr. T's DX Heaven (ST), Geerdes XPert 6 SWS (ST); books include *The Complete DX7* by Howard Massey, *Easy DX7* from Yamaha, *DX7 Synthesizer Set Ups* by Terry Fryer, *How to Understand and Program Your Yamaha DX7* by Lorenz Rychner, *Power Play DX7* by Steve DeFuria, *Programming DX7* by Ronnie Lawson and *FM Theory and Applications* by John Chowning and Dave Bristow; video: *Advanced DX7 Programming* by Hot Licks
Orig. price (1983):	$1895 (£1549)
Price in 1996:	$425 (£500)

"**T**he Synthesizer Redefined," says the heading on the DX7 brochure. You'd normally dismiss such trumpeting as typical marketing hogwash, but this time Yamaha was right, and there were very few people back in 1983 who, after hearing the instrument for even five minutes, voiced any other opinion.

The DX7 was immediately and universally praised and immediately and universally sought after. From 1983 to 1985, no other synth could get a look in. And this was not simply an important product in synth history; it was the key, pivotal instrument. The DX7 not only redefined what a synthesizer sounded like or could do but also redefined the synthesizer market. From the DX7 onwards, manufacturers' eyes were opened to the possibility that synthesizers could really *sell*.

The DX7 did not happen overnight. This was not some idea scratched out on the back of a cigarette packet and knocked out within the year. The first DX7s may have steamed out of Osaka in 1983, but the story actually began in California 15 years earlier.

Keyfax is not the framework for the full DX7 picture, but a thumbnail sketch shows Stanford University electronic music composition teacher John Chowning experimenting with vibratos in the late 1960s until he discovered that he could produce musically complex, harmonically interesting results by modulating one sine wave with the output from another, using high speed vibratos. Thus in 1967, the seeds of modern Frequency Modulation (FM) synthesis were sewn. (FM as a concept had already been broadly accepted, but Chowning's work made it controllable and valid in the musical mainstream.)

Chowning did not run from his studio on campus screaming "Eureka!" Instead, he tinkered away for a number of years, perfecting this, recalculating that, making noises and drawing the occasional scathing comment from colleagues who figured that he must be using up all the University's quota of oscillators, such was the succession of harmonically rich sounds that continued to emanate from his wooden hut of a studio on campus. Of course, he was not. He was using just two: one as a carrier, one as a modulator.

In 1971, digital synthesis guru Max Matthews of Bell Labs told Chowning that if he could tame his system to make recognizable brass and organ sounds, he might have a salable product on his hands. He approached the Stanford's Office of Technology Licensing with his discoveries, and they in turn approached a number of American organ manufacturers to see if they were interested in acquiring this new technology.

They were not. Wurlitzer, Lowry, Hammond and others all turned the offer down. One at least appreciated what Stanford had but couldn't see how the technology could fit into its own products, while the others couldn't see what was going on at all, and I'll spare the reddest of blushes by leaving it at that.

More as a last-ditch effort than anything else, Stanford turned to Yamaha, who produced a small range of Electone organs (at this time, everyone figured FM would only be of interest to organ manufacturers) and had an office in California.

A young engineer by the name of Mr. Ichimura was dispatched to Stanford to check things out. Mr. Ichimura understood digital and, as an engineer, appreciated the concept of FM in radio terms. So, it only took him about ten or fifteen minutes to comprehend the essence of what Chowning had cooking. Chowning knew that Ichimura was impressed by what he'd seen and heard and so was not surprised when he learned that Yamaha wanted to take out a year's exclusive option on FM.

In the ensuing few years, a number of things developed. Under the wing of Yamaha's organ division (the division that had actually taken out the option), a prototype FM instrument was built under the direction of Dr. Mochida, entitled the "MAD." This monophonic FM synth, built in 1973 by two young engineers by the names of Hirokato and Endos, is possibly the first all-digital synth ever made. By 1975, a polyphonic version had also been built.

Over at Stanford, meanwhile, things weren't quite so rosy. John Chowning's job was as an electronic music composer and teacher at Stanford, and the university's approach was very much this: "To hell with all this fancy synthesis stuff, where are the compositions?" To put it as bluntly as Californians get, they "let him go."

When Yamaha returned to Stanford in order to "do the big deal"—take out a ten-year license on FM—Chowning was nowhere to be seen (actually, he was in Europe). All very embarrassing. Somewhat hastily, the university contacted Chowning and offered him the post of research associate, a job he says he was by then in no position to turn down. Installed as director of the university's Center for Computer Research and Musical Acoustics (CCRMA, known as "carma"), Chowning was later offered a professorship in 1979.

As an aside, one of the many stories that grew up around FM is that Dr. Chowning received no monetary reward for his invention. Not true. As a member of the faculty in 1970, it was not compulsory to turn over licensing of any technology developed while at the university (as it is now) but it was the most obvious and perhaps the wisest move. Chowning signed the copyright of FM over to the university in return for a royalty, and in turn, the university assigned a license to Yamaha. Dr. Chowning may not presently be living in a Bel Air mansion, but he appears happy with what he made out of the deal. "People say to me, 'You'd be a billionaire if you'd kept it to yourself,'" he says. "And I say, right. Or I'd have got nothing." As it is, all parties appear to have been scrupulously diligent about royalty payments, and no whiff of dissent hangs in the air. While Chowning's deal with Stanford

is privileged information, the university itself is said to have reaped more than $20 million in license fees and outright payments, which it used, to its credit, to move CCRMA from its "shed" on campus to a splendid, brand-new, specially designed building.

But back to our story. With Chowning ensconced at Stanford again and a new ten-year license in place, serious work began on producing marketable products utilizing FM synthesis. There was, however, one final shootout between two technologies that Yamaha had been developing side by side: FM and a home-grown "summation" additive synthesis. Chowning, who by now was paying occasional visits to Japan, recalls a big meeting at which the two competing technologies were displayed and discussed. In the end, FM, which wasn't dependent upon digital filters that would have been very expensive to produce, won out. Not only was it more memory-efficient, but it also had the potential for far greater player control.

From then until the DX7's launch in 1983, John Chowning only occasionally heard whispers of "DX" as he slipped through factory corridors on his visits to Japan. The GS1 was the first FM-sporting instrument to be released, in 1981, though in spite of the ripple of excitement it caused in the industry, the GS series was always intended to be a market-tester.

With the launch of the DX7, all hell was let loose; Yamaha simply couldn't make enough of them. But by now, this was far removed from John Chowning's world. In fact, he saw and heard his first DX7 synthesizer in a bar in Palo Alto. Chowning remembers the occasion vividly: "My wife and I had been out to see a movie and we stopped off at a local bar for a nightcap. I knew the keyboard player in the bar, and when he saw me he waved me over excitedly to come and see this 'incredible new instrument' he had sitting on top of his piano. I was astonished. It was an awesome moment. I had no idea that people had been waiting in line to buy DX7s. I had no idea at all."

And so the product of Chowning's (and many, many others') labors ended up as a 16-voice polyphonic digital synthesizer, offering 32 internal memories plus a ROM/RAM cartridge slot. The DX7 keyboard is not weighted, but it responds to velocity and aftertouch. Further expression can be extracted from a Breath Controller, Yamaha's own invention, a mouthpiece/pacifier affair by which you can more or less convincingly simulate the breath-to-tone response of a wind instrument. (Unfortunately, very few players felt comfortable with this object stuffed into their mouths.)

The DX7 panel is not an object of particular beauty. There are plenty of dedicated controls, though switches are squishy "membrane" types and the display screen is minuscule. Along the top of the panel runs a collection of "algorithm" diagrams, so you can see at a glance the type of sound you are likely to produce (effectively) using each of these oscillator configurations. An envelope generator and a keyboard-level scaling graphic are perched on the end.

Chowning's FM theories manifest themselves on the DX7 as a series of "operators" (which can be thought of as oscillators) that the instrument offers to the user in a number of different configurations or "algorithms." The operators are all sine waves, and each can be either a carrier wave or a modulator wave, depending on its position or relationship with another wave in a particular algorithm. The DX7 can use six operators per voice.

DX7 programming is commonly, though not a little unfairly, perceived as impenetrable. Perhaps it was unwise of Yamaha to splash about words like "operator" and "algorithm" when "oscillator" or "voice" or "shape" might have been less intimidating.

In any given program, the novice programmer can simply switch operators on or off and begin to learn what role each performs within a sound, but things do get rather more involved when you consider that each operator can also specify a particular pitch, volume, envelope and such, and so each is almost a complete mini-synth in its own right. In a flat operator-plus-operator algorithm, the system can work as simply as drawbars on an organ, but once operators begin to interact, then the sonic results become vastly more complex and unpredictable (which is why the system sounds so good, of course). In fact, a maneuver such as changing an envelope setting of the top member in a stack of interacting operators can exert all manner of unexpected influences on those further down; it is this level of programming intensity that has led to the theory that the three essential ingredients of FM programming are trial, error and luck.

The individual parameters do not befuddle as much at the general level of interaction. Indeed, Yamaha retained many analog-style features and terminologies. The LFO, for instance, offers triangle, saw up/down, square, sine and random waves and can be set in terms of speed, delay, routing (pitch or volume) and amount. Although the envelope generators, which Yamaha bravely but wisely entombed in silicon rather than taking the "flexible" software route, have their rate and level system emblazoned on the control panel, such multistage envelopes are notoriously complex to set, especially without any help via movable graphics on the display screen. If I may borrow from Howard Massey's excellent book *The Complete DX7*, one rule of thumb is to remember that envelope generator control over a carrier will

affect volume over time and envelope generator control over a modulator will similarly affect tone. There is also a separate four-stage pitch envelope generator. (The tangible benefit of hardware envelopes, by the way, is speed.)

Many parameters that are sewn into the fabric of a program on more modern instruments are global parameters on the DX7. These include pitch bend range, mod wheel assignments, aftertouch response, glissando, poly/mono assign, etc. All of these are called Function parameters and are accessed using the same buttons as the presets or voice programming parameters. Said buttons—the offending squishy membranes—thus have three separate purposes.

Though FM programming has been somewhat unfairly classified as hopelessly complex, it is reasonable to say that 155,000 out of the instrument's 160,000 customers have been content to play the presets. Credit for this fact goes squarely to the two consultant programmers who voiced the DX7, Dave Bristow in the UK and Gary Leuenberger in the U.S. This Lennon-and-McCartney team of programmers, whose work spans from the GS1 to the SY series, extracted every possible ounce of musicianship from the DX7, ranging from the classic Fender Rhodes electric piano facsimile (which has since entered synth folklore, known as "DX piano" to all subsequent copyists) to the sonorous collection of fretted and fretless basses to hand percussion, bells, marimbas, ripping brass and sound effects.

Leuenberger explains how he created the DX piano: "It was a very intuitive thing that began on the GS series, which has just four pairs of operators. Having come from a background of B-3s, I knew what to expect by adding sine waves together. After learning what happens by changing the envelope for a modulator and a carrier, I made the foundation "rubbery" tone with one-to-one ratio but with different envelopes. Then I did the same using another pair of operators and detuned one against the other. With a third pair, I produced a sound like something hitting metal, which, to my intuitive sense, sounded like a "tine" [Rhodes metal rod] sound, so I added that in. Finally, by apportioning velocity control to these components, it turned into this beautiful, real-sounding musical instrument."

Bristow and Leuenberger also recommend embracing the concept of "stuff." Stuff is some character-inducing component part of a sound that can be used in several tones. Bristow explains creating a Wurlitzer tone: "I had this real high operator noise ["stuff"] which I added to 2:1 ratio square-wave, clarinet type of sound, so providing the fart necessary for a convincing Wurlitzer electric piano. Put a bunch of velocity on it and some tremolo...that's how it was made.

"Adding non-integer, weird ratios for just a fraction of a second colors your perception of a sound. Later I discovered that this wasn't actually FM at all, but AM, amplitude modulation—that the frequency is going up and down so much over a short period of time that they were creating their own side bands."

Bristow and Leuenberger's experiences with DX7 programming were moving (Bristow remembers the final sound presentation meeting in Japan at which all the engineers were packed into a room with tears in their eyes, some of them hearing music on this instrument for the first time after laboring over oscilloscopes and technical data for two years), madcap and occasionally murderous (they had just one week to compile the instrument's first 128 presets), but both agreed, when interviewed recently, that they would do it all again for the same unmentionably low fee. "But I bet your wives would issue divorce proceedings immediately," I quipped. "Well, actually, they did," both chorused.

At the end of this extremely long day, there can hardly have been a player in the 1980s who did not use the DX7 or one of its multifarious spinoffs. There also grew up a whole industry of DX7 add-ons and support products, such as Grey Matter's E! expansion kit, which bolsters the patch tally to 320—each one complete with its own dedicated function parameters—while improving the MIDI spec to include local on/off, full 16-channel access and wide-ranging MIDI filtering and also adding some simple tone controls and the possibility of patch layering.

A similarly user-installable mod from Group Center called DX Super Max beefs up the program count to 256, offers patch layering and function programming and the delights of a superb arpeggiator.

Many of these features were later to be found on the DX7II, a bold attempt to rectify the occasional DX7 foible, especially concerning the MIDI specs (the DX7 came out in the same year as MIDI and is understandably a bit limited—the ability to send out only on MIDI channel 1 and lack of a local off setting being the two biggest problems). It was unreasonable to expect the Mark II to live up to its illustrious forebear; most feel that some quite major improvements to the sound quality and improved programming possibilities through patch layering and microtonal tuning were offset by a sluggish keyboard response (too much processing going on).

As the collector's item that, in spite of the large numbers sold, the DX7 will surely become, only the plain DX7 will do. A masterful instrument, produced at the right time and the right price by the right people—always an irresistible combination.

Yamaha GS1 — Digital polyphonic synthesizer

THE FAX

Keyboard:	88-note
Programs:	16 ROM
External storage:	Voice cards
Polyphony:	16-voice
Oscillators per voice:	2 operators
Effects:	Chorus, vibrato, tremolo, detune, 3-band EQ
Connections:	Stereo ¼" and XLR audio
Dimensions:	1500mm x 826mm x 832mm
Weight:	90kg

THE FIGURES

Chief designers:	John Chowning (FM), Hans Yamada
Production run:	1982-4198
Approx. units sold:	100
Options:	BGS-1 Bench, FC-3A Foot Controller, Bank Selector (for 112-tone access)
Sounds:	Yamaha card library
Miscellaneous:	This is the sound of Toto's "Africa."
Orig. price (1982):	$16,000 (£11,995)
Price in 1996:	$3000 (£3000)

FM synthesis was forged in the research laboratories of Stanford University in California by John Chowning in the early 1970s. Through a process more fully described in the DX7 review, the technology was licensed to Yamaha, which spent almost ten years turning the theory into a highly polished sound-producing box, whereupon two young programmers in America and England turned the box into a musical instrument by constructing a sound set with depth, quality and expression that had never been heard before. It took Toto's David Paitch just a few minutes of playing about with the GS1's "Rhodes-into-brass" patch before he came up with the main riff of one of the band's biggest hits, "Africa." The GS1 is that sort of instrument.

The GS1 was FM's appetizer for Yamaha. It was never designed as a big seller in itself. Its sounds, aside from the odd minor tone enhancer, are preset. The whole package was presented to catch the public's ear and eye and to set up the programmable, affordable DX7 that would arrive in the following year.

With almost Clavinova styling, the GS1 contains 16 FM presets, and you can load in new sounds via lollipop-stick magnetic "voice cards," each storing 32 additional tones (half of which can be accessed by the instrument at any one time). A Bank Select modification was endorsed, though not made, by Yamaha at the time, providing access to 112 sounds. There is no display screen; presets are called up using individually numbered push buttons.

The GS1 is a player's instrument, pure and simple. The 88-note keyboard responds to both velocity and aftertouch (which can be switched off if necessary), the latter controlling different parameters for different sounds. The presets comprise classic FM types such as electric piano, brass, bells, etc., some of which appear layered and some as keyboard splits.

GS1 sounds can be adjusted rather than edited, parameters comprising detune (random or static), vibrato and tremolo (both with adjustable speed and depth), ensemble and EQ. The instrument's lack of programmability obviously focused attention on the presets, which had been programmed by Gary Leuenberger in the U.S. and Dave Bristow in the UK.

Leuenberger and Bristow's introduction to FM synthesis via the GS1's streamlined, two-operator style gave them a unique insight into the system's power and potential and was, according to Bristow, one of the main reasons they were able to produce the quality of sounds that they did for the six-operator DX7 two years later. He explains: "With that amount of time, that amount of exposure to two operators, a carrier and a modulator, you get a very deep, intuitive feel for how FM sounds, what you have to do to make it happen. By the time the DX7 came along with its 'algorithms' and six operators, I was ready."

With its brass castors, three pedals and 1/4-inch or XLR outputs, the GS1 wasn't just a showpiece but was designed to be used by the keyboard elite of its day. David Paitch was the highest-profile user.

Yamaha's organ division was who initially purchased the patent on Professor Chowning's FM, and the GS1, with its hefty price tag, lack of programmability and no less than 40 ICs (the DX7 got this tally down to two), is a fascinating behind-the-scenes glimpse into this heady East-West pooling of skills.

Few GS1s were made, and not many more of its younger brother, the portable GS2. Aside from the voice cards being somewhat prone to rejection or damage, the GS1 has no particular performance skeletons in its cupboard. This is a rare instrument, and one you'll seldom come across. However, though clearly rare, the GS1 has not yet become a darling in the world of collectors.

Yamaha KX88 Controller keyboard

THE FAX

Keyboard:	88-note
Programs:	16
External storage:	Sys Ex
Polyphony:	n/a
Oscillators per voice:	None
Effects:	Assignable controllers include 2 wheels, 2 footswitches, 2 pedals, 4 sliders, 7 panel buttons
Connections:	MIDI In/Out
Dimensions:	1441mm x 132mm x 347mm
Weight:	29kg

THE FIGURES

Production run:	1985-1995
Options:	Pedals and switches
Sounds:	n/a
Orig. price (1985):	$1695 (£1399)
Price in 1996:	$900 (£800)

Controller keyboards—"dumb" keyboards that make no sound but simply coordinate the sounds of others—have proved to be difficult items to sell. So for one of their rank not only to sell well but to achieve classic status is really quite a feat. As of this writing, the KX88 has just celebrated its tenth birthday, another extraordinary achievement given that controller keyboards are all about, well, control, and in terms of control, MIDI has changed beyond all recognition over the past ten years.

So what on earth is going on? What is it that people like about the KX88? Well, we can put its success down to two things: the name Yamaha and its 88-note weighted keyboard, which feels positive, is responsive and generally makes you feel like you're playing a real musical instrument rather than just operating a bank of switches.

This is all very well and commendable. But the KX88 was one of the very first dedicated controller keyboards, and as such has a limited MIDI spec in modern terms. Also, many of the limited features it does have are complex to set up, requiring at best patience and at worst knowledge of hexadecimal language and commands. (File under "Forget it" for most mortals.)

Some of the specifications would provoke howls of laughter from the high-flying controller keyboards of the 1990s. Just one MIDI Out and a mergeable In? Are you crazy? Sure, but at least you can send out on two MIDI channels simultaneously.

Sounds are controlled in A and B banks, each operating on a dedicated MIDI channel and capable of accessing a full 128 program change commands. Accessing, that is, in real time (i.e., from one of the panel sliders or buttons). For some reason, you can't store program change messages in any of the memories, which is a pretty big limiting factor.

However, controls and controllers are everywhere: wheels, sliders, five momentary switches, two toggle switches, foot controllers, a breath controller socket and, of course, the velocity/aftertouch-sensitive keyboard itself. All of these devices are definable and can be set independently to control pitch bend, volume, modulation, MIDI channel changes, portamento, transposition and even sequencer control (stop, start, song select and tempo). Sixteen such assignments can be stored in memory. Programming is a bit sluggish to take effect, but at least you can vaguely see what you're doing, since a healthy wodge of information is actually printed onto the control panel.

But that's not all. You can also redefine controller codes, completely reprogram DX instruments via System Exclusive messages and even tap into non-Yamaha SysEx codes via the Universal Parameter. However, back in 1985 when FM still ruled the racks, much of this, though still fairly incomprehensible to most mortals, was at least relevant in theory. Not today. Setting up such in-depth functions is downright unfriendly, since as often as not you'll be programming in hexadecimal. Moreover, since the KX88's Yamaha DX contemporaries operated with just 32 program memories, this is its default. To access a full complement of 128 programs, you must first do a fair amount of button-prodding to get into eight-Bank mode.

The KX88 is an odd mix of excess and paucity: You can tweak the pitch envelope of a passing DX7, but you can't store program changes or even step through program changes using a footswitch.

The KX88's continued popularity is firmly rooted in the feel of its 88-note weighted keyboard action. There are many controller keyboards on the market that are more immediately usable, but few with similar-quality keyboards and none that feel exactly like a KX88, of course. It depends on what you value the most: control or feel. If it's the latter, it still makes sense to look at the KX88.

The decision to buy a KX88 also makes sense for studio applications, where its lack of program memories and one or two curious programming omissions would not really matter. Although the feel is there, in a live setting you'd have to make sure you could live with limited keyboard zoning (only two sections), limited memories and the lack of slightly more current features, like a Panic button or card storage for backup. That said, you can prime a split-point setting and simply hit a note on the fly to set the new split, while the MIDI In's original intention of allowing you to plumb in a strap-on keyboard like Yamaha's KX5 remains a handy asset.

Considering its vintage, the KX88 is a truly remarkable instrument. Who on earth would have thought, back in 1985, that between the DX7 and KX88, it would be this baby that would still be doing the rounds?

The rarely-seen KX76 is identical but for a shorter (76-note), non-weighted keyboard.

Yamaha SY77 Digital keyboard workstation

THE FAX

Keyboard:	61-note
Programs:	128 ROM/64 RAM (single), 16 ROM/RAM (multi)
External storage:	Voice and Wave cards, disk drive
Polyphony:	32-voice
Oscillators per voice:	6 operators
Effects:	2 multieffects units
Connections:	2 stereo audio, phones, footwitches, sustain, breath controller, MIDI
Dimensions:	1046mm x 400mm x 117mm
Weight:	17kg

THE FIGURES

Production run:	1990-94
Options:	New Wave cards
Sounds:	Yamaha Voice/Wave cards, MetraSound, East-West, Voice Crystal, SoundSource, EMC, Valhalla, SoundSations, Pro Rec
Miscellaneous:	Books: *Yamaha SY77 Sound Making Book, Level 1* by Dan Walker, *Yamaha SY77 Sequencing Handbook* by Lorenz Rychner, *Yamaha SY77 Cheater's Guide and Cookbook* by Alexander and Mierkey; editors: Steinberg SY77/TG77 Synthworks (ST), Geerdes SY/TG77 SWS (ST), Sound Quest (Mac/ST/Amiga/PC)
Orig. price (1990):	$2995 (£1699)
Price in 1996:	$1000 (£750)

The DX7 was a hard act to follow. Not that the SY77 followed the DX in a strict sense; the Yamaha trail is in fact littered with keyboards that shuffled where the DX7 had marched triumphantly a few years prior. Nothing Yamaha has produced since has matched DX7 stature (nor, probably, ever will), but the power and range of the SY77 have made it last well. In record terms, you'd call the SY77 a sleeper. Released with the full wind of the Yamaha publicity machine in its sails, the SY77 met with some resistance from public and pundits alike, but as the years rolled on and "faults" (noisy effects, programming complexity, etc.) became part of the instrument's character, the SY77 is much appreciated and much used by FM aficionados looking for that sound and more in a modern work-station context.

Large and substantial-looking, with three perfor-mance wheels, a disk drive and a good-sized display, the SY77 bristles with technology labels—RCM, AWM 2, AFM—that describe (to some) the power under the hood. AWM 2 is the second generation of the Yamaha sampling technology used since the early days of the Clavinova digital pianos. AFM is "advanced" FM synthesis, based on FM techniques but with the helping hand of 16 waveforms rather than the sine wave-only oscillators on the DX et al. It also offers some additional looping facilities and new operator modulation inputs that allow sampled waves to act as modulators. This last enhancement really throws open the doors of FM. It is this interplay between FM and samples that is described in the RCM ("Realtime Convolution and Modulation") process. ("Convolution," aptly, is Yamaha's convoluted way of describing the Convolution filters; the word "filter" would have been just as descriptive and far easier to understand.)

A single SY77 voice is constructed using "ele-ments," which are complete voices based on either AWM samples or AFM waveforms. The element stage is where you can set splits, layers, velocity scalings and pan settings. Pan possibilities are great fun, because you can control pan position by note number or velocity or via the LFO. Fun, but you need to be disciplined, as listening to a sound that constantly pings around the stereo spectrum can be very tire-some.

Each element also has at its disposal two digital filters; one can be a dual resonant high- or lowpass, the other always lowpass. In dual-filter mode you can produce bandpass filtering effects. A five-stage enve-lope generator is also reserved for the filter section. Implemented for the first time here is the capability to loop between individual segments of the envelope generators, plus a delay factor.

Voice elements can be harnessed in a number of ways called "modes." These range from lone AWM or AFM elements to filtered versions of the same to sim-ple combinations or even intermodulating combina-tions. Your choice of mode governs the style of sound you will produce, and the SY77 can convincingly reproduce the sound of analog machines, hard-edged digital FM or even real instrument sample+ synthesis.

The sample+ synthesis side of the instrument fires up from a 2MB pool of waveform ROM contain-ing the building blocks of sound, from bits of piano and organ to scrapes, hits and gurgles to complete loops. Criticism was initially leveled at this waveform ROM in terms of range and sound quality. As time has

gone on, though, the application of new waves from cards, plus the realization that the instrument's con-siderable editing power lessens the need for "finished quality" waveform ROM, has silenced the critics.

The SY77 has a pair of digital multieffects units, mainly providing onboard reverb. Strangely, coming from a company that produced dedicated effects processors, the SY77's effects exert a dulling influence on the sounds. This is the one area of initial criticism that remains valid.

With full 16-part multitimbralism and a 16-track sequencer, the SY77 qualifies as a workstation. The sequencer offers both real-time and step program-ming, and you can offset tracks (alter relative track timing), record System Exclusive data and even pat-tern-record on track 16 for rolling, drum machine-type input.

The term "workstation" implies that all tasks can be undertaken from the one instrument, and the SY77 is well endowed with wheels (three) and external con-trollers like a breath controller and footpedals. On the down side, the keyboard has no release velocity and can only send out on one MIDI channel at a time, so it may not be ideal as a controller for a large multi-module rig. Polyphony is rated at 32-voice but in fact delivers 16 voices of AWM plus 16 voices of AFM, so there are restrictions.

You'd normally expect to find at least passable drum sounds on a workstation, but the standard SY77 drum voices are notoriously weak, totally lacking in depth. You can buy a new and vastly improved set of drum samples and program on card, which is essen-tial if you plan on sequencing in a wholly SY environ-ment.

Turning away from the SY's weaknesses, its many strengths include a range of expressive synth sounds (though orchestral sounds are not a strong point, either), where the blend of technologies combines crispness with warmth and musical response (the velocity options make it highly playable) with "effectsiness." A nice programming trick that has always worked well on FM synths is to layer a voice upon itself, pan one left and the other right and then detune one side. This works a treat on pianos or Clavinets, providing sounds that will really respond to the resultant chorus effect. Now add in some con-trolled panning and you're away.

The TG55 module is not an exact equivalent but rather the AWM2 side of the SY77 in a box, without the sequencer. The SY99, a bigger and improved ver-sion of the SY77, was released in the following year, but its increased price and size has allowed the SY77 to stay the distance best.

The SY77 never had time under the spotlight in the style of the DX7 or Roland's D-50. Its success has been quieter. However, once people come to grips with its none-too-obvious user interface and tortuous MIDI, the SY77 seems to become a favored axe.

Yamaha TX802 | Digital synthesizer module

THE FAX

Keyboard:	None
Programs:	128 ROM, 64 RAM single, 64 RAM multi
External storage:	Cartridge
Polyphony:	16-voice
Oscillators per voice:	6 operators
Effects:	None
Connections:	Stereo audio, 8 separate voice, MIDI
Dimensions:	480mm x 287mm x 94.5mm
Weight:	4.9kg

THE FIGURES

Production run:	1987-1990
Approx. units sold:	5000
Options:	None
Sounds:	Kid Nepro, Maartists, Sound Logic, SoundSations, Metrasound, Sound Source
Miscellaneous:	Editors: Steinberg DX/TX Synthworks (ST), Opcode 6-Op Lib/Ed (Mac), Sound Quest (ST, Amiga, PC); book: *The Yamaha TX802* by Lorenz Rychner
Orig. price (1987):	$1895 (£1329)
Price in 1996:	$350 (£350)

The DX7II never stood a chance of matching up to its illustrious predecessor, but the TX802, essentially a multitimbral DX7II in a box, has fared better. This is probably as sophisticated as plain FM got before Yamaha mixed and matched it with other forms of synthesis.

Designed for the studio-bound professional, the TX802 shares all the Mark II upgrades, such as microtuning, individual LFOs, velocity control over pitch and, most noticeably, 16-bit D/A converters. But where the DX7II disappointed a little—patch layering but no multitimbralism, a rather sluggish keyboard response—the TX802 delivers.

The styling of this 2U rackmount unit is clean and clear. It has a screen, beneath which are eight Tone Generator On/Off parameter select buttons, each with its own LED. Above the cartridge port are management buttons taking you into each of the prime areas: performance select, voice select, system setup, utility, performance edit, voice edit I and II, and store/compare. There is also a keypad and a failsafe, if tiresome, Enter button.

There are two ways of using a TX802: as a 16-voice FM expander or as a multitimbral FM module. The problem with the latter, as for any such pre-sample-based instrument, is lack of variety. There are no drum sounds here, no full range of acoustic guitars and acoustic pianos. All the tones are unashamedly and unmistakably FM. Not to say that's bad, of course,

but they conform to a type, and it's not often that you're going to need eight such types simultaneously.

But if and when you do, setting up, storing and using multitimbral patches is quite simple. The eight buttons beneath the display have the dual purpose of switching individual patches on and off (while you're playing, the buttons blink as they receive a Note On message) or activating one of the editable performance parameters (per voice) such as MIDI channel, note limit, volume, triggering mode, relative tuning and microtonal tuning scale.

Since the TX802 steps through sounds within a multi patch consecutively, you can do things like use similar but subtly different patches, which gives a sound a random but human feel. Voices can also be sent out and processed via separate outputs.

Individual voice editing comes in two forms, accessed by Voice Edit I and II. The first plugs you into programming the basic sound, which you do either onboard or from a DX7IID or compatible software, and the second gives various assignable controller routings for various function parameters, such as key mode or pitch or mod wheel ranges. Although programming basic sounds is much the same as on any six-operator, 32-algorithm FM synth, Yamaha does well to offer additional help in the way of some graphic displays for envelope setting, conglomerate operator frequencies and operator output level.

This is a powerful instrument, limited only by your love (or hatred) of FM sounds. At the original asking price, the lack of much tonal variety, or indeed any built-in effects, was to blame for the TX802's marginal sales performance. At more realistic second-hand prices, many people have picked up TX802s in order to add FM sparkle and spice to sample-based or even subtractive analog sounds or rigs.

One of the more interesting TX802 applications is as a voice in an electronic percussion system. Yamaha concurrently offered the PCM1 Percussion MIDI converter for transforming drum hits into MIDI messages; the TX802's eight-part multitimbralism can then be harnessed by individual drums within an electronic kit. The TX802 is particularly adept at sharp-tongued marimbas and chimes and assorted real and imaginary tuned percussion tones.

The Product Directory

Akai AX60
Polyphonic synthesizer

Country of origin	Japan
Orig. price (1986)	$895 (no UK price)
Price in 1996	$400 (no UK price)
Keyboard	61-note
Sound type	Analog, subtractive

Rare and early Akai synthesizer with knobs and switches and a digital sample input for processing samples direct from early Akai samplers. Only released in U.S.

Akai AX73
Polyphonic synthesizer

Orig. price (1986)	$1199 (£699)
Price in 1996	$350 (£250)
Keyboard	73-note
Sound type	Analog, subtractive

Similar to AX60 but longer keyboard and digital access control rather than knobs and switches. Quite good as a master keyboard. Internal sounds are a little thin.

Akai AX80
Polyphonic synthesizer

Orig. price (1984)	$1395 (£799)
Price in 1996	$600 (£350)
Keyboard	61-note
Sound type	Analog, subtractive

Akai's first dedicated musical instrument: pleasant-looking and -sounding but never caught on in a big way—and so rare.

Akai CD3000
Rackmount sampler

Orig. price (1993)	$3995 (£2399)
Price in 1996	$3000 (£1800)
Keyboard	3U module
Sound type	16-bit stereo sampler

Among Akai's 1993 batch of new 16-bit samplers. Initially, the CD only allowed sampling from its own CD player, though analog inputs were later offered. A great idea, though few people seem to have recognized it as such.

Akai MPC3000
Drum sampler

Orig. price (1993)	$3699 (£2799)
Price in 1996	$3000 (£2500)
Keyboard	n/a
Sound type	16-bit stereo

With 16 pressure-sensitive drum pads, the latest Roger Linn product was specifically designed for drum-oriented sampling and sequencing. As ever, bags of feel and groove, plus SMPTE, MTC and FSK onboard. A unique approach to sampling and one still favored by many pro producers.

Akai MWS76
MIDI master keyboard

Orig. price (1988)	No U.S. price (£2299)
Price in 1996	No U.S. price (£1200)
Keyboard	76-note
Sound type	n/a

Unusual blend of master keyboard with an Akai ASQ10 sequencer thrown in. Nice idea, but did anyone want it? Nah.

Akai MX73
MIDI master keyboard

Orig. price (1986)	$795 (£399)
Price in 1996	$425 (£200)
Keyboard	73-note
Sound type	n/a

Serviceable low-cost master keyboard, good for the money at the time but limited in its features and therefore appeal.

Akai MX76
MIDI master keyboard

Orig. price (1988)	No U.S. price (£1299)
Orig. price (1996)	No U.S. price (£500)
Keyboard	76-note
Sound type	n/a

Enjoyed only a very limited release. Rare, though not in the "sought-after" sense.

Akai PG2
Digital piano

Orig. price (1991)	$2666 (£1299)
Price in 1996	$1000 (£600)
Keyboard	88-note
Sound type	Sample

Slimmed down version of the earlier PG5 and PG3 pianos. Eight tones (based on Akai samples), but no tone mixing. Reverbs. Worthy more than exciting.

Akai PG3
Digital piano

Orig. price (1990)	$2666 (£1299)
Price in 1996	$1200 (£700)
Keyboard	88-note
Sound type	Sample

The "upright" version of Akai's eye-catching PG5 (see PG5 entry). Sounds based on Akai samples are strong and varied (24 of them). Reverb and chorus. Sounds can be split.

Akai PG5
Digital piano

Orig. price (1990)	$7000 (£3499)
Price in 1996	$3000 (£1800)
Keyboard	88-note
Sound type	Sample

Distinctive semi-grand design complete with opening lid. Good series of Akai sample-based sounds, plus reverb and chorus effects and a 4-track sequencer. Multitimbral and blessed with a mic input. Nice but far too expensive for a name not associated with pianos.

Akai S612
Rackmount sampler

See entry in Hot 100.

Akai S700
Rackmount sampler

Orig. price (1986)	$1699 (£999)
Price in 1996	$500 (£375)
Keyboard	2U module
Sound type	12-bit, mono

Halfway house between Akai's launch into sampling with the S612 and when things began to get serious with the S900. Limited with 2.8-inch Quick Disk but simple to use.

Akai S900
Rackmount sampler

See entry in Hot 100.

Akai S950
Rackmount sampler

See entry in Hot 100.

Akai S1000
Rackmount sampler

See entry in Hot 100.

Akai S1100
Rackmount sampler

Orig. price (1990)	$5999 (£3299)
Price in 1996	$3000 (£2000)
Keyboard	3U module
Sound type	16-bit, stereo

De rigeur chosen weapon for studio hounds from 1990 until the arrival of the 3000 series—and perhaps even after. Top quality sampling with plenty of expansions and options. Limited only by polyphony (16-voice), though the EX-1100 16-voice Expander was also made. Prices will vary depending on memory and upgrades.

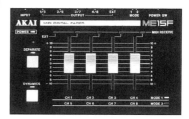

Akai S2000
Rackmount sampler

Orig. price (1995)	$1195 (£999)
Price in 1996	$1195 (£999)
Keyboard	3U module
Sound type	16-bit, stereo

What the S01 could or should have been. Low cost, high spec but simple to operate.

Akai S2800
Rackmount sampler

Orig. price (1993)	$1429 (£1299)
Price in 1996	$1300 (£1200)
Keyboard	3U module
Sound type	16-bit, stereo

Aimed at the S950 user now wanting to upgrade. Didn't work at its original price (almost twice current price) as it made little sense against the S3000. The limited memory expansion and limited outputs are not so critical at 1996 prices, considering the 32-voice polyphony and resonant filters. S2800 Studio comes with 8MB memory, SCSI and digital I/O.

Left: Alan Parsons mesmerized by a rare Akai keyboard: the MWS76;
Right: Another black box from Akai

Akai S3000(XL)
Rackmount sampler

Orig. price (1993)	$1995 (£1999)
Price in 1996	$1995 (£1500)
Keyboard	3U module (XL: 2U)
Sound type	16-bit, stereo

The "new" S1000 of its time, though by 1993, the competition from E-mu and Roland was far greater. Big items: polyphony (32-voice), resonant filters and Akai system loyalty. Plain S3000 priced at almost twice the above listed figure. XL version, which arrived late in 1995, though operating much the same, provided compatibility with Akai's Mac-based M.E.S.A™ editing system and use of standard SIMM memory. XL version: more for less.

Akai S3200(XL)
Rackmount sampler

Orig. price (1993)	$2995 (£2999)
Orig. price (1996)	$2995 (no UK price)
Keyboard	3U module
Sound type	16-bit, stereo

The bee's knees of samplers until E-mu's EIV series. Very professional and with plenty of expansions and upgrades available. Revamped to S3200XL status at end of 1995, which in addition to an almost 50 percent price drop, adds M.E.S.A™ software access and SIMM upgradability. Helluva lot for the money at 1996 prices.

Akai SG01
Polyphonic synthesizer module

Orig. price (1995)	No U.S. price (£399)
Price in 1996	No U.S. price (£399)
Keyboard	1U half-width module
Sound type	Sample

Small, silver range of expander modules containing: a GM sound set (SG01k), piano tones (SG01p) and a collection of vintage instruments (SG01v). All 32-voice polyphonic with 16-bit sounds taken from Akai's massive sound library. No frills and very limited editing but great value.

Akai S01
Rackmount sampler

Orig. price (1992)	$1500 (£799)
Price in 1996	$600 (£350)
Keyboard	2U module
Sound type	16-bit, mono

Akai's stab at the entry level/DJ market a few years too early. Excellent sound quality but very limited memory and facilities. Can expand internal memory from 1 to 2MB.

Akai VX90
Rackmount synthesizer

Orig. price (1986)	$699 (£499)
Price in 1996	$300 (£200)
Keyboard	2U module
Sound type	Analog, subtractive

Rack version of the AX73 with a healthy number of panel controls. Quite a bargain then and now.

Akai VX600
Polyphonic synthesizer

Orig. price (1986)	$900 (£600)
Price in 1996	$600 (£225)
Keyboard	37-note
Sound type	Analog

Short life span for this oddball analog. Run up the flagpole more than given a proper worldwide release.

Akai X7000
Keyboard sampler

Orig. price (1986)	$1699 (£999)
Price in 1996	$450 (£300)
Keyboard	61-note
Sound type	12-bit

Quite popular in its day though limited now due to 2.8-inch Quick Disk format. Sampling up to 40kHz was impressive at the time, but internal memory at a wafer thin 128KB.

Alesis QS6
Digital synthesizer

Country of origin	U.S.
Orig. price (1995)	$1099 (£999)
Price in 1996	$1000 (£900)
Keyboard	61-note
Sound type	Sample+ synthesis

Five-octave keyboard version of the Quadra-Synth, still 64-voice poly and generously voiced with internal, card and innovative Sound Bridge (Mac or PC sound assembly) options.

Alesis Quadrasynth
Digital synthesizer

Orig. price (1993)	$1499 (£1499)
Price in 1996	$750 (£750)
Keyboard	76-note
Sound type	Sample+ synthesis

Brave first attempt from effects specialists Alesis. Smooth looking but with a few rough edges, offers 64-voice polyphony and "Quadraverb style" effects processing. Direct link to ADAT.

Alesis Quadrasynth Plus Piano
Digital synthesizer

Orig. price (1995)	$1699 (£1499)
Price in 1996	$1200 (£1200)
Keyboard	76-note
Sound type	Sample+ synthesis

Updated version of the Quadrasynth with less rough edges and a spanking new multi-sampled stereo piano that takes up no less than 8MB waveform ROM.

Alesis S4
Digital synthesizer module

Orig. price (1994)	$999 (£999)
Price in 1996	$600 (£450)
Keyboard	1U rackmount module
Sound type	Sample+ synthesis

The world's first 64-voice sound module. Suffered at the hands of the QuadraSynth keyboard on which it is based, in that its release coincided with improvements Alesis had already made to the keyboard version. Optionally loaded with the new piano ROM.

Alesis S4 Plus
Digital synthesizer module

Orig. price (1995)	$1099 (£999)
Price in 1996	$800 (£800)
Keyboard	1U rackmount module
Sound type	Sample+ synthesis

Improved version of the S4 with ROM configurable to GM. Packed with sounds and high quality effects.

ARP 16-Voice
Electronic piano

Country of origin	U.S.
Orig. price (1979)	$2000 (£1100)
Price in 1996	$200 (£150)
Keyboard	73-note
Sound type	Preset, analog

Nice concept with some strong, interesting sounds (16 of them) and good processing (phaser, detune, vibrato), but the instrument was released with one or two chronic faults, making repairs ongoing and inevitable. This in no small way contributed to the downfall of ARP as a company. High risk.

ARP 2500
Modular synthesizer

Orig. price (1970)	$Variable: $2500-8500 (no UK price)
Price in 1996	$6000-7000 (£8000-9000)
Keyboard	Single or double manual 61-note models (separate)
Sound type	Subtractive, analog

Large and complicated series of synthesizer modules that use sliders instead of patch cords. Designed for education and electronic music studio use, it appeared before a wider audience in the film *Close Encounters of the Third Kind*, secreted in a custom shell and played by top ARP designer Philip Dodds. Stable, compared to Moog synths, but complex and expensive. ARP's debut product that went on to inspire the ARP 2600.

ARP 2600
Semi-modular synthesizer

See entry in Hot 100.

ARP Avatar
Guitar synthesizer

Orig. price (1977)	$3000 (£1500)
Price in 1995-6	$350 (£200)
Keyboard	Expander
Sound type	Subtractive, analog

Odyssey clone built for guitarists. A brave but ultimately doomed attempt to lure guitarists into the synthesizer fold. Pretty much wiped the company out.

ARP Axxe
Monophonic synthesizer

Orig. price (1975)	$780 (£400)
Price in 1995-6	$250 (£150)
Keyboard	37-note
Sound type	Subtractive, analog

Baby brother of the ARP Odyssey. Becoming sought after.

Left: Akai's mid-1990s top-of-the-line sampler: the S3200XL; Center: New kid on the keyboard block: Alesis' innovative Quadrasynth

ARP Odyssey
Monophonic synthesizer

See entry in Hot 100.

ARP Omni
String synthesizer

Orig. price (1975)	$2450 (£1200)
Price in 1996	$300 (£150)
Keyboard	49-note
Sound type	Subtractive, analog

Good all-purpose keyboard that became ARP's biggest-selling instrument and even appeared in Mark II form as well.

ARP Pro Soloist
Monophonic synthesizer

Orig. price (1972)	$1350 (£700)
Price in 1996	$300 (£150)
Keyboard	37-note
Sound type	Preset, analog

Useful and unusual through having presets to call upon but fairly unreliable.

ARP Pro/DGX
Monophonic analog synthesizer

Orig. price (1980)	$1200 (£600)
Price in 1996	$200 (£150)
Keyboard	37-note
Sound type	Preset, analog

Essentially a preset synth with sounds divided into "real instrument" categories. Some semblance of tone modifying is offered. Fairly good sounds for the type, price and era.

ARP Quadra
Synthesizer-string machine

Orig. price (1978)	$3700 (£2500)
Price in 1996	$500 (£400)
Keyboard	61-note
Sound type	Subtractive, analog

Mongrel keyboard blending ARP's Odyssey synth with string machine like Omni.

ARP Quartet
Analog string machine+

Countries of origin	U.S./Italy
Orig. price (1980)	$950 (£450)
Price in 1996	$175 (£100)
Keyboard	49-note
Sound type	Preset, analog

Polyphonic string machine+ made in conjunction with Siel in Italy. Tones are mixable, and it's easy to use but nothing much to write to home about.

ARP Solus
Monophonic synthesizer

Orig. price (1980)	$790 (£400)
Price in 1996	$300 (£125)
Keyboard	37-note
Sound type	Subtractive, analog

One of the final ARP products, similar to the Odyssey and Axxe. Dual oscillator and comes built into a flight case.

Bachmann PS2000
Digital piano

Country of origin	Italy
Orig. price (1991)	$2495 (no UK price)
Price in 1996	$850 (no UK price)
Keyboard	88-note
Sound type	Digital sample

Perfectly reasonable digital piano though without sufficient bells and whistles to seriously rival established digital piano manufacturers. Sounds hard-wired to certain effects, which is rather limiting, but some imaginative sound programming. PS1000 has 76-note keyboard, and GPS2000 is truncated grand piano cabinet version of the PS model.

Bachmann WS1(D)
Home keyboard

Orig. price (1992)	$1500 (no UK price)
Price in 1996	$600 (no UK price)
Keyboard	61-note
Sound type	Sample+ synthesis

Streamlined upgrades to the WS2 concept. Not a GM instrument, though close to the specification and there are a few less effects. The WS1D offers built-in disk drive that can accept standard MIDI files.

Bachmann WS2
Home keyboard

Orig. price (1990)	$3500 (no UK price)
Price in 1996	$1000 (no UK price)
Keyboard	61-note
Sound type	Sample+ synthesis

The mind of a professional workstation in a home keyboard setting. 32-voice polyphony, stereo digital effects, very high quality sounds and cannily programmed styles. The WS2 was Bachmann's (who is, in fact, GeneralMusic's U.S. trading brand name) first outing down this particular track.

Bachmann WS400
Home keyboard

Orig. price (1990)	$4000 (no UK price)
Price in 1996	$1300 (no UK price)
Keyboard	88-note
Sound type	Sample+ synthesis

Elongated and weighted action version of the WS2 with beefy 40W stereo amplification. The grand piano design GWS400 features enhanced amplification system.

Bachmann WX2
Home keyboard

Orig. price (1993)	$3000 (no UK price)
Price in 1996	$850 (no UK price)
Keyboard	61-note
Sound type	Sample+ synthesis

With sounds based upon the company's successful S2 pro synth, the WX2 took home keyboards on to greater heights. Peerless brass and guitar samples, serviceable sequencer and lyrics and some editing available on an external display. Superb demo song of Donald Fagen's "Kamakiriad" promises rather more sophistication than the styles subsequently deliver. WX400 is 88-note weighted keyboard version.

Baldwin DVP 50A
Digital piano

Country of origin	U.S.
Orig. price (1993)	$2500 (no UK price)
Price in 1996	No U.S. price (no UK price)
Keyboard	88-note
Sound type	Sampled (Ensoniq)

Digital piano (also the DVP25 and grand piano model DG100A) from important American acoustic piano builder Baldwin. For rock and pop markets, Baldwin's most notable claim to fame is Bruce Hornsby as an endorsee of the acoustics. Good sounds (samples licensed from Ensoniq), but Baldwin can hardly be accused of being a digital piano specialist.

Beilfuss Performance Synth
Polyphonic synthesizer

Country of origin	U.S.
Orig. price (1984)	$6000 (no UK price)
Price in 1996	No U.S. price (no UK price)
Keyboard	97-note
Sound type	Digital/analog hybrid

Implausible instrument from lone designer Keith Williams. Always "on the point of being released," but one questions whether it ever really was. Ten-voice polyphonic, a mix of digital and analog sound generation and an almost ridiculously long keyboard. Shiny black and elegant, also something of a black elephant.

Bit 01
Polyphonic synthesizer module

Country of origin	Italy
Orig. price (1985)	$899 (£499)
Price in 1996	$250 (£200)
Keyboard	2U module
Sound type	Analog

Rackmount version of the Bit 99. A strong and unusually already MIDI-ed analog synth. Rather more stable and usable than the Bit (Crumar in another hat) One.

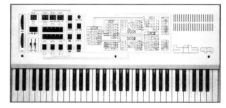

Bit 99
Polyphonic synthesizer

Orig. price (1985)	$999 (£599)
Price in 1996	$200 (£250)
Keyboard	61-note
Sound type	Analog

Source of quite strong analog sounds in a full MIDI setting with velocity keyboard. Never 100 percent reliable but good value at the time. Keyboard version of Bit 01.

Bit One
Polyphonic synthesizer module

See entry in Hot 100.

Buchla 100
Modular analog synthesizer

Country of origin	U.S.
Orig. price (1963)	No U.S. price (no UK price)
Price in 1996	$6000+ (£4000+)
Keyboard	n/a
Sound type	Subtractive, analog modules+

As with all subsequent Buchla products, hard to pin down in terms of price or performance—Buchla's point precisely. The design, including the lack of a recognizable keyboard, lends itself to experimental, atonal music rather than Top 40. The rarest earlier models are inscribed "San Francisco Tape Music Center" rather than "Buchla."

Buchla 200
Analog synthesizer modules

Orig. price (1973)	$5000+ (£3000+)
Price in 1996	$Variable (£variable)
Keyboard	n/a
Sound type	Subtractive, analog modules+

Superseding the 100 series but still made in unending variety and options, including the extremely expensive 361 package. Purist fodder only.

Buchla 300
Analog/digital synthesizer modules

Orig. price (1975)	No U.S. price (no UK price)
Price in 1996	$Variable (£variable)
Keyboard	n/a
Sound type	Hybrid digital/analog modules

Series of early microprocessor-controlled modules.

Buchla 400
Analog/digital synthesizer

Orig. price (1982)	$8000+ (no UK price)
Price in 1996	$Variable (£variable)
Keyboard	61-note
Sound type	Hybrid digital/analog

Despite being made in regular keyboard version, this is still not a synth for the faint hearted. Complex and still best for noises rather than tuned pitches for pop or rock music.

Casio AP-7
Digital piano

Country of origin	Japan
Orig. price (1990)	$2999 (£1699)
Price in 1996	$800 (£600)
Keyboard	88-note
Sound type	Digital, sampled

The first "Celviano" piano from Casio. A good effort, with interesting features like built-in CD player for music-minus-one playing. Eight fairly strong tones and a pleasant action, but as ever, Casio suffers at the hand of more "creditable" and established names in the field. AP-5 loses the CD player.

Casio AP-10
Digital piano

Orig. price (1996)	No U.S. price (£999)
Keyboard	88-note
Sound type	Digital, sampled

Five tones, small sequencer, plus reverb and chorus on this spring-weighted keyboard, latest digital from Casio.

Casio AP-20
Digital piano

Price in 1996	No U.S. price (£1499)
Keyboard	88-note
Sound type	Digital, sampled

Natural hammer action keyboard for its 10 tones, small sequencer, plus reverb and chorus, brilliance and variable touch response. Seems excellent value.

Casio AP-75
Digital piano

Orig. price (1995)	No U.S. price (£1999)
Price in 1996	No U.S. price (£1750)
Keyboard	88-note
Sound type	Digital, sampled

Natural hammer action keyboard, ten tones, small sequencer, reverb and chorus, even a built-in CD player on this 64-voice polyphonic 1995 model.

Casio AZ-1
Controller keyboard

Orig. price (1986)	$595 (£349)
Price in 1996	$150 (£100)
Keyboard	41-note
Sound type	n/a

Casio's lone excursion into controller keyboards in sling-on, over-the-shoulder style. Not a bad attempt, but no one has made a living out of this type of instrument, not even Casio. Dual MIDI channel output on hand and quite pleasant to play.

Casio CA Series
Home keyboards

Releases	1991+
Price	$150+ (£100+)
Keyboard	49-note
Sound type	Digital, preset

Small-key series of keyboards with okay sounds and features in a MIDI-free environment.

Casio CDP-3000
Digital piano

Orig. price (1988)	$1899 (£1299)
Price in 1996	$300 (£250)
Keyboard	88-note
Sound type	Digital

Casio's first semi-serious attempt in the digital piano arena. Nothing to write home about in the face of stiff competition from more established names.

Casio CK-500
Home keyboard

Orig. price (1985)	$499 (£345)
Price in 1996	$100 (£100)
Keyboard	49-note
Sound type	Digital/analog, preset

Mini-key keyboard with unusual addition of twin cassette decks.

Casio CPS-7
Digital piano

Orig. price (1995)	$499 (£399)
Price in 1996	No U.S. price (£350)
Keyboard	76-note
Sound type	Digital, preset

Unremarkable but good value digital piano with touch-sensitive keyboard and five tones.

Casio CPS-80S
Digital piano

Orig. price (1995)	£799
Price in 1996	£700
Keyboard	88-note
Sound type	Digital, preset

Ten tones and a small real-time sequencer. Not for sale in America. The CPS-50S has 76-note keyboard.

Casio CPS-700
Digital piano

Orig. price (1989)	$799 (£549)
Price in 1996	$150 (£150)
Keyboard	76-note
Sound type	Digital

Creditable attempt at a low-cost digital piano, using 12-bit PCM sampled sounds. A module, the CSM-10P, was quite a bargain at $399 (£199). Still is at greatly reduced prices. CPS-300 has 61-note keyboard.

Casio CSM-1
Tone module

Orig. price (1989)	$259 (£175)
Price in 1996	$100 (£80)
Keyboard	Module
Sound type	Digital, preset

Well kept secret and still a useful source of PCM sounds in 4-part multitimbral setting. Not GM, though. Shares sound engine with CT-640.

Casio CT-410
Home keyboard

Orig. price (1984)	$499 (£345)
Price in 1996	$100 (£75)
Keyboard	49-note
Sound type	Analog, preset

Sliver of editing on hand (filter with cutoff frequency and resonance, no less), but otherwise a fairly basic model. Can use filter on drum sounds, though, which is pretty hip.

Casio CT-450
Home keyboard

Orig. price (1987)	$299 (£249)
Price in 1996	$75 (£75)
Keyboard	49-note
Sound type	Digital/analog, preset

Aimed at budding percussionists with Casio DP-1 drum pad or SS1 sound-stick option. Neat features like being able to tap out a bass drum pattern using a footswitch. Indifferent tones, though, so limited (in 1987, never mind now) appeal.

Casio CT-460
Home keyboard

Orig. price (1988)	$399 (£279)
Price in 1996	$125 (£100)
Keyboard	49-note
Sound type	Digital/analog, preset

The first Casio to offer sound effects like crashing waves and space noises, plus some delays. Tone mixing makes it quite versatile. Ten-voice polyphonic. Fun in its day.

Left: Keen Casio Pro division endorsees Vince and Andy from Erasure; Center: Unusual audio cassette-sporting mini from Casio: the CK-500

Casio CT-510
Home keyboard

Orig. price (1987)	$399 (£349)
Price in 1996	$125 (£100)
Keyboard	49-note
Sound type	Digital/analog, preset

Full-size keys but only four octaves worth. Some very pleasant tones playable 8-note polyphonically. Drum pads on panel.

Casio CT-607
Home keyboard

Orig. price (1988)	$239 (£225)
Price in 1996	$100 (£75)
Keyboard	61-note
Sound type	Digital, preset

PCM sounds throughout so sounds relatively "modern." Tone mixing but no MIDI.

Casio CT-615
Home keyboard

Orig. price (1991)	$199 (£150)
Price in 1996	$85 (£75)
Keyboard	61-note
Sound type	Digital, preset

Full-size keys but no MIDI. PCM tones and 10-voice polyphonic. CT-625 has stereo speakers.

Casio CT-630
Home keyboard

Orig. price (1987)	$199 (£169)
Price in 1996	$75 (£75)
Keyboard	49-note
Sound type	Digital/analog, preset

No frills except PCM sampled drum sounds. No MIDI.

Casio CT-640
Home keyboard

Orig. price (1989)	$299 (£199)
Price in 1996	$100 (£85)
Keyboard	61-note
Sound type	Digital, preset

Ten-voice polyphony and a five-octave keyboard. Strong PCM tones (465 of them with Tone Mix).

Casio CT-647
Home keyboard

Orig. price (1992)	$199 (£175)
Price in 1996	$100 (£85)
Keyboard	61-note
Sound type	Digital, preset

Unglamorous but well made, with 16-voice polyphony, lots of tones and unusual "jukebox" song facility. No MIDI. CT-657 has more tones and a sequencer but still no MIDI.

Casio CT-660
Home keyboard

Orig. price (1988)	$499 (£325)
Price in 1996	$125 (£100)
Keyboard	61-note
Sound type	Digital/analog, preset

Five octave, full size keyboard, full MIDI version of the CT460. CT-640 is same minus sound effects.

Casio CT-670
Home keyboard

Orig. price (1990)	$399 (£379)
Price in 1996	$125 (£100)
Keyboard	61-note
Sound type	Digital, preset

Quite the rage in 1990, the CT-670 spearheaded a large series of CT-class Casios, including the CT-680 (same plus reverb), CT-656, CT-636 and CT-470 (49-note keyboard). All use PCM tone generation with tones mixable between banks. Auto accompaniments are now called Multi Accompaniment Systems. Some degree of control over sounds—attack and release.

Casio CT-770
Home keyboard

Orig. price (1992)	$479 (£399)
Price in 1996	$175 (£150)
Keyboard	61-note
Sound type	Digital, preset

Beefy keyboard with good tones and styles and velocity-sensitive keyboard and digital effects. CT-700 loses said effects and has less powerful amplification but is otherwise the same.

Casio CT-805
Home keyboard

Orig. price (1987)	$329 (£265)
Price in 1996	$100 (£85)
Keyboard	61-note
Sound type	Digital/analog, preset

Casio Melody Light teaching keyboard.

Casio CT-840
Home keyboard

Orig. price (1992)	$249 (£175)
Price in 1996	$100 (£85)
Keyboard	49-note
Sound type	Digital/analog, preset

Melody Light teaching keyboard without MIDI.

Casio CT-1000P
Home keyboard

Orig. price (1982)	$599 (£375)
Price in 1996	$100 (£100)
Keyboard	61-note
Sound type	Analog, preset/programmable

Offered a hint of what was to come, with neat, if simple, sound editing and a sophisticated arpeggiator. One of the best early Casios. No auto rhythms, etc.

Casio CT-6000
Home keyboard

Orig. price (1984)	$800 (£595)
Price in 1996	$200 (£150)

Keyboard	61-note
Sound type	Digital/analog, preset

With velocity and aftertouch-sensitive keyboard. Still a home keyboard with auto sections but a decent play.

Casio CT-6500
Home keyboard

Orig. price (1986)	$999 (£775)
Price in 1996	$250 (£200)
Keyboard	61-note
Sound type	Digital, preset

Tone mixing rather than programming; still a Phase Distortion instrument (same technology as CZ-101, etc.) but in a home keyboard setting.

Casio CTK-480
Home keyboard

Orig. price (1996)	No U.S. price (£149)
Keyboard	61-note
Sound type	Digital, preset/programmable

New 12-note polyphonic, 100 tone keyboard, battery operable.

Casio CTK-530
Home keyboard

Orig. price (1995)	No U.S. price (£349)
Price in 1996	No U.S. price (£325)
Keyboard	61-note
Sound type	Digital, preset/programmable

Multitimbral facility and velocity keyboard on this good value model.

Casio CTK-750
Home keyboard

Orig. price (1994)	$499 (£499)
Price in 1996	$250 (£250)
Keyboard	61-note
Sound type	Digital, preset/programmable

Bargain of a keyboard (and series) that includes generous tones, styles, motifs and so-named Magical Presets—a rag bag of frequently superb musical tricks with which to delight your audience. Not GM but definitely laid out in that sort of style. CTK-650 is similar but no pitch wheel and misses a few layering tricks. CT-550 has no MIDI. CT-450 similar and no velocity keyboard either.

Casio CTK-1000
Home keyboard

Orig. price (1993)	$595 (£595)
Price in 1996	$200 (£200)
Keyboard	61-note
Sound type	Digital, preset/programmable

Fancy sounding technologies lurk beneath this home keyboard exterior. Interesting interactive songwriting features and stereo speakers. Eight-part multitimbral. CTK-200 is same in small 49-key setting and no MIDI.

Casio CT-X1
Home synth

Orig. price (1990)	$375 (£325)
Price in 1996	$100 (£125)
Keyboard	49-note
Sound type	Digital, preset

Curious looking, humpbacked keyboard offering entry level synth parameters in a home keyboard (based around the CT-670) setting. Interesting, though not very well received.

Casio CZ-1
Polyphonic synthesizer

Orig. price (1986)	$1399 (£999)
Price in 1996	$300 (£300)
Keyboard	61-note
Sound type	Digital, programmable

Velocity keyboard version of the CZ-3000, which in turn is a double oscillator version of the CZ-100 and -1000. Additional "Operation Memories."

Casio CZ-101
Polyphonic synthesizer

See entry in Hot 100.

Casio CZ-230S
Home synthesizer

Orig. price (1986)	$399 (£345)
Price in 1996	$100 (£100)
Keyboard	49-note
Sound type	Digital, preset

A very interesting little keyboard using PD (same technology as CZ-101, etc.) synthesis. Though preset, there's a large collection of sounds, portamento, pitch wheel, programmable drums and a 4-track sequencer. Limitations include 4-note polyphony and small-key (not mini) keyboard. Was featured on the cover of *Keyfax 2*, incidentally. Well worth having as an extra source of PD sounds.

Casio CZ-1000
Polyphonic synthesizer

See Casio CZ-101 entry in Hot 100.

Casio CZ-3000
Polyphonic synthesizer

Orig. price (1986)	$899 (£695)
Price in 1996	$200 (£175)
Keyboard	61-note
Sound type	Digital, programmable

Same Phase Distortion power as the CZ-5000 but without sequencer and Cassette Interface.

Casio CZ-5000
Polyphonic synthesizer

Orig. price (1985)	$1199 (£875)
Price in 1996	$275 (£300)
Keyboard	61-note
Sound type	Digital, programmable

Full five-octave keyboard version of the groundbreaking CZ-101 and -1000 at twice the oscillator power. A small (and fairly useless) sequencer.

Casio DM-100
Home keyboard

Orig. price (1988)	$299 (£279)
Price in 1996	$100 (£100)
Keyboard	49-note & 32-note
Sound type	Digital/analog, preset

Unusual design—double manual, plus semblance of sampling offered. Tone mixing. Not very successful, though.

Casio FZ-1
Keyboard sampler

See entry in Hot 100.

Casio FZ-10M
Sampling module

See entry in Hot 100.

Casio FZ-20M
Sampling module

Orig. price (1989)	$2699 (£1899)
Price in 1996	$800 (£700)
Keyboard	module
Sound type	Digital sampling

Casio's final thoughts on pro samplers. Very much in line with FZ-1 and -10M except with SCSI and upgraded sampling tools (Loop Fade Optimizer, etc.). Came and went quickly.

Casio GK-700
Home keyboard

Orig. price (1995)	No U.S. price (£399)
Price in 1996	No U.S. price (£475)
Keyboard	61-note
Sound type	Digital, preset

Casio goes multimedia with this TV screen hook up-able home keyboard. The screen access is used for compositional mixing and matching of parts and phrases. GM compatible.

Casio GZ-5
GM sound module

Orig. price (1995)	No U.S. price (£65)
Price in 1996	No U.S. price (£65)
Keyboard	32-note
Sound type	Digital, preset

Mini keys, only 10 tones, but MIDI. Not available in U.S.

Casio GZ-50M
GM sound module

Orig. price (1995)	No U.S. price (£200)
Price in 1996	No U.S. price (£200)
Keyboard	Module
Sound type	Digital, preset

Casio's first General MIDI sound module, based on GZ-50M. Not available in U.S.

Casio GZ-500
Home keyboard

Orig. price (1995)	No U.S. price (£299)
Price in 1996	No U.S. price (£275)
Keyboard	61-note
Sound type	Digital, preset

Casio's first General MIDI keyboard. Not available in U.S.

Casio HT-700
Home synthesizer

Orig. price (1987)	$499 (£349)
Price in 1996	$150 (£125)
Keyboard	49-note
Sound type	Digital/analog, preset/programmable

Mid-size keys but a surprisingly strong range of programmable synth sounds. Came out around time of professional VZ-series synths.

Casio HT-3000
Home keyboard

Orig. price (1987)	$749 (£425)
Price in 1996	$200 (£175)
Keyboard	61-note
Sound type	Digital, preset

Full-size keyboard featuring strong, almost D-50-ish tones, drum sounds, etc. Stereo speakers. Expensive in its day but worthy.

Casio HZ-600
Polyphonic synthesizer

Orig. price (1987)	$499 (£349)
Price in 1996	$150 (£150)
Keyboard	61-note
Sound type	Digital/analog, programmable

Rogue release of analog type synth shortly after the runaway success of the digital CZ series. Nothing wrong really, but not in Casio's product range and therefore a bit of a lemon.

Casio KT-80
Home keyboard

Orig. price (1994)	$450 (£350)
Price in 1996	$200 (£175)
Keyboard	61-note
Sound type	Digital, preset

Offers CD player built in, plus similar range of features as on CTK-750, etc. CD player lets you perform music-minus-one type feats.

Casio MT Series
Home keyboards

Orig. release	1982+
Price	$200+ (£150+)
Keyboard	Various, but all mini-key
Sound type	Analog, preset

Most of the early MT series (MT-70, MT-800, MT-65) have educational overtones, using bar code readers and so-named Melody Lights. The MT-68 is the most serious of the vintage, offering embryonic synth-editing parameters and a large selection of accompaniment patterns.

Casio MT-210
Home keyboard

Orig. price (1985)	$249 (£225)
Price in 1996	$75 (£65)
Keyboard	49-note
Sound type	Digital/analog, preset

Good sound and useful little (small-key) keyboard with okay PCM-sampled drum sounds. Eight-note polyphonic.

Casio MT-400V
Home keyboard

Orig. price (1984)	$399 (£255)
Price in 1996	$75 (£50)
Keyboard	49-note
Sound type	Analog, preset

Mini-key version of the CT-410V.

Casio MT-500
Home keyboard

Orig. price (1986)	$299 (£255)
Price in 1996	$85 (£60)
Keyboard	49-note
Sound type	Digital/analog, preset

The first of many keyboards from Casio (and others) to sport drum pads on its front panel. With PCM drum sounds, plus a range of 20 so-so preset tones and stereo speakers, a reasonable buy in its day.

Left: High-powered "CZ": the CZ-3000

Casio MT-600
Home synthesizer

Orig. price (1987)	$299 (£225)
Price in 1996	$85 (£75)
Keyboard	49-note
Sound type	Digital, preset

A handy, 8-note polyphonic home synth with MIDI, small chord and pattern memory and 40 PCM presets. Mid-size keys.

Casio PMP-500
Home keyboard

Orig. price (1988)	$499 (£325)
Price in 1996	$125 (£100)
Keyboard	61-note
Sound type	Digital/analog, preset

Five-octave, full-size keyboard, full MIDI version of the CT-460.

Casio PT Series
Home keyboards

Releases	1983+
Price	$100+ (£150+)
Keyboard	Various, but all mini-key
Sound type	Digital/analog, preset

Casio's mini-key series began in 1983 and continued throughout the 1980s. Not toys exactly but hardly the thing to cart into the Record Plant for a session.

Casio RAP-1 Rapman
Home keyboard

Orig. price (1991)	$79 (£75)
Keyboard	32-note
Sound type	Digital, sampling

Brief flirtation with major success in 1991, but like all fashion items, hopelessly unsalable until retro interest kicks in. You can sample, scratch and play sundry hip-hop rhythms. Cheap thrills, in all senses.

Casio SK Series
Sampling home keyboards

Orig. release	1987
Price	$150+ (£130+)
Keyboard	32-note, 49-note
Sound type	PCM/sampling

Around the time of the FZ-series pro samplers, Casio made several home keyboards with sampling options. Sampling very rudimentary but okay for effects. Otherwise, tones, rhythms and speakers as normal. Include SK-5, SK-8 in 32-note keyboard variety and SK-100, SK-200 and SK2100 in 49-note keyboard versions. Sampling never exceeds a couple of seconds on any of them. The series is revived in 1996 with new SK-60 model due for late 1996 release.

Casio VA-10
Home keyboard

Orig. price (1993)	$199 (£199)
Price in 1996	$75 (£75)
Keyboard	32-note
Sound type	Digital/vocoding, preset

Another of Casio's occasional flights of fancy—this time into the world of vocoding. Six-voice polyphonic tones, rhythms and a teensy keyboard. Fashion item.

Casio VL-1
Home keyboard

Orig. release	1981
Price in 1996	$69+ (£35+)

Keyboard	29-note
Sound type	Analog, preset

The Casio that started the revolution. The VL-1 actually began life as a calculator. It has five monophonic tones, some preset rhythms and 100 memory "sequencer." Became hip in time (Yazoo, etc.).

Casio VZ-1
Polyphonic synthesizer

Orig. price (1988)	$1399 (£1299)
Price in 1996	$500 (£400)
Keyboard	61-note
Sound type	Digital, programmable

Second generation of Casio pro synths (after CZ series). Plenty of nice sounds and programming features but without the CZ's price structure, sold in numbers that any halfway decent synth would. Accordingly, a horrified Casio pulled the plug on the whole pro synth division. VZ-10M is the module.

Casio VZ-8M
Polyphonic synthesizer modular

Orig. price (1988)	$699 (£499)
Price in 1996	$150 (£200)
Keyboard	1U module
Sound type	Digital, programmable

Half of a VZ-1 in terms of polyphony (here 8-voice). With useful Mono mode for guitar controllers and interesting PD-ish digital sounds. Casio's final fling in terms of pro synths, though. Limited polyphony but quite a bargain and worth looking out for.

Casio WK-1500
GM Home keyboard

Orig. price (1996)	No U.S. price (no UK price)
Keyboard	76-note
Sound type	Digital, preset

Rare, sizable offering from Casio with 76-note keyboard, GM sounds, digital effects and multi-track recorder.

Cheetah Master Series 7P
Master keyboard

Country of origin	UK
Orig. price (1990)	$1425 (£699)
Price in 1996	$600 (£225)
Keyboard	88-note
Sound type	n/a

Cheetah's specialty was (the company stopped making musical instruments in 1993) master keyboards; this and the aftertouch-sporting Master Series 770 version were the top of the series. Plain-faced, with no sexy screens, these offered bags of programming power for the money, though their methods are at times a bit long-winded.

Cheetah MS6
Polyphonic synthesizer module

See entry in Hot 100.

Cheetah MS800
Polyphonic synthesizer module

Orig. price (1992)	$300 (£199)
Price in 1996	$125 (£100)
Keyboard	Half-width 1U module
Sound type	Digital, programmable

Impossibly difficult to program as only a design by a British Telecom engineer could be. Interesting wavetable synthesis, but very limited timbres—everything sounds metallic. Only limited release, so quite sought after by (some) collectors.

Cheetah SX16
Digital sampling module

Orig. price (1990)	$1599 (£799)
Price in 1996	$600 (£350)
Keyboard	1U module
Sound type	Digital sample

Ultra low-cost stereo sampler that has become popular—among DJs and "grain" enthusiasts—after the demise of Cheetah musical instrument division. Idiosyncratic.

Chroma Polaris
Polyphonic synthesizer

Country of origin	U.S.
Orig. price (1984)	$1495 (£1700)
Price in 1996	$600 (£650)
Keyboard	61-note
Sound type	Analog, programmable

ARP-designed synth released by Fender under the Chroma banner. Some nice features and one of the first instruments to hook up directly to a computer (Apple IIe), but had reliability problems and not very strong distribution. Chroma Expander one of the first keyboardless synths post-MIDI. Quite collectible. Called Fender Polaris in U.S..

Clavia Nord Lead
Virtual analog synthesizer

Country of origin	Sweden
Orig. price (1995)	$2395 (£1399)
Price in 1996	$2395 (£1399)
Keyboard	49-note
Sound type	Digital modeling

The hit of '95 in Europe from the unlikely source of Sweden. Although digital, the Nord Lead accurately (re)models many of the sounds and effects from the glory days of analog. With lots of finger-friendly knobs and switches and dressed in eye-catching red livery, this four-voice (expandable) instrument is the complete antithesis of the cloney workstations of the 1990s. Hands on, and thumbs up. Version 2.0 released in early 1996 added new analog drum sounds, 100 additional presets, a notch filter and the ability to process aftertouch. Expander version has all the knobs, too, just no keyboard.

Center: Post-FZ series Casio's sampling has been strictly street level

Commander Lynex
Sampling module

Country of origin	UK
Orig. price (1988)	No U.S. price (£1800)
Price in 1996	No U.S. price (£500)
Keyboard	1U module (with Atari ST)
Sound type	Digital sample

Flash-in-the-pan sampling system based around Atari ST computer that looked like temptingly good value. A sampling rate of 50kHz and 16-voice polyphony. Pretty impressive for the time, but in the way of so many British inventions, underfunded, undersold and eventually *went* under, too. The design (and designer) has sort of reappeared as a hard disk recording add-on (D2D) for the Falcon platform.

Control Synthesis Deep Bass Nine
Bass synthesizer

Country of origin	UK
Orig. price (1994)	$700 (£450)
Price in 1996	$550 (£350)
Keyboard	1U module
Sound type	Analog

Inspired by the retro revolution, especially Roland's TB-303 Bassline (see entry in Hot 100), a British music store put together the Deep Bass Nine module. Has a place and part to play but no memories, and rackmount design not ideal for twiddling. CV and gate ins and outs also.

Crumar Brassman
Multi-instrument keyboard

Country of origin	Italy
Orig. price (1975)	$500 (£300)
Price in 1996	$50 (£50)
Keyboard	49-note
Sound type	Analog

Specialist brass machine with some suitably windy features. Limited but interesting. A good buy, probably.

Crumar Compac
Electronic piano

Orig. price (1967)	$500 (£250)
Price in 1996	$50 (£50)
Keyboard	61-note
Sound type	Transistor

Widely used in the '60s, by such illustrious bands as The Beatles, no less. Distinctive '60s sound, one-paced and pretty clunky but a genuine period piece.

Crumar Composer
Multi-instrument keyboard

Orig. price (1982)	$1500 (£1300)
Price in 1996	$300 (£300)
Keyboard	49-note
Sound type	Analog

Fascinating attempt to be all things to all people. Mono and poly synth, plus strings and brass machine. Unique "side-to-side" key rocking vibrato feature and some strong sounds.

Crumar DP-80
Electronic piano

Orig. price (1982)	$1750 (£999)
Price in 1996	$175 (£150)
Keyboard	73-note
Sound type	Transistor

Twelve presets with reasonable control over tone and effects. Good gigging piano in its day. Also made at this time the DP50 and DP30, each with a few less features.

Crumar DS-1
Monophonic synthesizer

Orig. price (1978)	$800 (£500)
Price in 1996	$100 (£100)
Keyboard	49-note
Sound type	Analog

Analog synth with interesting DCOs and external input but never had the power—in any sense—of its American rivals. DS-2 combines this with a strings section. Designed by Bit One's Luciano Jura.

Crumar Multiman
Multi-instrument keyboard

Orig. price (1981)	No U.S price (£649)
Price in 1996	No U.S price (£200)
Keyboard	61-note
Sound type	Analog

Brass, piano, strings and bass. What else did you need in 1981? Some editing offered and a neat de-tune section where sounds can be combined and thickened. Feeble piano sound. Called Orchestrator in U.S..

Crumar Orchestrator
Multi-instrument keyboard

Orig. price (1981)	$999 (£575)
Price in 1996	$200 (£100)
Keyboard	61-note
Sound type	Analog

See Crumar Multiman entry.

Crumar Organizer TI/C
Multi-instrument keyboard

Orig. price (1981)	$895 (£575)
Price in 1996	$175 (£100)
Keyboard	61-note
Sound type	Analog

Organ-based instrument (with drawbars) with bass synth overtones. Limited but friendly.

Crumar Performer 2
Multi-instrument keyboard

Orig. price (1982)	$850 (£500)
Price in 1996	$150 (£150)
Keyboard	49-note
Sound type	Analog

Brass, strings and organ are the Performer (Performer 2 being the upgraded, smarter version) specialties. Serviceable and popular in its day but highly limited now.

Crumar Roadracer
Electronic piano

Orig. price (1979)	$500 (£379)
Price in 1996	$100 (£75)
Keyboard	61-note
Sound type	Transistor

Emergency-use-only Italian job. File under "best forgotten."

Crumar Roadrunner
Electronic piano

Orig. price (1983)	$450 (£300)
Price in 1996	$100 (£85)
Keyboard	61-note
Sound type	Transistor

Three Roadrunners were made in all, so the series was clearly popular. Sold on price rather than quality, though. Limited and dubiously piano-like collection of piano tones. Dullsville.

Crumar Roady
Electronic piano

Orig. price (1979)	$495 (£400)
Price in 1996	$100 (£75)
Keyboard	61-note
Sound type	Transistor

Better-than-average Crumar, with some lively tones and a separate bass section. Sturdy and serviceable for its vintage.

Crumar Spirit
Monophonic synthesizer

See listing in Hot 100.

Crumar Stratus
Multi-instrument keyboard/synth

Orig. price (1982)	$700 (£500)
Price in 1996	$100 (£100)
Keyboard	61-note
Sound type	Analog, preset/programmable

Synth-oriented keyboard with organ and strings presets in same, smaller mold as Trilogy.

Crumar Stringman
String synth

Orig. price (1975)	$600 (£400)
Price in 1996	$75 (£50)
Keyboard	49-note
Sound type	Analog

In the mold of the Brassman and accordingly some worthy string-oriented features. EQ and chorus. Another period piece.

Crumar Toccata
Organ

Orig. price (1981)	$500 (£325)
Price in 1996	$75 (£50)
Keyboard	49-note
Sound type	Analog, drawbars

Inexpensive and unspectacular electric organ.

Crumar Trilogy
Multi-instrument keyboard/synth

Orig. price (1982)	$600 (£400)
Price in 1996	$100 (£100)
Keyboard	61-note
Sound type	Analog, preset/programmable

Synth-orientated keyboard with organ and strings presets thrown in for good measure. Good tonal range and plenty of strong analog sounds. No storage and no MIDI.

Daewoo EU-20
Digital piano/multi-instrument keyboard

Country of origin	Korea
Orig. price (1993)	No U.S. price (£2000)
Price in 1996	No U.S. price (£1000)
Keyboard	88-note
Sound type	Sample

This weighted action keyboard has 84 tones and 16 rhythms, plus effects and a small play-sequencer.

Daewoo EX-5
Digital piano

Orig. price (1993)	No U.S. price (£2000)
Price in 1996	No U.S. price (£1000)
Keyboard	88-note
Sound type	Sample

High-gloss digital piano from Korean giant Daewoo. Twelve tones, including unusual "western piano" (honky tonk, we presume). EX-7 has smaller cabinet.

Daewoo EX-76
Digital piano

Orig. price (1993)	No U.S. price (£2000)
Price in 1996	No U.S. price (£1000)
Keyboard	76-note
Sound type	Sample

Keyboard truncated version of EX-7 with a few less tones in a curious looking three-legged cabinet rejected by Korg some years earlier.

Davis Clavitar
Remote keyboard

Country of origin	U.S.
Orig. price (1982)	$3000 (no UK price)
Price in 1996	$250 (no UK price)
Keyboard	49-note
Sound type	n/a

Rare bird from Californian Wayne Yentis—monophonic remote keyboard made for the likes of George Duke and Herbie Hancock. Can control parameters like filter cutoff and tuning. The Clavitron was made specifically for the Prophet-5. Both preempt MIDI.

Davoli Davolisint
Monophonic synthesizer

Country of origin	Italy
Orig. price (1972)	No U.S. price (£250)
Price in 1996	No U.S. price (£50)
Keyboard	37-note
Sound type	Analog

Oddball but popular (in Europe) effort from one of the many "who are they?" Italian companies that surfaced and sank in the 1970s. Several models were made, but very dubiously useful today.

Denon EP3300
Digital piano

Country of origin	Japan
Orig. price (1993)	No U.S. price (£1995)
Price in 1996	No U.S. price (£750)
Keyboard	88-note
Sound type	Sample

Professional offering from audio specialists Denon. Polyphony of 32 voices and 8 tones plus reverb.

Digisound
Modular synthesizers

Country of origin	UK
Releases	1985+
Price in 1996	No U. S. price (£variable depending on module/system)
Keyboard	49 & 61 note versions
Sound type	Analog

DIY analog synth kits and modules from Tim Higham's Digisound—an unusual choice of name for an analog specialist. Well made and worthy.

Digital Keyboards Synergy
Polyphonic synthesizer

Country of origin	U.S.

See entry in Hot 100.

Doepfer A-100
Analog synthesizer modules

Country of origin	Germany
Orig. price (1995)	$100-200 (£100-200)
Price in 1996	$100-200 (£100-200), $2300 for pre-assembled system, includes frame

Keyboard	n/a (rack modules)
Sound type	Analog

Quirky German manufacturer of analog equipment now coming into their own in the techno-obsessed 1990s. Huge range of modules, including many unusual ones (e.g., A-170 Slew Limiter, A-165 Dual Trigger Modifier, filter banks and a splendid vocoding system). Not particularly expensive and well made.

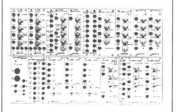

A-100

Analoges Modulsystem

Ausgabe März '96

DOEPFER MUSIKELEKTRONIK GMBH
Lenbachstr. 2 · D-82166 Gräfelfing
☎ 089 - 85 55 78 · Fax 089 - 854 16 98

Doepfer LMK1(+)
Controller keyboard

Orig. price (1990)	$695, LMK1+: $995 (no UK price)
Price in 1996	$695, LMK1: $995 (no UK price)
Keyboard	88-note
Sound type	n/a

Slimline but still flight-cased controller.

Doepfer LMK2(+)
Controller keyboard

Orig. price (1990)	$1100, LMK2+: $1300 (no UK price)
Price in 1996	$1100, LMK2+: $1300 (no UK price)
Keyboard	88-note
Sound type	n/a

Firm but not weighted keyboard as on LMK4. Plenty of features.

Doepfer LMK4(+)
Controller keyboard

Orig. price (1990)	$1500, LMK4+: $1725 (no UK price)
Price in 1996	$1500, LMK4+: $1725 (no UK price)
Keyboard	88-note
Sound type	n/a

Pre-flight-cased controller with weighted action, offering aftertouch and plenty of hand and foot controls.

Doepfer MS-404
Monophonic synthesizer

Orig. price (1994)	$499 (£345)
Price in 1996	$499 (£300)
Keyboard	n/a (1U module)
Sound type	Analog

With MIDI-to-CV interface, plenty of knobs and switches and 100 percent analog design, the 404 makes a good choice for purists who cannot find or cannot afford a genuinely "old" analog mono. Good firm sounds from this VCO box.

Dream GMX-1
GM sound module

Country of origin	France
Orig. price (1993)	$295 (£249)
Price in 1996	$150 (£150)
Keyboard	Module
Sound type	Digital, preset

Cheap if not exactly cheerful GM module from France. Sounds thin by comparison to Roland and Korg equivalents but you pays your money...

Dubreq Stylophone
Toy

Country of origin	France
Orig. price (1968)	No U.S. price (£20)
Price in 1996	No U.S. price (£20)
Keyboard	20-note
Sound type	Analog

Novelty item sold in toy stores that found its way onto David Bowie's *Space Oddity*, and also into the minds and hearts of a generation of British kids via Australian artist Rolf Harris. A joke, but a good one. Played by running a stylus (pen) up and down its "keyboard" contacts. And sounds? Unmistakably terrible. Like a mosquito on Ecstasy.

EDP Gnat
Monophonic synthesizer

Country of origin	UK
Orig. price (1980)	$230 (£100)
Price in 1996	$100 (£125)
Keyboard	25-note
Sound type	Analog

Smaller, one oscillator version of the Wasp. Still good sounds. Static keyboard. See Wasp entry for more details.

EDP Wasp
Monophonic synthesizer

See entry in Hot 100.

EKO Ekosynth
Monophonic synthesizer

Country of origin	Italy
Orig. price (1979)	$530 (£300)
Price in 1996	$100 (£60)
Keyboard	44-note
Sound type	Analog, preset

Surprisingly good little Italian mono synth. Fifteen presets with real time modifiers like filter and amplifier and LFO.

EKO Piano 200
Electronic piano

Orig. price (1980)	No U.S. price (£250)
Price in 1996	No U.S. price (£40)
Keyboard	61-note
Sound type	Analog

Undistinguished and inexpensive Italian electronic piano of the 1980s. Nuff said.

Center: Synthesizer as flight deck from Germans Doepfer and the A-100;
Right: UK's Gnat: flying in the face of (mid-1970s) fashion

Electro Harmonix Mini Synthesizer
Monophonic synthesizer

Country of origin	U.S.
Orig. price (1980)	$175 (£250)
Price in 1996	$100 (£100)
Keyboard	25-note
Sound type	Analog

Limited through its static and small keyboard but looks tempting and sounds, with its one oscillator, fairly pokey.

Electro Harmonix Super Replay
Sampling module

Orig. price (1984)	$675 (£500)
Price in 1996	$200 (£150)
Keyboard	Module
Sound type	Digital sampling

Sampling "box" whose innards would become the Akai 612 in due course. No keyboard, no MIDI, but quality is okay in a grainy sort of way.

Elgam Snoopy
Electronic piano

Country of origin	Italy
Orig. price (1977)	No U.S. price (£170)
Price in 1996	No U.S. price (£25)
Keyboard	44-note
Sound type	Analog

Not quite the silliest name in the business but close. The Snoopy poked its nose into the air in the late '70s and neither it nor Elgam seemed to have done much else since. Dull piano sounds in rickety casing.

Elka EK-22
Polyphonic synthesizer

Country of origin	Italy
Orig. price (1986)	No U.S. price (£999)
Price in 1996	No U.S. price (£200)
Keyboard	61-note
Sound type	Analog, programmable

Elka's mid-1980s assault on the professional keyboard market. Made some friends in Europe but so-so sounds meant it could never compete with the big boys from Japan. In-depth programming. EM-22 is a tabletop module.

Elka EK-44
Polyphonic synthesizer

Orig. price (1986)	No U.S. price (£1299)
Price in 1996	No U.S. price (£250)
Keyboard	61-note
Sound type	Digital, programmable

Litigation-inducing "FM" synth released alongside the EK-22. DX-ish sounds aplenty and some new programming twists as well. ER-44, EM-44 and ER-33 are tabletop, rackmount and half audio power versions respectively.

Elka MK-88
Controller keyboard

Orig. price (1987)	$2150 (£1299)
Price in 1996	$650 (£500)
Keyboard	88-note
Sound type	n/a

All-encompassing master keyboard-in-a-flight case, as is Italy's wont. Memories, lots of assignable wheels and sliders and, or perhaps so, quite complex to program. EK-55 has 61-note unweighted keyboard but is otherwise the same.

Elka Rhapsody 610
String synthesizer

Orig. price (1975)	$995 (£650)
Price in 1996	$100 (£100)

Keyboard	61-note
Sound type	Analog

Classic string machine used by the good and the great in the mid-'70s. Slider-controlled string sections, plus piano and clavichord tones. The four-octave Rhapsody 490 is strings only.

Elka Synthex
Polyphonic synthesizer

See entry in Hot 100.

Elka X-705
Stage organ

Orig. price (1977)	$3500 (£2500)
Price in 1996	$500 (£300)
Keyboard	49-note x 2
Sound type	Analog

Big and beefy stage organ complete with drawbars, tabs and synth section. Too much for the average player to handle, financially or otherwise. The X-605 also double manual but less tones.

Elvins TS-55
Electronic piano

Country of origin	UK
Orig. price (1979)	No U.S. price (£449)
Price in 1996	No U.S. price (£50)
Keyboard	61-note
Sound type	Analog

"The most realistic piano sound you have ever heard," proclaimed Londoner Pete Elvins in the TS-55 manual. Not exactly. Not then, never mind now. Creditable effort, though, with transposer and phaser on board, but still sank without trace.

EML
Monophonic synthesizer modules

Country of origin	U.S.
Orig. price (1968+)	$Variable (no UK price)
Price in 1996	$Variable (no UK price)
Keyboard	44-note on 101 and 500
Sound type	Analog

American producer of analog synthesizer modules from the late 1960s to mid 1980s. Mostly used in schools and colleges. Products sold under the Electrocomp name: 100, 101, 200, 300 etc. The Electrocomp 101 and 500 are single units with 44-note keyboard.

EMS Polysynthi
Polyphonic synthesizer

Country of origin	UK
Orig. price (1979)	No U.S. price (£990)
Price in 1996	No U.S. price (£250)
Keyboard	49-note
Sound type	Analog

Garish early polyphonic synth from the makers of the VCS3/Putney and Synthi 100. Trouble is it looks like a contraption knocked up by Little Tykes and sounds only marginally better. Complex. Interesting ideas (pressure-sensitive keyboard, full polyphony), but the sounds are raw and thin. Only a few were ever made, luckily.

EMS Synthi 100
Monophonic synthesizer

See entry in Hot 100.

EMS Synthi A
Monophonic synthesizer

See EMS VCS3 entry in Hot 100.

EMS Synthi AKS
Monophonic synthesizer

See EMS VCS3 entry in Hot 100.

EMS VCS3
Monophonic synthesizer

See entry in Hot 100.

E-mu Classic Keys
Polyphonic synthesizer

Country of origin	U.S.
Orig. price (1994)	$849 (£647)
Price in 1996	$575 (£475)
Keyboard	1U module
Sound type	Sample+ synthesis

No super filters, but 512 preset classic keyboards sounds in a Proteus-style environment, plus effects.

E-mu EII
Digital sampler

See entry in Hot 100.

E-mu EIII
Digital sampler

See entry in Hot 100.

E-mu EIV
Digital sampler

See entry in Hot 100.

E-mu E4K
Digital sampling keyboard

Price in 1996	$3995 (£3499)
Keyboard	76-note
Sound type	Digital sampling (stereo)

The heart of an EIV sampler in plush setting of 76-note weighted keyboard piano type instrument. Comes with 270MB internal hard drive, from which you can load up finished sounds at almost synth-preset speed, plus 4MB RAM as standard. With SMF scratchpad sequencer and 8 outputs, a very tempting proposition. Either 64-voice or 128-voice versions.

Center: EMS appeal: Wear black and be German

E-mu E64
Digital sampler

Orig. price (1995)	$3295 (£2700)
Price in 1996	$3000 (£2500)
Keyboard	2U module
Sound type	Digital sampling (stereo)

Half the polyphony of an EIV and slightly fewer windows on the future in terms of expansion ports. Bargain.

E-mu Emax
Digital sampler

Orig. price (1986)	$2999 (£2199)
Price in 1996	$600-800 (£400-600)
Keyboard	61-note
Sound type	Digital sampling (mono)

E-mu's series of samplers for the mid-price market. Good value (in home territory U.S., anyway) if purveyor of slightly time-consuming procedures. Always a good library in tow. Came in four varieties: (original) Emax, Emax Rack, Emax HD (built-in hard disk) and Emax Rack HD. The Emax SE adds additive synthesis tools.

E-mu Emax II
Digital sampler

Orig. price (1989)	$3495 (£1999)
Price in 1996	$1200-2000 (£700-1100)
Keyboard	61-note
Sound type	Digital sampling (stereo)

Complete re-bore of the original Emax, including a new 16-bit stereo sampling sound chip, digital filters and such. At one point the Emax II looked more sophisticated than E-mu's top-of-the-line EIII. Offered in rack and keyboard forms and also "Turbo" with 8MB RAM.

E-mu Emulator
Digital sampler

See entry in Hot 100.

E-mu ESI32
Digital sampler

Orig. price (1994)	$1495 (£1250)
Price in 1996	$900 (£850)
Keyboard	2U module
Sound type	Digital sampling (stereo)

The brain of an EIII in an only partially trimmed package that makes it outstanding value. Expandable up to 32MB. Can read EIII library and Akai S1000/S1100 over SCSI.

E-mu Modular
Monophonic synthesizer modules

Releases	1972+
Price	$Variable (no UK price)
Keyboard	61-note (separate, monophonic and polyphonic)

A huge series of modules that was E-mu's stock in trade for much of the 1970s. Extremely well made and much sought after by the rich and famous. E-mu's work on digitally scanning keyboards began here and was later used on Oberheim and Sequential instruments.

E-mu Morpheus
Polyphonic synthesizer

See entry in Hot 100.

E-mu MPS
Polyphonic synthesizer

Orig. price (1992)	$1695 (£1295)
Price in 1996	$850 (£600)
Keyboard	61-note
Sound type	Sample+ synthesis

Rare bird, as it was the sole Proteus instrument to come in keyboard form. Launched in UK in 1992 and basically bombed. Proteus family's only failure. Bit of a mismatch of sounds, keyboard, features and system. But apart from that...

E-mu Orbit
Polyphonic synthesizer module

Price in 1996	$995 (£895)
Keyboard	1U module
Sound type	Sample+ synthesis

Launched amid techno heaven (or hell) at Frankfurt 1996, Orbit is a module full of sweeps, swishes and swooshes, plus some canny sequenced loops, razor sharp filters and good MIDI clocking features, wrapped up in a friendly Proteus-style package. Aimed at, but not limited to, the dance market. Laptop real-time controller Launch Pad due for release later in 1996.

E-mu ProFormance
Digital piano module

Orig. price (1991)	$295 (£349)
Price in 1996	$180 (£175)
Keyboard	Module
Sound type	Sample, preset

Fifteen piano-type presets in a squat little box with a couple of knobs. A great price. People tend to love it or hate it, and with no editing to speak of, neither camp can be persuaded away from their opinion. Makeover in 1993 to ProFormance Plus comprised some judicious tweaking (nothing radical) and a knob re-spray.

E-mu Proteus
Polyphonic synthesizer

See entry in Hot 100.

E-mu Proteus 2
Polyphonic synthesizer

See E-mu Proteus entry in Hot 100.

E-mu Proteus 3
Polyphonic synthesizer

See E-mu Proteus entry in Hot 100.

E-mu Proteus FX
Polyphonic synthesizer

Orig. price (1994)	$749 (£610)
Price in 1996	$475 (£400)
Keyboard	1U module
Sound type	Sample+ synthesis

As name implies, Proteus with digital effects offered in two banks, sensibly, as a final stage feature, so sounds are not attaching themselves to and then having to detach themselves from the effects when it comes to using the instrument multitimbrally.

E-mu Sound Engine
GM one module

Orig. price (1993)	No U.S. price (no UK price)
Price in 1996	No U.S. price (no UK price)
Keyboard	Module
Sound type	Digital sample

Desktop GM module that E-mu slipped out in 1993. No one, including E-mu it seems, was very pleased with it, so it quietly went away. Until now.

E-mu UltraProte
Polyphonic synthesizer

Orig. price (1994)	$1699 (£1499)
Price in 1996	$1000 (£850)
Keyboard	1U module
Sound type	Sample+ synthesis

Souped up version of the original Proteus, with extensive filtering options (and so highly "playable"), plus expanded and improved sound hierarchy.

E-mu Vintage Keys
Polyphonic synthesizer

Orig. price (1993)	$1095 (£870)
Price in 1996	$500 (£450)
Keyboard	1U module
Sound type	Sample+ synthesis

Brilliant idea. A Proteus-style module full of all the great keyboard sounds, from the Hammond to Minimoog to Rhodes piano, Farfisa organs, etc. Sort of works. Inevitably a lot gets lost in the translation, but it'll get you out of jail, and it's a lot lighter than a B3. E-mu Vintage Plus has sound expansion.

Ensoniq ASR-10
Digital sampler

Country of origin	U.S.
Orig. price (1993)	$2695 (£2345)
Price in 1996	$1350 (£1200)
Keyboard	61-note
Sound type	Sample

Extension of the EPS system, though improved to genuine performance status, complete with top notch built-in effects and an 8-track sequencer. SIMMs upgradable and SCSI option. Made in keyboard and module versions.

Left: E-mu's option- and version-laden Emax samplers; Center: Options, options, options on the groundbreaking EII sampler

Ensoniq EPS
Digital sampler

Orig. price (1988)	$1995 (£1695)
Price in 1996	$700 (£500)
Keyboard	61-note
Sound type	Sample

Polyphonic aftertouch revamp of the Mirage. In various forms and powers, the EPS has been a long-lived, successful series. Quirky, though, and some vintages have been prone to bouts of unreliability.

Ensoniq EPS-16 Plus
Digital sampler

Orig. price (1991)	$2395 (£1940)
Price in 1996	$900 (£750, for basic model)
Keyboard	61-note
Sound type	Sample

Long-serving sampler released in several versions and formats. Used extensively in live performances thanks to the handy and rare additional features of built-in effects and multitrack sequencer.

Ensoniq ESQ-1
Polyphonic synthesizer

See entry in Hot 100.

Ensoniq KS-32
Polyphonic synthesizer

Orig. price (1992)	$2195 (£1895)
Price in 1996	$1300 (£900)
Keyboard	76-note
Sound type	Sample+ synthesis

The sounds of an SQ-2 (which itself is based upon the SQ-1) with a weighted action 76-note keyboard. Good stacking features but small screen and no disk drive.

Ensoniq KT-76
Polyphonic synthesizer

Orig. price (1994)	$2495 (£1999)
Price in 1996	No U.S. price (no UK price)
Keyboard	76-note
Sound type	Sample+ synthesis

Not so much rehash as rethink. Genuine workstation with top quality sounds and effects, plus a friendly sequencer and a highly playable keyboard. Only limitation is lack of disk drive. GM mode available.

Ensoniq Mirage
Digital sampler

See entry in Hot 100.

Ensoniq Mirage DSK
Digital sampler

See Ensoniq Mirage entry in Hot 100.

Ensoniq SD-1
Polyphonic synthesizer

Orig. price (1991)	$2695 (£1995)
Price in 1996	$1300 (£800)
Keyboard	61-note
Sound type	Sample+ synthesis

Relaunch of the VFX-SD(II) with some cosmetic changes and a couple of additional ROM waves. Better bet by far than original VFX.

Ensoniq SDP-1
Digital piano

Orig. price (1986)	$1395 (£1125)
Price in 1996	$500 (£400)

Keyboard	76-note
Sound type	Sample

Fleeting outing for Ensoniq and one the company quickly withdrew from when they saw how tough and impenetrable the competition. Okay sounds that have later adorned Baldwin pianos, in fact, but the whole package simply didn't add up. A module SPM-1 was also made.

Ensoniq SQ-1 (Plus)
Polyphonic synthesizer

Orig. price (1990)	$1595 (£1349)
Price in 1996	$650 (£450)
Keyboard	61-note
Sound type	Sample+ synthesis

Heart of a VFX in a streamlined, cost-effective package. Less voice stacking and small screen but still has a generous sequencer and plenty of sounds. Originally 16-voice polyphonic, upgraded to 32-voice polyphonic in 1992. SQ-1 Plus features additional 1MB piano samples. SQ-R module has half waveform ROM.

Ensoniq SQ-2
Polyphonic synthesizer

Orig. price (1991)	$1795 (£1599)
Price in 1996	$900 (£750)
Keyboard	76-note
Sound type	Sample+ synthesis

The SQ-1 in a 76-key version. Reasonable halfway house: good value for the keyboard, but you lose some voice-stacking features (3 max) and Patch Select buttons. Upgraded to 32-voice polyphony (from the curious 21-voice) in 1992.

Ensoniq SQ-80
Polyphonic synthesizer

Orig. price (1988)	$1895 (£1395)
Price in 1996	$500 (£300)
Keyboard	61-note
Sound type	Digital/analog, programmable

Polyphonic, aftertouch, enhanced waveform ROM version of the ESQ-1 synth.

Ensoniq TS-10
Polyphonic synthesizer

Orig. price (1993)	$2495 (£1995)
Price in 1996	$1750 (£1250)
Keyboard	61-note
Sound type	Sample+ synthesis

Back to classic Ensoniq vacuum display here on this clever blend of synth and sampler with 24-track sequencer and creamy effects in tow. A genuine contender for workstation status.

Ensoniq TS-12
Polyphonic synthesizer

Orig. price (1994)	$2795 (£2199)
Price in 1996	$2200 (£1500)
Keyboard	76-note
Sound type	Sample+ synthesis

The TS-10 in 76-key, weighted keyboard version. Equally clever and complete with helpful features like SoundFinder to help you navigate

around its 600+ library of sounds. A big instrument.

Ensoniq VFX
Polyphonic synthesizer

Orig. price (1989)	$1995 (£1350)
Price in 1996	$600 (£450)
Keyboard	61-note
Sound type	Sample+ synthesis

The first of a line of instruments based around Ensoniq's wavetable-like Transwaves system. Plain VFX had many problems, but as the series developed—VFX SD (with sequencer), VFX SD (II) (same but with new piano samples)—problems were ironed out. Quirky, but has many loyal fans.

Evolution EVS-1
Polyphonic synthesizer

Country of origin	UK
Orig. price (1990)	$599 (£299)
Price in 1996	$200 (£150)
Keyboard	1U module
Sound type	Analog synthesis (various)

Oddball module from UK that promised much but fell short on delivery. Editing only via external computer hook up, though plenty of unusual sounds thanks to a bewildering array of synthesis-type and sundry mysterious sounding features.

Fairlight CMI
Music computer system

Country of origin	Australia

See entry in Hot 100.

Farfisa Compact
Stage organ

Country of origin	Italy

See entry in Hot 100.

Farfisa DP-18
Digital piano

Orig. price (1992)	$499 (£350)
Price in 1996	$200 (£150)
Keyboard	61-note
Sound type	Digital

Not innovative but functional and well made series of inexpensive digital pianos from Farfisa. Well balanced tones and a playse-quencer. Nice little package. DE20, released in 1995, had additional orchestral tones and DPR22 additional rhythms.

Farfisa F1
Home keyboard

Orig. price (1993)	$3000 (£2000)
Price in 1996	$1500 (£1200)
Keyboard	76-note
Sound type	Multi synthesis

First of a new line from Farfisa based on a multimillion-dollar investment in new technology from the IRIS research center in Rome. Still

---

Center: Sounds aplenty on Ensoniq's synth/sampler hybrid: TS-10; **Right: First Ensoniq wavetable synth:** VFX-SD (sequencer model)

essentially a home keyboard but with expandability in terms of sound and style editing, no less than eight simultaneous effects, mic input and quite the snazziest stand and speakers arrangement ever made.

Farfisa F5
Home keyboard

Orig. price (1994)	$2500 (£1750)
Price in 1996	$1500 (£1000)
Keyboard	61-note
Sound type	Multi synthesis

Punchy but trimmed version of the F1. Some operational differences but much the same power, sonically. The F6 (1995) is similar to the F5 but loses aftertouch and some control features.

Farfisa F7
Home keyboard

Price in 1996	No U.S. price (no UK price)
Keyboard	61-note
Sound type	Multi synthesis

Almost indistinguishable to the naked eye from past F-series instruments but with GM sounds, lots of effects, karaoke style sequencer and disk drive still full of features. The F8 is a more preset version.

Farfisa Syntorchestra
Multi-instrument keyboard

Orig. price (1976)	$600 (£375)
Price in 1996	$100 (£70)
Keyboard	37-note
Sound type	Analog

Serviceable but undististinguished string machine of mid-'70s vintage.

Farfisa TK-100
Home keyboard

Orig. price (1987)	No U.S. price (£699)
Price in 1996	No U.S. price (£100)
Keyboard	61-note
Sound type	Analog

TK series encompassed the TK-100, TK-80 and TK-90. Based on the promising sounding Sampled Wave Technology, the series did not, however, deliver. Best forgotten.

Fender Rhodes
Electric piano

Country of origin	U.S.

See entry in Hot 100.

Forat F16
Digital sampler

Country of origin	U.S.
Orig. price (1987)	$2000 (no UK price)
Price in 1996	No U.S. price (no UK price)
Keyboard	4U module
Sound type	Sample

Limited availability module from Forat, Californian fixit company. Good value, drum-based sampler with up to 60kHz sample rate and variable RAM and voices. Rare knob editing rather than onscreen.

Freeman String Symphoniser
String machine

Country of origin	UK
Orig. price (1966)	No U.S. price (no UK price)
Price in 1996	No U.S. price (no UK price)
Keyboard	61-note
Sound type	Analog

Eponymous creation by Ken Freeman (*War of the Worlds* and general star session player of the 1970s in UK). Rare and rather wonderful.

Furstein Night & Day
Acoustic/digital piano

Country of origin	Italy
Orig. price (1993)	No U.S. price (2999)
Price in 1996	No U.S. price (£1750)
Keyboard	88-note
Sound type	Acoustic/digital

Furstein is Farfisa. Highly innovative creation of acoustic piano with built-in digital sounds for "silent" practice through a pedal that can lock the acoustic sound of the strings. Yamaha and others have leaped onto this particular bandwagon, leaving Furstein somewhat out in the cold. Hard old world, isn't it?

GEM CD3
Home keyboard

Country of origin	Italy
Orig. price (1993)	No U.S price (£500)
Price in 1996	No U.S. price (£250)
Keyboard	61-note
Sound type	Sample+ synthesis

Entry-level home keyboards with some of the earlier sound quality. Disk drive and even a small slice of RAM in which to load samples. Wobbly GM specification (five-part multitimbrality) but generally good value. CD2 loses disk drive (a major loss because then you can't load in new sounds and styles), and CD1 has but 4-track sequencer and no "joy ball," GEM's delightful name for the pitch and mod controller.

GEM DP20
Digital piano

Orig. price (1990)	$1499 (£949)
Price in 1996	$600 (£450)
Keyboard	76-note (S3 76-note)
Sound type	Digital sample

Along with the 88-note keyboard models DP25, DP30 and DP40, a no nonsense digital piano with slender polyphony (16-voice) and just eight tones, but pleasant sounding for the time and money.

GEM DSK3/4
Home keyboard

Orig. price (1987)	No U.S. price (£399)
Price in 1996	No U.S. price (£100)
Keyboard	61-note
Sound type	Analog/PCM

Before GEM (now GeneralMusic) became a serious high-tech producer, its stock in trade was inexpensive home keyboards and organs. No MIDI and limited programming skills in evidence.

GEM DSK5/6
Home keyboard

Orig. price (1986)	No U.S. price (£549)
Price in 1996	No U.S. price (£125)
Keyboard	61-note
Sound type	Analog/PCM

MIDI version of the above with some editing and sound layering. Rather ancient now for its type.

GEM DSK7/8
Home keyboard

Orig. price (1987)	No U.S. price (£699)
Price in 1996	No U.S. price (£125)
Keyboard	61-note
Sound type	Analog/PCM

Slightly more grown-up versions of the above. The DS8 with its custom drum memory and arrangement potential is the best of this somewhat undistinguished bunch.

GEM PS2000
Digital piano

Orig. price (1991)	No U.S price (£1399) (see Bachmann PS2000)
Price in 1996	No U.S price (£450)
Keyboard	88-note
Sound type	Digital sample

Perfectly reasonable digital piano though without sufficient bells and whistles to seriously rival established digital piano manufacturers. Sounds hard-wired to certain effects, which is rather limiting, but some imaginative sound programming. PS1000 has 76-note keyboard, and GPS2000 is truncated grand piano cabinet version of the PS model.

GEM WS1(D)
Home keyboard

Orig. price (1992)	No U.S price (£1000) (see Bachmann WS1D)
Price in 1996	No U.S price (£500)
Keyboard	61-note
Sound type	Sample+ synthesis

Streamlined upgrades to the WS2 concept. Not a GM instrument, though close to the specification and there are a few less effects. The WS1D offers built-in disk drive that can accept standard MIDI files. Branded Bachmann in U.S.

GEM WS2
Home keyboard

Orig. price (1990)	No U.S price (£2000) (see Bachmann WS2)
Price in 1996	No U.S price (£550)
Keyboard	61-note
Sound type	Sample+ synthesis

The mind of a professional workstation in a home keyboard setting. 32-voice polyphony, stereo digital effects, very high quality sounds and cannily programmed styles. The WS2 was Bachmann's (who is, in fact, GeneralMusic's U.S. trading brand name) first outing down this particular track. Called Bachmann WS2 in U.S.

GEM WS400
Home keyboard

Orig. price (1990)	No U.S price (£3000) (see Bachmann WS400)
Price in 1996	No U.S price (£1000)
Keyboard	88-note
Sound type	Sample+ synthesis

Elongated and weighted action version of the WS2 with beefy 40W stereo amplification. The grand piano design GWS400 features enhanced amplification system. Branded Bachmann in U.S.

GEM WX2
Home keyboard

Orig. price (1993)	No U.S price (£2000) (see Bachmann WX2)
Price in 1996	No U.S price (£850)
Keyboard	61-note
Sound type	Sample+ synthesis

With sounds based upon the company's successful S2 pro synth, the WX2 took home keyboards on to greater heights. Peerless brass and guitar samples, serviceable sequencer and lyrics and some editing available on an external display. Superb demo song of Donald Fagen's "Kamakiriad" promises rather more sophistication than the styles subsequently deliver. WX400 is 88-note weighted keyboard version.

GeneralMusic RPS
Digital piano

Country of origin	Italy
Price in 1996	No U.S. price (no UK price)
Keyboard	88-note (S3: 76-note)
Sound type	Digital sample

With 64-note polyphony, highly accurate sound generation, including one of the best Rhodes samples in the business, the RPS even includes a form of half-pedaling, natural string reverberation effect. Series comprises RP1, RP2 and RP3, plus grand piano design GRP3.

GeneralMusic S2
Polyphonic synthesizer

Orig. price (1992)	$2900 (£1699)
Price in 1996	$1750 (£750)
Keyboard	61-note
Sound type	Sample+ synthesis

Originally released as GEM (the company changed its name to GeneralMusic in 1994), this is a pro synth with some first rate sampled sounds (soft sax a specialty), innovative editing procedures, good effects, large screen and good sound library. The only limit is the professionals' acceptance of a new name. The S3 has 76-note keyboard. A "Turbo" kit boosts polyphony from 16- to 32-voice and expands the waveform ROM.

GeneralMusic SX3
Home keyboard

Orig. price (1995)	$2795 (£1995)
Price in 1996	£2000 (£1200)
Keyboard	76-note
Sound type	Sample+ synthesis

GEM changed its name to GeneralMusic in 1994. This grown-up home keyboard is in the mold of the Korg i-series. Excellent style programming, top notch sounds, practical editing and helpful external display hookup possible. Aimed at the working pro in club or lounge situations.

GeneralMusic WK3
Home keyboard

Price in 1996	No U.S. price (no UK price)
Keyboard	61-note
Sound type	Sample+ synthesis

Powerful but good value home keyboard workstation from GeneralMusic, launched at Frankfurt in 1996. Some 32 layers or splits possible, dual MIDI ports, extensive editing—even on-the-fly—plus SMF disk drive, effects and extensive range of GM sounds. WK4 has large square display screen.

Gleeman Pentaphonic
Polyphonic synthesizer

Country of origin	U.S.

See entry in Hot 100.

Godwin Strings
String machine

Country of origin	Italy
Orig. price (1980)	No U.S. price (£450)
Price in 1996	No U.S price (£75)
Keyboard	49-note
Sound type	Analog

Italian string machine. Not the best, not the worst. Generic.

Goldstar GEK S230
Home keyboard

Country of origin	Korea
Orig. price (1993)	No U.S. price (under £500)
Price in 1996	No U.S. price (no UK price)
Keyboard	61-note
Sound type	PCM

Inexpensive route into General MIDI with keyboard. Along with GEK S330, S325 and S525 (which are not GM), the sounds and styles are rather budget. You pays your money...

Goldstar GS1000
Home keyboard

Orig. price (1993)	No U.S. price (£1500)
Price in 1996	$750 (no UK price)
Keyboard	61-note
Sound type	Sample+ synthesis

Creditable attempt at new angles on a home keyboard with some music teaching facilities and nice effects. Weak sounds let it down. GS1000R is rack version.

Greengate DS3
Sampling system

Country of origin	UK
Orig. price (1986)	$2000 (£1800+)
Price in 1996	$500 (£300)
Keyboard	61-note
Sound type	Sample

Apple IIe computer-based sampling system from Molloy and Munro, a pair of British songwriters. Had a brief day in court. Started life as a sampling drum machine before blossoming into a polyphonic system complete with extensive editing, digital synthesis. Similar to Fairlight but at a fraction of the cost. Went belly-up eventually, as do most such British endeavors.

Greengate DS4
Sampling system

Orig. price (1986)	$2500+ (£1750-2100)
Price in 1996	$2500+ (£1800+)
Keyboard	61-note
Sound type	Sample

Hardware version of DS3 in rackmount unit offering 44.1kHz sampling, 8-voice polyphony, sequencer, digital synthesis and more. Looked highly promising but was only made in small quantities before the end of Greengate.

Hammond A-100
Home organ

Country of origin	U.S.
Orig. price (1959)	No U.S. price (no UK price)
Price in 1996	$1200 (£1000)

Keyboard	60-note x 2
Sound type	Tonewheel

Similar sounding to the B-3 and C-3 but later model and with built-in amplification and spring reverb. Aimed more at home users.

Hammond B-3
Stage organ

See entry in Hot 100.

Hammond C-3
Stage organ

See Hammond B-3 entry in Hot 100.

Hammond D-100
Home organ

Orig. price (1963)	No U.S. price (no UK price)
Price in 1996	$1200 (£1000)
Keyboard	60-note x 2
Sound type	Tonewheel

Imposing B-3 and C-3 soundalike with built-in amplification.

Hammond E-100
Home organ

Orig. price (1965)	No U.S. price (no UK price)
Price in 1996	$1200 (£1000)
Keyboard	60-note x 2
Sound type	Tonewheel

One set of drawbars per manual.

Hammond H-100
Home organ

Orig. price (1965)	No U.S. price (no UK price)
Price in 1996	$1200 (£1000)
Keyboard	44-note x 2
Sound type	Tonewheel/transistors

Mixture of tonewheel and transistorized sound generation.

Hammond HA-2500
Digital piano

Countries of origin	U.S./Japan
Orig. price (1993)	No U.S. price (£1899)
Price in 1996	No U.S. price (£1000)
Keyboard	88-note
Sound type	Digital

Along with accompanying models HA-3500 and HA-1500, a serviceable digital piano, featuring half a dozen piano-based tones, reverb and chorus, playsequencer, MIDI and built-in amplification. Well made if somewhat unexciting.

Hammond L-100
Home/stage organ

Orig. price (1961)	$1100 (£450)
Price in 1996	$400 (£500)
Keyboard	44-note x 2
Sound type	Tonewheel

Small (compared to B3), strange organ that one Keith Emerson used to delight in sticking knives into as he slithered across stage with the instrument on his chest. Not the majesty of a B3 but a Hammond nonetheless.

Hammond M-100
Home/stage Organ

Orig. price (1961)	$1300 (£650)
Price in 1996	$450 (£500)

Left: Punchy WK4 "World keyboard" from GeneralMusic; Center: Greengate DS3: Apple-based sampling system circa 1984

| Keyboard | 44-note x 2 |
| Sound type | Tonewheel |

Similar but marginally enhanced compared to the L series.

Hammond XB-2
Stage organ

Countries of origin	U.S./Japan
Orig. price (1992)	$1799 (£1399)
Price in 1996	$2195 (£1599 new, not second hand)
Keyboard	61-note
Sound type	Digital

Hammond as in Hammond-Suzuki rather than the traditional U.S. organ manufacturer. Even so, a creditable attempt at offering Hammond B-3-type sounds and facilities in a modern MIDI environment. Editing a bit fiddly, but the sounds are as good as they come in sample-based organs and the look—and name—is just right too. Has special 11-pin Leslie connections. XB-3 and XB-5 are double manual spinet styled versions; pedalboard on XB-3. The so-named Version 2 XB-2 improves on some programming limitations and offers more sounds.

Helpinstill Roadmaster
Electro-acoustic piano

Country of origin	U.S.
Orig. price (1979)	$2495 (£1950)
Price in 1996	$500 (£300)
Keyboard	88-note
Sound type	Electro-acoustic

Pickup manufacturers Helpinstill's one-time launch into the world of complete instruments. Good to play (favored by Rabbit from The Who, among many others), but as simply a pre-electrified acoustic piano, always going to be difficult to defeat major players like Yamaha. PG-21 a grand piano design.

Hohner ADAM
Home keyboard

Country of origin	Germany
Orig. price (1995)	No U.S. price (£2999)
Price in 1996	No U.S. price (no UK price)
Keyboard	61-note
Sound type	Digital/analog

Large and expensive project for Hohner in the 1990s, in development for two or three years. Essentially a high-end home keyboard with advanced synth system (PCM/FM), sequencer and the rare ability to load styles from other manufacturers. Not available in U.S..

Hohner Clavinet
Electric clavichord

See entry in Hot 100.

Hohner Duo
Electronic piano plus

Orig. price (1978)	$1750 (£495)
Price in 1996	$500 (£500)
Keyboard	60-note
Sound type	Electro-acoustic

Mix of Clavinet and Pianet, complete with tone mixing. Almost unfeasibly heavy, but now fashionable thanks to the return of the Clavinet (sound) in the 1990s.

Hohner EK4 Opus
String machine

Orig. price (1981)	No U.S. price (£285)
Price in 1996	No U.S. price (£50)
Keyboard	49-note
Sound type	Electro-acoustic

Looks like a dog but in fact capable of some powerful, interesting sounds. Short keyboard but variable attack and sustain and useful sound combinations.

Hohner HS1
Digital sampler

Orig. price (1987)	No U.S. price (£1599)
Price in 1996	No U.S. price (£400)
Keyboard	61-note
Sound type	Digital

Casio FZ sampler rebadged as Hohner for the European market. Bargain route into "Casio FZ sampling" if that is your requirement.

Hohner HS2
Polyphonic synthesizer

Orig. price (1988)	No U.S. price (£1199)
Price in 1996	No U.S. price (£250)
Keyboard	61-note
Sound type	Digital

Casio VZ-1 rebadged as Hohner for European market. Not especially successful for Casio or Hohner.

Hohner K11
Piano/strings machine

Orig. price (1980)	$1295 (£741)
Price in 1996	$200 (£150)
Keyboard	61-note
Sound type	Analog

Large and heavy piano and strings instrument with piano, harpsichord and strings (including good cello and bass tones). Split keyboard facility. Some okay sound combinations.

Hohner Pianet
Electronic piano

See entry in Hot 100.

Jen Musipack
Music computer system

Country of origin	Italy
Orig. price (1984)	No U.S. price (£995)
Price in 1996	No U.S. price (no UK price)
Keyboard	61-note
Sound type	Apple sound generator card

Creditable early attempt at an Apple-based music computer. All-in-one system of sound creation and sequencing but limited and only of (vague) historic interest today.

Jen Piano 73
Electronic piano

Orig. price (1982)	$500 (£345)
Price in 1996	$80 (no UK price)
Keyboard	73-note
Sound type	Electronic

Three tones, two speakers and pair of tubular steel legs. Old-fashioned, even in 1982.

Jen SX-1000
Monophonic synthesizer

Orig. price (1981)	$300 (£159)
Price in 1996	$100 (no UK price)
Keyboard	37-note
Sound type	Analog

Unremarkable single oscillator synth from Italy. Good for beginners in 1980s. No performance controls. Called the Jen "Synthetone" SX-1000 in U.S.

Jennings Univox
Monophonic synthesizer

| Country of origin | UK |

No price details on this very early "synthesizer" reportedly used on The Tornados "Telstar" recording in 1962.

(Jeremy) Lord Skywave
Monophonic synthesizer

Country of origin	UK
Orig. price (1978)	No U.S. price (£750)
Price in 1996	No U.S. price (£200)
Keyboard	49-note
Sound type	Analog

Just the name should tell you most of what you need to know. Idiosyncratic British analog monosynth—large, be-knobbed, worthy but flawed and a total commercial failure. The joystick was unusual, but the programming was tortuous and the sounds not sufficiently interesting to propel users along even a gentle learning curve, much less the Skywave's Himalayan trek.

JHS Harmonizer
Multi-instrument keyboard

Countries of origin	Italy/UK
Orig. price (1980)	No U.S. price (£499)
Price in 1996	No U.S. price (no UK price)
Keyboard	49-note
Sound type	Analog

Rather grim offering from Brits that JHS made under license in Italy. All tones (strings, reeds, piano, organ, brass) saturated with electronics.

JHS Pro 6
Electronic piano

Orig. price (1983)	No U.S. price (£299)
Price in 1996	No U.S. price (no UK price)
Keyboard	73-note
Sound type	Analog

Classic (if that's the word for it) early 1980s, Italian-designed electronic piano. Not nice. Avoid.

JVC KB-300
Home keyboard

Country of origin	Japan
Orig. price (1984)	$559 (£359)
Price in 1996	$75 (no UK price)
Keyboard	49-note
Sound type	Analog

Nice (at the time) offering from hi-fi specialists JVC. Also KB-500 and KB-700. Not worth hunting down but well made items, with features commensurate with their vintage.

Kawai CA330
Digital piano

Country of origin	Japan
Orig. price (1993)	$2800 (£1699)
Price in 1996	$1250 (£750)
Keyboard	88-note
Sound type	Digital sampled

Featuring Kawai's AWA weighted action along with seven tones, reverb and 15-voice polyphony. Not enough to match the gloss of Technics and Yamaha for most people. Also in series: CA130 (no reverb, 76-note keyboard) and CA230 (10W amplification in place of CA330's 20W system).

Kawai CA800
Digital piano

| Orig. price (1993) | $4000 (£2399) |
| Price in 1996 | $2000 (£1250) |

Keyboard	88-note
Sound type	Digital sampled

Similar to CA330 but far more sophisticated sampling techniques employed when acquiring the sounds and a better (longer keys) action. CA600 loses some punch in bass amplification system and reverts to CA330 type action. CA500 has smaller amplification system.

Kawai EP608
Electro-acoustic piano

Orig. price (1983)	$2400 (£1495)
Price in 1996	$500 (£500)
Keyboard	75-note
Sound type	Electro-acoustic

Serviceable and sturdy electric piano employing real strings and hammer action. Degree of portability but still weighs in at 63kg. EP308 the grand piano design version.

Kawai EP705M
Electro-acoustic piano

Orig. price (1985)	$2400 (£1990)
Price in 1996	$600 (£750)
Keyboard	75-note
Sound type	Electro-acoustic

Modernized version of the EP608. Same good-quality feel and sounds but improved casing. The "M" model is MIDI-ed. No "M," no MIDI.

Kawai FS640
Home keyboard

Orig. price (1992)	No U.S. price (from £200)
Price in 1996	No U.S. price (£variable)
Keyboard	61-note
Sound type	PCM digital presets

A large series of home keyboards starting with the non-MIDI FS640 and working up to the FS2000 (see following entry) via the FS730 (with velocity keyboard); the FS690 (that adds a degree of programmability); the MIDI-ed, sequencer-sporting but preset FS750; the semi-programmable FS780; the pitch and mod wheel sprouting FS800 and finally the FS900 that comes with a small mixing panel and drum pads. A theme of reasonably interesting sounds and innovative features.

Kawai FS2000
Home keyboard

Orig. price (1992)	$1500 (£1000)
Price in 1996	$750 (£400)
Keyboard	61-note
Sound type	PCM

Apart from a lack of GM (not yet born), the "Super Lab" still makes a good home keyboard today. Strong sounds, embryonic programmability and neat, customizable auto accompaniment features.

Kawai GMega
GM Sound module

Orig. price (1993)	$499 (£349)
Price in 1996	$350 (£250)
Keyboard	n/a
Sound type	Sample+ synthesis

A rather good GM module owing a lot to Kawai's K11 keyboard synth. A lot of tones, different tuning temperaments, editable effects and direct Macintosh interface. GMega LX is streamlined equivalent computer desktop model without a screen.

Kawai K1
Polyphonic synthesizer

See entry in Hot 100.

Spawned numerous modules and spin-offs including K1M (tabletop) and K1r (rackmount) and also K1II (see below).

Kawai K1II
Polyphonic synthesizer

Orig. price (1989)	$995 (£695)
Price in 1996	$350 (£300)
Keyboard	61-note
Sound type	Sample+ synthesis

Spurred on by the success of the K1, Kawai produced the K1II, adding drum sounds and digital effects. Modular K1rII has no effects, as it happens, but does have the punchy Kawai drum sounds.

Kawai K3
Polyphonic synthesizer

Orig. price (1986)	$1095 (£1045)
Price in 1996	$300 (£300)
Keyboard	61-note
Sound type	Digital/analog

Interesting hybrid synth based on 32 digital waveforms but with resonant filtering, EGs, etc. Thinnish sounds, best on plucky synth guitars, but becoming quite sought after. K3M a rackmount module.

Kawai K4
Polyphonic synthesizer

Orig. price (1990)	$1445 (£895)
Price in 1996	$500 (£400)
Keyboard	61-note
Sound type	Sample+ synthesis

Quite similar in approach to K1 (see main entry), founded on PCM or DC (Digital Cyclic) waveforms. Digital filtering (resonant) gives it plenty of zip, but keyboard is sluggish and the module K4R, for some inexplicable reason, comes without the effects.

Kawai K5
Polyphonic synthesizer

See entry in Hot 100.

Kawai K11
Polyphonic synthesizer

Orig. price (1993)	$899 (£749)
Price in 1996	$500 (£450)
Keyboard	61-note
Sound type	Sample+ synthesis

High resolution (18-bit) sampled waveforms in otherwise standard sample+ synthesis GM synthesizer. Programming includes digital resonant filters, but screen is small. Sounds unspectacular.

Kawai K5000W
Workstation

Orig. price (1996)	No U.S. price (no UK price)
Keyboard	61-note
Sound type	Advanced additive

Big additive synthesis workstation. Interesting.

Kawai KC10 Spectra
Polyphonic synthesizer

Orig. price (1991)	$695 (£449)
Price in 1996	$200 (£200)

Keyboard	61-note
Sound type	Sample+ synthesis

Homey version of the K4 using PCM and DC waves. Minimum editing available (no filtering as such) but comes with selection of drum patterns—useful for grooving over. Multitimbral.

Kawai KC20
Polyphonic synthesizer

Orig. price (1993)	$699 (£499)
Price in 1996	$400 (£275)
Keyboard	61-note
Sound type	PCM

General MIDI synth along GMega lines, with thoughtful quick setup MIDI features.

Kawai KSP30
Digital piano

Orig. price (1994)	$4000 (£3199)
Price in 1996	$1500 (£1000)
Keyboard	88-note
Sound type	Digital sampled

GM Home keyboard meets digital piano. KSP10 has smaller sequencer, and KSP5 has just 76-note keyboard.

Kawai M8000
Controller keyboard

Orig. price (1987)	$1895 (£1497)
Price in 1996	$750 (£700)
Keyboard	88-note
Sound type	NA

Weighted action controller, well presented and with just the right amount of control. Four MIDI Outs, four zones, aftertouch okay, but Kawai's lack of presence in high-end circles meant not many were sold.

Kawai MDK61
Controller keyboard

Orig. price (1993)	$499 (£399)
Price in 1996	$200 (£150)
Keyboard	61-note
Sound type	n/a

Slimline controller aimed at computer musicians. Capable of dialing up 1000 Program Change messages. The MIDIKEY II version claims be able to access 16,384 patches and also, rather more usefully, clips for "sling-on" roving keyboard playing.

Kawai MR300
Digital piano

Orig. price (1991)	$3000 (£1699)
Price in 1996	$750 (£500)
Keyboard	88-note
Sound type	Digital sampled

Surprisingly well executed digitals that "got away." Probably better than later CA models for the time. MR series includes MR120, -210, -3000 and -380.

Center: K1II: drum- and FX-sporting successor to Kawai's popular K1; Right: Kawai's undermarketed but sexy M8000 controller keyboard

Kawai P160
Digital piano

Orig. price (1988)	No U.S. price (£999)
Price in 1996	No U.S. price (£250)
Keyboard	76-note
Sound type	Digital sampled

The P series also includes 88-note models: the P260, -360, -1000 and -2500. All sport 10 piano-based tones capable of adding chorus and (on some) tremolo. Kawai's sampling technology still needed some work at this time.

Kawai PHm
Sound module

Orig. price (1989)	$375 (£350)
Price in 1996	$75 (£75)
Keyboard	n/a
Sound type	PCM

Another Kawai K1 reworking (see main entry) in plain-Jane black box form. Good value but could never compete with Roland MT-32 at the time.

Kawai PV35
Home keyboard

Orig. price (1991)	$2300 (£1499)
Price in 1996	$500 (£400)
Keyboard	61-note
Sound type	PCM

Home keyboard in digital piano hat. Disk drive, sequencer, EQ, chorus, reverb, plus 12 tones playable to 32-voice polyphony. Not bad effort. Also in the series: the PV30 (chorus, no reverb and card slot in place of disk drive) and PV10 (no sequencer, less power).

Kawai PX30
Home keyboard

Price in 1995	$599 (£349)
Price in 1996	$500 (£300)
Keyboard	61-note
Sound type	PCM

Kawai SX210
Polyphonic synthesizer

Orig. price (1983)	$1595 (£999)
Price in 1996	$200 (£175)
Keyboard	61-note
Sound type	Analog

DCO-based synth similar to SX240 without the MIDI, sequencer, chord memory and most of the other goodies that make the SX240 desirable. No mod wheel, either, quite a common Kawai anomaly.

Kawai SX240
Polyphonic synthesizer

See entry in Hot 100.

Kawai X20
Home keyboard

Orig. price (1993)	$250 (£175)
Price in 1996	$100 (£85)
Keyboard	61-note
Sound type	PCM

Small home keyboard but with 100 good PCM tones. X30 has semi velocity-sensitive (over three levels) keyboard and small playsequencer. X40D becomes a GM keyboard, and "Ad Lib" customizable arrangements and X50D add quality reverb and fairly useful sequencer. The X65D completes the current series. The "D" stands for the instruments "3D" sound. Well...

Kawai XS1
Sound module

Orig. price (1992)	$275 (£175)
Price in 1996	$100 (£85)
Keyboard	n/a
Sound type	PCM

Pre GM module along K4 lines incorporating PCM and DC waveforms. Multitimbral, with 16 multi locations, boasts some punchy Kawai drum sounds. Overshadowed by GMega.

Kawai Z1000
Home keyboard

Orig. price (1996)	No U.S. price (no UK price)
Keyboard	61-note
Sound type	Sample+ synthesis

"Entertainment keyboard" along similar lines of Technics KN series.

Keytek CTS 2000
Polyphonic synthesizer

Country of origin	Italy
Orig. price (1987)	$1995 (no UK price)
Price in 1996	$250 (no UK price)
Keyboard	61-note
Sound type	Digital sample

Short-lived "name" manufactured by Siel, who in turn was acquired by Roland a year or so after the CTS 2000. Interesting D50-ish concept, but factory programs were poor and programming hardly a breeze. CTS 400 a budget version (don't bother), and CTS 5000 76-note digital piano of similar ilk. All rather forgettable, I'm afraid.

Kinetic Sound Prism
Digital synthesizer

Orig. price (1982)	$29,000-46,000 (no UK price)
Price in 1996	No U.S. price (no UK price)
Keyboard	61-note x 2
Sound type	Multi (digital)

A large, fabulously expensive and horribly impractical multi synthesis (pre) workstation produced in limited (one?) quantities in the early 1980s. Sounded and looked incredible but offered too much, for too much, too soon.

Korg 01/W
Polyphonic synthesizer

Country of origin	Japan

See listing in Hot 100.

Korg 03/R
Polyphonic synthesizer module

Orig. price (1992)	$1299 (£999)
Price in 1996	$450 (£300)
Keyboard	n/a
Sound type	Sample+ synthesis

The modular equivalent of the 01/W (as the M3 is to the M1), which is to say very similar but with some key features missing. In this instance, no waveshaping parameter (for analog effects) and no sequencer. An early GM module with accordingly hesitant results. RE1 editor might save you going blind—or just mad—trying to program the thing.

Korg 05R/W
Polyphonic synthesizer module

Orig. price (1993)	$636 (£599)
Price in 1996	$400 (£300)
Keyboard	n/a
Sound type	Sample+ synthesis

Brilliant GM module with editing, effects and direct computer access to Mac or PC thrown in

for good measure. Superb drum kits and spacious 01/W-type sounds. The GM spec works fine with only minor aberrations.

Korg 707
Polyphonic synthesizer

Orig. price (1988)	$899 (£599)
Price in 1996	$250 (£200)
Keyboard	49-note
Sound type	Digital

Pretty much a cut-down DS-8, though with its radical looks and low cost, strangely a better buy and a more viable product. Dead easy to use, though not spectacularly powerful, useful and fun to look at. Made in a range of colors.

Korg 770
Monophonic synthesizer

Orig. price (1975)	$1099 (£475)
Price in 1996	$150 (£100)
Keyboard	32-note
Sound type	Analog

Neat and compact early Korg mono with two VCOs, filter, envelope generator, LFO, etc., plus ring mod and portamento. Never a classic but old and rare.

Korg 800-DV
Dual voice synthesizer

Orig. price (1975)	$1750 (£850)
Price in 1996	$200 (£200)
Keyboard	44-note
Sound type	Analog

"Performance" synth, curtailed and built for onstage use with no less than two voices playable simultaneously. Ancient Korg curio; interesting for its range of control inputs and obviously rare but not terribly valuable.

Korg 900-PS Preset
Monophonic synthesizer

Orig. price (1975)	$1200 (£550)
Price in 1996	$200 (£125)
Keyboard	37-note
Sound type	Analog

Fun little synth with unique touch bar running along the front panel for vibrato, portamento and other effects. Presets span tubas, bassoon, mandolin and funky trumpet (no less), plus there are many synth-like controls and effects.

Korg Audio Gallery
GM module

Orig. price (1993)	$330 (£399)
Price in 1996	$200 (£200)
Keyboard	n/a
Sound type	Digital samples

Computer module (32-voice) incorporating Korg's AI2 sound generation as found on the 01/W series pro synths. Tones are editable but only from a connected Mac computer via the built-in interface. Strong sounds and good features though not perhaps as universal as Roland's Sound Canvas equivalents.

Korg BX-3/CX-3
Stage organ

See Korg CX-3 entry in Hot 100.

Korg Concert C-15S
Digital piano

Orig. price (1993)	$1800 (£999)
Price in 1996	$1200 (£700)
Keyboard	88-note
Sound type	Digital samples

No effects on this basic but still top audio-quality digital.

Korg Concert C-30
Digital piano

Orig. price (1990)	$2750 (£1795)
Price in 1996	$800 (£650)
Keyboard	88-note
Sound type	Digital samples

Curious looking with two front legs, plus sort of plinth that houses the pedals. Revamped keyboard action and fancy-sounding technologies but the appearance, which makes it look as if it's about to topple over, was a major hindrance. Also C-40 and double polyphony (to 32-voice) C-50.

Korg Concert C-55
Digital piano

Orig. price (1991)	$2999 (£1999)
Price in 1996	$1000 (£750)
Keyboard	88-note
Sound type	Digital samples

Ten tones and generous 32-voice polyphony, plus digital effects. Heads up a series that is all 16-voice poly and includes the C-45, -35, -25 and -15. With each, you lose the odd tone or effect. C-15S has no effects at all, in fact. All reasonable pianos, though. The C-50G and C-50FP are grand piano design versions that also add brass and choir tones.

Korg Concert C-56
Digital piano

Orig. price (1993)	$4195 (£2600)
Price in 1996	$2000 (£1250)
Keyboard	88-note
Sound type	Digital samples

Plush, upmarket digital that came hot on the heels of Korg's weird three-legged C-55 series. Good range of 10 32-voice polyphonic tones and effects, plus small playsequencer. C-46 drops to 16-voice poly, C-36 loses one or two tones, C-26 loses the rather splendid strings tone and C-15S loses the effects section. C-56M is a rogue three-legged version of the C-56.

Korg Concert C-56G
Digital grand piano

Orig. price (1994)	$6350 (£3600)
Price in 1996	$4500 (£1950)
Keyboard	88-note
Sound type	Digital samples

Grand piano design using C-56 technology. The C-56FP "French Polished" version lists at $7200.

Korg Concert C-303
Digital piano

Orig. price (1994)	$2700 (£1499)
Price in 1996	$1500 (£750)
Keyboard	88-note
Sound type	Digital samples

With Steinway samples and new crossfade sampling technology, plus top quality reverbs, the C-303 can also respond multitimbrally to playback from a connected sequencer. Also slightly smaller C-505.

Korg Concert C-600
Digital piano

Orig. price (1989)	$2100 (£1160)
Price in 1996	$600 (£400)
Keyboard	76-note
Sound type	Digital samples

Six good quality tones on this short scale keyboard with modest 8W amplification system. C-800 adds surround sound reverb and 88-note keyboard.

Korg Concert C-3500
Digital piano

Orig. price (1987)	$2295 (£1499)
Price in 1996	$500 (£500)
Keyboard	88-note
Sound type	Digital samples

First of Korg's now long line of Concert Series digital pianos. Limited to five tones and modest speaker power but a reasonable play. Also C-2500, which has just three tones.

Korg Concert C-5000
Digital piano

Orig. price (1988)	$2795 (£1799)
Price in 1996	$600 (£600)
Keyboard	88-note
Sound type	Digital samples

Slightly modified version of C-3500, with five presets, plus some stereo reverbs. In this series, the top of the line. The C-7000 has stereo piano sample, too. The C-6000 has two additional presets.

Korg Concert C-5500
Digital piano

Orig. price (1990)	$2895 (£1899)
Price in 1996	$750 (£700)
Keyboard	88-note
Sound type	Digital samples

Interim model with nice action and seven presets. Quickly overshadowed by the C-30/50, etc. Also reverb-less C-4000.

Korg Concert C-9000
Digital piano

Orig. price (1989)	$4995 (£3700)
Price in 1996	$1500 (£1200)
Keyboard	88-note
Sound type	Digital samples

Grand piano casing version of the C-7000 with added sostenuto pedal. The C-7500 is an exact, upright equivalent. Pricey.

Korg Delta
Multi-instrument keyboard

Orig. price (1981)	$995 (£699)
Price in 1996	$200 (£200)
Keyboard	49-note
Sound type	Analog

Poor relation to the Trident. Synthy string machine in unspectacular style.

Korg DP-80
Digital piano

Orig. price (1986)	$1299 (£649)
Price in 1996	$400 (£200)
Keyboard	76-note
Sound type	Digital

Light-action keyboard but serviceable tones (16 of them) and a reasonable MIDI spec for the time.

Korg DP-2000C
Digital piano

Orig. price (1987)	$1999 (£999)
Price in 1996	$400 (£250)
Keyboard	76-note
Sound type	Digital

Okay feel and 30 tones to choose from on this pre Concert series digital and its 88-note partner, DP-3000C. EQ, ROM card loading of new sounds and a small playsequencer complete an attractive picture. You can also split and layer tones on the DP-3000C.

Korg DS-8
Polyphonic synthesizer

Orig. price (1987)	$1295 (£1099)
Price in 1996	$300 (£325)
Keyboard	61-note
Sound type	Digital

Analog-style version of FM synthesis on this oddball offering shortly before the amazing M1 technology started ruling the earth. Interesting for those after something different, but rather insipid sounds only partially offset by the good quality digital effects section.

Korg DSS-1
Digital sampler

Orig. price (1986)	$2499 (£2259)
Price in 1996	$750 (£500)
Keyboard	61-note
Sound type	Samples

Decidedly unique sampler which, aside from the modular DSM, proved to be Korg's first and last attempt at such an instrument (to date, anyway). Had some great sounds and features but eternally slow and a complete pain to use. Some still swear by it. Normal people would swear at it.

Korg DW-6000
Analog/digital synthesizer

Orig. price (1985)	$1195 (£774)
Price in 1996	$200 (£175)
Keyboard	61-note
Sound type	Analog/digital hybrid

Innovative but unrefined forerunner of the DW-8000 (see Hot 100) and beyond. Digital waveforms and analog editable but limited with non-velocity keyboard.

Korg DW-8000
Analog/digital synthesizer

See listing in Hot 100.

Korg EPS-1
Multi-instrument keyboard

Orig. price (1982)	$995 (£1099)
Price in 1996	$175 (£200)
Keyboard	76-note
Sound type	Analog

Ground-breaking with its 76-note velocity keyboard, but sounds, spanning pianos and strings, are uniformly average. Not hopeless, but no classic.

Korg i-1
Home keyboard

Orig. price (1995)	$5750 (£3300)
Price in 1996	$5000 (£2500)
Keyboard	88-note
Sound type	Sample+ synthesis

An i-3 with an 88-note weighted action keyboard, 40W stereo amplification system and enhanced user style memory.

Korg i-3
Home keyboard

Orig. price (1993)	$3250 (£2199)
Price in 1996	$2500 (£1200)
Keyboard	61-note
Sound type	Sample+ synthesis

Home keyboard for grown-up musicians. Caused shock throughout the industry upon its launch, due at least in part to this styles-based keyboard arriving without built-in speakers. Heart of an X series pro synth but with wonderfully intuitive backings and auto functions. Got off to difficult start, but with subsequent launch of other i-series instruments, Korg's message looks to be getting through. i-2 is the 76-note keyboard version ($3999).

Korg i-4S
Home keyboard

Orig. price (1995)	$2799 (£1599)
Price in 1996	$2000 (£1200)
Keyboard	61-note
Sound type	Sample+ synthesis

An i-3 with some new style components and 15W built-in amplification/speaker system. i-5S ($1399) is 61-note keyboard version.

Korg Lambda
Multi-instrument keyboard

Orig. price (1979)	$1650 (£999)
Price in 1996	$200 (£150)
Keyboard	48-note
Sound type	Analog

Organ, string, strings, brass machine of no particular merit. Brass sounds stand out from its otherwise undistinguished range of sounds. Poor value when new.

Korg LP-10
Electronic piano

Orig. price (1981)	$596 (£425)
Price in 1996	$100 (£75)
Keyboard	61-note
Sound type	Analog

Three tones, plus graphic equalizer. Doesn't look too bad, but sounds and features are fairly dismal. One of the first sightings of a key transposer.

Korg M-500 Micro Preset
Monophonic synthesizer

Orig. price (1978)	$700 (£300)
Price in 1996	$125 (£75)

Keyboard	32-note
Sound type	Analog

Tiny synth-cum-string machine following on from the M-500SP but with no speaker system. The fact that you can play two sounds at once, plus the smattering of synth controls, made this a fun piece of kit at the time.

Korg M-500SP Micro Preset
Monophonic synthesizer

Orig. price (1977)	$800 (£350)
Price in 1996	$125 (£85)
Keyboard	32-note
Sound type	Analog

Small preset synth with 30 "real instrument" sounds, plus sundry "synths." Internal speaker. Rare but of no special value

Korg M1
Polyphonic synthesizer

See listing in Hot 100.

Korg M3r
Polyphonic synthesizer module

Orig. price (1990)	$1000 (£899)
Price in 1996	$450 (£350)
Keyboard	n/a
Sound type	Sample+ synthesis

Slimmed down M1 but with fewer PCM samples, making sounds nontransferable between them. RE1 editor makes the otherwise tedious programming easier. Price difference between M3 and M1 module eroded over the years, making the M3 rather less desirable by comparison.

Korg Mini Korg 700S
Monophonic synthesizer

Orig. price (1973)	$999 (£350)
Price in 1996	$150 (£100)
Keyboard	37-note
Sound type	Analog

Korg's first synth: dual oscillator, monophonic, complete with curious features such as the Traveler (slider-operated filter mod), singing level and expand switch, in addition to two VCOs, VCF and simple envelope generator. Of considerable historic interest if nothing else.

Korg Mono/Poly
Analog synthesizer

See listing in Hot 100.

Korg MS-10/20
Analog synthesizer

See listing in Hot 100.

Korg MS-50
Analog synthesizer

Orig. price (1979)	$750 (£400)
Price in 1996	$125 (£150)
Keyboard	n/a
Sound type	Analog

An extension of the MS-20 (see Hot 100) but without a keyboard. All modules within this patch bay tabletop unit are independent, making this a programmer's dream. Quite sought after.

Korg OASYS
Polyphonic synthesizer

Orig. price (1996)	No U.S. price (no UK price)
Keyboard	61-note
Sound type	Physical modeling+

Wondersynth from the Korg satellite team based in Milpitas, California, that hailed from Sequential Circuits. Open-ended synthesis techniques, spearheaded by physical modeling. Still in development, though previewed—far too early—at the 1995 Winter NAMM show. Expensive.

Korg P3
Digital piano module

Orig. price (1988)	$595 (£399)
Price in 1996	$200 (£150)
Keyboard	n/a
Sound type	Digital samples

Highly underrated piano (plus) module, with cracking acoustic piano samples, plus ROM card slot for additional tones. Dead easy to use and a sound quality that belies its size and price. Well worth looking out for.

Korg PE-1000
Multi-instrument keyboard

Orig. price (1977)	$2100 (£900)
Price in 1996	$150 (£100)
Keyboard	60-note
Sound type	Analog

Seven presets, all in the piano category (Clavi, harpsichord, pianos, etc.), grace this tolex-clad semi-synth keyboard.

Korg PE-2000
Multi-instrument keyboard

Orig. price (1976)	$2300 (£950)
Price in 1996	$150 (£100)
Keyboard	48-note
Sound type	Analog

Three-oscillators per voice offered by this elderly, chunky synth-cum-strings/brass, organ instrument. Sophisticated controls for the era.

Korg Poly-61
Polyphonic synthesizer

See listing in Hot 100.

Korg Poly-800
Polyphonic synthesizer

See listing in Hot 100.

Korg Polysix
Polyphonic synthesizer

See listing in Hot 100.

Korg Prophecy
Monophonic synthesizer

Orig. price (1995)	$1250 (£999)
Price in 1996	$1000 (£900)
Keyboard	37-note
Sound type	Physical modeling+

First of Korg's mid-1990s physical modeling technology instruments: a dedicated lead-line synth to satisfy the current craze for synths "as they used to be." Wonderful to look at and play with pitch ribbon and inviting hands-on controls, multimode filters and effects and heartily endorsed by synth soloist supreme Rick Wakeman.

Korg PS-3200
Polyphonic synthesizer

See listing in Hot 100.

Korg PS-3300
Polyphonic synthesizer

Orig. price (1977)	$7000 (£5000)
Price in 1996	$4000+ (£3000+)
Keyboard	48-note
Sound type	Analog

A completely polyphonic synthesizer? Not even in the mid-1990s is there such a thing. But the PS-3300 does in fact boast some 48 separate and complete synthesizer circuits—one for each note on its externally connected keyboard. Related, of course, to the PS-3200 (see entry in Hot 100) with equally lush sounds. Rare, wonderful and valuable.

Korg RK-100
Remote keyboard

Orig. price (1984)	$495 (£499)
Price in 1996	$150 (£125)
Keyboard	41-note
Sound type	n/a

Solid sling-on released, in the first flush of enthusiasm for such instruments, in a range of four colors. Not a good seller but not a bad instrument.

Korg SAS-20
Home keyboard

Orig. price (1983)	$995 (£599)
Price in 1996	$175 (£75)
Keyboard	61-note
Sound type	Analog

Korg's first home keyboard, a full decade before its "first home keyboard" in the i-series. Oddball but not at all a bad effort with lots of flashing lights, reasonable tones and cunning "compu magic" chord recognition feature. Ahead of its time but only of (mild?) historic interest today.

Korg SG-1D
Digital piano

See entry in Hot 100.

Korg Sigma
Multi-instrument keyboard

Orig. price (1979)	$1400 (£700)
Price in 1996	$259 (£200)
Keyboard	37-note
Sound type	Analog

Could have been Korg's Yamaha CS80, but it wasn't to be. Nice ideas on this large synth-cum-organ/string/brass machine, but the sad fact is it doesn't sound very good.

Korg SP-80(S)
Electronic piano

Orig. price (1982)	$995 (£999)
Price in 1996	$175 (£125)
Keyboard	76-note
Sound type	Analog

Korg's debut into the home piano market. Touch-sensitive keyboard, speakers and (on "S" model) strings as additional preset. Good effort for the time though unlikely to have lasting value.

Korg Symphony
Multi-instrument module

Orig. price (1988)	$595 (£399)
Price in 1996	$125 (£100)
Keyboard	n/a
Sound type	Digital samples

Symphonic version of the P3 piano module. Simple to use and great preset sounds. Never caught on in the way it should have. A bargain.

Korg Synthe-Bass
Bass synthesizer

Orig. price (1978)	$800 (£350)
Price in 1996	$100 (£100)
Keyboard	25-note
Sound type	Analog

Tolex-clad bass synth with sine, square, pulse and sawtooth waveforms, plus rudimentary synth controls over tone and envelope. Packs up into a briefcase.

Korg T1
Polyphonic synthesizer

Orig. price (1989)	$5669 (£3700)
Price in 1996	$2000 (£1500)
Keyboard	88-note
Sound type	Sample+ synthesis

Inflated version of the M1 (see entry in Hot 100) physically and in terms of memory and upgradability (T1 can load in Korg DSS sample data). Weighted 88-note keyboard and built-in hard drive. T2 has 76-note synth action keyboard and none of the add-on/memory bells and whistles, and T3 has 61-note keyboard. "EX" versions of these instruments are expanded with sample RAM.

Korg Trident MkII
Polyphonic synthesizer

See entry in Hot 100.

Korg Trinity
Polyphonic synthesizer

Orig. price (1995)	$3599 (£2395)
Price in 1996	$3000 (£2000)
Keyboard	61-note
Sound type	Sample+ synthesis

New look and sounds from Korg midway through the decade. TouchView screen is slow but eye-catching and the sounds brilliant and lush as could only come from the peerless Korg voicing department. Still essentially analog editing applied to sample snippets, albeit expanded and expandable and with an effects section that's almost large enough to solve the single sound/multi sound effects problem. The synth to aspire to in the current marketplace. Trinity Plus ($3999) comes with added Korg Prophecy sound source as well. Trinity Pro ($4799) has 76-note keyboard, and Trinity Pro X ($6999) has 88-note weighted keyboard and the (current future) option of hard-disk recording, in order to add audio to the instrument's MIDI sounds and sequencing potential.

Korg VC-10
Vocoder

Orig. price (1978)	$1750 (£750)
Price in 1996	$300 (£200)
Keyboard	32-note
Sound type	Analog

Chunky unit resembling the MS-10 patch bay synth. With VU meter, minimal controls over input and output signals, plus vibrato and five jack patch bay, friendly yet exciting to use. Rare. Quite sought after.

Korg Wavestation
Polyphonic synthesizer

See entry in Hot 100.

Korg X3
Polyphonic synthesizer

Orig. price (1993)	$1999 (£1399)
Price in 1996	No U.S. price (no UK price)
Keyboard	61-note
Sound type	Sample+ synthesis

Pared-down version of 01/W launched, some said, to nail the M1 in its coffin. That didn't work, but the X series itself has proved popular nonetheless. Less physical gloss than 0 series but great sounds. X3R is the module. X2 is 76-note keyboard version and additional piano sample, released in 1995.

Korg X5D
Polyphonic synthesizer

Orig. price (1995)	$895 (£1300)
Price in 1996	$800 (£1000)
Keyboard	61-note
Sound type	Sample+ synthesis

Keyboard version of slightly earlier success story, the 64-voice polyphonic, half rack X5DR. Time-honored AI2 synthesis engine with 8MB PCM waveform memory and built-in PC interface. For the computer-inclined who wants to have a crack at playing.

Kurzweil 1000 Series
Polyphonic synthesizer modules

Country of origin	U.S.
Orig. price (1987)	$2495 (£2200)
Price in 1996	$1000 (£800)
Keyboard	n/a
Sound type	Digital

Quality modules drawing on the 250 sound library based on the K1000. All rated at 20-voice polyphony and offering at-the-time-peerless examples of their namesake, the series included the general instrument PX Professional Expander, HX Horn Expander, GX Guitar Expander and SX String Expander. "Plus" versions with additional sounds also made. And, just to confuse and befuddle a little more, the AX Plus is a combination of SX and HX units. Have a drink!

Kurzweil 150
Fourier synthesizer

Orig. price (1987)	No U.S. price (no UK price)
Price in 1996	No U.S. price (no UK price)
Keyboard	n/a
Sound type	Additive, Fourier

Innovative but limited appeal additive synth utilizing some 240 independent oscillators, which can be used to "model" sound parameters. Sound Lab Apple IIe editing and programming package made available, but the 150 was far too ahead of its time to catch on with the general public.

Kurzweil 250
Digital sampler

See entry in Hot 100.

Kurzweil 250 RMX
Digital sampler

See Kurzweil 250 entry in Hot 100.

Kurzweil EGP-K
Digital piano

Orig. price (1987)	$2500 (£2200)
Price in 1996	$750 (£800)
Keyboard	76-note
Sound type	Digital

Slimmed down, tabletop version of Ensemble Grande with 76-note keyboard. Wide range of presets (100) for what was essentially designed as a digital piano. 12W stereo amplification.

Kurzweil Ensemble Grande
Digital piano

Orig. price (1987)	$2500 (no UK price)
Price in 1996	$750 (no UK price)
Keyboard	88-note
Sound type	Digital

Most commonly seen in its Mark III and Mark IV versions. Home pianos, nicely finished with rosewood cabinets. 100 presets taken from Kurzweil 250 library.

Kurzweil K1000
Polyphonic synthesizer

Orig. price (1987)	$2495 (£2195)
Price in 1996	$650 (£500)
Keyboard	76-note
Sound type	Sample+ synthesis

Full keyboard version of Kurzweil's (perhaps better known) PX modules—all of whom plunder 250 library of samples for their sound generation. Convoluted life, with many expansions and versions: SE, SE II and SE II/EXT indicating upgrades to the software. Good sounds and polyphony (24-voice) for the time. Good buy second-hand.

Kurzweil K1200
Polyphonic synthesizer

Orig. price (1991)	$2599 (£1899)
Price in 1996	$700 (£800)
Keyboard	88-note
Sound type	Sample+ synthesis

Another in the everlasting series of Kurzweil instruments whose sounds are based upon the 250 sample library. Generous (for 1991) 6MB sample memory and equally generous storage potential of some 1000 edited programs. Kurzweil Pro-76 is a 76-note keyboard version

Kurzweil K2000
Polyphonic synthesizer

See entry in Hot 100.

Kurzweil K2500
Polyphonic synthesizer/sampler

Orig. price (1995)	$4720 (£3500)
Price in 1996	$4720 (£3500)
Keyboard	76-note
Sound type	Digital/sampling

Extension of the phenomenally successful K2000 (see entry in Hot 100) but with 48-voice polyphony, vast amounts of sample memory, major sequencer and, even on this basic model, a 76-note keyboard. Available in many forms, from the rackmount K2500R (also available in RS, "S" for user sampling option), K2500S (ditto) and top of the line K2500-SX ($6085), featuring an 88-note weighted keyboard, user sampling and maximum memory expansion.

Kurzweil Mark 5
Digital piano

Orig. price (1993)	$2895 (£2589)
Price in 1996	$2000 (£2000)
Keyboard	88-note
Sound type	Digital

In Kurzweil's home-based series. Pleasant-looking digital with 32-voice polyphony, 23 tones and a 25W quad amplification system. Multi-timbral.

Kurzweil Mark 10
Digital piano/home keyboard

Orig. price (1993)	$4295 (£3699)
Price in 1996	$3500 (£3000)
Keyboard	88-note
Sound type	Digital

Large, impressive-looking piano-cum-home keyboard complete with 86 tones and 32 preset music accompaniment styles. With its 130W quad amplification system, a heavyweight performer.

Kurzweil Mark 12
Digital piano

Orig. price(1996)	No U.S. price (no UK price)
Keyboard	88-note
Sound type	Digital

Current new kid on the block—a supercharged version of the Mark 10 in slimmer, more traditional upright form.

Kurzweil Mark 150
Grand piano/home keyboard

Orig. price (1993)	$10,000 (£8000)
Price in 1996	$7500 (£5500)
Keyboard	88-note
Sound type	Digital

Grand piano version of the Mark 10. Even more impressive, visually and aurally, with its massive 200Wt amplification system.

Kurzweil MicroPiano
Digital piano module

Orig. price (1994)	$525 (£625)
Price in 1996	$450 (£400)
Keyboard	n/a
Sound type	Digital

With essentially the same voice-producing capability of Kurzweil's Mark 150, the Micro-Piano is a bargain, price and spacewise. Not a great deal of control offered but 32 tones and 32-voice polyphony, plus reverbs and chorus. Simple to operate. Recommended.

Kurzweil MIDIBoard
Master keyboard

Orig. price (1986)	$2495 (£1835)
Price in 1996	$1000 (£750)
Keyboard	88-note
Sound type	n/a

Luxurious controller keyboard; great to play if less than wholly reliable or fathomable. Lots of controls and controllers, but well past its sell-by date.

Kurzweil PC-88
Polyphonic synthesizer

Orig. price (1994)	$2495 (£2100)
Price in 1996	$2200 (£1750)
Keyboard	88-note
Sound type	Sample+ synthesis

Smart master keyboard meets synthesizer, plus, on the latest "MX" version ($2950), master keyboard meets synth meets GM module.

Strong sounds, easy to operate and nice, mid-weight action keyboard.

Kurzweil Pro 1
Polyphonic synthesizer

Orig. price (1991)	$2599 (£1899)
Price in 1996	$700 (£700)
Keyboard	n/a
Sound type	Digital

Module of the K1200.

Kurzweil RG-100
Digital piano

Orig. price (1994)	$1495 (£999)
Price in 1996	$1495 (£999)
Keyboard	88-note
Sound type	Digital

Simple, streamline piano ideal for gigging or rehearsing. Built-in speakers and just four tones. No frills but good action and seemingly well made.

Kurzweil RG-200
Digital piano

Orig. price (1994)	$2395 (£1750)
Price in 1996	$2000 (£1750)
Keyboard	88-note
Sound type	Digital

Similar to RG-100 but with 12 tones and digital effects. Quite a lot more money for features that could be supplied externally.

Kustom 88
Digital piano

Orig. price (1981)	No U.S. price (no UK price)
Price in 1996	No U.S. price (no UK price)
Keyboard	88-note
Sound type	Digital

Baldwin-built early digital that came and went in a flash in the early 1980s. Few were made, so rare but hardly sought after.

Logan String Melody
String machine 78

Country of origin	Italy

See entry in Hot 100.

Lync LN-4
Remote keyboard

Country of origin	U.S.
Orig. price (1988)	$1325 (no UK price)
Price in 1996	$450 (no UK price)
Keyboard	49-note
Sound type	n/a

Phallic remote keyboard; sleek, stylish and pricey. Had a brief flurry of name user interest

Right: Missing Lync? Jan Hammer in ecstasy over the Lync controller

164

but never crossed over into general public acceptance. Can communicate on four MIDI channels simultaneously and access 64 MIDI programs. The LN-1, even rarer and more expensive than the LN-4, was released as early as 1985.

Lync LN-1000
Remote keyboard

Orig. price (1992)	$799 (£599)
Price in 1996	$350 (£350)
Keyboard	49-note
Sound type	n/a

Lync's more sensibly priced version of the LN-4. Full 128 MIDI program access, but one channel at a time. Aftertouch keyboard, pitch and a second assignable wheel and nice big volume knob. Good keyboard, but Lync went AWOL before the LN-1000's undoubted appeal could convert into meaningful sales.

Marion Systems MSR-2
Polyphonic synthesizer module

Country of origin	U.S.
Orig. price (1993)	$1695 (£1349)
Price in 1996	$1200 (£1200)
Keyboard	n/a
Sound type	Analog

Good value for analog lovers who need all the programming bells and whistles and don't mind working fairly hard for the results. Flexible in terms of MIDI and voices (you can double the 16-voice polyphony with slot-in "ASM" card).

Marion Systems ProSynth
Polyphonic synthesizer module

Orig. price (1995)	$1149 (£699)
Price in 1996	$1149 (£600)
Keyboard	n/a
Sound type	Analog

Brave attempt to offer an inexpensive glimpse into the past from one of the synthesizer's founding fathers, Tom Oberheim. Eight-voice analog system in slimline rackmount format. Sounds are somewhat lackluster though.

Mellotron 400
Multi-instrument keyboard

Country of origin	UK
Orig. price (1970)	No U.S. price (£800)
Price in 1996	No U.S. price (£1500+)
Keyboard	35-note
Sound type	Analog tape replay

Slimmed down, single keyboard Mellotron, generally more rugged and therefore practical to own. See entry in Hot 100.

Mellotron Mark I
Multi-instrument keyboard

Orig. price (1963)	No U.S. price (£1000)
Price in 1996	No U.S. price (no UK price)
Keyboard	35-note (x2)
Sound type	Analog tape replay

First (British) Mellotron very firmly based on the American Chamberlin. Tape-based monster of an instrument that plays back recordings of "real" instruments or vocals. Valve amplification and suitably snarly and noisy. Museum piece.

Mellotron Mark II
Multi-instrument keyboard

Orig. price (1964)	No U.S. price (£1000)
Price in 1996	No U.S. price (£2000+)
Keyboard	35-note x 2
Sound type	Analog tape replay

Revamped and vaguely more reliable version of the Mark I. The "Melly" was used on most of the classic '60s and '70s recordings (Beatles, Moody Blues, etc.). A labor of love to own, more collector's piece than serious piece of musical equipment for prolonged, active use. See entry in Hot 100.

Mellotron "Novatron"
Multi-instrument keyboard

Orig. price (1978)	No U.S. price (£1400)
Price in 1996	No U.S. price (£2000+)
Keyboard	35-note
Sound type	Analog tape replay

Late model "Mellotron" produced as the company was changing its name. See Mellotron entries in Hot 100.

Moog Liberation
Remote monophonic synthesizer+

Country of origin	U.S.
Orig. price (1980)	$1395 (£800)
Price in 1996	$1000 (£500)
Keyboard	44-note
Sound type	Analog

High-profile sling-on keyboard with sounds. Used by people like Devo, Tom Coster and Herbie Hancock. Dual oscillator synth with raspy Moog filtering, aftertouch keyboard and pitch ribbon. Slider controls an additional polyphonic organ tone. Heavy.

Moog Memorymoog
Polyphonic synthesizer

See entry in Hot 100.

Moog Micromoog
Monophonic synthesizer

Orig. price (1976)	$895 (£800)
Price in 1996	$300 (£300)
Keyboard	32-note
Sound type	Analog

One oscillator version of the Mini. Pink noise, 24dB/oct self-oscillating lowpass filter, pitch ribbon and mod wheel. Reasonable substitute for Minimoog though with less power.

Moog Minimoog
Monophonic synthesizer

See entry in Hot 100.

Moog Multimoog
Monophonic synthesizer

See entry in Hot 100.

Moog Opus 3
Multi-instrument keyboard

Orig. price (1981)	$1995 (£700)
Price in 1996	$250 (£250)
Keyboard	49-note
Sound type	Analog

Poorly received, if not conceived, synth-cum-string machine. Substantially different from Moog's regular instruments with its quasi drawbar organ sliders, multi-pitched brass tone and strings section, the Opus was aimed at the instant gratification market. A small envelope generator, simple filter, chorus and vibrato can be used to modify tones—in real time only.

Moog Polymoog
Polyphonic synthesizer

Orig. price (1977)	$5295 (£3000)
Price in 1996	$1000 (£600)
Keyboard	71-note
Sound type	Analog

One of the earliest polyphonic synthesizers and so important for that fact alone. Eight presets, modifiable using numerous front and rear panel buttons, switches and sliders. With polyphony available through use of shared, divide-down oscillators, the sound is comparatively weak if still unique. There are keen users and collectors, though not this author.

Moog Polymoog Keyboard
Polyphonic synthesizer

Orig. price (1978)	$3995 (£2100)
Price in 1996	$800 (£500)
Keyboard	71-note
Sound type	Analog

Streamlined version of the above with 14 presets modifiable with simple vibrato, filter and envelope controls. Pitch ribbon. Sold well, so not terribly rare, but will only appeal to purists looking for a genuine old Moog.

Moog Prodigy
Monophonic synthesizer

See entry in Hot 100.

Moog Rogue
Monophonic synthesizer

Orig. price (1981)	$545 (£325)
Price in 1996	$200 (£175)
Keyboard	32-note
Sound type	Analog

Rather ordinary late-model mono synth with nothing spectacular onboard. Dual oscillators, though not fully independent, and simple envelope generator shared between filter and amplifier. Some people appreciate its simplicity and appreciate one or two of its control features, but most people view the Rogue as a poor relation.

Moog Satellite
Monophonic synthesizer

Orig. price (1974)	$750 (£375)
Price in 1996	$150 (£125)
Keyboard	37-note
Sound type	Analog

Made under license by Thomas Organs, a starter Moog mainly as add-on instrument for organists. Single oscillator design within a range of "real instrument" facsimiles. Not terribly inspiring.

Moog Sonic Six
Duophonic synthesizer

Orig. price (1974)	$1500 (£900)
Price in 1996	$500 (£400)
Keyboard	37-note
Sound type	Analog

Center: Seventies pro vocoder from synth specialists Moog

Portable 2-voice analog with speakers in Minimoog vein. Good control features. Quite rare.

Moog Source
Monophonic synthesizer

See entry in Hot 100.

Moog Taurus Pedals
Bass pedals

Orig. price (1976)	$1300 (£700)
Price in 1996	$350 (£350)
Keyboard	13-note
Sound type	Analog

Clumpy set of synth bass pedals with three presets, plus semi-programmable tone that, on plain Taurus setting or with a little detune, delivers wall-crumbling bass that no other instrument can come close to. A one-trick pony, perhaps, but some trick. Taurus II has 18 notes.

Multivox MX-880
Multi-instrument keyboard

Orig. price (1978)	$1300 (£700)
Price in 1996	$2500 (£200)
Keyboard	37-note
Sound type	Analog

Preset synth meets string/brass machine of no high distinction.

Multivox MX-3000
Multi-instrument keyboard

Orig. price (1978)	$3000 (£1300)
Price in 1996	$300 (£250)
Keyboard	61-note
Sound type	Analog

Large, quite sophisticated but still over-priced instrument that borrowed heavily from its more established peers. Programmable synth features sit uneasily alongside piano, strings and brass presets.

Novation BassStation
Bass synthesizer

Country of origin	UK
Orig. price (1994)	$649 (£299)
Price in 1996	$600 (£250)
Keyboard	37-note
Sound type	Digital/analog

Dedicated monophonic bass synth from experienced British design team under new company banner of Novation. Smattering of presets, plus remarkably full complement of programming parameters complete with auto-glide, portamento and choice of 24dB/oct or "TB-303-style 12dB/oct filtering." Great fun to play and, over MIDI, the keyboard itself kicks out full polyphony. BassStation Rack has improved high end, many more memories and more MIDI control such as MIDI-clockable LFO.

Novation MM10
Controller keyboard

Orig. price (1991)	$219 (£99)
Price in 1996	$100 (£50)
Keyboard	25-note
Sound type	n/a

Dinky controller keyboard whose initial inspiration was to alleviate the problems associated with playing one of Yamaha's QY-10 "Walkstations." Tiny but portable, surprisingly flexible and with full-size keys. MM10X replaces the LED screen with LCD and irons out some of the original model's quirkiness. Essentially the same beast.

Right: Heart of Oberheim's pre-MIDI "system": the OB-Xa

Oberheim 4-voice
Polyphonic synthesizer

Country of origin	U.S.

See entry in Hot 100.

Oberheim 8-voice
Polyphonic synthesizer

See Oberheim 4-Voice entry in Hot 100.

Oberheim DPX-1
Sample playback module

Orig. price (1987)	$2095 (£1549)
Price in 1996	$500 (£300)
Keyboard	n/a
Sound type	Samples

2U module for sample playback, tapping into disk libraries of (at the time) E-mu, Sequential, Ensoniq and Akai. Great idea that never caught on. Happy users no doubt exist but supremely brave to investigate for the first time, some 10 years after its release.

Oberheim Eclipse
Digital piano

Countries of origin	U.S./Italy
Orig. price (1993)	$2495 (no UK price)
Price in 1996	$2000 (no UK price)
Keyboard	88-note
Sound type	Sample

Produced with Viscount of Italy for U.S. market only. Simple but effective piano offering good sounds and effective rather than extensive MIDI control in pre flight cased design. Additional strings tone on a slider.

Oberheim Matrix-6
Polyphonic synthesizer

Orig. price (1985)	$1695 (£1350)
Price in 1996	$400 (£350)
Keyboard	61-note
Sound type	Analog

Produced long after departure of Tom Oberheim and certainly not viewed (yet, anyway) as a classic. Spongy little keyboard and only 6-voice polyphony but capable of attractive sounds and useful as programmer for Matrix-1000 with whom it shares a basic voice architecture. Produced in module form as Matrix-6R.

Oberheim Matrix-12
Polyphonic synthesizer

See entry in Hot 100.

Oberheim Matrix-1000
Polyphonic synthesizer module

See entry in Hot 100.

Oberheim OB-1
Monophonic synthesizer

See entry in Hot 100.

Oberheim OB-3
Stage organ/module

Countries of origin	U.S./Italy
Orig. price (1995)	$799 (no UK price)
Price in 1996	$500 (no UK price)
Keyboard	61-note
Sound type	Electronic

Produced in conjunction with Viscount in Italy, initially just as a tabletop unit but later in keyboard version as well. Workaday as opposed to inspired, but with strong, hands-on organ tones employing drawbar control, plus sensible

presets and lifelike rotary speaker, overdrive and key click features. Only 8-voice. Released in 1996: 24-voice polyphony, OB-3 2 (squared) version ($1295), stereo, with added reverb.

Oberheim OB-8
Polyphonic synthesizer

See entry in Hot 100.

Oberheim OB-8K
Polyphonic synthesizer

Orig. price (1989)	$1295 (no UK price)
Price in 1996	No U.S. price (no UK price)
Keyboard	61-note
Sound type	Analog

Eight-voice multitimbral synth that trickled out at the end of the 1980s. Basically an 8-voice version of the Matrix-6 meets Oberheim XK controller keyboard. Very few ever saw the light of day.

Oberheim OB-MX
Polyphonic synthesizer

Orig. price (1994)	$2995+ (£1799+)
Price in 1996	$2000+ (£1500+)
Keyboard	n/a
Sound type	Analog

Folly produced by Oberheim—by now little more than a paper company within the Gibson empire—with help from synth pioneer Don Buchla. Interesting concept of hands-on module combining Oberheim, Moog and other technologies and filter designs but miserably uncontrollable (surprise, surprise) and most of the sounds ex-factory are abysmal. Price is for 2-voice system. Expandable.

Oberheim OB-SX
Polyphonic synthesizer

Orig. price (1980)	$2995 (£1500)
Price in 1996	$600 (£500)
Keyboard	61-note
Sound type	Analog

Minimally editable Oberheim released in several memory/factory program versions. Real-time controls do extend to LFO rate, filter cutoff, etc., plus there's chord/note hold feature, portamento and unison. Good value for analog sounds, without specific programming features.

Oberheim OB-X
Polyphonic synthesizer

Orig. price (1979)	$5995 (£3250)
Price in 1996	$600 (£500)
Keyboard	61-note
Sound type	Analog

First of Oberheim's classic OB synths very much in mold of Prophet-5 et al. Produced in a number of polyphony versions, from 2-voice to 8-voice. Warm sounds but only 2-pole filtering.

Oberheim OB-Xa
Polyphonic synthesizer

Orig. price (1981)	$5995 (£3250)
Price in 1996	$700 (£600)

Keyboard	61-note
Sound type	Analog

Similar to OB-X with additional split/layer feature and program memories. Filter has choice of 2-pole/4-pole. Just pre-MIDI though kits were made. OB-Xa was centerpiece of Oberheim's recording system that included DMX drum machine and DSX sequencer.

Oberheim SEM
Monophonic synthesizer module

See Oberheim 4-voice entry in Hot 100.

Oberheim XK
Remote keyboard

Orig. price (1985)	$995 (£1150)
Price in 1996	$250 (£300)
Keyboard	61-note
Sound type	n/a

Not bad effort with release velocity and aftertouch, plus zoning, memories, arpeggiator, chord latch, etc., but produced at a critically bad time in Oberheim's eventful, yo-yo life and, therefore, failed to make much impact.

Oberheim Xpander
Polyphonic synthesizer

See Oberheim Matrix-12 entry in Hot 100.

Octave Cat
Duophonic synthesizer

Country of origin	U.S.
Orig. price (1977)	$799 (£792)
Price in 1996	$150 (£150)
Keyboard	37-note
Sound type	Analog

Mass market mono (okay, duo) synth of late '70s that sort of climbed on board the ARP bandwagon. Light on performance controls and not very user friendly. Released in "SRM" and "SRM II" versions. Wow, or perhaps that should be Meow!

Octave Kitten
Monophonic synthesizer

Orig. price (1978)	$599 (£575)
Price in 1996	$100 (£100)
Keyboard	37-note
Sound type	Analog

One-oscillator version of the above. Same reservations, worse sound.

Octave-Plateau Voyetra Eight
Polyphonic synthesizer

See entry in Hot 100.

Orla Commander
Controller keyboard

Country of origin	Italy
Orig. price (1993)	No U.S. price (£1180)

Price in 1996	No U.S. price (£800)
Keyboard	88-note
Sound type	n/a

Flight-cased heavyweight from Italy with lots of dedicated knobs and sliders, four MIDI Outs and the chance to coordinate not just MIDI sound patches but sequences and tempo as well. Comprehensive unit and good value.

Orla Concerto C10-H
Digital piano

Orig. price (1995)	No U.S. price (no UK price)
Price in 1996	No U.S. price (no UK price)
Keyboard	88-note
Sound type	Digital samples

"H" for Hammer Action option on this, the first in a series of Orla digitals that includes C-30, plus the accompaniment-sporting C-40 and C-50D. C-10 starts with just six main tones, plus three background tones, while the C-50D's offering is in the hundreds.

Orla Concerto C-8800
Digital piano

Orig. price (1991)	No U.S. price (£1399)
Price in 1996	No U.S. price (£650)
Keyboard	88-note
Sound type	Digital samples

Low cost digital from Italian organ specialists. Sixteen tones and 16-voice, with 25W stereo amplification. Nothing staggering, but a bargain original list price.

Orla KX-750
Home keyboard

Orig. price (1993)	No U.S. price (£1899)
Price in 1996	No U.S. price (£850)
Keyboard	61-note
Sound type	Sample+ synthesis

Organ-oriented home keyboard, featuring actual drawbars in addition to presets, styles, effects and built-in amplification system.

Oxford Synthesizer Company OSCar
Duophonic synthesizer

Country of origin	UK

See entry in Hot 100.

Pearl PK-801
Multi-instrument keyboard

Country of origin	U.S.
Orig. price (1979)	$1995 (£995)
Price in 1996	$200 (£125)
Keyboard	73-note
Sound type	Analog

Oddball one-off release. Looks a bit like a Polymoog (heaven help it) and features a number of keyboard and orchestral instrument presets on which some tweaking can be carried out. Sturdy and well thought out, but as Pearl's one and only (?) keyboard offering, it clearly didn't sell.

Peavey C8
Controller keyboard

Country of origin	U.S.
Orig. price (1992)	$1999 (£1799)
Price in 1996	$1200 (£1200)
Keyboard	88-note
Sound type	n/a

Majestic offering available in range of glossy colors. Nice, if not peerless, to play and offers a wide, though not exhaustive, range of MIDI control. Features include 4 MIDI Outs, channel aftertouch, large display and DOS-compatible disk drive. Looks the biz. C8p ($1599) is

slightly more portable, loses the disk drive, is less glossy, but adds a data wheel. Designed for stage use.

Peavey Cyberbass
Polyphonic synthesizer module

Orig. price (1994)	$999 (£899)
Price in 1996	$900 (£750)
Keyboard	n/a
Sound type	Sample

Interesting 1U module housing a wide range of synth and drum samples, plus the chance to load in additional user samples. Six polyphonic outputs, dual effects, 16-voice poly, memory card.

Peavey DK 20 Millenium
Digital piano

Orig. price (1994)	$2599 (no UK price)
Price in 1996	$1750 (no UK price)
Keyboard	88-note
Sound type	Digital samples

Dogged effort from Peavey that was riddled with awkward sounds and feel upon release but has been slowly upgraded and improved with age. Peavey is not known for its pianos and here's why. DK 40 not only has additional sounds but plug-in daughterboard option for upgrading with non-Peavey material.

Peavey DPM 2
Polyphonic synthesizer

Orig. price (1990)	$1299 (£999)
Price in 1996	$500 (£500)
Keyboard	61-note
Sound type	Sample+ synthesis

Peavey's second synth following on the heels of the DPM 3 to which it is very similar. Digital Phase Modulation-based (sample+ synthesis by another name), a good all-round synth with okay sounds, effects, drum kits and, in true Peavey fashion, oodles of upgrades. Module is DPM V2.

Peavey DPM 3
Polyphonic synthesizer

Orig. price (1990)	$1299 (£999)
Price in 1996	$650 (£500)
Keyboard	61-note
Sound type	Sample+ synthesis

Peavey's debut synth and not a bad effort either. Trail-blazer in upgradability though the network of add-ons and enhancements make it a nightmare to judge on the second hand market (indicated 1996 s/h price is for basic model). Interesting, rather than special. DPM V3 quite a pleasant and good value 1U module.

Peavey DPM 4
Polyphonic synthesizer

Orig. price (1993)	$2299 (£1999)
Price in 1996	$1200 (£1500)
Keyboard	61-note
Sound type	Sample+ synthesis

Left: 1983: Bad time to launch initially non-MIDI Voyetra Eight; Right: Peavey's first ever synth: the DPM3

You can almost seamlessly upgrade from a DPM 3 to a DPM 4 using Peavey's generous system of upgrades and add-ons. An out of the box DPM 4 comes with 10MB sample waveform and 512KB of user sample memory. 32-voice poly, two multi effects processors and 100 programs complete an attractive, if not earth-shattering picture.

Peavey DPM 488
Polyphonic synthesizer

Orig. price (1993)	$2799 (£2499)
Price in 1996	$2200 (no UK price)
Keyboard	88-note
Sound type	Sample+ synthesis

Fully expanded DPM 3 in a beautiful wooden cabinet with controller keyboard features aplenty. Bit of a mishmash of applications, but pretty to look at and pleasing to play.

Peavey DPM SI
Polyphonic synthesize

Orig. price (1993)	$1699 (£1399)
Price in 1996	$1200 (£1000)
Keyboard	76-note
Sound type	Sample+ synthesis

Extra keyboard length version of the DPM 2 with most of that instrument's trimmings as standard. Expandable itself to 500 sounds using card option. Positive feel keyboard and good internal effects.

Peavey DPM SP
Sample playback module

Orig. price (1991)	$999 (£379)
Price in 1996	$300 (£300)
Keyboard	n/a
Sound type	Digital samples

Highly cost-effective sampling system comprising SP playback module, available in memory upgradable versions from 2 to 32MB. Peavey's dual-pronged approach to sampling includes the DMP SX module, which you need if you also want to record samples yourself. SP offers fine complement of digital editing tools, plus analog-style editing with filters and envelopes. Small screen editing not brilliant but bargain-priced system where you only pay for what you need. Price listed is for SP unit only. SX (now in Mark II mode) lists new at $399. SP Plus ($1299) doubles polyphony to 32-voice and can load Akai S1000 library from SCSI. Regular SP unit also has Akai-loading upgrade available.

Peavey Spectrum Bass
Bass synthesizer module

Orig. price (1992)	$299 (£279)
Price in 1996	$250 (£200)
Keyboard	n/a
Sound type	Sample+ synthesis

Generous number of programs (200) on this sample playback module full of bass sounds—fingered, Moog, slap, upright, FM, vocal, you name them. Editing over MIDI SysEx only, but simple panel, immediate control and good price should suffice. Not overly powerful but wide range of sounds. Spectrum Bass II ($399) is programmable (even if it still requires some form of external programming device) with 64 RAM locations and is 12-voice polyphonic.

Peavey Spectrum Organ
Organ module 95

Orig. price (1995)	$399 (£349)
Price in 1996	$350 (£300)
Keyboard	n/a
Sound type	Sample+ synthesis

Good value organ module with huge span of organ tones. Minimal editing by itself, but with Peavey's PC1600 MIDI sliders in tow, you can edit and even record real-time tonal changes into your sequencer.

Peavey Spectrum Synth
Polyphonic synthesizer

Orig. price (1992)	$399 (£349)
Price in 1996	$250 (£250)
Keyboard	n/a
Sound type	Sample+ synthesis

Dual oscillator module with almost 1000 "classic" synth presets offered in multitimbral, 12-voice polyphony format. Minimal editing and simple control panel. Excellent value if not for purists.

PPG PRK
Controller keyboard

Country of origin	Germany
Orig. price (1984)	$5000 (£3666)
Price in 1996	No U.S. price (no UK price)
Keyboard	72-note
Sound type	n/a

Processor Keyboard produced by PPG to accompany its Waveterm-based sampling and recording system in the mid-1980s. High-speed disk drive and wooden keyboard action made it expensive—too expensive to be viable, in fact.

PPG Realizer
Polyphonic synthesizer

Orig. price (1986)	No U.S. price (£30-40,000)
Price in 1996	$1200 (£1200)
Keyboard	n/a
Sound type	Multi synthesis

A wonderful idea whose day is perhaps even yet to come. Back in 1986, an instrument capable of replicating different synthesis and recording technologies in software was little more than a dream. Indeed, sadly, that is what the Realizer turned out to be. Few, if any, production models were made, and PPG itself soon splintered into a number of separate OEM design houses.

PPG Wave 2.2/2.3
Polyphonic synthesizer

See PPG Wave 2.3 entry in Hot 100.

PPG Wave Computer 340/380
Modular synthesizer system

Orig. price (1979)	No U.S. price (no UK price)
Price in 1996	No U.S. price (no UK price)
Keyboard	n/a
Sound type	Digital wavetable

Forerunner of Wave keyboard synths. Initially built for Tangerine Dream and subsequently used by Thomas Dolby on such memorable early tracks as "Windpower," on which Dolby attributes the germ of the idea to the Wave Computer's inherent fuzziness and crunchiness of its "incompatible" waves and (the sequenced 16ths) in "Flying North."

PianoDisk Series
Acoustic/MIDI player pianos

Country of origin	U.S.
Orig. price (1993)	$5500+ (no UK price)
Price in 1996	No U.S. price (no UK price)
Keyboard	88-note
Sound type	Acoustic

Large series of add-on and pre-fitted units/-instruments that give MIDI input control to an acoustic piano. Series embraces small upright models to full size grands complete with sequencing and jukebox facilities. Well established company in this curious but fast-growing field.

Quasimidi Quasar
Polyphonic synthesizer module

Country of origin	Germany
Orig. price (1994)	$1795 (£995)
Price in 1996	$1500 (£900)
Keyboard	n/a
Sound type	Multi synthesis

Module full of hard-edged sounds beloved by the techno boys. Multi synthesis is interesting if complex, but with drum kits, effects, arpeggiator and even GM compatibility, a splendid offering if you want "different" sounds in a quirky but modern (1996) musical environment.

Quasimidi Technox
Polyphonic synthesizer module

Orig. price (1995)	No U.S. price (£749)
Price in 1996	No U.S. price (£700)
Keyboard	n/a
Sound type	Sample+ synthesis

Slimmed down version of the Quasar not currently being made available to U.S. market.

Quasimidi Raven
Polyphonic synthesizer

Orig. price (1995)	$2195 (£1599)
Price in 1996	$2000 (£1500)
Keyboard	61-note
Sound type	Multi synthesis

Center: Control and storage elements of PPG's complex sampling system; Right: Quasimidi (Raven, Quasar...) was initially a software company.

Dance floor keyboard in Quasar mold with some handy real-time controls and 16-part multitimbral sequencer. Rave on!

Quasimidi Cyber-6
Controller keyboard

Orig. price (1995)	$1395 (£999)
Price in 1996	$1395 (£999)
Keyboard	61-note
Sound type	Sample+ synthesis

New fun approach to the genre, complete with 8-track sequencer, "motivator" super arpeggiator and 8-zone control. In eye-catching red livery.

Rhodes Chroma
Polyphonic synthesizer

Country of origin	Japan

See entry in Hot 100.

Rhodes MK-80
Stage piano

Orig. price (1990)	$2795 (£1799)
Price in 1996	$750 (£650)
Keyboard	88-note
Sound type	Digital (SAS)

Roland-built digital piano with Rhodes marque somewhat gratuitously applied. Good instrument, though, with comfortable keyboard action, eight quality piano tones, effects, editability, stretch tuning and reasonable 16-voice polyphony. MK-60 is 64-key version with no display.

Rhodes Model 660
Polyphonic synthesizer

Orig. price (1989)	$1595 (£999)
Price in 1996	$650 (£450)
Keyboard	61-note
Sound type	Digital (RS-PCM)

Roland U-series type sounds within this immediate and friendly sample playback "synth." Not especially glamorous, but functional for its time and price.

Rhodes Model 760
Polyphonic synthesizer

Orig. price (1990)	$2095 (£1288)
Price in 1996	$850 (£550)
Keyboard	76-note
Sound type	Digital (RS-PCM)

Released after Model 660 but still essentially 76-note version of Roland U series sample playback synths. The 128 tones are tweakable rather than editable. Suited to club player looking for no hassle, instant results on a decent action "synth" with good Rhodes tones.

Rhodes Pianos

See Fender Rhodes entry in Hot 100.

Rhodes VK-1000
Electronic organ

Orig. price (1990)	$3295 (£1999)
Price in 1996	$1100 (£650)
Keyboard	76-note
Sound type	Digital (SAS)

Big and beefy stage organ with 64 preset tones, drawbars and effects, including built-in rotary speaker and pro XLR outputs. Never really caught on, though. Sounds are strong, but the whole package just doesn't quite hang together. Built by Roland. Nothing to do with Harold Rhodes, Rhodes Chroma, Cecil Rhodes...

Riday T-91
Controller keyboard

Country of origin	U.S.
Orig. price (1994)	No U.S. price (no UK price)
Price in 1996	No U.S. price (no UK price)
Keyboard	49-note
Sound type	n/a

Preposterous design employing rows of tabs in order to "unify" different keyboard configurations/fingerings that occur when playing in different keys on a conventional keyboard. Surely operates well in the hands of its designers, but seems unlikely to catch on in a big way.

RMI Keyboard Computer
Polyphonic synthesizer

Country of origin	U.S.

See entry in Hot 100.

Roland A-30
Controller keyboard

Country of origin	Japan
Orig. price (1993)	$795 (£499)
Price in 1996	$300 (£200)
Keyboard	76-note
Sound type	n/a

Non sling-on version of the AX-1. In other words, GS/GM panel controls tailored to Roland Sound Canvas modules. Battery power option is handy. Thirty-two user patches. As simple as the A-50 is complex.

Roland A-33
Controller keyboard

Orig. price (1995)	$695 (£499)
Price in 1996	$695 (£499)
Keyboard	76-note
Sound type	n/a

Simple operation controller with GS/GM specific controls. Dual MIDI Outs and 32 MIDI program memories.

Roland A-50
Controller keyboard

Orig. price (1989)	$1795 (£1395)
Price in 1996	$900 (£600)
Keyboard	76-note
Sound type	n/a

Murderous to program but pleasant to play. A-80 is the 88-note weighted keyboard version. Lots of control—if your name is Einstein.

Roland A-90EX
Stage piano/controller keyboard

Price in 1996	$2995 (£1999)
Keyboard	88-note
Sound type	n/a

Futuristic stage piano-cum-controller blessed with those lovely knobby push buttons last seen on the JD-800. Armed with 24MB piano samples playable 64-voice polyphonically across its weighted, hammer action keyboard, there are also extensive controller features such as eight keyboard zones, 64 performance memories, real-time sliders, wheels and buttons. Purchasable with or without voices (as plain A-90) or with additional GS sound set. Frightening.

Roland Alpha-Juno 1
Polyphonic synthesizer

Orig. price (1986)	$895 (£695)
Price in 1996	$225 (£175)
Keyboard	49-note
Sound type	Analog

Compact late analog poly with one or two neat features (chord memory, chorus, noise, time and level type EGs) but generally thin sounds and non-velocity keyboard. Also produced in "Home Synth" version as HS-10.

Roland Alpha-Juno 2
Polyphonic synthesizer

Orig. price (1986)	$1095 (£995)
Price in 1996	$400 (£225)
Keyboard	61-note
Sound type	Analog

Longer (and velocity sensitive) keyboard version of A-J 1 with cartridge option. A much better bet.

Roland AX-1
Remote keyboard

Orig. price (1982)	$795 (£535)
Price in 1996	$500 (£400)
Keyboard	45-note
Sound type	n/a

Revival of the Axis; still blood red and stylish but this time with dedicated GS controls, pitch ribbon and handy battery power option. Small and light (3kg), the new "Axis" seems to have found a niche in the Sound Canvas/General MIDI market.

Roland Axis
Remote keyboard

Orig. price (1985)	$695 (£500)
Price in 1996	$300 (£175)
Keyboard	45-note
Sound type	n/a

Flashy (red, "stabilizer bar") sling-on controller with oodles of control features and pleasantly firm and roomy keyboard. Fiddliness and worldwide lack of interest in the whole concept of remote keyboards at the time were its undoing.

Roland CM-32L
Polyphonic synthesizer module

"Computer" version of MT-32 (see Roland MT-32 entry in Hot 100).

Roland D-5
Polyphonic synthesizer

Orig. price (1989)	$895 (£599)
Price in 1996	$400 (£375)
Keyboard	61-note
Sound type	Digital (LAS)

Budget version of the D-10. Sounds are a little naked without an effects section, but compensatory features of chord memory, harmony,

---

Center: Roland-built curio that has nothing in common with Rhodes pianos; Right: Axis bold and beautiful from Roland chase play and arpeggiator are fun and multi-timbrality is useful.

Roland D-10
Polyphonic synthesizer

Orig. price (1988)	$1395 (£850)
Price in 1996	$400 (£300)
Keyboard	61-note
Sound type	Digital (LAS)

Second generation of D-series synth after the D-50. Multitimbral, with some great catchy drum loops and plenty of "D-50-ish" sounds. Slim on effects and almost impenetrable programming, but something still hooks you in. D-20 adds an 8-track sequencer and D-110 is 1U module version (no sequencer) with six assignable outputs.

Roland D-20
Polyphonic synthesizer

Orig. price (1988)	$1795 (£1165)
Price in 1996	$600 (£475)
Keyboard	61-note
Sound type	Digital (LAS)

D-10, plus a multitrack sequencer/drum machine and built-in disk drive. Good for hotel room practice. Overpriced when new.

Roland D-50
Polyphonic synthesizer

See entry in Hot 100.

Roland D-70
Polyphonic synthesizer

Orig. price (1990)	$2595 (£1799)
Price in 1996	$750 (£700)
Keyboard	76-note
Sound type	Digital (LAS)

Extension of D-50, with its RS-PCM samples abetting "advanced" LA synthesis. Capable of some splendidly complex sounds and the keyboard a pleasure to play, but the programming is a nightmare. Used by many top acts (e.g., Simply Red: strings on "Something Got Me Started," Tears for Fears: Space Dream and Prologue presets used on "Tears Roll Down") who can presumably afford to hire a programmer.

Roland DJ-70
Keyboard sampler

Orig. price (1992)	$3495 (£1799)
Price in 1996	$900 (£750)
Keyboard	37-note
Sound type	Digital samples

Preempting the mid-1990s explosion of "DJ as musician," this short keyboard sampler is based on Roland's pro S-750 sampling module. With large "scratch pad" and plenty of tools for quick looping and tempo setting, plus a handy phrase sequencer for those who feel moved to actually play. A niche product but a successful one. An upgraded DJ-70 MkII was launched at Frankfurt in 1996.

Roland E-20
Home keyboard

Orig. price (1988)	$2000 (£1500)
Price in 1996	$600 (£450)
Keyboard	61-note
Sound type	Digital (LAS)

Made in Roland's then-recently-acquired Italian production facility (ex-Siel), the E-20 and E-10 helped define a new professionalism in the

world of home keyboards. Grown-up synth-based sounds and genuinely musical style programming, plus small multitrack sequencer. Expanded and enhanced on subsequent E-series instruments, but this is where it all started.

Roland E-30
Home keyboard

Orig. price (1990)	$2000 (£1500)
Price in 1996	$700 (£550)
Keyboard	61-note
Sound type	Digital (LAS)

Similar to E-20 but more accessible tones, more of them and one or two new features like Arranger Loop for practice/jamming.

Roland E-66
Home keyboard

Orig. price (1994)	$1500 (£1500)
Price in 1996	$900 (£800)
Keyboard	61-note
Sound type	Digital (LAS)

Streamlined reworking of E-86 with, they say, higher clock resolution sequencing. Class performer still.

Roland E-70
Home keyboard

Orig. price (1991)	$2000 (£1500)
Price in 1996	$600 (£550)
Keyboard	61-note
Sound type	Digital (LAS)

GS version of E series with more standardized 24-voice polyphony. Custom styles can be written and sequencer simplified. Has held up well. E-35 released alongside with no programming facility and reduced power amplification. E-15 exchanges multitrack sequencer for simple playsequencer.

Roland E-86
Home keyboard

Orig. price (1993)	$2500 (£2000)
Price in 1996	$1000 (£850)
Keyboard	61-note
Sound type	Digital (LAS, PCM)

Imposingly large with big screen, 32-voice polyphonic and additional JV-80 style sounds on board. Disk drive for storing/loading SMF data. E-56 ditches JV-80 sound bank and disk drive, and E-36 caters to the novice player with its Easy Eight styles. E-16 offers additional one touch play features.

Roland EP-09
Electronic piano

Orig. price (1980)	No U.S. price (no UK price)
Price in 1996	No U.S. price (no UK price)
Keyboard	61-note
Sound type	Analog

Not to be confused with later EP models, this electronic piano sits alongside the Saturn and other '80s 09-series instruments. An arpeggia-

tor enlivens five understandably old-fashioned piano tones.

Roland EP-5
Digital piano

Orig. price (1990)	$795 (£530)
Price in 1996	$300 (£200)
Keyboard	61-note
Sound type	Digital (PCM)

Roland revived the EP class in 1990 with a series of low cost digitals, foolproof to use and quite pleasant to play. Simple playsequencer is handy and 24-voice polyphony quite sufficient in this context. EP-3 loses sequencer and keyboard dynamics, the latter a major loss.

Roland EP-9
Digital piano

Orig. price (1992)	$1650 (£1199)
Price in 1996	$500 (£400)
Keyboard	88-note
Sound type	Digital (PCM)

Inexpensive route into full 88-note (semi-weighted) piano playing. Eight tones, plus reverb and chorus effects playable at 28-voice polyphony. Playsequencer. Coincided with a revamped EP-7 called the EP-7IIE ($1345), which has same features on 76-note keyboard.

Roland EP-50
Electronic piano

Orig. price (1985)	$785 (£665)
Price in 1996	$100 (£75)
Keyboard	61-note
Sound type	Analog

Marketed as electronic piano with MIDI controller capabilities. Four tones, chorus, speakers. HP-100 the same instrument in different suit of clothing (wood grain rather than plain black) clothing.

Roland EP-6060
Electronic piano

Orig. price (1982)	$850 (£525)
Price in 1996	$175 (£125)
Keyboard	61-note
Sound type	Analog

Produced long before Roland had a piano division and before the advent of digital pianos. Range of so-so quality piano tones but with internal speaker system and well-presented arpeggiator. Curio value only.

Roland FP-1
Digital piano

Orig. price (1985)	$2545 (£1799)
Price in 1996	$1650 (£1000)
Keyboard	88-note
Sound type	Digital

Little to remind you of the earlier FP-8 but a good all-around performer with six piano-/string tones, nice chorus and reverb effects and discrete speaker system. Not as eye-catching as the FP-8.

Roland FP-8
Digital piano

Orig. price (1991)	$2895 (£1799)
Price in 1996	$1300 (£1000)
Keyboard	88-note
Sound type	Digital (Advanced SAS)

Eye-catching design on this stage portable digital and offered in range of colors too. Sixteen tones, plus reverb and chorus and a handy 10W stereo speaker system. Perfect instrument for gigging or rehearsals.

Roland G-800
Home keyboard

Orig. price (1995)	$2995 (£1999)
Price in 1996	$2500 (£1500)
Keyboard	76-note
Sound type	Digital

Giant of an instrument in all senses, from the weighted 76-note keyboard to the arsenal of nearly 700 tones, SMF disk drive, 32-part multitimbrality, 64-voice polyphony, 128 music styles, 25 drum kits...the list goes on and on. Aside from the provocative, "Who needs a band?" nonsense in the glossy brochure (damned cheek!), a superb effort. Certainly the most advanced Roland home keyboard currently—if not the most advanced from anyone.

Roland HP-70
Electronic piano

Orig. price (1982)	$850 (£660)
Price in 1996	$100 (£75)
Keyboard	75-note
Sound type	Analog

Early HP model with commensurate sounds and features. HP-60 and HP-30 also made. The latter not touch sensitive. A bit of a bloomer, even in 1982, though it does sport an arpeggiator by way of compensation.

Roland HP-100
Electronic piano

Orig. price (1985)	$795 (£625)
Price in 1996	$100 (£75)
Keyboard	76-note
Sound type	Analog

Four tones, plus chorus, small speaker system and MIDI. Serviceable for the time but of no particular value today. Same as EP-50 in different styling.

Roland HP-300
Electronic piano

Orig. price (1983)	$1295 (£990)
Price in 1996	$200 (£175)
Keyboard	74-note
Sound type	Analog

Early dedicated home piano with basic MIDI spec, six tones, plus chorus and tremolo on the HP-400, the 88-note keyboard version.

Roland HP-350
Electronic piano

Orig. price (1983)	$1295 (£990)
Price in 1996	$200 (£175)
Keyboard	74-note
Sound type	Analog

Marginally MIDI enhanced version of the HP-300, as is the HP-450.

Roland HP-600
Digital piano

Orig. price (1987)	$2000 (£950)
Price in 1996	$450 (£375)
Keyboard	76-note
Sound type	Digital (SAS)

Five tones at 15-voice polyphony, plus chorus and multitimbral MIDI control. Non-weighted keyboard. HP-700 is 76-note weighted action version; HP-800 is the full 88-note model.

Roland HP-2000
Digital piano

Orig. price (1986)	$2600 (£1399)
Price in 1996	$400 (£400)
Keyboard	76-note
Sound type	Digital (SAS)

Part of an absurdly convoluted series of mid-'80s HP series that includes 88-note models HP-3000S and HP-4500S. All share 16-voice polyphony, eight tones and chorus and tremolo effects. "S" action smoother, but the (non-S) HP-2000 has a bit more bite if you like that kind of thing.

Roland HP-2500
Digital piano

Orig. price (1989)	$2499 (£1599)
Price in 1996	$500 (£500)
Keyboard	88-note
Sound type	Digital (SAS)

Big improvement in polyphony (31-voice) over its predecessors. Eight tones with chorus, tremolo and reverb enhancers. HP-2500 anchored and launched Roland's ISM system of sequencer-inspired music teaching. HP-1000 of similar specification and vintage but with just five tones and no reverb.

Roland HP-2900G
Digital piano

Orig. price (1992)	$3799 (£2295)
Price in 1996	$1500 (£1000)
Keyboard	88-note
Sound type	Digital (Advanced SAS)

Unusual in its offering of a full complement of Sound Canvas-style GS tone bank in addition to the five quality pianos. Reverb and chorus effects, plus a disk drive for multitimbral sequence storage. Built-in sequencer can accommodate just five tracks, but with a tally of more than 200 sounds onboard playable from its first rate keyboard, a most useful instrument. Only the polyphony, at 24-voice, is a little on the light side.

Roland HP-3700
Digital piano

Orig. price (1990)	$3799 (£2800)
Price in 1996	$800 (£700)
Keyboard	88-note
Sound type	Digital (Advanced SAS)

Advanced SAS technology employs digital recreation of string reverberation for more life-like sounds. A big instrument with six tones, two of which are indistinguishable. Range of tuning temperaments offered for classical buffs. Also in series: HP-2700 (reduced polyphony from 32-voice to 24-voice and smaller amplification system), HP-1700 (no sostenuto pedal and just five tones) and HP-900 (76-key version of HP-1700).

Roland HP-3800
Digital piano

Orig. price (1993)	$4900 (£2899)
Price in 1996	$2000 (£1250)
Keyboard	88-note
Sound type	Digital (Advanced SAS)

Sober looking but authoritative digital with seven tones playable at 28-voice polyphony. Big 40W stereo amplification system. Two track playsequencer but no other obvious bells and whistles. HP-2800 has reduced power speaker system, HP-1800 has more portable physical design and loses one of the acoustic piano tones (no loss as two are similar to the point of twinning) and HP-1500's amplification is reduced still further.

Roland HP-5500
Digital piano

Orig. price (1986)	$3000 (£2200)
Price in 1996	$400 (£450)

Keyboard	88-note
Sound type	Digital, SAS

First of the Structured Adaptive Synthesis (SAS) generation digitals and very successful at the time. Eight quality tones playable 16-voice polyphonically, with chorus and brilliance thrown in as well. HP-5600 has walnut finish. Models suffixed "S" feature subsequently improved keyboard action.

Roland HP-5700
Digital piano

Orig. price (1991)	$11,299 (£4500)
Price in 1996	No U.S. price (no UK price)
Keyboard	88-note
Sound type	Digital (Advanced SAS)

Smart looking digital, almost absurdly over-priced, though, with just seven tones, plus effects, albeit delivered through a high quality 40W stereo amplification system. Tone layering adds to the sonic potential and a new (then) hammer action is a joy to play. HP-7700 is grand piano version—even more pricey but rarely seen and so, one must presume, a bit of a liability.

Roland HP-6000
Digital piano

Orig. price (1988)	$5995 (£2995)
Price in 1996	$1500 (£750)
Keyboard	88-note
Sound type	Digital, SAS

Top of its particular tree in 1988: 16-voice polyphony, 8 tones and (new feature back then) digital reverb in addition to chorus and tremolo. Big sound system with useful audio input jacks.

Roland HS-10
Polyphonic synthesizer

See Roland Alpha-Juno 1 entry.

Roland JD-800
Polyphonic synthesizer

See entry in Hot 100.

Roland JD-990
Polyphonic synthesizer module

Orig. price (1993)	$2095 (£1445)
Price in 1996	$900 (£700)
Keyboard	n/a
Sound type	Sample+ synthesis

Intriguing mix of many a Roland luminary but most closely related to JD-800. High level of programming, though curtailed number of effects algorithms. Polyphony light at 24-voice. Class sounds, of course.

Roland JS-30
Sampling workstation

Orig. price (1995)	$1795 (no UK price)
Price in 1996	No U.S. price (no UK price)
Keyboard	n/a
Sound type	Sample

Sampling workstation offering SCSI access to outside world of sound libraries and digital input, along with 44.1kHz sampling and SIMMs memory expandability (up to 4MB). With its real-time phrase sequencer, the perfect environment for a serious DJ/programmer.

Roland Juno-6
Polyphonic synthesizer

See Roland Juno-60 entry in Hot 100.

Roland Juno-106
Polyphonic synthesizer

Orig. price (1984)	$1095 (£880)
Price in 1996	$450 (£400)
Keyboard	61-note
Sound type	Analog

Essentially a MIDI version of the Juno-60 but with a facelift and the arrival of portamento and departure of chord hold and the arpeggiator. 128 program memories. Has become highly sought after in mid-1990s.

Roland Jupiter-4
Polyphonic synthesizer

Orig. price (1978)	$2895 (£1810)
Price in 1996	$450 (£450)
Keyboard	48-note
Sound type	Analog

Pretty much of a preset synth on the cusp of organ synthesizer. Single oscillator design makes for thin tones but good filtering, arpeggiator and the chance to store modifications in eight memory locations. Four-voice polyphony. Hip at the time.

Roland Jupiter-6
Polyphonic synthesizer

Orig. price (1983)	$2295 (£1999)
Price in 1996	$600 (£500)
Keyboard	61-note
Sound type	Analog

Dual oscillator and six-voice polyphony, priced and styled midway between Jupiter-8 and Juno-106. Flexible filtering within a decent range of programming tools but lacks the bite and power of Jupiter-8. No chorus but good arpeggiator. Okay as Jupiter-8 substitute but not the real thing.

Roland Jupiter-8
Polyphonic synthesizer

See entry in Hot 100.

Roland JV-30
Polyphonic synthesizer

Orig. price (1992)	$1195 (£985)
Price in 1996	$500 (£400)
Keyboard	61-note
Sound type	Sample+ synthesis

Slimline GS keyboard released alongside, but substantially different from, the JV-80. Tally of 445 tones is impressive, and the real time edit sliders are useful.

Roland JV-80
Polyphonic synthesizer

Orig. price (1992)	$1895 (£1499)
Price in 1996	$750 (£650)
Keyboard	61-note
Sound type	Sample+ synthesis

Well-planned instrument compatible with JD-800 sounds but fully multitimbral and with a refreshingly intuitive user interface. Sample

waveform memory can be expanded, though internal program memory is rather light. Top quality sounds. JV-880 is 1U module version.

Roland JV-90
Polyphonic synthesizer

Orig. price (1995)	$2050 (no UK price)
Price in 1996	No U.S. price (no UK price)
Keyboard	76-note
Sound type	Sample+ synthesis

Extended JV-80 in keyboard length, sounds and multitimbral possibilities (24 parts). Still a dedicated synth, not a workstation, but highly desirable with well programmed voices. 61-note keyboard JV-50 released alongside, which, like JV-30 before it, offers GS/GM format sounds with the addition of an SMF player and disk drive, features not found on the otherwise identical JV-35. All three are expandable using VE-JV Voice Expansion cards.

Roland JV-1000
Polyphonic synthesizer

Orig. price (1993)	$2995 (£1859)
Price in 1996	$1100 (£850)
Keyboard	76-note
Sound type	Sample+ synthesis

Synth designed by committee with features from a range of Roland synths and sequencers dotted all over its football pitch sized control panel. All sounds great in theory. In practice, the dual displays, the S-MRC style sequencing, the expansion boards with Sound Canvas GS/GM tones make for a confusing life aboard this roomy, less-than-the-sum-of-its-parts instrument.

Roland JV-1080
Polyphonic synthesizer module

Orig. price (1994)	$1895 (£1085)
Price in 1996	$1000 (£900)
Keyboard	n/a
Sound type	Sample+ synthesis

Everything that a modern module should be: GM compatible but not shackled to GM, lots of high quality sounds and effects, good-sized screen, upgradable with voice expansion boards, six outputs...still hard to beat.

Roland JW-50
Polyphonic synthesizer

Orig. price (1993)	$2000 (£1500)
Price in 1996	$800 (£600)
Keyboard	61-note
Sound type	Digital (LAS, RS-PCM)

Innards of a Sound Canvas in sequencer-sporting, SMF style-touting keyboard form. An unusual mix of technologies and features, which has not, it has to be said, been eagerly snapped up.

Roland JX-1
Polyphonic synthesizer

Orig. price (1991)	$895 (£535)
Price in 1996	$250 (£200)
Keyboard	61-note
Sound type	Sample+ synthesis

Great little synth that was received very badly and quickly disappeared without a trace. High quality presets with some editing potential courtesy of immediate and obvious panel sliders. No hassle operation all round and excellent sounds. Go figure!

Roland JX-3P
Polyphonic synthesizer

See entry in Hot 100.

Roland JX-8P
Polyphonic synthesizer

Orig. price (1985)	$1695 (£1325)
Price in 1996	$400 (£400)
Keyboard	61-note
Sound type	Analog

DCO-based 8-voice poly with plenty of buttons but no knobs or sliders (separate programmer PG-800 covered this purpose). Sleek and stylish in looks and sound but not yet deemed a classic.

Roland JX-10
Polyphonic synthesizer

Orig. price (1986)	$2750 (£1800)
Price in 1996	$600 (£450)
Keyboard	61-note
Sound type	Analog

Still a good looker some 10 years on but a flawed masterpiece. Can be thought of as two JX-8Ps in one unit with plenty of rich, textural sounds in its armory. Not noted for envelope speed, so better at smooth tones than hard-edged ones. Rather wobbly SysEx implementation. MKS-70 is the module, featuring useful Mode 2 mono mode for guitarists.

Roland KR-100
Home keyboard

Orig. price (1991)	$2000 (£1500)
Price in 1996	$500 (£450)
Keyboard	61-note
Sound type	Digital (LAS)

The KR series is Roland's rag-bag range of deliberately nontechnical home keyboards. Downbeat in looks, but this one has accomplished styles and "D-50" type sounds and effects.

Roland KR-650
Home keyboard

Orig. price (1992)	$2500 (£2000)
Price in 1996	$600 (£500)
Keyboard	76-note
Sound type	Digital (PCM)

Roughly equivalent to E-15 home keyboard but in typically low-key KR styling. SMF disk drive and 200+ strong PCM tones. KR-350 has less tones and, at 24-voice, four notes less of polyphony. KR-4500, meanwhile, has full 88-note keyboard with weighted piano action and full complement of GM tones and 6-track sequencer. KR-3500 slices off two tracks worth of sequencing power and loses the disk drive, while the KR-5500 adds JV-80 style sounds and boasts a massive 60W stereo amplification system.

Roland MC-202
Monophonic synthesizer

See entry in Hot 100.

Roland MC-303 Groovebox
Bass synthesizer/sequencer

Orig. price (1996)	$799 (£599)
Keyboard	n/a
Sound type	Digital

Took Frankfurt '96 by storm. Though sample-based, presents the essence of TB-303 Bassline and SH-101 synths, plus TR-909 and 808 drum machines. Complete with "accent" control, arpeggio, real-time filter cutoff and resonance controls, plus modern facilities like reverb and chorus and, of course, MIDI. A joy to play on its little tab-style keypad and equally a joy to listen to.

Roland M-DC1
Vintage synth module

Orig. price (1995)	$795 (£499)
Price in 1996	No U.S. price (no UK price)
Keyboard	n/a
Sound type	Digital (RS-PCM)

Module dedicated to drum sounds in Roland's five-unit haul of sharply focused rackmount modules. All your favorite Roland drum sounds represented as well as rhythms and sundry cut-and-paste sounds and effects and loops.

Roland MGS-64
Polyphonic synthesizer module

Orig. price (1995)	$895 (£599)
Price in 1996	$700 (£500)
Keyboard	n/a
Sound type	Digital (RS-PCM)

Top dog in Roland's thoroughly drab-looking series of Sound Canvas style rack expansion modules. Features here include onboard editing and 64-voice polyphony. Lots of power if little fizz.

Roland MKB-200
Controller keyboard

Orig. price (1986)	$899 (£599)
Price in 1996	$200 (£200)
Keyboard	61-note
Sound type	n/a

Short-lived controller: compact and cost-conscious. Semi-weighted keyboard and 128 memories.

Roland MKB-1000
Controller keyboard

Orig. price (1984)	$2195 (£1665)
Price in 1996	$600 (£450)
Keyboard	88-note
Sound type	n/a

Fabulous actioned controller keyboard with limited but still quite sufficient range of MIDI controls and controllers. Small screen and heavy but 128 memories. MKB-300 is the 76-key synth action version.

Roland MKS-10
Piano module

Orig. price (1984)	$1095 (£990)
Price in 1996	$100 (£150)
Keyboard	n/a
Sound type	Analog

Very early MIDI module, and one of the first dedicated to piano tones (based on the HP-400). Eight tones, modifiable with chorus, tremolo and flanger, plus brilliance. Not brilliant, but good source of '80s piano tones and useful 16-voice polyphony at the current level of price/interest.

Roland MKS-20
Digital piano module

See Roland RD-1000 entry in Hot 100.

Roland MKS-30
Polyphonic synthesizer module

Orig. price (1984)	$995 (£875)
Price in 1996	$300 (£250)

Keyboard	n/a
Sound type	Analog

Six-voice poly in JX-3P mold (see JX-3P entry in Hot 100). Additionally capable of responding to incoming velocity control from suitably endowed MIDI keyboard.

Roland MKS-70
Polyphonic synthesizer module

See Roland JX-10 entry.

Roland MKS-80
Polyphonic synthesizer module

See entry in Hot 100.

Roland MKS-100
Digital sampling module

Orig. price (1987)	$1300 (£900)
Price in 1996	$325 (£300)
Keyboard	n/a
Sound type	Sample

Modular equivalent of Roland S-10 keyboard sampler. Not a big success at the time.

Roland M-OC1
Orchestral sound module

Orig. price (1995)	$795 (£499)
Price in 1996	$650 (£400)
Keyboard	n/a
Sound type	Digital (RS-PCM)

Slightly more successful than the equivalent Strings module, but still not up to E-mu Proteus 2 Orchestral standards.

Roland MP-600
Electronic piano

Orig. price (1979)	$1250 (£695)
Price in 1996	$200 (£175)
Keyboard	61-note
Sound type	Analog

Understandably dated. As a pro stage-oriented instrument, the MP-600 has fared better than a gaggle of similar though even later vintage HP models. Just three tones but handy graphic EQ and tone mixing with sliders. Would always get you out of trouble.

Roland MS-1
Sampling module

Orig. price (1994)	$695 (no UK price)
Price in 1996	No U.S. price (no UK price)
Keyboard	n/a
Sound type	Samples

Canny tabletop sampler for instant/DJ market. Streamlined operation still offers sample rate choices from 44.1kHz to grainy 16kHz and built-in flash ROM protects against time-consuming loading. Single track sequencer for recording phrases that can be played back from panel pads. All in all a fun gadget with pro audio overtones.

Roland M-SE1
String ensemble module

Orig. price (1995)	$795 (£499)
Price in 1996	$650 (£400)
Keyboard	n/a
Sound type	Digital (RS-PCM)

String sounds aplenty but not, sadly, culled from the stunning S-series sampler library. The "3D" RSS processing is scant compensation. Nice idea, only partially successful.

Roland MT-32
Polyphonic synthesizer module

See entry in Hot 100.

Roland MT-120
Polyphonic synthesizer module

Orig. price (1992)	$1000 (£825)
Price in 1996	$400 (£275)
Keyboard	n/a
Sound type	Digital (LAS, RS-PCM)

Brains of a standard SC-55 Sound Canvas with sequencer. MT-120S model comes with speaker. Good for lone players as one-man band backing device.

Roland MV-30
Music production module

Orig. price (1990)	$2600 (£1690)
Price in 1996	$500 (£450)
Keyboard	n/a
Sound type	Digital (RS-PCM)

Box of tricks housing 128 RS-PCM tones and 16-track Roland MC style sequencer. In spite of innovative features (real-time phrase sequencer seen extensively on subsequent instruments), okay effects and real-time mixing, the MV-30 was greeted with almost total indifference. Then again, so was the MC-202 and TB-303 for the first 10 years of their lives, so watch out!

Roland M-VS1
Vintage synth module

Orig. price (1995)	$795 (£499)
Price in 1996	$650 (£400)
Keyboard	n/a
Sound type	Digital (RS-PCM)

Probably best of the bunch in this M series of dedicated instrument sound/type modules. Tones trawling the Roland archives including D-50, SH-101, TB-303, JX-3P as well as classic emulations of Moog, ARP and other manufacturers.

Roland P-55
Digital piano module

Orig. price (1993)	$695 (£469)
Price in 1996	$325 (£250)
Keyboard	n/a
Sound type	Digital (SAS, PCM)

Piano module available within the GM format with 4MB sounds drawn from Roland's long experience in digital pianos, harpsichords, etc. Three-part multitimbrality and a modicum of editing available in terms of tuning, velocity response and effects. 28-voice polyphonic.

Roland P-330
Digital piano module

Orig. price (1989)	$895 (£430)
Price in 1996	$350 (£300)
Keyboard	n/a
Sound type	Digital (SAS)

Tweakable piano sounds in SAS style but without the edge and sparkle of the MKS-20. Still a quality animal.

Roland PC-200
Controller keyboard

Orig. price (1991)	$595 (£499)
Price in 1996	$200 (£175)
Keyboard	49-note
Sound type	n/a

Built in gray for the computer market. (Roland super GM format) GS-friendly panel controls, compact and inexpensive. Also PC-150, which has non-velocity keyboard.

Roland RAP-10
Polyphonic synthesizer/sampling card

Orig. price (1993)	$599 (£449)
Price in 1996	$175 (£175)
Keyboard	n/a
Sound type	Digital (LAS, RS-PCM)

PC sound card incorporating Sound Canvas styles synthesis, plus direct-to-disk digital recording up to 44.1kHz with digital filtering. Great value for PC users. Sold within ATW-10 recording package.

Roland RD-250S
Digital piano

Orig. price (1987)	$1995 (£1350)
Price in 1996	$450 (£400)
Keyboard	76-note
Sound type	Digital (SAS)

Neat, no-nonsense stage piano in RD-1000 (see entry in Hot 100) tradition. Improved MIDI control but less editable sounds than RD-1000; though with smoother keyboard, less satisfying to play. RD-300S is 88-note keyboard version.

Roland RD-500
Digital piano

Orig. price (1994)	$2895 (£1999)
Price in 1996	$2250 (£1500)
Keyboard	88-note
Sound type	Digital (SAS, PCM)

Daunting, initially, with its panel full of sliders and switches, but the value of controller keyboard features within a top flight digital piano is not to be shunned. Twelve basic tones, editable and storable within 31 user programs, plus reverb, EQ and chorus effects. Synths and strings tones add range. Polyphony quoted as 32-voice but still easy to eat up with layered and combination programs.

Roland RD-1000
Digital piano

See entry in Hot 100.

Roland RS-09
Multi-instrument keyboard

Orig. price (1978)	$895 (£530)
Price in 1996	$150 (£150)
Keyboard	44-note
Sound type	Analog

Shot in the dark organ/string machine with the build quality of Roland SH-series synths. Friendly to use and capable of some great textures.

Roland RS-505 Paraphonic
Multi-instrument keyboard

Orig. price (1978)	$1895 (£991)
Price in 1996	$350 (£250)
Keyboard	49-note
Sound type	Analog

Billed as an "ensemble synthesizer" back in 1978, this organ, strings, brass machine was well made and delivered its component musical parts from separate sections and even separate outputs. Useful more than spectacular. Not a classic but the subject of reasonable interest among collectors.

Roland S-10
Sampling keyboard

Orig. price (1986)	$1799 (£999)
Price in 1996	$200 (£150)
Keyboard	49-note
Sound type	Digital samples

Major misreading of the sampler market in 1986. Short scale keyboard and cost-cutting features including 2.8 inch Quick Disk. Not a success. S-10 and later the S-220 modules (double polyphony at 16-voice) were released to little avail until the Quick Disk storage was superseded by standard 3 1/2-inch drives.

Roland S-50
Sampling keyboard

Orig. price (1986)	$2900 (£2300)
Price in 1996	$800 (£500)
Keyboard	61-note
Sound type	Digital samples

Got off to a weak start but than picked up, especially in module form as S-550. External monitoring useful and sound quality deemed rich and rounded, especially responsive to bass samples. Twelve-bit sampling that only extends to 30kHz sample rate, plus programming is a bit of a nightmare, but it's well executed and large sound library is still available. S-330 module is a 1U reduced memory version of S-550.

Roland S-330
Sampling module

See Roland S-50 entry.

Roland S-750
Sampling module

Orig. price (1991)	$4995 (£3175)
Price in 1996	$2000+ (£1500+)
Keyboard	n/a
Sound type	Digital samples

Roland's mainstay pro sampler. Not the easiest to fathom but capable of delivering top quality audio and control features. Best features include the filters, re-sampling and a massive library of peerless quality work. S-770, complete with internal 40MB hard drive and digital I/O came out a year earlier, and S-700 playback unit (SCSI but no disk drive) came out two years later.

Roland S-760
Sampling module

Orig. price (1991)	$1699 (£1799)
Price in 1996	$1100 (£900)
Keyboard	n/a
Sound type	Digital samples

Elegant solution to high quality but low-cost (and relatively low brain power required) sampling. Streamlining of S-750 approach with 24-voice polyphony. Sampling up to 48kHz and expansion to 32MB. Digital I/O an option. Can read Akai library over SCSI.

Roland Saturn-09
Electronic organ

Orig. price (1980)	$795 (£449)
Price in 1996	$175 (£125)
Keyboard	44-note
Sound type	Analog

Similar in looks and features to the RS-09 string machine, except the Saturn is dedicated to organ sounds. Just four basic tones accessible via drawbars, plus two speed chorus and one or two tone-enhancers (percussive, accent). Full polyphony. Curious, but curiously useful and well made.

Roland SC-7
Polyphonic synthesizer module

Orig. price (1993)	$399 (£279)
Price in 1996	$175 (£150)
Keyboard	n/a
Sound type	Digital (LAS, RS-PCM)

Displayless gray computer module based on Sound Canvas SC-55. Limited to 128 Capitol Tones only and no RAM for user programs.

Roland SC-33
Polyphonic synthesizer module

Orig. price (1994)	$675 (£449)
Price in 1996	$300 (£200)
Keyboard	n/a
Sound type	Digital (LAS, RS-PCM)

Entry level tabletop Sound Canvas. No user program storage.

Roland SC-50
Polyphonic synthesizer module

Orig. price (1994)	$695 (£549)
Price in 1996	$375 (£300)
Keyboard	n/a
Sound type	Digital (LAS, RS-PCM)

Same improved audio quality of SC-55 MkII but a few less features (like, no program memories). Good value.

Roland SC-55 MkII
Polyphonic synthesizer module

Orig. price (1994)	$795 (£649)
Price in 1996	No U.S. price (no UK price)
Keyboard	n/a
Sound type	Digital (LAS, RS-PCM)

Improved version of original Sound Canvas. Cleaner sounds and direct Mac or PC digital interface. See Roland Sound Canvas entry in Hot 100.

Roland SC-88
Polyphonic synthesizer module

Orig. price (1994)	$1095 (£799)
Price in 1996	$625 (£425)
Keyboard	n/a
Sound type	Digital (LAS, RS-PCM)

Double helping of Sound Canvas magic on this 64-voice polyphonic, 645-tone little monster. Same Sound Canvas simplicity of operation. New tones culled from JV-80 synths.

Roland SC-155
Polyphonic synthesizer module

Orig. price (1994)	$895 (£715)
Price in 1996	$375 (£300)
Keyboard	n/a
Sound type	Digital (LAS, RS-PCM)

Tabletop version of Sound Canvas SC-55 MKII.

Center: Roland's S-750: pricey, of quality, complex

Roland SCC-I
Polyphonic synthesizer sound card

Orig. price (1993)	$499 (£299)
Price in 1996	$225 (£150)
Keyboard	n/a
Sound type	Digital (LAS, RS-PCM)

Sound card for PC based on Sound Canvas. Some limitations (no storage of edited sounds) but also handy MT-32 mode for vintage computer game enthusiasts.

Roland SD-35
Polyphonic synthesizer module

Orig. price (1994)	$1085 (£759)
Price in 1996	$450 (£400)
Keyboard	n/a
Sound type	Digital (LAS, RS-PCM)

Tabletop version of SC-55 with additional MIDI File player built in. Disk drive reads DOS-formatted disks as well as Roland format. Also has useful utility for converting Type 1/Type 0 Standard MIDI Files.

Roland SH-1
Monophonic synthesizer

Orig. price (1978)	$895 (£529)
Price in 1996	$225 (£200)
Keyboard	32-note
Sound type	Analog

Briefcase-residing single oscillator mono (plus sub osc) with 24dB/oct lowpass filtering, white and pink noise, CV and Gate outputs...most of what you need. Not deemed classic but well made and always worth a play.

Roland SH-2
Monophonic synthesizer

Orig. price (1979)	$995 (£549)
Price in 1996	$350 (£300)
Keyboard	37-note
Sound type	Analog

Excellent little dual oscillator synth complete with, astonishingly enough, one of the best owners manuals ever written. All the features you need to learn about and produce classic subtractive synthesis sounds.

Roland SH-3
Monophonic synthesizer

Orig. price (1979)	$1199 (£795)
Price in 1996	$300 (no UK price)
Keyboard	44-note
Sound type	Analog

Longer keyboard version of Roland SH-2.

Roland SH-5
Monophonic synthesizer

Orig. price (1976)	$2000 (no UK price)
Price in 1996	$500 (no UK price)
Keyboard	44-note
Sound type	Analog

Rare but worthy early Roland synth with studious-looking vertical control panel.

Roland SH-7
Monophonic synthesizer

Orig. price (1978)	$1800 (no UK price)
Price in 1996	$800 (no UK price)
Keyboard	45-note
Sound type	Analog

Heavily slidered control panel gives this early Roland mono a tactile appeal. Rare.

Roland SH-09
Monophonic synthesizer

Orig. price (1980)	$595 (£299)
Price in 1996	$250 (£150)
Keyboard	32-note
Sound type	Analog

Neat and compact mono much in style of SH-1 aside from unique oatmeal-colored keys. Single oscillator, plus sub osc. Limited but simple and fun.

Roland SH-101
Monophonic synthesizer

See entry in Hot 100.

Roland Sound Canvas
Polyphonic synthesizer module

See entry in Hot 100.

Roland Studio M
Music production module

See Roland MV-30 entry.

Roland System 100M
Modular synthesis system

Orig. price (1975)	$Variable (£variable)
Price in 1996	No U.S. price (no UK price)
Keyboard	n/a
Sound type	Analog

Large range of component parts, including keyboards and modules beloved by many serious pros in the late 1970s (Robert Fripp a notable user). Well made and relatively friendly. Made in small quantities until well into the 1980s. Collectible.

Roland TB-303 Bassline
Bass synthesizer

See entry in Hot 100.

Roland U-20/220
Polyphonic synthesizer/module

See U-20 entry in Hot 100.

Roland U-110
Polyphonic synthesizer module

Orig. price (1989)	$1599 (£599)
Price in 1996	$250 (£200)
Keyboard	n/a
Sound type	Digital (PCM)

Noisy but useful PCM sample-based module improved and expanded upon within the U-20/220. However, still a wonderful source of "slotter" sounds, with a graininess that is part of the appeal and value within the often transparently clean modern digital environment. 31-voice polyphony not to be sneezed at, either.

Roland VK-1
Electronic organ

Orig. price (1980)	$1595 (£850)
Price in 1996	$200 (£150)
Keyboard	61-note
Sound type	Analog

Roland's failed attempt at the portable Hammond, a niche occupied by Korg with the BX/CX3. Drawbar control, plus percussive harmonics, chorus and vibrato but no real bite.

Roland VK-09
Electronic organ

Orig. price (1981)	$995 (£525)
Price in 1996	$200 (£175)
Keyboard	61-note
Sound type	Analog

Drawbar-based organ, even if the drawbars do not perform in quite the standard method. Better than VK-1. Just.

Roland Vocoder Plus
Vocoder/string machine

See Vocoder entry in Hot 100.

Roland W-30
Sampling workstation

Orig. price (1989)	$2295 (£1599)
Price in 1996	$650 (£750)
Keyboard	61-note
Sound type	Samples

Unique sampling workstation combining Roland style sampling with Roland style sequencing. Not the greatest marriage on earth but has many loyal users among pro songwriting fraternity.

Roland XP-10
Polyphonic synthesizer

Orig. price (1995)	$895 (£699)
Price in 1996	$895 (£699)
Keyboard	61-note
Sound type	Sample+ synthesis

Straight ahead synth packed with sample-based sounds and effects.

Roland XP-50
Polyphonic synthesizer

Orig. price (1995)	$2195 (£1599)
Price in 1996	$1700 (£1100)
Keyboard	61-note
Sound type	Sample+ synthesis

Lots of punchy, in-your-face, dance-oriented sounds and features on this S-MRC style sequencing workstation. Aside from impenetrable owners manual and somewhat flimsy keyboard, an exciting, inspiring instrument.

Roland XP-80
Polyphonic synthesizer

Price in 1996	$2595 (£1799)
Keyboard	76-note
Sound type	Sample+ synthesis

Longer keyboard, big screen version of XP-50. Sixty-four voice polyphony.

RSF Kobol
Monophonic synthesizer

Country of origin	France

See entry in Hot 100.

RSF Polykobol
Polyphonic synthesizer

Orig. price (1983)	$8000 (£5000)
Price in 1996	No U.S. price (no UK price)
Keyboard	61-note
Sound type	Analog

Left: Early Roland mono, SH-5, catches the eye more than ear

Ambitious project that stretched the limits of conventional subtractive synthesis but scuppered RSF in the process. Only made in tiny quantities.

Samick SGP-101P
Digital piano

Country of origin	Korea
Orig. price (1984)	$1500 (£1200)
Price in 1996	No U.S. price (no UK price)
Keyboard	88-note
Sound type	Digital samples

Blessed with sounds from E-mu ProFormance piano module and with a reasonable keyboard, plus 25W stereo amplification system. Lacks the high gloss finish of Technics and Yamaha but interesting. SGP-101G is grand piano design version.

Samick SXP-501
Digital piano

Orig. price (1995)	No U.S. price (no UK price)
Price in 1996	No U.S. price (no UK price)
Keyboard	88-note
Sound type	Digital samples

Substantial-looking digital piano plus, complete with SMF access and karaoke features. SXP-511 model adds auto accompaniment styles.

Sequential Max
Polyphonic synthesizer

Country of origin	U.S.
Orig. price (1984)	$795 (£725)
Price in 1996	$250 (£200)
Keyboard	49-note
Sound type	Analog

Unwise move for Sequential into the realms of mass market keyboards. That said, a multitimbral synth was almost unheard of at the time (therefore unappreciated, too) and with its reliance upon external programming (based around Commodore 64 computer), lack of performance controls and unusual looks, it never really stood a chance.

Sequential Multi-Trak
Polyphonic synthesizer

Orig. price (1985)	$1499 (£1565)
Price in 1996	No U.S. price (no UK price)
Keyboard	61-note
Sound type	Analog

Upgraded version of Sequential's (and the world's) first multitimbral synth, the Six-Trak,

Left: No-holds-barred attempt to sell multitimbralism concept in 1984; Center: Snazzy packaging from Prophet-makers Sequential Circuits; Right: Multitimbralism began here on Sequential's 1984 Six-Trak

with 100 program storage, multitrack sequencer and arpeggiator. Troublesome but talented.

Sequential Pro One
Monophonic synthesizer

See entry in Hot 100.

Sequential Prophet
Remote Controller keyboard

Orig. price (1981)	$895 (£727)
Price in 1996	$250 (£200)
Keyboard	61-note
Sound type	n/a

Rare pre-MIDI sling-on remote keyboard designed for use with Prophet-5. Can access Prophet programs using panel buttons and connected via proprietary digital interface along with CV for filter and amplifier control. Limited appeal in its day. Almost useless aside from historical value today.

Sequential Prophet-5
Polyphonic synthesizer

See entry in Hot 100.

Sequential Prophet-10
Polyphonic synthesizer

See Sequential Prophet-5 entry in Hot 100.

Sequential Prophet-600
Polyphonic synthesizer

See entry in Hot 100.

Sequential Prophet-2000
Digital sampling keyboard

Orig. price (1986)	$2599 (£1999)
Price in 1996	$500 (£400)
Keyboard	61-note
Sound type	Digital samples

Innovative approach to sampling that never really caught on. Twelve-bit format, though up to 41.1kHz sample rate. You can mix preset waves with user samples. Good range of edit parameters. Mac editing software available at the time. Marred by squishy membrane panel controls and less than 100 percent reliability. Prophet-2002 somewhat improved modular version. Eight-voice poly.

Sequential Prophet-3000
Digital sampling module

Orig. price (1987)	$5000 (£3795)
Price in 1996	$850 (£750)
Keyboard	2U module
Sound type	Digital samples

Sequential's swan song and what could have been a major influence on sampler design with

its separate laptop controller, macro templates and streamlined sampling procedures. High quality unit (16-bit, 48kHz sampling) made in tiny numbers before Sequential was swallowed up and subsequently put on hold by Yamaha.

Sequential Prophet-T8
Polyphonic synthesizer

See entry in Hot 100.

Sequential Prophet-VS
Polyphonic synthesizer

See entry in Hot 100.

Sequential Six-Trak
Polyphonic synthesizer

Orig. price (1984)	$895 (£850)
Price in 1996	$300 (£250)
Keyboard	49-note
Sound type	Analog

The world's first MIDI multitimbral synthesizer, even if at the time no one quite knew why we should be needing it. Multitimbral facility monophonic allows you to stack up different mono tones or sequence six different lines. Sounds themselves not in Prophet-5 class but okay and programming rather tortuous. Not terribly reliable.

Sequential Split-Eight
Polyphonic synthesizer

Orig. price (1984)	No U.S. price (no UK price)
Price in 1996	No U.S. price (no UK price)

Japanese-designed instrument made for Sequential when times were getting extremely rough for the company. Cut down "Prophet" sounds in a rather plasticky casing. Made primarily for Japanese market and sold mainly in Japan.

Sequential Studio 440
Drum sampler/sequencer

Orig. price (1987)	$3999 £3000)
Price in 1996	$1000 (£750)
Keyboard	Tabletop
Sound type	Digital samples

Sophisticated 12-bit drum sampler and sequencer in manner of Linn/Akai MPC instruments. However...considerably less than 100 percent reliability undermined its appeal to the point of extinction. Way ahead of its time with SCSI, MTC, disk drive, 32-track sequencing, plus host of digital control and analog edit parameters. A currently working model would be a rare and valued find.

Siel Cruise
Multi-instrument keyboard

Country of origin	Italy
Orig. price (1982)	$595 (£549)
Price in 1996	$175 (£175)
Keyboard	49-note
Sound type	Analog

Complicated yet ultimately dreary mono/poly synth mishmash. Has one or two good settings (combining mono and poly sections) but no storage facilities and polyphonic tones are weak.

Siel DK-70
Polyphonic synthesizer

Orig. price (1986)	$795 (£549)
Price in 1996	$150 (£100)
Keyboard	49-note
Sound type	Analog

Trimmed DK-80 with sling-on possibilities. Fearful keyboard action. Best avoided.

Siel DK-80
Polyphonic synthesizer

Orig. price (1985)	$995 (£799)
Price in 1996	No U.S. price (£150)
Keyboard	61-note
Sound type	Analog

Brave attempt at producing an interesting-sounding, flexible synth that stood out from the Japanese pack, but cheap and nasty keyboard action let it down severely. Onboard sequencer, 6-voice dual oscillator design but with limited filtering. Expander 80 is modular version.

Siel DK-600
Polyphonic synthesizer

Orig. price (1983)	$1295 (£999)
Price in 1996	$300 (£175)
Keyboard	61-note
Sound type	Analog

Originally released as the Opera 6. Six-voice dual oscillator design capable of some okay brass patches. Let down by keyboard action, so "Expander" might be better bet for those interested.

Siel MK-900
Home keyboard

Orig. price (1984)	$695 (£399)
Price in 1996	$100 (£75)
Keyboard	61-note
Sound type	Analog

Good in its day for its age and type, but this synth-orienated MIDI home keyboard has no current relevance, no value.

Siel Mono
Monophonic synthesizer

Orig. price (1982)	$449 (£249)
Price in 1996	$125 (£75)
Keyboard	37-note
Sound type	Analog

One of Siel's more attractive offerings. Essentially the mono section of Siel Cruise and all the better for it.

Siel Piano Quattro
Electronic piano

Orig. price (1983)	$995 (£985)
Price in 1996	$200 (£200)
Keyboard	72-note
Sound type	Analog

A big boy and quite interesting. Different piano sounds, tweakable and strong on weird effects.

Siel Prelude
Electronic piano

U.S. name of PX Piano. See Siel PX Piano entry.

Siel PX JR
Electronic piano

Orig. price (1984)	$595 (£399)
Price in 1996	$100 (£100)
Keyboard	72-note
Sound type	Analog

A lot of keyboard for the money, then and now, so good value source of '80s style electronic piano tones. And with a touch-sensitive keyboard no less.

Siel PX Piano
Electronic piano

Orig. price (1983)	$795 (£599)
Price in 1996	$174 (£125)
Keyboard	72-note
Sound type	Analog

Another reasonable effort and good value for this vintage of piano tone. Ten tones, plus tremolo and chorus.

Solton MS5
Home keyboard

Country of origin	Germany
Orig. price (1991)	$2158 (£2000)
Price in 1996	$700 (£650)
Keyboard	61-note
Sound type	Multi synthesis

Employing subtractive analog, PCM and FM technologies to produce a wide range of tone colors in a style-based and therefore deemed "home keyboard" setting. No speakers. Programmable. Excels at organ tones. MS4 a tabletop expander.

Solton MS50
Home keyboard

Orig. price (1994)	$2200 (£1799)
Price in 1996	$1750 (£1500)
Keyboard	61-note
Sound type	Multi synthesis

Multimedia music workstation (i.e., style-generating synthesizer with lyrics-on-display feature). Offers grown-up sounds, especially strong on organs, in home keyboard setting. GM compatible and with good effects processing. Speakers only on MS50S (also known as MS60) model. MS40 a tabletop module in similar vein complete with disk drive.

Solton MS100
Home keyboard

Orig. price (1995)	No U.S. price (no UK price)
Price in 1996	No U.S. price (no UK price)
Keyboard	76-note
Sound type	PCM

With 540MB hard drive on board, 256 tones, 11 drum kits and high quality effects, this GM home keyboard is both powerful and different. Only Solton's comparative lack of corporate muscle counts against it.

Studio Electronics SE1
Monophonic synthesizer module

Country of origin	U.S.
Orig. price (1994)	$1395 (£1526)
Price in 1996	$1200 (£1500)
Keyboard	2U rackmount
Sound type	Analog

Three oscillators and Moog and ARP style filtering on this well made rackmount MIDI-ed mono. Ring mod, multiple triggering and 99 program memories. All credit to Studio Electronics for substantially stoking if not sparking the analog revival of the 1990s.

Studio Electronics SE6
Polyphonic synthesizer module

Orig. price (1995)	$4495 (£4500)
Price in 1996	$4495 (£4500)
Keyboard	2U rackmount
Sound type	Analog

Six-voice polyphonic version of SE1.

Technics SX-AX70
Home keyboard/synthesizer

Country of origin	Japan
Orig. price (1989)	No U.S. price (£1299)
Price in 1996	No U.S. price (£350)
Keyboard	61-note
Sound type	PCM2

Fascinating glimpse into Technics future WSA professional synthesizers on this home keyboard meets synth released some six years earlier. PCM "squared" technology of the time, reminiscent of subsequent Physical Modeling in its mixing and matching of instrument characteristics (and even, amazingly enough, in the advertising of the time which depicted mongrel "guitaraxophones" and such, very much in the manner of WSA series synth ads). Plenty of editable/programmable tones split up into PCM Attack and Body Sources from which all manner of faux instruments can be constructed. Styles also present, plus reasonable little sequencer. Not received well, unfortunately and duly abandoned. AX5 and AX3, similar but with less features and tones, both met with the same end: oblivion. Shame.

Technics SX-K700
Home keyboard

Orig. price (1987)	No U.S. price (£899)
Price in 1996	No U.S. price (£250)
Keyboard	61-note
Sound type	PCM

Early Technics home keyboard with high quality if conservative style and sound programming. Comprehensive sequencing facilities—both scratchpad type and more in-depth 4-track, with rudimentary sound editing available. First indication that Technics was capable of producing world-class instruments in this field. Also of this vintage, the far less inspiring four-octave K350 and K500.

Technics SX-KN400
Home keyboard

Orig. price (1990)	$1500 (£750)
Price in 1996	$600 (£300)
Keyboard	61-note
Sound type	PCM

Streamlined and limited by its mere 11-voice polyphony version of KN800. Still high quality sounds and 56 styles (some of which are a bit glitchy if you start playing challenging chord fingerings). Nowhere near as good as its predecessor KN200 limited still further by no velocity keyboard. Okay, but not two of Technics' best.

Technics SX-KN570
Home keyboard

Orig. price (1993)	$2500 (£1000)
Price in 1996	$700 (£600)

Left: Weak SIEL: flimsy sounds and keyboard on Italian DK-600

| Keyboard | 61-note |
| Sound type | PCM |

Less sexy-looking (LED as opposed to LCD) version of KN650 but still offers 200 tones, layerable, effects and 3-track sequencer. KN470 scaled down further in terms of memories and sequencer storage. Neither advertises itself as GM—a bit of a blunder by now.

Technics SX-KN650
Home keyboard

Orig. price (1992)	$2500 (£1000)
Price in 1996	$700 (£500)
Keyboard	61-note
Sound type	PCM

Cut down version of KN1000. Polyphony still a healthy 32-voice but comparatively straight-jacket effects and a certain wheeziness to some of the PCM tones. Pianos, organs, guitars, the best tones. Eight-track sequencer. Admirably straightforward to operate. KN550 has half the number of tones (100) and no provision for user style writing. KN750, meanwhile, adds a disk drive and large (7000-note capacity) sequencer and user style bank.

Technics SX-KN701
Home keyboard

Orig. price (1995)	$1695 (£899)
Price in 1996	$1500 (£750)
Keyboard	61-note
Sound type	PCM

Mid-priced keyboard with lots of good sounds and styles but no disk drive and smallish internal sequencer. KN-501 ($1195) is similar but has GM organized sounds.

Technics SX-KN800
Home keyboard

Orig. price (1989)	$3500 (£1500)
Price in 1996	$750 (£500)
Keyboard	61-note
Sound type	PCM

If the K700 was the first indication that Technics was capable of leading the field in home keyboards, the KN800 was the first to actually do so. With editable sounds, usable accompaniment patterns, crisp effects and sleek looks, the only complaint at the time was figuring out some of its many features. Disk drive SY-FD20 could be retrofitted. KN600 is 16-voice poly (as opposed to KN800's 23-voice) and has no onboard effects.

Technics SX-KN901
Home keyboard

Orig. price (1995)	$2500 (£999)
Price in 1996	$2000 (£800)
Keyboard	61-note
Sound type	PCM

Affordable home keyboard for those who drooled over the KN1000, KN2000 and still can't afford a KN3000. Thirty-two-voice polyphony and far more conservative styling (conventional 2 x 16 character display) but fully GM compatible and brim full of top quality sounds, rhythm patterns and complete styles. Also nine different temperaments offered.

Technics SX-KN1000
Home keyboard

Orig. price (1991)	$4000 (£2000)
Price in 1996	$1000 (£700)
Keyboard	61-note
Sound type	PCM

Technics hit the jackpot once again with this home keyboard—32-voice poly, 120 top quality PCM tones (editable to quite a wide degree) and stylish accompaniment patterns that can expand or contract in their intensity depending upon player dynamics. Disk drive was optional until close to the end of its life when it became a standard fixture. Music Disk Collection software for new styles and registrations loadable via the disk drive.

Technics SX-KN1200
Home keyboard

Orig. price (1994)	$2500 (£1399)
Price in 1996	$1500 (£750)
Keyboard	61-note
Sound type	PCM

With its range of soft breathy saxes and emotive jazz harmonica, the KN1200 is a delight to play as is. Impressively synth-like features also, though, with powerful easy edit sound editing. SMF-friendly disk drive, composer and 100 styles—a mid-priced GM keyboard for the inquiring mind. Handy APC Sound Arranger that helps choose sounds to go with each automatic accompaniment style is also found on slightly curtailed cousin KN700 and baby KN500.

Technics SX-KN2000
Home keyboard

Orig. price (1993)	$5000 (£2000)
Price in 1996	$2000 (£1000)
Keyboard	61-note
Sound type	PCM

Only something as impressive as the KN2000 stood a chance of stemming the flow of KN1000 customers. Another big, impressive instrument with giant screen, 64-voice polyphony, hundreds of styles—internally or off disk—editable sounds and almost note-perfect chord recognition. A creamy acoustic piano heads up the classy list of tones that can be coerced into GM mode, though the instrument makes no GM claims on the front panel. Sixteen-track sequencer can load in SMF.

Technics SX-KN3000
Home keyboard

Orig. price (1995)	$4995 (£2500)
Price in 1996	$4500 (£2000)
Keyboard	61-note
Sound type	PCM

Big screen, 400 styles, organ drawbar on screen, 64-voice poly, GM optional HD, high level voice editing.

Technics SX-PC100
Digital piano

Orig. price (1994)	$1495 (no UK price)
Price in 1996	$1200 (no UK price)
Keyboard	76-note
Sound type	PCM

U.S. model of Technics PX100 (see PX100 entry). Also PC-200 ($2595), which has 88-note keyboard, larger (25W stereo) amplification system and small playsequencer, plus two headphones sockets—good for education. PX-111 very similar model sold in UK.

Technics SX-PR35
Home keyboard

Orig. price (1991)	$5000 (£3000)
Price in 1996	$2000 (£1000)
Keyboard	88-note
Sound type	PCM

Weighted 88-note piano action type of home keyboard—a blend of KN and PX technologies and features. HSS technology employed here (see PX66 entry), manifesting itself as 40 layerable tones. Accompaniments are musical more than flashy and can be added to using Music Disk Collection data loaded from the internal disk drive. On PR250, the disk drive is optional and PR50 has just 12 tones and no obvious means of adding a disk drive. All with 32-voice poly.

Technics SX-PR110
Home keyboard

Orig. price (1993)	$3000 (£1500)
Price in 1996	$1750 (£850)
Keyboard	76-note
Sound type	PCM

Entry level, auto-accompaniment, piano-style home keyboard with 16 tones and 16 styles, plus plain reverb. No disk drive but a reasonable 15W stereo amplification system. Good bet if you can't run to Technics' full 88-note models, which tend to be frighteningly expensive.

Technics SX-PR307
Home keyboard

Orig. price (1994)	$8695 (£4000)
Price in 1996	$4000 (£2500)
Keyboard	88-note
Sound type	PCM

General MIDI finally catches up with Technics' piano styled home keyboards. Some 200 tones offered accompanied by 100 styles, reverb, 60W stereo amplification and built-in disk drive. PR305 slims down to 180 tones, 83 styles and 50W stereo system, while the PR303 plummets to just 16 tones and 70 styles.

Technics SX-PR370
Home keyboard

Orig. price (1993)	$5000 (£3000)
Price in 1996	$2200 (£1100)
Keyboard	88-note
Sound type	PCM

Super HSS technology (see PX74 entry) employed on this 58 tone, 32-voice poly accompaniment sporting piano action keyboard. Handy "Pianist" mode accompaniment takes its cue from what you play over the entire keyboard range, not just left hand "chord position." Eight-part sequencer can save or load data via internal disk drive. PR270 has but 40 tones and is physically styled a little different, while the PR170 has 30 tones, less powerful amplification, no third sostenuto pedal and optional disk drive.

Technics SX-PV10
Digital piano

Orig. price (1984)	No U.S. price (£899)
Price in 1996	No U.S. price (£200)
Keyboard	61-note
Sound type	PCM

Ten tones on this early digital. Passable pianos and a good acoustic guitar. Chorus, celeste and phaser.

Technics SX-PX1
Digital piano

Orig. price (1986)	No U.S. price (£3599)
Price in 1996	No U.S. price (£1000)
Keyboard	88-note
Sound type	PCM

First serious attempt by Technics to branch into digital piano market. Endorsed wholeheartedly by Rick Wakeman among others and indeed a fine job for the time. Extensive multi-sampling carried out for smoothness of tone and authenticity. Six-toned, plus chorus and tremolo and a 2-track sequencer. Replaced 20 times over by now but still a commendable play.

Technics SX-PX6
Digital piano

Orig. price (1987)	No U.S. price (£1399)
Price in 1996	No U.S. price (£500)
Keyboard	88-note
Sound type	PCM

Sparse-featured second generation of Technics digitals offering just six tones at 16-voice polyphony with chorus as a lone optional effect. Good speaker system. PX4 is 76-note model.

Technics SX-PX9
Digital piano

Orig. price (1986)	No U.S. price (£1599)
Price in 1996	No U.S. price (£500)
Keyboard	88-note
Sound type	PCM

PX1 quality sounds on more basic keyboard. Five tones, plus 2-track sequencer, chorus and tremolo. PX7 sports a less loungy look and PX5 has just a 76-note keyboard.

Technics SX-PX30
Digital piano

Orig. price (1988)	$2500 (£1699)
Price in 1996	$1000 (£700)
Keyboard	88-note
Sound type	PCM

Featuring Technics' then-new Concert Touch keyboard action, which is slick and fast. Eleven meticulously sampled tones, plus chorus, EQ and reverb and a 2-track (not separate sound per track, though) sequencer. PX20: same animal with slightly reduced power amplification and minus the sequencer.

Technics SX-PX66
Digital piano

Orig. price (1990)	$4999 (£2000)
Price in 1996	$1750 (£850)
Keyboard	88-note
Sound type	PCM

Harmonic Source Sampling made its debut here, a Technics technology employing a pot-pourri of close-miked, direct and reverberant sound recording for its samples. Ten tones include a spanking new Steinway sample, plus splendidly warm electric piano, along with reverb and celeste effects. Amplified using a massive 50W stereo system. PX55 loses one or two tones and half the amplification wattage while PX44 drops down to 16-voice polyphony. Both PX66 and PX55 are 32-voice.

Technics SX-PX74
Digital piano

Orig. price (1992)	$5299 (£2000)
Price in 1996	$1850 (£850)
Keyboard	88-note
Sound type	PCM

After Harmonic Source Sampling...Super Harmonic Source Sampling (see PX66 entry) on the PX74, which reveals itself as a stereo sampling version of the same. Ten suitably expansive tones, plus reverb and celeste, plus 2-track sequencer. Can function multitimbrally over MIDI. PX73 loses four (of the most indifferent) tones and reduces amplification from 50W stereo to 20W stereo, while PX71 is standard HSS (i.e., not using stereo samples) and jettisons the sequencer. Strangely enough, Super

HSS makes a fairly marginal difference, and the sequencer is strictly limited. Ergo PX71 (some $2000 less than PX73 on U.S. list price) makes a good buy.

Technics SX-PX100
Digital piano

Orig. price (1994)	No U.S. price (£1099)
Price in 1996	No U.S. price (£600)
Keyboard	76-note
Sound type	PCM

Low cost but still high quality digital using just 76-note keyboard. Six tones, but impressive 32-voice polyphony and reverb and celeste effects. Called PC100 in U.S.

Technics SX-PX106
Digital piano

Orig. price (1994)	$6799 (no UK price)
Price in 1996	$2500 (no UK price)
Keyboard	88-note
Sound type	PCM

Very similar to PX107, which came out a year earlier, but with older style keyboard action (lighter than PX107) yet beefier amplification system (80W stereo) and more memory for the sequencer (8000 notes). A polished performer, only made available in U.S.

Technics SX-PX107
Digital piano

Orig. price (1993)	$6799 (£2599)
Price in 1996	$2000 (£1200)
Keyboard	88-note
Sound type	PCM

RIP HSS (see PX66 entry). In 1993, the fashion was DA (Dynamic Acoustics), whose difference is, to say the least, subtle. Still a great piano, offering 10 tones, plus reverb and celeste in a whopping 60W stereo amplification setting. First class keyboard action, if quite heavy and impressive half-pedaling effects on, well, foot. Mega 64-voice polyphony. PX103 reduced to 32-voice and arrives minus the strings tone (dreary, no loss), while the PX101 has no vibes nor rock piano tone and no 2-track sequencer as featured on PX107 and PX103.

Technics SX-PX111
Digital piano

Orig. price (1995)	No U.S. price (£1599)
Price in 1996	No U.S. price (£1000)
Keyboard	88-note
Sound type	PCM

Similar if not identical to PC200 (see Technics PC200 entry) as sold in U.S.

Technics SX-PX203
Digital piano

Orig. price (1995)	$3795 (no UK price)
Price in 1996	$2500 (no UK price)
Keyboard	88-note
Sound type	PCM

More DA (Dynamic Acoustics) from Technics on this 32-voice poly, 50W stereo amplified digital, sporting clean, open lines; functional more than flash. The PX201 drops the PX203's 2-track sequencer and drops to 40W stereo amplification. Both instruments available in black or simulated wood grain finish.

Technics SX-PX207
Digital piano

Orig. price (1995)	$6295 (£2599)
Price in 1996	$5000 (£2250)
Keyboard	88-note
Sound type	PCM

Solid and impressive performer employing ear-catching wrap-around speaker system utilizing the front grille and state-of-the-art Technics sampled sounds. Grand piano, upright, electric grand, pair of electrics, harpsichord, voice and strings can be played in isolation or layered. Max 64-voice polyphony. Digital effects and filter. Class animal. Also PX205, which loses the odd voice and a few watts of power.

Technics SX-WSA1
Polyphonic synthesizer

Orig. price (1995)	$4995 (£2936)
Price in 1996	$3000 (£2500)
Keyboard	61-note
Sound type	Acoustic modeling synthesis

Technics finally leaves home keyboards behind and produces a fully professional, future tech synth with all the trimmings. Creamy quality sounds and, for the most part, fathomable programming. Only Technics reputation in the leisure market has pro users uncertain. Rick Wakeman a noted fan. 256 preset tones culled from numerous resonators and drivers, accompanied by expressive, real-time controllable digital effects and a full-scale 16-track sequencer. Expandable in terms of outputs and wave memory. Also SX-WSA1R 3U rackmount version.

Teisco 100P
Monophonic synthesizer

Country of origin	Japan
Orig. price (1981)	No U.S. price (£650)
Price in 1996	No U.S. price (£125)
Keyboard	37-note
Sound type	Analog

Kawai-made, organ-inspired mono with presets. S-60P similar with less presets.

Unique DBM
Controller keyboard

Country of origin	Italy
Orig. price (1986)	$1199 (no UK price)
Price in 1996	$150 (£175)
Keyboard	72-note
Sound type	n/a

Unique was one of Crumar's multifarious *nom de plumes* under which the world's keyboard market was periodically assaulted. (Unique keyboards sold in the UK under the name of Bit or occasionally Chase.) Notable facilities include sequencer, two MIDI Outs, 3-zone splits and aftertouch keyboard. However, its weird positioning of pitch and mod wheels, featherlite action and the fact that Unique, Bit, Chase, Crumar and various other horses they rode in on have now all galloped off into the sunset, make this a dubious, indeed high-risk, prospect.

Viscount D9
Stage organ

Country of origin	Italy
Orig. price (1991)	$1295 (£699)
Price in 1996	No U.S. price (£300)
Keyboard	61-note
Sound type	Analog

Useful, drawbar-laden stage organ, which along with module D9E, is also seen in U.S. branded as the Oberheim OB-3. Slim on polyphony but some strong tones and, as all such instruments should be, hands on and dead easy to use. Also appeared in UK under the name of Fujiha D9 in splendidly Italian cavalier style to make people assume Japanese parentage.

Viscount Classico SV-80
Digital piano

Orig. price (1993)	$3200 (£1799)
Price in 1996	$2000 (£1000)
Keyboard	88-note
Sound type	Digital samples

Perfectly reasonable offering from Viscount, suffering only through lack of corporate muscle and international marketing savvy. Good, clean range of tones, nice effects and amplification. Just nothing special. Also SV-100, the home-style version of the pre flight cased, rock 'n' roll FK-1000 (see FK-1000 entry).

Viscount FK-1000
Digital Piano

Orig. price (1993)	No U.S. price (£999)
Price in 1996	No U.S. price (£650)
Keyboard	88-note
Sound type	Digital sample

Sold as Oberheim Eclipse in U.S. Well made 32-voice digital with limited, but responsive and robust, range of piano tones, plus handy slider-operated strings. Comes hard-wired into its flight case and gets on with the job very well. Pleasant rather than startling keyboard action. Good value.

Voce DMI-64
Organ module

Country of origin	U.S.
Orig. price (1991)	$800 (no UK price)
Price in 1996	$500 (no UK price)
Keyboard	1U rackmount
Sound type	Digital samples

Powerful if somewhat impenetrable specialist organ module based on 64 organ samples stored within 99 presets. Later accompanied by MIDI Drawbar Controller to make things easier. Voce has since moved on to better and more usable things in the field.

Voce Electric Piano
Piano module

Orig. price (1995)	$549 (£500)
Price in 1996	$500 (£400)
Keyboard	1U half width rackmount
Sound type	Additive synthesis

A module full of classic electric piano tones. Unusually, not sample-based but additive synthesis-based. Thirty-two tones cover Wurlitzers to Rhodes to Clavi but specifically no acoustic pianos. Not everyone's cup of tea but keenly priced with some good effects (wah-wah, tremolo...) and refreshingly different.

Voce Micro B
Organ module

Orig. price (1993)	$499 (£499)
Price in 1996	$350 (£300)
Keyboard	1U half width rackmount
Sound type	Digital samples

Plenty of polyphony in this tiny module. Good, strong sounds, if a tad sharp on the attack side, but with some MIDI limitations and inflexible effects. Subsequent Micro B II ($579) a far better and more controllable bet. No physical drawbars, of course.

Voce V3
Organ module

Orig. price (1995)	$1195 (£995)
Price in 1996	$900 (£700)

Keyboard	1U rackmount
Sound type	"Digital tone wheels"

Major performer in the organ module game. Bags of power sonically, polyphonically and in terms of control. Optional MIDI Drawbar Controller ($299) would complete a very happy picture. Onboard effects include Voce's own Leslie simulator, Spin, though there's an actual Leslie connector at the back if you're something of a purist. Probably the best in its field.

Vox Continental
Stage organ

Country of origin	UK

See entry in Hot 100.

Vox Jaguar
Stage organ

Orig. price (1962)	$200 (£75)
Price in 1996	$200 (£150)
Keyboard	49-note
Sound type	Transistor

Baby brother to the Vox Continental but just as popular at the time and, to some extent, even more so as a vintage keyboard. Uses rocker switches as opposed to drawbars. Simple, fun, raucous, very '60s and sought after if hardly in the "priceless" category yet.

Waldorf MicroWave
Polyphonic synthesizer module

Country of origin	Germany

See entry in Hot 100.

Waldorf Wave
Polyphonic synthesizer

Orig. price (1993)	$8000 (£5000)
Price in 1996	No U.S. price (£4000)
Keyboard	61-note
Sound type	Wavetable

Gorgeous instrument with large highly tactile control panel and presently available in a range of colors and polyphonies. Had difficult birth but produces PPG-like sounds in an inimitable but vaguely modern fashion. Big, boisterous, in permanent multitimbral mode, expensive, fairly complex to operate.

Wersi Pegasus
Polyphonic synthesizer

Country of origin	Germany
Orig. price (1993)	$5000 (£3500)
Price in 1996	No U.S. price (no UK price)
Keyboard	61-note
Sound type	Digital

Hit-and-miss distribution has limited all Wersi products outside Germany. Sleek home synth in Korg i-Series class though understandably more inclined to European ears on its styles (marches, etc.). A highly sophisticated performer, though, with 54-voice polyphony, touch screen, expandable, 24-bit effects... Pegasus 2 adds more styles, sounds and effects. Rackmount Pegasus Expander also.

Will Systems MAB-303
Monophonic synthesizer module

Country of origin	Germany
Price in 1996	$500 (£350)
Price in 1996	No U.S. price (no UK price)
Keyboard	1U half width rackmount
Sound type	Analog

One of an increasing number of TB-303 clones coming out of Germany. With 18dB filtering, Accent, Slide on and off, this tiny rack unit's filter and oscillator even respond to aftertouch. Limited release outside Germany at time of writing.

Wurlitzer EP-200
Electronic piano

Country of origin	U.S.

See entry in Hot 100.

Wurlitzer WX-2
Home keyboard

Orig. price (1994)	$3895 (no UK price)
Price in 1996	No U.S. price (no UK price)
Keyboard	61-note
Sound type	Digital samples

SMF incorporating with huge array of tones, plus GM set, styles, disk drive, even lyrics and melody display. Sample RAM expansion available. Made also under GeneralMusic banner.

Yamaha CBXK1
Controller keyboard

Country of origin	Japan
Orig. price (1995)	No U.S. price (£129)
Price in 1996	No U.S. price (£100)
Keyboard	37-note
Sound type	n/a

Bargain controller keyboard aimed at the computer market. Thirty-seven mini keys, battery operable and impressive level of assignable controllers for the money and size.

Yamaha CE20
Multi-instrument keyboard

Orig. price (1982)	$1395 (£999)
Price in 1996	$85 (£150)
Keyboard	49-note
Sound type	Digital (FM)

Fascinating early glimpse into the power of FM synthesis as would later be revealed on the DX7. Here, tones offered as presets in mono and poly categories for the most part outstanding examples of FM (flute, trombone especially). Dead easy to use. CE25 is 8-voice poly version with 20 presets.

Yamaha CLP50
Digital piano

Orig. price (1986)	$2799 (£1500)
Price in 1996	$600 (£450)
Keyboard	88-note
Sound type	Digital (AWM)

Best of the series Clavinova digital piano in 1986. 20W stereo amplification and three top quality tones. CLP30 and CLP20 have smaller amplification systems.

Yamaha CLP123
Digital piano

Orig. price (1994)	$4000 (no UK price)
Price in 1996	$2500 (no UK price)
Keyboard	88-note
Sound type	Digital (AWM)

Center: World's most beautiful synth? The wondrous Wave from Waldorf

Yamaha CLP124
Digital piano

Orig. price (1992)	$5275 (£2399)
Price in 1996	$2000 (£1000)
Keyboard	88-note
Sound type	Digital (AWM)

The Clavinova series received a new sound chip and new stereo samples for the CLP124 and associates. Effects include reverbs and Yamaha's own "Cosmic" (swirly phasing) and amplification is a weighty 50W stereo. CLP123 is quite drastic reduction in tones, power and effects (just reverb), while CLP122S ditches strings (so no classic piano+strings patches), and CLP121S moves down to 14-voice polyphony from its 76-note keyboard.

Yamaha CLP153sg
Digital piano

Orig. price (1995)	$2655 (£1399)
Price in 1996	No U.S. price (no UK price)
Keyboard	88-note
Sound type	Digital (AWM)

Low-cost but high-quality Clavinova with five layerable tones, reverb, metronome, plus two headphones sockets. No frills; good for teachers. CLP152S with 76-note keyboard

Yamaha CLP155
Digital piano

Orig. price (1995)	$4435 (no UK price)
Price in 1996	No U.S. price (no UK price)
Keyboard	88-note
Sound type	Digital (AWM)

More high-quality AWM tones from 30W amplification system in the Clavinova series. CLP156 offers built-in disk drive and LED display. CLP157 has additional effects and more powerful amplification.

Yamaha CLP300
Digital piano

Orig. price (1987)	$2399 (£1499)
Price in 1996	$600 (£450)
Keyboard	88-note
Sound type	Digital (AWM)

Respectable if modest piano with five tones and pleasantly weighted keyboard. CLP200 has 76-note keyboard, loses a couple of tones and has 8W, in place of the CLP300's 20W amplification.

Yamaha CLP500
Digital piano

Orig. price (1987)	$2599 (£1899)
Price in 1996	$700 (£575)
Keyboard	88-note
Sound type	Digital (AWM)

Replacement for and development of CLP50. "New" AE keyboard action, plus 10 sparkling AWM tones and crisp 30W stereo amplification. Chorus and tremolo only. No reverb or multitimbral application, which means you really have to like the tone quality. Pure and simple.

Yamaha CLP560
Digital piano

Orig. price (1990)	$2999 (£2450)
Price in 1996	$1500 (£1000)
Keyboard	88-note
Sound type	Digital (AWM)

Nothing especially flash on this quality Clavinova. Can be 3-part multitimbral over MIDI but no chorus (just reverb and brilliance) and flat tone mixing as opposed to adjustable layering. CLP760 adds a third acoustic piano tone, can split tones across the keyboard and revives the effects of chorus, detune and tremolo, while CLP360 loses the strings and vibes tones and is 26-voice polyphonic and CLP260 loses the second acoustic piano and has no effects whatsoever.

Yamaha CLP650
Digital piano

Orig. price (1988)	$2999 (£1999)
Price in 1996	$1000 (£750)
Keyboard	88-note
Sound type	Digital (AWM)

Rare (for the time) 32-voice polyphony on this heavyweight Clavinova with 10 layerable tones and top quality effects. CLP550 halves polyphony and features seven tones, and CLP350 has just five. CLP570 and CLP670 are simply upgraded cabinet versions of CLP550 and CLP650. Got it?

Yamaha CP7
Electronic piano

Orig. price (1983)	$445 (£369)
Price in 1996	$50 (£50)
Keyboard	61-note
Sound type	Analog

Inoffensive, bespeakered, but pre-MIDI, just four tones and not a lot of use.

Yamaha CP10
Electronic piano

Orig. price (1980)	$495 (£399)
Price in 1996	$30 (£30)
Keyboard	61-note
Sound type	Analog

Not much good in 1980. Almost indescribably disposable now.

Yamaha CP11
Electronic piano

Orig. price (1981)	$595 (£439)
Price in 1996	$50 (£40)
Keyboard	61-note
Sound type	Analog

Arpeggiator the only chink of light in this dismal piano, plus drum patterns/accompaniments keyboard.

Yamaha CP20
Electronic piano

Orig. price (1981)	$1125 (£999)
Price in 1996	$150 (£150)
Keyboard	61-note
Sound type	Analog

Touch-sensitive keyboard, but little else to recommend about this 4-tone wood-finish piano.

Yamaha CP25
Electronic piano

Orig. price (1982)	$1995 (£1279)
Price in 1996	$200 (£200)
Keyboard	61-note
Sound type	Analog

Synth-like electronic piano, unusually programmable courtesy of mixing four waveforms and tweaking filter and envelope. Sixteen-voice polyphonic. Flanger makes ear-catching noise, too. CP35 is 73 note version with XLR outputs and Yamaha's pre-MIDI Key Code digital interface.

Yamaha CP30
Electronic piano

Orig. price (1978)	$1695 (£1279)
Price in 1996	$200 (£200)
Keyboard	76-note
Sound type	Analog

Big and heavy early Yamaha electronic with reasonable degree of control over its tones. Still outmoded.

Yamaha CP60
Electro-acoustic piano

Orig. price (1986)	$4500 (£2799)
Price in 1996	$1750 (£750)
Keyboard	76-note
Sound type	Acoustic

Upright version of the classic CP70 and CP80 with MIDI. Never as successful but still a good performer and useful compromise between electric and acoustic technology: real strings, pre-miked, plus MIDI, 7-band EQ, tremolo.

Yamaha CP70M
Electric grand piano

See Yamaha CP80 entry in Hot 100.

Yamaha CP80
Electric grand piano

See entry in Hot 100.

Yamaha CS01
Monophonic synthesizer

Orig. price (1982)	$275 (£189)
Price in 1996	$85 (£50)
Keyboard	32-note
Sound type	Analog

Innovative small-key synth offering Breath Control over filter cutoff or volume, shoulder straps, internal speaker, battery power option... Single oscillator design with 12dB/oct filtering, so not huge sounding. Fun and inexpensive. CS01II has brighter livery.

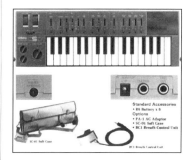

Yamaha CS1X
Polyphonic synthesizer

Price in 1996	No U.S. price (£599)
Price in 1996	No U.S. price (no UK price)
Keyboard	61-note
Sound type	Digital (AWM 2)

Left: Yamaha's ill-fated rescue of Sequential; Right: Yamaha's innovative and popular late mono: the CS01

Eye-catchingly blue, hands-on synth for the knob-twiddling dance/techno market. Analog sounds in digital domain, with interesting new concepts like "scene controller" (instant changes in sound texture), plus an arpeggiator, drums, effects, pitch and mod wheel, 32-voice polyphony and a great sticker price.

Yamaha CS5
Monophonic synthesizer

Orig. price (1979)	$485 (£349)
Price in 1996	$75 (£125)
Keyboard	37-note
Sound type	Analog

Single oscillator with clean, more than powerful, sounds. Good panel layout, multimode filtering. Safe bet.

Yamaha CS15
Monophonic synthesizer

Orig. price (1979)	$835 (£589)
Price in 1996	$175 (£150)
Keyboard	37-note
Sound type	Analog

Dual oscillator version of CS5—in fact, dual everythings: filters, VCAs, envelope generators. Portamento, brilliance, plus pitch bend give tactile edge to this complex but quite powerful mono.

Yamaha CS15D
Preset monophonic synthesizer

Orig. price (1980)	$1095 (£739)
Price in 1996	$175 (£150)
Keyboard	37-note
Sound type	Analog

Unusual preset synth offering 29 sounds, plus single live configuration. Confusingly, has little in common with CS15 physically, though similar range of parameters.

Yamaha CS20M
Monophonic synthesizer

Orig. price (1980)	$1595 (£1179)
Price in 1996	$200 (£200)
Keyboard	37-note
Sound type	Analog

Eight memories in this large but still mono synth. Dual oscillator, plus noise, multimode filtering (12dB/oct), portamento or glissando and pro XLR output. Not terribly exciting but a useful performer.

Yamaha CS40M
Duophonic synthesizer

Orig. price (1980)	$2195 (£1599)
Price in 1996	$200 (£200)
Keyboard	44-note
Sound type	Analog

Big and expensive at the time but, armed with four VCOs, ring modulator, multimode filtering, some 20 patch memories and a roomy 44-note keyboard, not a rip-off. Well made and good fun for serious programmers.

Yamaha CS60
Polyphonic synthesizer

Orig. price (1978)	$4950 (£2290)
Price in 1996	$450 (£450)
Keyboard	61-note
Sound type	Analog

Cut down version of CS80 (see entry in Hot 100). Thinner sounds and non-velocity, though (curiously) still aftertouch sensitive keyboard. Not really the same animal though similar operation. Also CS50 with 49-note keyboard and 4-voice polyphony.

Yamaha CS70M
Polyphonic synthesizer

Orig. price (1981)	$2999 (£1899)
Price in 1996	$300 (£400)
Keyboard	61-note
Sound type	Analog

Bill Nelson was an ardent fan of CS70M long after this bulky 6-voice poly had its brief heyday. Dual oscillators, full complement of programmable parameters, effects of ensemble and tremolo, portamento, four independent tracks' worth of sequencing and even external storage via magnetic data cards. Sounds have a tendency towards harshness.

Yamaha CS80
Polyphonic synthesizer

See entry in Hot 100.

Yamaha CVP75
Home keyboard/piano

Orig. price (1991)	No U.S. price (£3500)
Price in 1996	No U.S. price (£1200)
Keyboard	88-note
Sound type	Digital (AWM)

Piano style home keyboard in the Clavinova

series. Somewhat curious looking but firm AE weighted action keyboard, 12 immediately accessible tones, plus a further 50 "hidden" ones and 24 styles with user programming available. Disk drive and effects complete this powerful mixture of digital piano and home keyboard. CVP65 slightly less powerful in amplification, CVP55 has less hidden tones and CVP35 loses disk drive and is just 16-voice polyphonic.

Yamaha CVP87A
Home keyboard/piano

Orig. price (1993)	No U.S. price (£3500)
Price in 1996	No U.S. price (£1750)
Keyboard	88-note
Sound type	Digital (AWM)

Piano style home keyboard with built-in teaching system (Guide System). Disk drive that can accept SMF, plus Yamaha Disk Orchestra, etc. Somewhat curious GM mode whereby GM tones can only be called up by a GM sequence. Big 80W stereo amplification. CVP85A loses third pedal and audio inputs. CVP83S has 40W stereo.

Yamaha CVP89
Home keyboard/piano

Orig. price (1995)	$10,655 (£4999)
Price in 1996	No U.S. price (no UK price)
Keyboard	88-note
Sound type	Digital (AWM)

Bells and whistles, style-sporting digital piano in the Clavinova series. Lots of everything—voices, polyphony, styles, amplification... Also in the series, CVP79, -69, -59 and -49, which all progressively shave off voices and features but share 88-note weighted keyboard (except CVP49: 76-note) and GM-compatible AWM tones.

Yamaha CX5M
Music computer system

Orig. price (1984)	$669 (£549)
Price in 1996	$100 (£100)
Keyboard	YK-01: 49-note, YK-10: 61-note
Sound type	Digital (FM)

Music computer system based around MSX computer, comprising FM tones, simple sequencing, accompaniments with add-ons for sound editing, multitimbral sequencing and more. The MSX as a computer platform failed, however, which scuppered any chance the CX5M might have had at bringing computer-based music to the masses. Accordingly of no real value today. Even the subsequent CX5MII/128, with a then-whopping 128KB of RAM and SFG05 Tone Generator onboard failed to ignite worldwide interest. This later unit was sold in Japan as CX7M/128.

Yamaha Disklavier
MIDI player piano

See entry in Hot 100.

Yamaha DSR1000
Home keyboard

Orig. price (1987)	$1399 (£719)
Price in 1996	$350 (£250)
Keyboard	61-note
Sound type	Digital (FM)

Easily digestible FM sounds, PCM drum patterns (16 preset, 16 programmable), 2-track sequencer, speakers and MIDI. DSR-2000 has 5-track sequencer and velocity keyboard. Equivalent to DX-11 sounds in nonpatronizing home keyboard setting.

Yamaha DX1
Polyphonic synthesizer

Orig. price (1984)	$10,900 (£9499)
Price in 1996	No U.S. price (no UK price)
Keyboard	73-note
Sound type	Digital (FM)

Hand-finished "Rolls Royce" of FM keyboards, made in limited quantities. Essentially two DX7s though with better, more visual displays and panel controls. ROM/RAM cartridge storage, split or layered sounds, plus 64-channel performance memory. Designed as a flagship, and an impressive one, too.

Yamaha DX5
Polyphonic synthesizer

Orig. price (1985)	$3495 (£2999)
Price in 1996	$750 (£600)
Keyboard	76-note
Sound type	Digital (FM)

Similar to DX5 in its "dual DX7" design with 32-voice polyphony, performance memories and plenty of panel controls to steer you through the maze of FM programming. A stylish instrument and still a joy to play.

Yamaha DX7
Polyphonic synthesizer

See entry in Hot 100.

Yamaha DX7IID
Polyphonic synthesizer

Orig. price (1987)	$2195 (£1699)
Price in 1996	$500 (£450)
Keyboard	61-note
Sound type	Digital (FM)

"The DX7 is dead. Long live the DX7." Something along those lines is how the DX7II, in both its "D" and "FD" (with built-in disk drive) manifestations, was ushered in. Though innumerable original DX7 faults, limitations, anomalies, etc. were fixed—split/layered tones available, assignable sliders, increased bit-rate and so better audio quality, micro tuning, decent MIDI—many were not. Most notably, multitimbral function that was made available courtesy of third party mod from Grey Matter, entitled E! Plenty of classic FM tones but lacks the charm of the original.

Yamaha DX7S
Polyphonic synthesizer

Orig. price (1987)	$1495 (£1295)
Price in 1996	$400 (£350)
Keyboard	61-note
Sound type	Digital (FM)

A DX7II without the split/layering capability and with old-style DX7 size display screen. Multitimbral upgrade E! could be fitted, thus leapfrogging over its basic inherent limitations.

Yamaha DX9
Polyphonic synthesizer

Orig. price (1983)	$1395 (£949)
Price in 1996	$200 (£175)
Keyboard	61-note
Sound type	Digital (FM)

Baby brother of the DX7, released concurrently and, one suspects, produced in order to sell DX7s as opposed to generating sales of itself. With its 4-operator FM system, just 20 memories and no cartridge slot, there are a lot of minuses. Still 16-voice poly. The dearth of DX7s still around make the DX9 not a particularly attractive buy on the second-hand market.

Yamaha DX11
Polyphonic synthesizer

Orig. price (1988)	$995 (£675)
Price in 1996	$375 (£275)
Keyboard	61-note
Sound type	Digital (FM)

Multitimbral FM synth along lines of TX81Z module. 128 preset tones, plus 96 memories, with flexible tone/keyboard mapping—even in terms of tuning. Some Quick Edit parameters speed up the grisly business of FM programming. Used and long admired by Bill Bruford as tone expander for his Simmons SDX drum sampling system.

Yamaha DX21
Polyphonic synthesizer

Orig. price (1985)	$795 (£800)
Price in 1996	$250 (£200)
Keyboard	61-note
Sound type	Digital (FM)

Part of second generation of 4-operator FM synths—a little more controllable, split/layering and with one or two superb features such as being able to pitch bend a single note within a chord. Non-velocity keyboard a bit of a boob, though velocity can be received over MIDI.

Yamaha DX100
Polyphonic synthesizer

Orig. price (1986)	$599 (£399)
Price in 1996	$150 (£175)
Keyboard	49-note
Sound type	Digital (FM)

192 tones' worth of 4-operator FM on this short-scale keyboard. Can be used in sling-on mode. Shallow, light keyboard which is non-velocity. DX27 ($799) identical except 61-note full-size keyboard.

Yamaha EMT1
Polyphonic synthesizer module

Orig. price (1988)	$500 (£330)
Price in 1996	$85 (£75)
Keyboard	1U half width module
Sound type	Digital (FM)

Simple box of 32 FM tones. No hassle operation. Released alongside EMT10 though never quite as popular.

Yamaha EMT10
Polyphonic synthesizer module

Orig. price (1988)	$550 (£330)
Price in 1996	$75 (£65)
Keyboard	1U half width module
Sound type	Digital (AWM)

Foolproof box of 12 AWM sampled tones ranging from acoustic pianos to choir to bass. Limited to 8-voice polyphony but very high quality for the price. Rick Wakeman a big fan at one point.

Yamaha FB01
Polyphonic synthesizer module

Orig. price (1986)	$350 (£325)
Price in 1996	$85 (£75)
Keyboard	1U half width module
Sound type	Digital (FM)

Multitimbral FM tone module. Tabletop design housing 240 presets and room for 96 externally edited (via computer and FB editor software) tones. Four-operator FM. Very popular in its day and, though now considered noisy and dated, a very cost-effective route into some FM sounds. Only 8-voice polyphony.

Yamaha Gran Touch
Digital piano

Orig. price 1996	No U.S. price (no UK price)
Keyboard	88-note
Sound type	Digital samples

The latest in Yamaha's seemingly endless range of acoustic-meets-electric pianos. As name implies, the key here is keyboard action, faithfully reproduced, shanks, hammers and all, from a Yamaha acoustic piano. Sounds are samples from Yamaha Concert Series CFIIIS stored in 30MB waveform ROM and played back via a 60W stereo amplification system. With extensive MIDI controls and obvious "silent" potential.

Yamaha GS1
Polyphonic synthesizer

See entry in Hot 100.

Yamaha GS2
Polyphonic synthesizer

See Yamaha GS1 entry in Hot 100.

Yamaha KX5
Remote keyboard

Orig. price (1984)	$495 (£449)
Price in 1996	$100 (£100)
Keyboard	37-note
Sound type	n/a

Almost a success at the time, which would have made it unique among this first generation of "dumb" controller keyboards. Some features slanted towards DX7, which made it more viable then and less viable now. Pitch ribbon plus Breath Controller input give it distinction.

Yamaha KX76
Remote keyboard

Orig. price (1986)	$1750 (no UK price)
Price in 1996	$400 (no UK price)
Keyboard	76-note
Sound type	n/a

76-note keyboard version of KX88 (see entry in Hot 100).

Left: First presentation of the DX7; Center: Yamaha DX100: good value FM in 1986

Yamaha KX88
Controller keyboard

See entry in Hot 100.

Yamaha MIDI Grand
Acoustic/MIDI piano

Orig. price (1988)	$17,999 (£10,999)
Price in 1996	No U.S. price (no UK price)
Keyboard	88-note
Sound type	Acoustic

Yamaha Concert Grand with MIDI Out built in. Not to be confused with Disklavier "player piano" models, which can be driven from a sequencer and have motorized keys, the MIDI Grand is strictly for real-time human control. From its swanky, high tech control panel, all manner of MIDI layerings and trickery can be masterminded and stored within 64 performance memories. Not what you'd call fool-proof to operate but a joy to play. Two models: C3E and the longer and 50 percent more expensive C7E.

Yamaha MK100
Home keyboard

Orig. price (1984)	$425 (£269)
Price in 1996	$75 (£75)
Keyboard	49-note
Sound type	Digital

Creditable attempt at a home keyboard that doesn't insult the intelligence. Patterns okay, but Multi Menu allows you to construct new sounds, plus pattern sequencer. Speakers, battery power option. A lot of fun at the time.

Yamaha MU5
Polyphonic synthesizer module

Orig. price (1995)	$299 (£239)
Price in 1996	$250 (£200)
Keyboard	1U half width rackmount
Sound type	Digital (AWM 2)

Basic MU series model with just 128 GM tones. Direct computer interface. Not terribly exciting.

Yamaha MU50
Polyphonic synthesizer module

Orig. price (1995)	$499 (£429)
Price in 1996	$450 (£400)
Keyboard	1U half width rackmount
Sound type	Digital (AWM 2)

Low-cost XG format module packed with 700+ sounds and more than respectable digital effects.

Yamaha MU80
Polyphonic synthesizer module

Orig. price (1995)	$895 (£699)
Price in 1996	$650 (£500)
Keyboard	1U half width rackmount
Sound type	Digital (AWM 2)

GM module replacing the TG300 et al. Massive 32-part multitimbrality, with 64-voice polyphony, 660 tones, 18 drum kits, EQ and four effects processors. Marks the debut of Yamaha's "super GM" XG format.

Yamaha P50M
Digital piano module

Price in 1996	No U.S. price (£399)
Price in 1996	No U.S. price (no UK price)
Keyboard	1U half width rackmount module
Sound type	Digital (AWM 2)

Simple box of digital piano sounds trawled from Yamaha's long experience in the field.

6MB waveform ROM spans CP80 to DX7 over 20 tones (32-voice poly), with onboard reverb and chorus, plus slider controllable EQ. Can be incorporated into XG/GM environment.

Yamaha P150
Digital piano

Orig. price (1995)	$2295 (no UK price)
Price in 1996	$2000 (no UK price)
Keyboard	88-note
Sound type	Digital (AWM)

Interesting blend of piano and organ features.

Yamaha P300
Digital piano

Orig. price (1995)	$3995 (£2500)
Price in 1996	$3200 (£2250)
Keyboard	88-note
Sound type	Digital (AWM 2)

Affordable version of the P500 released one year later. Eleven piano voices playable at 32-voice polyphony, plus effects, panel EQ and plenty of MIDI performance control. Not in the same gob smacking class of looks as the P500 but much the same sounds and feel.

Yamaha P500
Digital piano

Orig. price (1994)	$8265 (£5999)
Price in 1996	$6000 (£4000)
Keyboard	88-note
Sound type	Digital (AWM 2)

Eye-catching, modern design on this 32-voice digital with 11 AWM sampled tones, creamy effects (two separate processors) and a host of MIDI performance controls and memories. Very expensive, but if looks are as important as the sound...

Yamaha PDP40
Home keyboard/piano

Orig. price (1985)	$4875 (no UK price)
Price in 1996	$4250 (no UK price)
Keyboard	88-note
Sound type	Digital (AWM)

88-note keyboard version of the PDP100 with GM-compatible tones and the all-important disk drive missing on its predecessor.

Yamaha PDP100
Home keyboard/piano

Orig. price (1984)	No U.S. price (£1500)
Price in 1996	No U.S. price (£850)
Keyboard	76-note
Sound type	Digital (AWM)

PDP stands for Personal Digital Piano, another hybrid in the home keyboard/digital piano stakes. GM compatible, with quality AWM tones, plus 99 styles, effects. Keyboard action stiff rather than weighted but roomier (than most) at 76-notes. Lack of disk drive rather a blunder with GM.

Yamaha PF10
Digital piano

Orig. price (1983)	$995 (£1099)
Price in 1996	$250 (£225)
Keyboard	76-note
Sound type	Digital (FM)

Splendid for the time, early digital with 10 inspiring FM tones and a pleasant keyboard. Speakers, plus stereo outputs. PF15 ($1595) is 88-note weighted keyboard version. A bit more satisfying to play and definitely worth paying extra for. Lack of MIDI the only real drawback.

Yamaha PF70
Digital piano

Orig. price (1986)	$995 (£999)
Price in 1996	$275 (£400)
Keyboard	76-note
Sound type	Digital (FM)

Upgraded and MIDI-ed extension of the PF10 (along with its big brother PF80 [$1099] an extension of the PF15), with new tones, chorus and tremolo and EQ. Tones less radical than PF10/15 but MIDI control, plus some operational improvements (like being able to switch off the internal speakers) make this a more generally usable instrument. Weighted keyboard action on both models.

Yamaha PF85
Digital piano

Orig. price (1987)	$1995 (£1350)
Price in 1996	$500 (£400)
Keyboard	88-note
Sound type	Digital (AWM)

Performance piano in similar styling to PF70. Five Clavinova-type tones including superb electric piano. Chorus, 20W amplification and 16-voice polyphony. Keyboard equivalent to TX1P piano module.

Yamaha PF2000
Digital piano

Orig. price (1988)	$1995 (£1249)
Price in 1996	$600 (£400)
Keyboard	88-note
Sound type	Digital (FM)

Overlooked but stylish hybrid digital piano, synth and controller keyboard. A dozen FM tones and Clavinova AE action with capability of loading in DX7II sound cartridges. Great idea.

Yamaha PF P100
Digital piano

Orig. price (1993)	No U.S. price (£1799)
Price in 1996	No U.S.price (£650)
Keyboard	88-note
Sound type	Digital (AWM)

Portable stage piano in PF tradition with speakers, effects, 10 tones and highly playable keyboard action. Tones can be split or layered, detuned, transposed and tweaked in terms of velocity response. Effectively there are 10 MIDI memories, making this a good blend of MIDI controller and piano. Weighs 34kg.

Yamaha PSR6
Home keyboard

Orig. price (1988)	$199 (£149)
Price in 1996	$50 (£50)
Keyboard	49-note
Sound type	Digital (FM)

Impressively synth-like features on this small key keyboard. One hundred preset FM tones, plus rhythms and accompaniments.

Yamaha PSR16
Home keyboard

Orig. price (1988)	$299 (£199)
Price in 1996	$60 (£60)
Keyboard	49-note
Sound type	Digital (FM)

"Digital synthesizer" with 32 FM voices and impressively simple sound editing. Auto Bass Chord, etc. Good example of the type.

Yamaha PSR21
Home keyboard

Orig. price (1986)	$399 (£299)
Price in 1996	$75 (£50)
Keyboard	49-note
Sound type	Digital (FM)

Early FM home keyboard with alarmingly simple but effective FM editing potential. Though seemingly similar, 61-note keyboard PSR31 uses non-editable PCM voices. PSR22 and PSR32 released 1987 and appear indistinguishable from their 21/31 counterparts.

Yamaha PSR36
Home keyboard

Orig. price (1988)	$399 (£299)
Price in 1996	$85 (£75)
Keyboard	61-note
Sound type	Digital (FM)

Highly versatile accompaniment permutations on this 32 FM voice (editable), PCM drum sound, MIDI-sporting home synth.

Yamaha PSR50
Home keyboard

Orig. price (1988)	$600 (£479)
Price in 1996	$100 (£75)
Keyboard	49-note
Sound type	Digital (FM)

MIDI makes its appearance on simple PSR-style FM home keyboard. Also in series: PSR60 (more voices), PSR80 with interesting Voice Variator feature (simple editing tool) and PSR90, which adds cartridge storage and LCD screen. PSR70 would seem to lie within this series but doesn't (see PSR70 entry).

Yamaha PSR70
Home keyboard

Orig. price (1985)	No U.S. price (£699)
Price in 1996	No U.S. price (£125)
Keyboard	61-note
Sound type	Digital (FM)

Mono and poly FM voices in similar vein to PSR6100. New feature of "endings" within auto accompaniment menu implemented here. Also PSR60 and PSR50 (no solo section).

Yamaha PSR420
Home keyboard

Orig. price (1995)	$599 (£399)
Price in 1996	No U.S. price (no UK price)
Keyboard	61-note
Sound type	Digital (AWM)

GM tones and plenty of auto features on this big screen model but no disk drive. PSR520 has even larger screen and pitch wheel and PSR620 adds disk drive.

Yamaha PSR500
Home keyboard

Orig. price (1991)	$899 (£499)
Price in 1996	$250 (£225)
Keyboard	61-note
Sound type	Digital (AWM)

Standard, if basic, AWM tones, playable multitimbrally on a 5-octave velocity keyboard. Lively styles, effects and limited scratchpad sequencing. Also in this series: PSR400, which loses reverb section; PSR300 loses pitch wheel and half the styles and PSR200, -150, -100, -75, -19 and -3 all base themselves around the same philosophy but do not sport MIDI. PSR3, -19 and -100 are, in fact, FM tone keyboards, inferior to their AWM tone big brothers.

Yamaha PSR510
Home keyboard

Orig. price (1993)	$999 (£699)
Price in 1996	$350 (£250)
Keyboard	61-note
Sound type	Digital (AWM)

GM AWM tones on this mid-priced home keyboard. Orchestration feature encourages tone mixing but otherwise fairly standard fair. PSR410 has a few less styles and loses an effects section, and PSR310 reduces its tone count to below GM requirements. PSR210 and -110 still AWM tones but no MIDI. Jam Track music-minus-one facilities as replacements.

Yamaha PSR600
Home keyboard

Orig. price (1992)	$1199 (£650)
Price in 1996	$350 (£250)
Keyboard	61-note
Sound type	Digital (AWM)

AWM tones enhanced by user sample loading—to be played back as keyboard tones or from panel pads. Eight-track sequencing, style-writing and Yamaha's clever Note Effects performance phrases. Lots of features, lots of fun. GM too. No user sampling on the PSR1700.

Yamaha PSR2700
Home keyboard

Orig. price (1994)	$1199 (£1500)
Price in 1996	$350 (£750)
Keyboard	61-note
Sound type	Digital (AWM)

28-voice poly home keyboard workstation with disk drive AWM sounds, plus the rare ability to store up 99 user samples. Sophisticated "interactive" styles onboard.

Yamaha PSR4500
Home keyboard

Orig. price (1989)	$2200 (£750)
Price in 1996	$450 (£300)
Keyboard	61-note
Sound type	Digital (AWM)

Striking AWM keyboard with plenty of quality sounds (pianos especially good), plus accompaniments. PSR4600 produced a year later, almost indistinguishable.

Yamaha PSR5700
Home keyboard

Orig. price (1993)	No U.S. price (£1750)
Price in 1996	No U.S. price (£850)
Keyboard	61-note
Sound type	Digital (AWM)

Yamaha's best-of-the-series home keyboard for 1993. Excellent tones, especially the pianos and general keyboards. Professional look and performance, plus handy helpers like Phrase Pads, sequencer and disk drive. Not GM as such, but a GM mode lets you configure what there is to GM.

Yamaha PSR6000
Home keyboard

Orig. price (1995)	No U.S. price (no UK price)
Price in 1996	No U.S. price (no UK price)
Keyboard	61-note
Sound type	Digital (AWM)

Bells and whistles General MIDI AWM home keyboard with large screen and interactive styles a go-go. Custom editing in the voice department, plus 8-track sequencing. Effects in both reverb and modulation types. 38-voice polyphony.

Yamaha PSR6100
Home keyboard

Orig. price (1984)	$1499 (£1089)
Price in 1996	$250 (£200)
Keyboard	76-note
Sound type	Digital (FM)

First of a long line of grown-up home keyboards in Yamaha's PS series. FM tones (18 poly, 18 mono), 64 drum patterns, auto bass chord, embryonic sequencer. MIDI.

Yamaha PSR6300
Home keyboard

Orig. price (1987)	$1999 (£1499)
Price in 1996	$300 (£250)
Keyboard	61-note
Sound type	Digital (FM)

Poly and mono FM voices, plus 24 PCM drum patterns and reasonable quality sequencer. Quite synthy with portamento, pitch/mod wheel, cartridge port, MIDI. A home keyboard workstation.

Yamaha PSR6700
Home keyboard

Orig. price (1991)	$2999 (£1500)
Price in 1996	$700 (£600)
Keyboard	76-note
Sound type	Digital (AWM)

Large and 40-note polyphonic keyboard with high-quality tones, layerable or mixable, that can be enhanced with 33 reverb/effect types. Similarities with Yamaha SY (synth) programming, along with "interactive" (styles can change based on your keyboard dynamics) accompaniments that offer good programmability but incline towards business. 8-track sequencer also.

Yamaha PSR7000
Home keyboard

Orig. price (1995)	$2999 (£1999)
Price in 1996	No U.S. price (no UK price)
Keyboard	61-note
Sound type	Digital (AWM)

Brim full of tones (almost 500 of them), styles (120), effects and gadgets such as mic input and TV-sized display. Unusual separate organ section, complete with rotary speaker effect on tap and option of incorporating MIDI bass pedals. Sequencer 16-tracks but quite basic compared to everything else on this impressive home keyboard workstation.

Yamaha PSR-SQ16
Home keyboard

Orig. price (1991)	$2250 (£1250)
Price in 1996	$650 (£500)
Keyboard	61-note
Sound type	Digital (AWM/PCM)

Released shortly after PSR6700. Complex looking, with 56-note polyphony and full 16-track sequencer. Innovative Note Processor feature to inject performance characteristics into your playing. GM drum mapping available not fully GM as an instrument. Disk drive reads SMF, though.

Yamaha QS300
Home keyboard

Price in 1996	$1895 (£1199)
Price in 1996	No U.S. price (no UK price)
Keyboard	61-note
Sound type	Digital (AWM 2)

Home keyboard for grown-ups rather in the manner of Korg's i-series instruments. Voices based loosely on the SY85 and sequencer on the QY300. Toss in three effects units, phrases, styles and drum kits and it adds up to a useful package. No speakers (though an "s" version is bound to appear in due course) and a generally pro approach to the genre.

Yamaha QY8
Music processor

Orig. price (1994)	$299 (£225)
Price in 1996	No U.S. price (no UK price)
Keyboard	25-note
Sound type	Digital (AWM)

Low cost "Walkstation." What the QY10 could and should have been: powerful yet still easy to use. 6000-note sequencer, 98 tones, 50 preset patterns and input possible of some 24 chord shapes. Four sequence tracks available.

Yamaha QY10
Music processor

Orig. price (1991)	$399 (£249)
Price in 1996	$125 (£85)
Keyboard	25-note
Sound type	Digital (AWM)

First of what went on to become a new type of instrument—the roving, pocket-sized music processor, on which styles and mini sequences could be played, written and stored. 32-voice polyphonic, 8-part multitimbral and great sounds. The buttons and programming layout and the 25-notes worth of squishy rubber pads that serve as keys are fiddly to use. Novation produced the MM-10 dedicated controller keyboard (see separate entry). Improved upon subsequently, notably by QY20.

Yamaha QY20
Music processor

Orig. price (1992)	$599 (£449)
Price in 1996	$275 (£200)
Keyboard	25-note
Sound type	Digital (AWM)

Full 16-part multitimbralism on this extension of the QY10. Patterns improved and extended, with pattern recording in both real- and step-time and higher (96 ppqn) resolution. Square LCD also makes this far easier to fathom than QY10. Novation keyboard still usable with adapter. Video manual plus booklet produced.

Yamaha QY22
Music processor

Orig. price (1995)	$595 (£449)
Price in 1996	No U.S. price (no UK price)
Keyboard	25-note
Sound type	Digital (AWM)

"Walkstation thingy" nestled in between entry-level QY8 and high-end QY300. Very similar to QY20. Full 128 GM sound bank, with 8-track sequencer, 28-voice polyphony, squishy buttons for keys and, as ever, lots of fun.

Yamaha QY300
Music processor

Orig. price (1994)	$1299 (£899)
Price in 1996	No U.S. price (no UK price)
Keyboard	25-note
Sound type	Digital (AWM)

GM on a Yamaha "Walkstation." Still blessed with AWM tones, effects, styles, etc., but with addition of disk drive and full size computer-like keyboard. 16MB waveform ROM playable 64-voice polyphonically. A big performer all around.

Yamaha QY700
Music processor

Orig. price (1996)	No U.S. price (£699)
Keyboard	25-note
Sound type	Digital (AWM 2)

Enhanced XG format GM "project studio in a box" as Yamaha calls it. Some 480 AWM 2 tones playable 32-voice polyphonic taken from the QY's 32-bit waveform ROM. Three effects units and 110,000 note sequencer. Pattern-based recording, offering 3000 built-in musical phrases. Huge display screen. Disk drive DD/HD capable of both Type 1 and Type 0 file formats.

Yamaha Silent Piano Series
Acoustic/digital piano

Series of regular acoustic pianos that have MIDI tone modules fitted for alternative "silent" playing on headphones. Models include MP100. MP80 and MP80T. AWM tones plus reverb. Great idea, even if Yamaha was not the first to offer it (Furstein Night & Day came out several years earlier).

Yamaha SK15
Multi-instrument keyboard

Orig. price (1981)	$895 (£789)
Price in 1996	$100 (£100)
Keyboard	49-note
Sound type	Analog

Appeared after and is modeled after the worthy SK20 to which it is happily similar. Cheaper list price and slightly curtailed features.

Yamaha SK20
Multi-instrument keyboard

Orig. price (1980)	$1395 (£1089)
Price in 1996	$225 (£200)
Keyboard	61-note
Sound type	Analog

Straight ahead organ/strings/brass machine with some useful features (key split, ensemble, tremolo, organ "drawbars" and tone mixing. Good quality tones. SK10 nowhere near as good. Avoid. SK30 well overpriced at the time ($2825) adds aftertouch keyboard, solo voices and more synth-like parameters.

Yamaha SK50D
Multi-instrument keyboard

Orig. price (1980)	$3875 (£2799)
Price in 1996	$350 (£300)
Keyboard	61-note x 2
Sound type	Analog

Based on SK30 but with added bass tones and double manual. Big, physically and aurally. Probably too big to be of much current value on the vintage scene.

Yamaha SU10
Digital sampling module

Orig. price (1996)	No U.S. price (£299)
Keyboard	none
Sound type	Digital samples

QY style phrase sampler offering 4-voice polyphony and capable of housing some 48 samples (up to 44.1kHz) in memory. Scratch-pad sequencer and indeed a "scratch" button for the dance inclined. Very clever and great fun, but not intended as a rival to an Akai S3000.

Yamaha SY22
Polyphonic synthesizer

Orig. price (1990)	$1095 (£649)
Price in 1996	$450 (£375)
Keyboard	61-note
Sound type	Sample+ synthesis, Vector synthesis

The only hint of a legacy from Yamaha's ill-fated buyout of Sequential Circuits in the late 1980s. The wave-mixing Vector synthesis harks back to the Prophet-VS and (subsequent to the SY22) inclines onto the Korg Wavestation (see Prophet-VS and Korg Wavestation entries in the Hot 100), both of which also grew out of the Sequential team in California. The SY22's Vectoring prowess concerns the real-time blending of its FM and AWM (sampled) waveforms. Simple but cheery and interesting results, abetted by a small bank of digital effects. Only 16-voice polyphony and 8-part multitimbralism. TG33 ($999) module doubles polyphony and adds more outputs. TG33 the better bet, frankly.

Yamaha SY35
Polyphonic synthesizer

Orig. price (1992)	$899 (£659)
Price in 1996	$400 (£300)
Keyboard	61-note
Sound type	Sample+ synthesis, Vector synthesis

AWM and FM voice components on this revamp of the SY22. More samples on hand but still 64 single and 16 multitimbral programs storable, plus 64 presets. "Improved" audio quality distinguishes SY35 from SY22.

Yamaha SY55
Polyphonic synthesizer

Orig. price (1990)	$1595 (£799)
Price in 1996	$450 (£350)
Keyboard	61-note
Sound type	Sample+ synthesis (AWM 2)

Half of an SY77, with sounds based solely on AWM 2 samples. Good filtering (high, resonant low- or bandpass with own EG), but overall the instrument is limited due to its slimline 74 waveform library of raw samples. Effects workmanlike more than inspired. Sequencer. TG55 ($995) module drops the sequencer and sprouts additional audio outs. TG55 probably the better bet if you want these sounds.

Yamaha SY77
Polyphonic synthesizer

See entry in Hot 100.

Yamaha SY85
Polyphonic synthesizer

Orig. price (1992)	$1995 (£1499)
Price in 1996	$900 (£700)
Keyboard	61-note
Sound type	Sample+ synthesis (AWM 2)

Yamaha finally cuts free of FM programming on this plain AWM sample-based workstation. User sample loading is possible. Maybe a little confusing to seasoned Yamaha programmers in that a single sample+ filter, EG, etc. make up the single voices (previously four "elements" made up a sound) though a '"performance" here can avail itself of up to four voices. Easy edit panel sliders, powerful multimode filtering, excellent effects and 8-track sequencing.

Yamaha SY99
Polyphonic synthesizer

Orig. price (1991)	$3995 (£2499)
Price in 1996	$1500 (£1200)

Keyboard	76-note
Sound type	Sample+ synthesis (RCM, FM)

Similar fundamentals to SY77 (see SY77 entry in the Hot 100) but expanded in keyboard length, waveform ROM (267 AWM samples stored therein), plus user sample loading via up to 3MB battery backed RAM. Programming still "samples within FM" but new features notably include sync. Sequencer, 16-track and bigger memory than SY77 with Type 1 and Type 0 MIDI Files loadable. Never the easiest system to maneuver around, but this is a class animal.

Yamaha TG33
Polyphonic synthesizer module

See Yamaha SY22 entry.

Yamaha TG55
Polyphonic synthesizer module

See Yamaha SY55 entry.

Yamaha TG77
Polyphonic synthesizer module

See Yamaha SY77 entry in Hot 100.

Yamaha TG100
Polyphonic synthesizer module

Orig. price (1992)	$449 (£349)
Price in 1996	$200 (£175)
Keyboard	Half width, 1U rackmount
Sound type	Sample+ synthesis (AWM 2)

Yamaha's first dedicated GM module and the first from anyone to offer direct link to a host computer (no need for separate MIDI/computer interface). Polyphony no more than reasonable at 28-voice but plenty of lively tones (minimal editing possible internally) and handy audio inputs. CBXT3 is same in dedicated computer livery with no screen. Outlasted the subsequent TG300 and TG500, which must say something!

Yamaha TG300
Polyphonic synthesizer module

Orig. price (1993)	$799 (£649)
Price in 1996	$300 (no UK price)
Keyboard	Half width, 3U rackmount
Sound type	Sample+ synthesis (AWM)

Enhanced TG100 with nearly 500 tones, 32-voice polyphony and new DSP chip allowing up to three simultaneous effects. Overshadowed and replaced by newer MU series modules.

Yamaha TG500
Polyphonic synthesizer module

Orig. price (1993)	$1495 (£999)
Price in 1996	$600 (£450)
Keyboard	1U rackmount
Sound type	Sample+ synthesis (AWM 2)

Similar but not exact equivalent to SY85. 64-voice polyphony is impressive and was unique upon release, and 8MB sample ROM makes this a powerful resource. No sequencer but some 570 patches in total. Only possible negative is lack of SIMM-based sample RAM. Good value if now replaced by newer MU series modules.

Yamaha TQ5
Music production module

Orig. price (1989)	$499 (£449)
Price in 1996	$175 (£175)
Keyboard	n/a
Sound type	Digital (FM)

Stand-alone module of YS200 home keyboard. FM sounds and 8-track sequencing with volatile RAM and only card or SysEx storage—no disk drive.

Yamaha TX1P
Digital piano module

Orig. price (1987)	$895 (£629)
Price in 1996	$300 (£225)
Keyboard	n/a
Sound type	Digital (AWM)

Useful piano module of five AWM tones, plus chorus, transpose, delay, chord memory. Not multitimbral but 16-voice polyphony, and the effect type features are surprisingly creative.

Yamaha TX7
Polyphonic synthesizer module

Orig. price (1985)	$845 (£699)
Price in 1996	$175 (£150)
Keyboard	Tabletop module
Sound type	Digital (FM)

Module of DX7 (see DX7 entry in Hot 100) with 32 program memories. Can only be programmed externally using DX7 or equivalent.

Yamaha TX16W
Digital sampling module

Orig. price (1988)	$2895 (£1799)
Price in 1996	$450 (£400)
Keyboard	n/a
Sound type	Digital samples

One of Yamaha's rare excursions into user sampling. Though blessed with some loyal users (and in due course, clubs, software, newsgroups, etc.), neither a commercial nor technical success at the time. 12-bit sampling with stereo capability, with digital filters and impressive edit parameters in terms of LFOs, EGs, performance control. Library is a bit hit-and-miss, and the operating system, whose routines are notoriously long-winded, has to be booted up from disk.

Yamaha TX802
Polyphonic synthesizer module

See entry in Hot 100.

Yamaha TX816
Polyphonic synthesizer module

Orig. price (1984)	$4995 (£4199)
Price in 1996	$800 (£750)
Keyboard	Rackmount
Sound type	Digital (FM)

Rackfull of (8) DX7s, each referred to as a TFI module and each capable of housing 32 tones and function parameters and responding 16-voice polyphonically. One of the earliest cases of multitimbralism, even if few figured out why it was needed at the time. Capable of massive power in providing a component part of one single, complex FM patch across all eight modules. TX216 ($2095) the same but with just two TFIs.

Yamaha TX81Z
Polyphonic synthesizer module

Orig. price (1987)	$450 (£449)
Price in 1996	$175 (£175)

Keyboard	1U rackmount
Sound type	Digital (FM)

Multitimbral FM module in more flexible though still similar 8-voice style as FB01. Just 128 tones, but you can edit directly from the control panel and store in 32 program memories. Found favor as module for both wind and guitar controllers. Interesting use of sound parameters mimics reverb and delay processing.

Yamaha V50
Polyphonic synthesizer

Orig. price (1989)	$1895 (£1239)
Price in 1996	$550 (£450)
Keyboard	61-note
Sound type	Digital (FM)

First Yamaha FM synth to get serious about built-in digital effects. Accordingly, the V50's slant on FM was, indeed remains, substantially different from the comparatively naked and dry DX7 et al. Only 4-operator (DX21 style) FM but with effects, PCM drum sounds and a sequencer, a reasonable package. Not fashionable as of writing but worth a second glance.

Yamaha VL1
Duophonic synthesizer module

Orig. price (1994)	$4995 (£3499)
Price in 1996	$4000 (£2000)
Keyboard	49-note
Sound type	Digital (Physical Modeling)

First of the new generation of Virtual Acoustic synthesizers based upon Physical Modeling technology licensed by Yamaha from the same Stamford University out of which emerged FM two decades earlier. Beautifully presented with wood grain panel and gold hardware, the VL1 specializes in wind instrument facsimiles, offering various foot and mouth controllers including the BC-2 Breath Controller as standard. Undoubtedly expressive beyond any normal synth's wildest dreams but, like a "real instrument," it takes time to master. Price, complexity and lack of polyphony limit its appeal, but the VL1 has been an excellent flagship for Yamaha's "towards 2000" synthesizer technology.

Yamaha VL1M
Duophonic synthesizer module

Orig. price (1995)	$2995 (£2199)
Price in 1996	$2000 (£1500)
Keyboard	3U rackmount
Sound type	Digital (Physical Modeling)

Module of VL1.

Yamaha VL7
Monophonic synthesizer

Orig. price (1995)	$2995 (£2199)
Price in 1996	$2250 (£1500)
Keyboard	49-note
Sound type	Digital (Physical Modeling)

Mono version of the ground—and wallet—breaking VL1. Strict mono playback.

Yamaha W5
Polyphonic synthesizer

Orig. price (1995)	$2495 (£1649)
Price in 1996	$1800 (£1350)
Keyboard	76-note
Sound type	Sample+ synthesis (AWM 2)

Workstation with oodles of sounds, effects and

Left: TG100: first GM module with direct computer access

sequencing power. Looks like a Korg. Templates aid voice editing but still not the easiest instrument to understand overall. Expansion boards available for Vintage Sounds, Concert Grand piano and Rhythm Section. A class performer. Also 61-note keyboard version, W7 ($1995).

Yamaha YP9
Digital piano (portable)

Orig. price (1986)	$599 (£395)
Price in 1996	$150 (£100)
Keyboard	61-note
Sound type	Digital (FM)

Home piano with small internal amplification system with five FM tones, playsequencer, chorus and MIDI access from light but touch-sensitive keyboard. YPR7, without the sequencer, chorus, or MIDI, is a waste of time by comparison.

Yamaha YPP35
Digital piano (portable)

Orig. price (1992)	$675 (£480)
Price in 1996	$350 (£200)
Keyboard	61-note
Sound type	Digital (AWM)

Just eight tones but 32-voice polyphony and small playsequencer. Good value, uncomplicated digital piano. YPP15 loses three tones and sequencer.

Yamaha YPP45
Digital piano (portable)

Orig. price (1994)	No U.S. price (no UK price)
Price in 1996	No U.S. price (no UK price)
Keyboard	76-note
Sound type	Digital (AWM)

No-nonsense, plain-Jane digital with eight tones playable at 32-voice polyphony. Not vastly different from YPP35 but longer keyboard and large amplification (10W) system. As ever, a good value.

Yamaha YPP50
Digital piano (portable)

Orig. price (1995)	$1000 (£1499)
Price in 1996	No U.S. price (no UK price)
Keyboard	76-note
Sound type	Digital (AWM)

Seven tones on this simple 8-voice polyphonic, no-frills digital. YPP55 adds a few extra tones and zooms up to 32-voice polyphony.

$\mathcal{I}$ndex

Acknowledgments

Many thanks to the following people and organizations for supplying some of the artwork in this edition:

Matthius Becker
Originalton West Sound & Vision

Malcolm Doak

Al Goff
Goff Professional (Hammond services)
(860) 667-2358

Kenny Howes
c/o Numerous Complaints Music

David Kean
Mellotron Archives
(818) 754-1191

Michael Mendelson
(Photographed the Roland Juno-60 and Juno-106)

Dave Netting
Ensoniq
155 Great Valley Parkway
Malvern, PA 19355

George Petersen

Tim Smith
Smith-Weyer Labs

David Hillel Wilson
New England Synthesizer Museum
(603) 881-8587

Chris Youdell
Analogue Modular Systems Inc.
(213) 850-5216

Frank Stratton
SRC Music
(510) 559-8618

A Music Bookstore At Your Fingertips...

FREE!